THE
HANDY
AMERICAN
GOVERNMENT
ANSWER
BOOK

ALSO FROM VISIBLE INK PRESS

The Handy African American History Answer Book
by Jessie Carnie Smith
ISBN: 978-1-57859-452-8

The Handy American History Answer Book
by David L. Hudson Jr.
ISBN: 978-1-57859-471-9

The Handy Anatomy Answer Book, 2nd edition
by Patricia Barnes-Svarney and Thomas E. Svarney
ISBN: 978-1-57859-542-6

The Handy Answer Book for Kids (and Parents), 2nd edition
by Gina Misiroglu
ISBN: 978-1-57859-219-7

The Handy Art History Answer Book
by Madelynn Dickerson
ISBN: 978-1-57859-417-7

The Handy Astronomy Answer Book, 3rd edition
by Charles Liu
ISBN: 978-1-57859-190-9

The Handy Bible Answer Book
by Jennifer Rebecca Prince
ISBN: 978-1-57859-478-8

The Handy Biology Answer Book, 2nd edition
by Patricia Barnes Svarney and Thomas E. Svarney
ISBN: 978-1-57859-490-0

The Handy Boston Answer Book
by Samuel Willard Crompton
ISBN: 978-1-57859-593-8

The Handy California Answer Book
by Kevin S. Hile
ISBN: 978-1-57859-591-4

The Handy Chemistry Answer Book
by Ian C. Stewart and Justin P. Lamont
ISBN: 978-1-57859-374-3

The Handy Civil War Answer Book
by Samuel Willard Crompton
ISBN: 978-1-57859-476-4

The Handy Communication Answer Book
by Lauren Sergy
ISBN: 978-1-57859-587-7

The Handy Diabetes Answer Book
by Patricia Barnes-Svarney and Thomas E. Svarney
ISBN: 978-1-57859-597-6

The Handy Dinosaur Answer Book, 2nd edition
by Patricia Barnes-Svarney and Thomas E. Svarney
ISBN: 978-1-57859-218-0

The Handy English Grammar Answer Book
by Christine A. Hult, Ph.D.
ISBN: 978-1-57859-520-4

The Handy Geography Answer Book, 3rd edition
by Paul A. Tucci
ISBN: 978-1-57859-215-9

The Handy Geology Answer Book
by Patricia Barnes-Svarney and Thomas E. Svarney
ISBN: 978-1-57859-156-5

The Handy History Answer Book, 3rd edition
by David L. Hudson, Jr.
ISBN: 978-1-57859-372-9

The Handy Hockey Answer Book
by Stan Fischler
ISBN: 978-1-57859-513-6

The Handy Investing Answer Book
by Paul A. Tucci
ISBN: 978-1-57859-486-3

The Handy Islam Answer Book
by John Renard Ph.D.
ISBN: 978-1-57859-510-5

About the Author

 **Gina Misiroglu** is the author or editor of more than three dozen books in the popular culture, biography, American history, folklore, and women studies genres. She holds two degrees from UCLA and has worked in various editorial capacities for publishers such as Price Stern Sloan, New World Library, Visible Ink Press, Cengage, Penguin Books, Facts On File, and Routledge. Her most notable works include the three-volume *American Countercultures: An Encyclopedia of Nonconformists, Alternative Lifestyles, and Radical Ideas in U.S. History*, which won the 2010 RUSA Award for Outstanding Reference Source; *The Superhero Book: The Ultimate Encyclopedia of Comic-Book Icons and Hollywood Heroes* (2012); and the trade anthology *Girls Like Us: 40 Extraordinary Women Celebrate Girlhood in Story, Poetry, and Song* (1999), winner of the New York Public Library's "Best Book for Teens" Award. Misiroglu has contributed to or authored many "Handy Answer Book" titles, including *The Handy Answer Book for Kids (and Parents)*, *The Handy Politics Answer Book*, and *The Handy Presidents Answer Book*. She is proud to say she votes in every national and local election.

The Handy Law Answer Book
by David L. Hudson Jr.
ISBN: 978-1-57859-217-3

The Handy Literature Answer Book
by Dan Burt and Debbie Fielder
ISBN: 978-1-57859-635-5

The Handy Math Answer Book, 2nd edition
by Patricia Barnes-Svarney and Thomas
    E. Svarney
ISBN: 978-1-57859-373-6

The Handy Military History Answer Book
by Samuel Willard Crompton
ISBN: 978-1-57859-509-9

The Handy Mythology Answer Book
by David A. Leeming, Ph.D.
ISBN: 978-1-57859-475-7

The Handy New York City Answer Book
by Chris Barsanti
ISBN: 978-1-57859-586-0

The Handy Nutrition Answer Book
by Patricia Barnes-Svarney and Thomas
    E. Svarney
ISBN: 978-1-57859-484-9

The Handy Ocean Answer Book
by Patricia Barnes-Svarney and Thomas
    E. Svarney
ISBN: 978-1-57859-063-6

The Handy Pennsylvania Answer Book
by Larry Baker
ISBN: 978-1-57859-610-2

The Handy Personal Finance Answer Book
by Paul A. Tucci
ISBN: 978-1-57859-322-4

The Handy Philosophy Answer Book
by Naomi Zack
ISBN: 978-1-57859-226-5

The Handy Physics Answer Book, 2nd edition
By Paul W. Zitzewitz, Ph.D.
ISBN: 978-1-57859-305-7

The Handy Politics Answer Book
by Gina Misiroglu
ISBN: 978-1-57859-139-8

The Handy Presidents Answer Book, 2nd edition
by David L. Hudson
ISBN: 978-1-57859-317-0

The Handy Psychology Answer Book, 2nd edition
by Lisa J. Cohen
ISBN: 978-1-57859-508-2

The Handy Religion Answer Book, 2nd edition
by John Renard
ISBN: 978-1-57859-379-8

The Handy Science Answer Book, 4th edition
by The Carnegie Library of Pittsburgh
ISBN: 978-1-57859-321-7

The Handy Supreme Court Answer Book
by David L Hudson, Jr.
ISBN: 978-1-57859-196-1

The Handy Technology Answer Book
by Naomi Bobick and James Balaban
ISBN: 978-1-57859-563-1

The Handy Weather Answer Book, 2nd edition
by Kevin S. Hile
ISBN: 978-1-57859-221-0

PLEASE VISIT THE "HANDY ANSWERS" SERIES
WEBSITE AT WWW.HANDYANSWERS.COM.

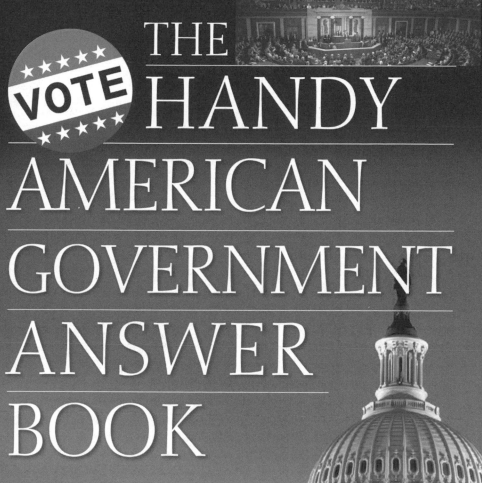

THE HANDY AMERICAN GOVERNMENT ANSWER BOOK

How Washington, Politics, and Elections Work

Gina Misiroglu

Detroit

THE HANDY AMERICAN GOVERNMENT ANSWER BOOK

How Washington, Politics, and Elections Work

Visible Ink Press®
43311 Joy Rd., #414
Canton, MI 48187–2075
Visible Ink Press is a registered trademark of Visible Ink Press LLC.

Most Visible Ink Press books are available at special quantity discounts when purchased in bulk by corporations, organizations, or groups. Customized printings, special imprints, messages, and excerpts can be produced to meet your needs. For more information, contact Special Markets Director, Visible Ink Press, www.visibleink.com, or 734–667–3211.

Managing Editor: Kevin S. Hile
Art Director: Mary Claire Krzewinski
Typesetting: Marco DiVita
Proofreaders: Carleton Copeland and Shoshana Hurwitz
Indexer: Larry Baker
Cover images: Shutterstock.

Front cover photos: Vote button and U.S. Capitol images from Shutterstock; President Obama before joint session of Congress from the White House archive.

Back cover photos (top to bottom): Library of Congress, U.S. Navy, Shutterstock.

ISBN: 978–1–57859–639–3
eBook ISBN: 978–1–57859–674–4

Cataloging–in–Publication data is on file at the Library of Congress.

Printed in the United States of America.

10 9 8 7 6 5 4 3 2 1

Table of Contents

INTRODUCTION TO THE DEMOCRATIC REPUBLIC ... 1

THE U.S. CONSTITUTION ... 21

FEDERALISM ... 57

THE U.S. CONGRESS ... 73

THE PRESIDENT ... 117

THE COURTS ... 147

Acknowledgments

Photo Sources

AgnosticPreachersKid (Wikicommons): pp. 138, 276.

Elvert Barnes: p. 261.

Matthew G. Bisanz: p. 136.

Boston Centinel: p. 94.

Collection of the Supreme Court of the United States: p. 159.

CriticalThinker (Wikicommons): p. 241.

Gadol87 (Wikicommons): p. 231.

Victor Grigas: p. 266.

Harper's New Monthly Magazine: p. 32.

Historical Society of Pennsylvania: p. 38.

The History of North America. London: E. Newberry, 1789: p. 33.

Paul Hughes: p. 203.

Kmusser (Wikicommons): p. 28.

Michael Kranewitter: p. 133.

Kurz & Allison, Art Publishers, Chicago, U.S.A.: p. 62.

Peter Larson/Medill News Service: p. 103.

Library of Congress: pp. 12, 22, 46 (right), 64, 79, 95, 131, 246, 248, 270.

Mitchell Map Company: p. 25.

Larry D. Moore: p. 308 (right).

National Archives and Records Administration: pp. 55, 209, 211.

National Gallery of Art: p. 153.

National Portrait Gallery, Washington, D.C.: p. 52.

Timeline

Year	Event
1774	Colonists form First Continental Congress as Britain closes down Boston Harbor and deploys troops in Massachusetts
1775	George Washington leads Continental Army to fight against British rule in American Revolution
1775–1791	Continental Congress issues first U.S. paper currency, known as "continentals"
1776	Declaration of Independence signed; colonists declare independence
1778	The U.S. Treasury system is reorganized
1781	Rebel states form loose confederation, codified in Articles of Confederation, after defeating the British at the Battle of Yorktown
1783	Britain accepts loss of colonies, signing the Treaty of Paris
1787	Founding Fathers draw up new constitution for United States of America; constitution goes into effect in 1788
1787	Northwest Ordinance establishes how the Northwest Territory is to be organized and eventually organized into states
1789	U.S. Constitution approved, replacing the Articles of Confederation and establishing a stronger, centralized, federal government
1789	George Washington becomes first president of the United States
1789	Judiciary Act establishes the U.S. district courts to serve as the federal trial courts for admiralty and maritime cases
1789	The first U.S. veterans pension law for invalid Revolutionary War soldiers is approved during the first session of Congress
1789	Congress establishes the U.S. Customs Service
1789	President George Washington approves Congress's proposal to create the Department of the Treasury
1789	Congress establishes the U.S. Postal Service

Year	Event
1789	The Department of War is established
1790	The first decennial federal census is conducted
1791	The Bill of Rights, Amendments 1–10 of the U.S. Constitution, guarantees individual freedoms
1791	At the urging of Treasury Secretary Alexander Hamilton, Congress establishes the First Bank of the United States
1797	John Adams is elected president for the Federalist Party; *The Federalist Papers* explain the Constitution to the American people and promote the concept of federalism
1798	The Anti-Federalist Party is renamed the Democratic-Republican Party, supporting states' rights and a strict interpretation of the Constitution
1798	Alien and Sedition Acts are signed into law by President John Adams, these laws included new powers to deport foreigners and make it harder for immigrants to vote
1800	Thomas Jefferson, leader of the Democratic-Republican Party, is elected the third president of the United States
1802	*Marbury v. Madison* establishes the principle of judicial review
1803	The Louisiana Territory is purchased from France, doubling the size of the United States
1804	Continental Congress creates the U.S. Treasury
1808	Trans-Atlantic slave trade is abolished
1809	James Madison follows Jefferson as leader of Democratic-Republican Party
1820	Congress passes Missouri Compromise, admitting Missouri as a slave state and Maine as a free state; prohibits slavery in the Louisiana Territory north of the 36° 30" latitude line
1823	President James Monroe lays out his cornerstone of U.S. foreign policy in the Monroe Doctrine, stating that the United States would not interfere in the internal affairs of, or wars between, European powers
1825	John Quincy Adams becomes the last president under the Democratic-Republican ticket.
1834	The Indian Department is established in the War Department
1846	President James K. Polk signs the Oregon Treaty with Great Britain, gaining territory in the northwest
1846	The Smithsonian Institution is established
1848	With the Treaty of Guadalupe Hidalgo, the United States gains California and southwest territories in the wake of the Mexican War
1849	Department of the Interior established
1850	Compromise of 1850 is signed, making California a free state, and the new Utah Territory and New Mexico Territory are able to decide on slavery through popular vote

Year	Event
1854	Opponents of slavery establish the Republican Party
1856–1857	U.S. Supreme Court decides on Dred Scott case, ruling that slaves are not citizens of the United States and cannot sue in federal courts; declares the Missouri Compromise unconstitutional
1860	Congress establishes the Government Printing Office
1861	Republican Abraham Lincoln is elected president
1861	Eleven pro-slavery southern states secede and form the Confederate States of America under the leadership of Jefferson Davis, triggering civil war with abolitionist northern states
1861	Congress authorizes the first Medals of Honor
1862	Homestead Act allows citizens to acquire 160 acres of land by farming it for five years
1862	Department of Agriculture is established
1862	Morrill Act establishes the federal government to allot land to townships for public schools
1862	Army Medal of Honor is established
1863	Habeas Corpus Suspension Act authorizes the president of the United States to suspend the writ of habeas corpus
1863	Lincoln issues Emancipation Proclamation, declaring slaves free
1863	National Banking Act establishes a national currency
1865	The 13th Amendment abolishes slavery and involuntary servitude; Lincoln is assassinated
1865	National Soldiers & Sailors Asylum Act establishes aid to disabled veterans of the Union Army's volunteer forces
1867	Purchase of the Alaska Territory
1868	Impeachment trial of President Andrew Johnson
1868	14th Amendment signed, guaranteeing citizenship rights and equal protection under the laws, especially to the newly emancipated African Americans after the Civil War
1869	The two-party system of the Democrats and Republicans is firmly established in the United States; continues to present day
1870	Department of Justice established, expanding the duties of the Attorney General
1870	15th Amendment prohibits denial of the right to vote to any citizen based on that citizen's "race, color, or previous condition of servitude"
1871	U.S. Commission on Fish and Fisheries created
1876	Sioux Indians defeat U.S. troops at Battle of Little Big Horn
1882	Chinese Exclusion Act creates a ten-year suspension of immigration of Chinese laborers; Chinese forbidden from becoming citizens
1887	Interstate Commerce Act
1890	U.S. troops defeat Sioux Indians at Wounded Knee

Year	Event
1890	Sherman Antitrust Act outlaws practices deemed monopolistic to consumers and the market economy
1891	Evarts Act gives the U.S. Courts of Appeals jurisdiction over the majority of appeals from U.S. district and circuit courts
1893	Court of Appeals of the District of Columbia is established to hear appeals from the Supreme Court of the District of Columbia
1895	American Historical Association advocates greater use of archival sources
1898	U.S. gains Puerto Rico, Guam, the Philippines, and Cuba following the Spanish-American War; U.S. annexes Hawaii
1899	Rivers and Harbors Appropriation Act makes it a misdemeanor to discharge refuse matter into navigable waters or tributaries without permit
1902	U.S. Reclamation Service establishes the U.S. Geological Survey; in 1923, it is re-named the Bureau of Reclamation
1903	President Theodore Roosevelt establishes the first wildlife refuge at Pelican Island National Bird Reservation
1906	President Roosevelt signs the Antiquities Act, the first U.S. law to provide general protection for any general kind of cultural or natural resource
1906	Bureau of Immigration and Naturalization is established and naturalization papers become standardized and contain more detail about aliens
1906	Pure Food and Drugs Act outlaws the misbranding of food and drug products moving in interstate commerce
1911	The Judicial Code of 1911 abolishes the U.S. circuit courts, transferring their jurisdiction to the U.S. district courts and making the district courts the sole trial courts of general jurisdiction in the federal judiciary
1913	Sixteenth Amendment establishes the first constitutionally mandated income tax
1913	President William Taft signs a bill authorizing the planning of a national archives of three million cubic feet
1913	President Woodrow Wilson signs the Federal Reserve Act, establishing the Federal Reserve System
1914	Clayton Antitrust Act builds on the 1890 Sherman Antitrust Act by enabling the federal government to outlaw practices that it foresees as potentially damaging to consumers and the competitive market
1915	Naval Appropriations Act establishes the National Advisory Committee for Aeronautics
1915	Federal Trade Commission is established to protect consumers and promote competition
1916	National Park Service created
1919	Treaty of Versailles ends World War I and includes the League of Nations Covenant
1919	Volstead Act implements Prohibition
1920	Nineteenth Amendment gives women the right to vote
1921	Congress establishes the Veterans Bureau and consolidates federal programs for veterans

Year	Event
1921	Quota Act establishes the annual immigrant admissions per country using a formula based on the 1910 federal population census
1924	Immigration Act of 1924 limits the number of immigrants allowed entry into the United States through a national origins quota; excludes immigrants from Asia
1924	Congress gives indigenous people right to citizenship
1929–1933	Thirteen million people become unemployed after the Wall Street stock market crash of 1929 triggers the Great Depression; President Herbert Hoover rejects direct federal relief
1933	President Franklin D. Roosevelt launches "New Deal" recovery program, which includes major public works
1934	President Roosevelt signs An Act to Establish a National Archives of the United States Government, which also establishes the National Historical Publications Commission
1935	Banking Act removes the Treasury Secretary and the Comptroller of the Currency from the federal governing board
1935	The Federal Register Act establishes the publication of government documents within the National Archives
1935	Social Security Act establishes a system of federal old-age benefits
1937	Federal Aid in Wildlife Restoration Act allocates federal funds to be available for state wildlife protection and propagation
1938	Civil Aeronautics Act creates the Civil Aeronautics Authority and Air Safety Board to regulate commercial air operations
1938	Food, Drug, and Cosmetic Act provides that all new drugs have to be reviewed by the Food and Drug Administration to ensure that they are safe prior to marketing
1940	Fish and Wildlife Service is created within the Department of the Interior
1941	The Franklin D. Roosevelt Library becomes first presidential library
1941	U.S. Army Air Forces is established
1941	Japanese warplanes attack U.S. fleet at Pearl Harbor in Hawaii; U.S. declares war on Japan; Germany declares war on U.S, which thereafter intervenes on a massive scale in World War II, eventually helping to defeat Germany
1942–1945	The U.S. military, the National Resources Planning Board, and the Office of Strategic Services station employees in the National Archives Building in Washington, D.C., for research in records and intelligence gathering
1944	The "G.I. Bill" or Servicemen's Readjustment Act of 1944 provides new education, training, housing, and rehabilitation benefits; declares the Veterans Administration an essential war agency
1945	Fifty nations convene at the United Nations Conference in San Francisco, creating the United Nations
1945	The United States drops two atomic bombs on Hiroshima and Nagasaki; Japan surrenders

Year	Event
1947	President Truman signs the National Security Act amendments, ordering a reorganization of the U.S. military; creating the National Security Council (NSC), the Central Intelligence Agency (CIA), and Department of the Air Force; merging the War Department and Navy Department into a single Department of Defense, all under the direction of the Secretary of Defense
1947	With the Truman Doctrine, President Truman requests $400 million in aid from Congress to combat Communism, emphasizing Greece and Turkey; Cold War with Soviet Union begins
1947	Secretary of State George C. Marshall proposes his Marshall Plan, a program of massive aid to help Europe rebuild after World War II; known as the European Recovery Program, some $13 billion is dispersed from 1948 to 1952
1948	President Truman signs Executive Order 9981, ordering integration of all military forces
1949	National Security Act of 1947 is amended, creating the executive department of the Department of Defense to oversee the military services
1949	North American Treaty Organization (NATO) is established
1949	Geneva Conventions define the basic rights of wartime prisoners and establish protections for civilians in and around a war zone
1950	National Science Foundation is established
1950–1954	Senator Joseph McCarthy carries out a crusade against alleged Communists in government and public life; the campaign and its methods become known as McCarthyism
1952	National Security Agency (NSA) is established to conduct communications intelligence (COMINT) activities for the military
1954	The Atomic Energy Act creates the Atomic Energy Commission (AEC)
1954	Senator McCarthy is formally censured by the Senate
1954	Racial segregation in schools becomes unconstitutional; start of campaign of civil disobedience to secure civil rights for Americans of African decent
1958	Congress establishes the National Aeronautics and Space Administration (NASA)
1958	President Dwight D. Eisenhower signs the Federal Aviation Act, creating the Federal Aviation Agency (FAA)
1960	Democratic Party candidate John F. Kennedy elected president, narrowly defeating Republican Richard Nixon
1961	Bay of Pigs invasion, an unsuccessful attempt to invade Cuba by Cuban exiles, is organized and financed by Washington
1962	U.S. compels Soviet Union to withdraw nuclear weapons from Cuba in what has becomes known as the Cuban Missile Crisis
1963	President John F. Kennedy assassinated; Lyndon Johnson becomes president
1964	Civil Rights Act outlaws discrimination based on race, color, religion, sex, or national origin
1964	Wilderness Act creates the National Wilderness Preservation System

Year	Event
1964	Indian Reorganization Act (aka the Wheeler–Howard Act) decreases federal control, increases Indian self-government and responsibility, stops allotment of tribal lands to individuals, and returns surplus lands to tribes; amended and extended in 1960s and 1970s
1965	Voting Rights Act prohibits racial discrimination in voting
1965	Immigration and Nationality Act abolishes the national origins quota system, replacing it with a preference system that focuses on immigrants' skills and family relationships with citizens or U.S. residents
1966	President Lyndon Johnson signs the Department of Transportation Act, bringing thirty-one previously scattered federal elements under one Cabinet department
1966	Freedom of Information Act (FOIA) identifies the kinds of executive branch agency records that can be disclosed
1968	Black civil rights leader Martin Luther King Jr. assassinated
1969	Republican Party candidate Richard Nixon elected president amid growing public opposition to Vietnam War; U.S. military presence in Vietnam exceeds 500,000 personnel
1969	National Environmental Policy Act (NEPA) is passed to help assess the impacts of major federal development projects on fish and wildlife
1970	Congress passes Clean Air Act, authorizing the development of federal and state regulations to limit emissions from industrial sources
1973	Endangered Species Act provides for the conservation of species and their ecosystems that are endangered or threatened
1974	U.S. House of Representatives begins impeachment process against President Richard M. Nixon
1974	In a TV address, Nixon announces his resignation in the wake of the Watergate scandal over a 1972 break-in at the Democratic Party headquarters; Vice President Gerald Ford is sworn in as his successor
1975	Nuclear Regulatory Commission established; Atomic Energy Commission dissolved
1976	Democratic Party candidate Jimmy Carter elected president
1978	Foreign Intelligence Surveillance Act (FISA) prescribes procedures for requesting judicial authorization for electronic surveillance and physical search of persons engaged in espionage or international terrorism against the United States on behalf of a foreign power
1978	Foreign Intelligence Surveillance Court allows federal district court judges to review applications for warrants related to national security investigations
1978	The Presidential Records Act makes all presidential records created after 1981 the property of the United States
1978	Information Security Oversight Office (ISOO) established
1979	U.S. embassy in Tehran, Iran, seized by radical students; the 444-day hostage crisis that followed, including a failed rescue attempt in 1980, damages Carter's popularity and dominates the 1980 presidential election campaign

Year	Event
1980	Monetary Control Act requires federal government to establish reserve requirements for all eligible financial institutions
1980	Republican Party's Ronald Reagan is elected president; Reagan will adopt tough anti-Communist foreign policy and tax-cutting policies, which lead to a large federal budget deficit
1981	Iran frees the fifty-two U.S. embassy hostages on the same day of President Reagan's inauguration
1984	Ronald Reagan re-elected president, beating Democratic Party candidate Walter Mondale
1986	Space shuttle *Challenger* explodes shortly after takeoff from Cape Canaveral, killing all seven crew members; manned space flights are suspended until September 1988
1986	U.S. warplanes bomb Libyan cities; "Irangate" scandal uncovered, revealing that proceeds from secret U.S. arms sales to Iran were used illegally to fund Contra rebels in Nicaragua
1988	George H. W. Bush, Reagan's vice president, is elected president
1988	Veterans Administration is elevated to Cabinet-level department and renamed the Department of Veteran Affairs
1989	U.S. troops invade Panama, oust its government, and arrest its leader, one-time CIA informant General Manuel Noriega, on drug-trafficking charges
1989	Nazi War Crimes Disclosure Act declassifies wartime and postwar records from World II, mostly relating to war crimes and war criminals
1991	U.S. forces play dominant role in war against Iraq, which was triggered by Iraq's invasion of Kuwait and ended with the expulsion of Iraqi troops from that country
1992	Democratic Party candidate Bill Clinton elected president
1992	Congress passes North American Free Trade Agreement (NAFTA), which is intended to create free-trade bloc between the United States, Canada, and Mexico
1995	Oklahoma City bombing kills more than 160 people in worst-ever incident of domestic terrorism up to that time
1996	Clinton re-elected, beating Republican rival Bob Dole
1998	Scandal over Clinton's purported sexual impropriety with White House worker Monica Lewinsky dominates domestic political agenda and leads to impeachment proceedings in Congress
1999	U.S. plays leading role in NATO bombardment of Yugoslavia in response to Serb violence against ethnic Albanians in the province of Kosovo
2000	Republican Party's George W. Bush, son of George H. W. Bush, wins the presidency
2001	Terrorist attack on the World Trade Center and the Pentagon on September 11 prompts United States to embark on a "War on Terror," which includes the invasion of Afghanistan and Iraq
2001	U.S. leads massive campaign of air strikes against Afghanistan and helps opposition forces defeat the Taliban regime and find Saudi-born dissident Osama bin Laden, suspected of masterminding the September 11 attacks

Year	Event
2001	USA Patriot Act increases the number of judges on the Foreign Intelligence Surveillance Court from 7 to 11; establishes a Foreign Intelligence Surveillance Court of Review
2001	Energy giant Enron declares bankruptcy after massive fraudulent accounting practices are exposed
2002	E-Government Act of 2002 promotes the use of the Internet and new technologies for improved efficiencies across the government and greater public access to federal government information and services
2002	President Bush, during his State of the Union Address, references Iraq, Iran, and North Korea as an "Axis of Evil"
2002	Telecommunication giant WorldCom's multi-billion-dollar accounting fraud is revealed, eclipsing the Enron scandal to become the biggest business failure in U.S. history
2002	President Bush signs into law a bill creating a Department of Homeland Security, the biggest reorganization of federal government in more than fifty years; the department is tasked with protecting the U.S. against terrorist attacks
2003	U.S. Customs and Border Patrol established
2003	Space shuttle *Columbia* breaks up while reentering the atmosphere, killing the seven astronauts on board
2003	Missile attacks on Baghdad mark the start of a U.S.-led campaign to topple Iraqi leader Saddam Hussein
2004	George W. Bush wins a second term
2005	Office of the Director of National Intelligence (ODNI) opens; John Negroponte serves as first director
2006	Congress renews the Patriot Act, a centerpiece of the government's fight against terrorism, after months of debate about its impact on civil liberties
2006	Millions of immigrants and their supporters take to the streets to protest against plans to criminalize illegal immigrants
2006	Democratic Party wins control of the Senate and House of Representatives in midterm elections; Defense Secretary Donald Rumsfeld steps down
2008	Turmoil in the U.S. and international financial markets arises as major Wall Street investment bank Lehman Brothers collapses
2008–2009	With hundreds of billions of dollars lost in bad loans and a prolonged property slump, leading to worst financial crisis since the Great Depression
2009	Democratic senator Barack Obama becomes the first black president of the United States
2009	First Tea Party rally held in protest at Obama administration's plans to bail out banks and introduce health care reform; the populist and libertarian movements serve as the focus for conservative opposition to the president's reform plans.
2009	President Barack Obama issues Executive Order 13526, prescribing a uniform system for classifying, safeguarding, and declassifying national security information, including information relating to defense against transnational terrorism

Year	Event
2010	Democrats in Congress succeed in passing a bill on health care reform
2010	U.S. and Russia announce agreement on a new nuclear arms reduction treaty to replace the 1991 Strategic Arms Reduction Treaty
2010	President Obama unveils a new defense policy significantly curtailing the circumstances in which the U.S. would use nuclear weapons
2010	Deepwater Horizon oil rig spill in the Gulf of Mexico is America's biggest to date
2010	Republicans make sweeping gains in mid-term elections, regaining control of the House of Representatives
2011	U.S. forces kill al Qaeda leader Osama bin Laden in an operation in the Pakistani city of Abbottabad
2011	The final space shuttle mission is completed with the landing of *Atlantis*, bringing about the end of the thirty-year program
2011	Across the United States, anti-capitalist protesters march under the slogan "Occupy Wall Street" against so-called corporate greed and increasing government debt; the protests inspire marches in other cities worldwide
2012	President Obama unveils a revised defense strategy involving budget cuts, but insists the country will maintain its military superiority; Tea Party opposes Obama
2012	The U.S. ambassador to Libya is killed when armed men storm the consulate in Benghazi
2012	President Obama wins re-election by a narrow margin over Republican contender Mitt Romney
2013	A compromise bill prevents the U.S. from falling off the "fiscal cliff" with a set of scheduled tax increases and sharp spending cuts likely to trigger a new recession
2013	President Obama inaugurated for a second and final term
2013	Twin bomb blasts targeting the Boston Marathon kill three people and injure more than 170; Soviet-born Islamic extremist Dzhokhar Tsarnaev is charged
2013	Former National Security Agency (NSA) contractor Edward Snowden flees to Russia via Hong Kong after leaking information on extensive Internet and telephone surveillance by U.S. intelligence; Russia later refuses a U.S. demand for his extradition
2013	Cross-party deal is reached to end a sixteen-day partial government shutdown, which began when Congress failed to agree on a budget
2014	President Obama orders curbs on the use of bulk data collected by U.S. intelligence agencies, in response to criticism sparked by the Snowden leaks
2014	U.S. Senate sends the president a bill to raise the country's borrowing limit for another year, ending a series of political standoffs over the issue
2014	The shooting of an unarmed black teenager by a white policeman sparks weeks of riots in the Missouri town of Ferguson; a grand jury's decision not to charge the officer with murder sets off new unrest
2014	Republicans win a Senate majority in mid-term elections, gaining control of both houses of Congress
2014	President Obama says he will use executive powers to allow four million illegal immigrants to apply for work permits, bypassing the Republic-controlled Congress

Year	Event
2014	U.S. Congressional leaders reach $1.1 trillion spending bill deal to fund federal government until September 2015 and avoid a January shutdown
2014	U.S. and Cuba begin steps to normalize diplomatic relations after more than fifty years of stand-off
2015	President Obama announces that 10,000 U.S. troops will remain in Afghanistan as advisors and trainers until 2016
2015	Police kill two Islamists who opened fire on a Texas conference to draw cartoons of the Muslim Prophet Muhammad; Islamic State armed group claims responsibility
2015	National Guard pulls out of Baltimore and curfew ends after a week of riots sparked by death of a black man in police custody
2015	U.S. accuses Chinese hackers of massive breach of personal data of nearly four million government workers; China denies any role
2015	White supremacist shoots dead nine African American worshippers in a church in Charleston, North Carolina, prompting demands for end to public display of Confederate Civil War-era symbols
2015	Cuba and U.S. reopen embassies
2015	FBI states that a Muslim couple who shot dead fourteen people and wounded twenty-one others at an office party in San Bernardino, California, were Islamist extremists who had prepared the attack (the worst on U.S. soil since September 2001) in advance
2016	Republican candidate Donald Trump wins presidential election, defeating Democratic candidate Hillary Clinton in one of the most heated political campaigns in U.S. history
2017	President Trump signs several executive orders, including a travel ban on anyone arriving from seven Muslim-majority countries, a four-month suspension of the U.S. refugee program, pulling the U.S out of the Trans-Pacific Partnership trade deal, and strengthening border security
2017	A rally for white nationalists in Charlottesville, Virginia, is organized to protest the removal of a statue of General Robert E. Lee. Anti-white national demonstrators confront them and violence breaks out, killing one woman and injuring other protesters. The almost immediate result is the accelerated removal of Confederate memorials.

Introduction

"What is government itself but the greatest of all reflections on human nature? If men were angels, no government would be necessary. If angels were to govern men, neither external nor internal controls on government would be necessary." Although James Madison wrote these words in *The Federalist* No. 51 more than two centuries ago, his words are still relevant today.

Recent events such as heated national elections, the escalation of global terrorism, and the effect of big money on political decision making and its relationship to various corporate financial scandals have forced people to pause and consider realities that our Founding Fathers never dreamed of. Clarification is not easily obtained; television, radio, and newspapers, those repositories of America's basic freedom to express opinions, however misinformed, frequently mean to seduce with spin and sell products rather than serve anything resembling truth. Yet in the midst of the overheated rhetoric of the moment, Americans are responsibly rethinking their role in history and their place as citizens in a free democracy. In the twenty-first century, people across the political spectrum are seeking a better understanding of international issues such as terrorism and national issues like immigration and Internet privacy. They are turning to their leaders and asking them hard questions about how they are going to govern our land and relate to the unprecedented situations of this fast-changing, crisis-dominated world.

The Handy American Government Answer Book: How Washington, Politics, and Elections Work is set against this political backdrop. It is designed to answer basic questions about how our very complex government operates and what it promises, thereby removing the barriers to understanding current political drama. Its straightforward, easily understood, question-and-answer format addresses contemporary issues, as well as the fundamental basics of government in the United States. It traces the historic development of the government and demystifies the departmental labyrinth, providing clear and concise definitions of who does what and why. Meant to inform and entertain, this at-a-glance resource is for those who want to revisit the best snippets of their high school civics class, as well as those who desire a more detailed background on today's headlines. Organized into easily accessible, topic-oriented chapters, over 1,000 most-asked, useful questions are presented.

Interspersed are trivia-oriented and off-the-cuff questions that you might not have considered since you last watched *Jeopardy*. In sum, the book presents an overarching look at government and politics, its key players, and notable events since the time of the early republic. The book begins by exploring the origins of American government. From early colonial governments to the Revolutionary War and the Declaration of Independence, the red, white, and blue shines through in these chapters. You'll be reminded why the English philosopher John Locke's ideas were an inspiration to the new republic, who founded the early colonies, and how an emerging spirit of independence changed the shape of a tenuous America and laid the foundation for a national government. A careful look at the Constitution, our Founding Fathers, and the concept of federalism make up this first section.

Even government and politics aficionados can use some brushing up on how the three branches of the government interact with one another and work to serve the American people. The executive, legislative, and judicial branches are rigorously covered in chapters of the book. Related concepts, such as democracy, limited government, bureaucracy, separation of powers, and check and balances, are examined. What is the president's job description? How does a bill become a law? What is a quorum? A whip? A filibuster? Logrolling? What is the difference between a veto and a pocket veto? How do Supreme Court justices interpret the Constitution? How does a case reach the Supreme Court?

What follows is an intricate look at civil rights and civil liberties, those fundamental freedoms so many Americans feel are slipping away in these tenuous times. In 1755 Benjamin Franklin said, "Those who would give up essential liberty, to purchase a little temporary safety, deserve neither liberty nor safety." Civil liberties are under fire in this age of unprecedented wiretapping, data collection, Internet regulation, microchip implants, and increased federal law enforcement powers. Read about these issues: why there is so much controversy over school prayer, whether random drug tests for student athletes violate their right to privacy, if burning the American flag is considered free speech, how worldwide terrorism, beginning with the events of September 11, has ushered in a new era of restricted freedoms, and much more.

Political opinion and political behavior—in short, the way government behaves—make up the bulk of the book. Readers glean little-known facts about the role of interest groups and what they do to gain influence, political parties, campaigns and elections, how liberals and conservatives differ, and how the media works. But the book is also directly relevant to *you*. You'll learn why trust in government has declined, what Americans think of their president, and what the average citizen can do to get involved. Questions like "Why should a person vote?" "Is the government responsive to public opinion?" and "What is the history of women and minorities in government and politics?" round out the book.

No work of this kind would be whole without acknowledging the numerous resources available to those who want to learn more about the workings of American government and current political trends. For this reason, the concluding pages of the book function as their own mini-resource section, complete with original documents like the Declaration of Independence, the U.S. Constitution (including amendments), and the Articles of Confederation. Here you'll find recommended reading lists and lists of websites for further study.

"The best political community is formed by citizens of the middle class," said Aristotle, a citizen of an early democracy. An informed citizenry is the best defense against political and corporate chicanery, and an active electorate presents the greatest opportunity for democracy to flourish. *The Handy American Government Answer Book* provides some basic illumination in that quest.

—Gina Misiroglu

"The essential principles of our Government ... form the bright constellation which has gone before us and guided our steps through an age of revolution and reformation. The wisdom of our sages and blood of our heroes have been devoted to their attainment. They should be the creed of our political faith, the text of civic instruction, the touchstone by which to try the services of those we trust; and should we wander from them in moments of error or of alarm, let us hasten to retrace our steps and to regain the road which alone leads to peace, liberty and safety."

—Thomas Jefferson, First Inaugural Address, 1801

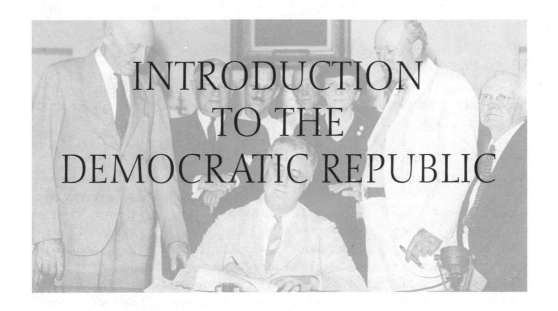

INTRODUCTION TO THE DEMOCRATIC REPUBLIC

POLITICS AND GOVERNMENT

What is politics?

In the broadest sense, politics can be defined as the process of resolving conflicts and deciding which individuals get what, when, and how. More specifically, politics is the struggle over power or influence within organizations or groups that can grant benefits or privileges. Politics can be found in schools, businesses, social groups, and any other organized collection of individuals.

What is government?

Government is the preeminent institution within society in which decisions are made that resolve conflicts and allocate benefits and privileges. It is different from other institutions because it has the ultimate authority for making these decisions.

How does government differ from politics?

Generally, "government" is the word used to describe the formal institutions through which a land and its people are ruled. ("To govern" means to rule.) The term "politics," however, refers to conflicts over the character, leadership, membership, and policies of a government. The goal of politics is to have a voice, or representation, in the government's leadership, organization, and policy making because this representation leads to political power or influence. Political activities include things like raising funds for candidates, lobbying, or attempting to influence public opinion. Americans obtain access to their government through political participation, whereby they can debate and remedy the issues of leadership, structure, and policy of the government that arise.

1

What is the difference between politics and political science?

"Politics" refers to the conduct of government, especially the making of government policies and government organization. Political science is the academic study of political systems and theories.

How is the government involved in my daily life?

Although you can ignore politics, it is impossible to ignore government. Step outside your home, for example, and you almost immediately find yourself walking down a government-owned street or driving on a government-owned highway. The water you drink and the air you breathe are beholden to government pollution standards. The government records your birth. Your public school is a government-funded and government-regulated educational institution; home schools and private schools must meet government educational standards all the way through college. Later in life, your driver's license will be issued by the government, and if you start earning money at any job, you will begin paying payroll and income taxes to the government. When you spend money—currency issued by the federal government—you will pay sales tax on those goods. And if you need assistance from the government, there are government programs to help, including the federal health care program Medicare. When you die, the county government will record your death, and a government judge will oversee the distribution of your estate to your heirs.

What does government do?

Since government is the institution through which a land or a society is ruled, it is the institution that enforces the land's public policies. In its simplest sense, public policies

One of the benefits of government that people might take for granted is the highway system, which would not be possible without taxpayer-funded improvements in infrastructure. The same could be said for such essentials as water lines and sewer systems.

are all the things that the government decides to do, such as impose an income tax, service its armed forces, protect the environment, and hold businesses to certain standards. In a democratic United States, the people elect representatives to the government to enact the popular will. The people who exercise the powers of the government include legislators, who make the law; executives and administrators, who administer and enforce those laws; and judges, who interpret the law.

Why do we need government?

People need government for many reasons. A thread that is common to all governments is the desire to provide a sense of order to the land. All governments tax, penalize, restrict, and regulate their people. A democracy exists to give voice to the people and protect their inalienable rights, as English philosopher John Locke (1632–1704) suggested it should. In contrast, a totalitarian government exists to benefit the state or those in charge and empowers its leaders to rule in any way they see fit. In this type of government, the people's personal freedom is not recognized.

What is the purpose of government in the United States?

In the United States, the purpose of the government is outlined in the Preamble to the Constitution: to form a more perfect union, to establish justice, to ensure domestic tranquility, to provide for the common defense, to promote the general welfare, and to secure the blessings of liberty. In sum, the American government provides citizens with an organized system by which they can live as a nation in peace.

DEMOCRACY AND OTHER FORMS OF GOVERNMENT

What role do authority and legitimacy play in different forms of government?

In order for a government to function, it must have authority—the right and power to enforce its decisions. A government's authority ultimately rests on its control of the armed forces and police. In a healthy society, the government's authority has broad popular support; that is, people accept the government's right to establish laws. When this is the case, a government has legitimacy.

Authority without legitimacy is often a characteristic of oppressive regimes, such as the dictatorships in Egypt, Libya, and Tunisia in the early 2010s.

How are various governments classified?

Several basic features are used to classify governments. They include the geographic distribution of power, which divides the definitions of government between unitary, federal, and confederate; the relationship between the legislative and executive branches,

Gradually, however, liberalism embraced democracy along with equality and liberty for all people. In the eighteenth century, liberal revolutions burst out over much of Western Europe, with the sentiment that dramatic change was possible. It was from this cultural milieu that many of the principles foundational to individual liberty—such as free speech, free assembly, and free conscience—were born. The concept of a limited government and power in the hands of the people were key to the American Revolution of 1776.

Seventeenth-century English philosopher John Locke said that governments should only rule with the consent of the people.

Is there a philosophical basis to limited government?

The philosophical basis of a government that has limitations on its power and that gives a voice to its people can be traced back to the ideas of English philosophers John Locke (1632–1704) and John Stuart Mill (1806–1873) and Scottish economist Adam Smith (1723–1790). Locke challenged the concept of a king's divine right to rule and instead introduced the concept of the "social contract" of government. He believed that government should only exist with the consent of the people and that the only legitimate reason for its existence is to preserve and protect the inalienable rights that people possess.

Fellow philosopher John Stuart Mill believed passionately in the importance of individual freedom against the power of the state. He also came to believe that one of the goals of society should be to offer all its citizens economic security. Today, his name is most associated with a philosophical school called utilitarianism, the main tenet of which is that we should make our ethical decisions on the basis of which action will bring the greatest amount of happiness to the greatest number of people.

In 1776, when the thirteen American colonies of Great Britain declared their independence from their mother country, Adam Smith published *The Wealth of Nations*, considered the first true work of economics and believed to be the most important book in the development of capitalism. In his book, Smith champions a free-market economy and proposes that supply and demand (instead of government laws) are the best regulators of an economic system. Together, these three men represent the early philosophical thought that led to the concept of limited government in the United States.

What are the major concepts of American government?

Three major concepts define American government. First, it is a representative democratic type of government, outlined in and enforced by the Constitution of the United States, that serves the will of the people and gives them direct access to their govern-

> ## Do all governments have constitutions?
>
> No. A constitution, which serves to outline the fundamental laws that establish government organization, determine the roles and duties of segments of the government, and clarify the relationship between the people and their government, is a characteristic of a democracy. The U.S. Constitution was created in 1787 and ratified in 1788.

ment through the political process. Second, it is federal, with powers divided between a central government and several local governments. Third, it is limited in nature in that the government does not have ultimate authority over the people, and each individual has certain rights that the government cannot take away. Associated with its limited nature is the government's distribution of power among its three branches, maintained by a system of checks and balances. Together, these concepts ensure that the American government lies in the hands of the people.

What does the word "democracy" mean?

The word "democracy" comes from the ancient Greek word *demokratia*. *Demos* means "the people," and *krateo* means "to rule." A democracy, then, is a form of government in which the people rule. The power lies in the hands of the people, who may either govern directly or govern indirectly by electing representatives. The American government is a democracy, and the Constitution of the United States ensures this. Under this "social contract," the people of the United States established a government, endowed it with powers, placed upon it certain limitations, set up an administrative structure, and provided the means of control over it. At the heart of democracy lies the concept of popular sovereignty—the idea that the people are the supreme authority and that sovereignty rests in the body of citizens, not one supreme ruler.

What is the difference between representative democracy and direct democracy?

A system of government that provides its citizens with a regular and ongoing opportunity to elect top government officials is known as a representative democracy. A system that allows citizens to vote directly on laws and policies is termed a direct democracy. The government of the United States is a representative democracy at the national level since citizens vote for government officials but do not vote on legislation. Certain states, however, allow for direct legislation through popular referendums. In these states, the voters decide on state legislation through the voting process.

What is considered the purest model of direct democracy?

In ancient Greece, the Athenian system of government is usually considered the purest model of direct democracy because the citizens of that community debated and voted directly on all laws, even those put forward by the city's ruling council. The most important feature of Athenian democracy was that the legislature was composed of all the citizens, each of whom enjoyed a high level of participation. Direct democracy has been practiced in New England town meetings in the United States and at a local level in Switzerland.

Are democracy and limited government the same thing?

The concept of democracy contains the concept of limited government almost inherently in that a government created "by and for the people" puts the power in the hands of many rather than in the hands of one. Guarding against the abuse of power was so important to the Founding Fathers (who had just claimed independence from tyrannical England) that when they created the Constitution, they established a system of separation of powers in order to keep the federal government limited in scope and authority. The separation of powers is maintained by a system of checks and balances, whereby each of the three branches of government—executive, legislative, and judicial—is able to participate in and influence the activities of the other branches. Examples of this include the president's veto power over congressional legislation, the Senate's power to approve presidential appointments, and the Supreme Court's power to review congressional enactments.

What are the essential differences between a presidential and parliamentary system of democracy?

When governments are viewed in terms of the relationship between their legislative and executive agencies, they can be called either presidential or parliamentary. A presidential government, such as exists in the United States, has a separation of powers between the executive and legislative branches. The executive branch is that of the president, while the legislative branch is that of Congress, which is made up of the Senate and the House of Representatives. While the branches are independent of one another and equal in weight, each is accountable to the other, and thus, a system of checks and balances ensures that each branch can restrain actions of the other branch.

In a parliamentary government, such as that of the United Kingdom and most other European nations, the executive branch is made up of a prime minister or premier and that official's cabinet. They are members of the legislative branch, which is called the parliament. The prime minister is the leader of the majority party in parliament and is chosen by that party, making him or her a part of the legislature and subject to its control. There is no system of checks and balances because the chief executive is responsible to and holds office in the legislature.

Is one system better than another?

Many scholars argue that the parliamentary form of government is more expeditious because it does not have one of the major problems that a presidential government has: there is no conflict or deadlock on issues between the executive and legislative branches, which may not always see eye-to-eye on issues. Under the parliamentary system there is never an instance of "divided government" as has occurred in the United States, when

Great Britain's House of Parliament is in London, England. Parliamentary systems dominate most European countries, as well as such nations as India, Australia, and Japan.

one major political party holds the presidency and another controls Congress. Although the American system of government works best when the same party controls its executive and legislative branches, the separation of powers and independent spirit that a democracy ensures does not guarantee this situation. The parliamentary system, on the other hand, does not have a system of checks and balances in place, thus increasing the possibility of abuse of power.

Why is America's democratic system considered so precious?

Although Americans have their own reasons for treasuring democracy, there are several underlying concepts that make a democracy a valued system of government. First, there is a respect for the fundamental worth of the individual, which allows for each person to be viewed as a separate and distinct human being. Second, a democracy stresses the equality of all individuals as it involves equality of opportunity and equality before the law. Third, it is the will of the people and not the will of a select ruling leadership that determines public policy. This is most commonly referred to as "majority rule and minority rights." Fourth, a democracy holds individual freedom to be key to its society while recognizing that there must be balance between the rights of the individual and the rights of society at large. Finally, a democracy upholds individual decision making, both in private life and in government participation; that is, people in a democracy make their own decisions because, according to the definition, people who cannot choose for themselves are not really free.

FUNDAMENTAL VALUES

What is political culture?

In its broadest sense, political culture is the political atmosphere or climate of a nation's government as perceived by its people. It is based upon a shared identity or system of belief in the government and its functions. Although a wide variety of responses might come from people who are asked, "What do you think of your government?", few would disagree that the American political culture embraces values such as democracy, equality, independence, and liberty.

What is liberty?

Since America's founding, perhaps its most fundamental ideal has been that of liberty. This ideal is found in all of the country's early documents: the Declaration of Independence named "Life, Liberty, and the pursuit of Happiness" as three inalienable rights of the people, and the Bill of Rights was created to preserve individual liberties. Because the concept of democracy recognizes the fundamental worth of the individual, liberties are personal freedoms to which we are entitled as human beings. Personal freedom also means freedom from government control, and all democratic governments minimize the role that government plays in the lives of their people.

What is laissez-faire capitalism, and how does it relate to government?

Closely related to the idea of personal liberty, or personal freedom, is the concept of economic freedom. Since the origin of America, economic freedom has been associated with the concepts of capitalism, free competition, and the protection of private property. Laissez-faire, which is translated "to let do" and interpreted as "to let [people] do [as they choose]," is a concept that opposes government influence on economic affairs beyond the minimum necessary to maintain peace and property rights. Laissez-faire capitalism was the economic philosophy introduced during the country's formation to encourage minimal government involvement in business affairs in order to maximize individual freedom of choice and expression. Americans continue to value economic freedom, recognizing that state and federal governments need to impose certain business restrictions to protect the public, including health and safety laws, environmental protection laws, and regulations in the workplace. Born out of the Industrial Revolution and the Progressive Movement, the concept of what industry can and cannot do at the expense of the individual continues to be fine-tuned as government laws are enacted.

What is equality?

Few people fail to recognize the statement in the Declaration of Independence that "all men are created equal." Democracy is based on a fundamental belief in the individual as a unique human being. The democratic concept of equality means that all people are inherently equal and because of this are entitled to both equality of opportunity and

Striving for social and political equality is an ongoing struggle, as these people demonstrate in the 2013 March on Washington, commemorating the fiftieth anniversary of Rev. Dr. Martin Luther King Jr.'s protest at the nation's capital.

equality before the law. The concept of liberty requires limits on government so that personal freedom can be recognized. The concept of equality, by contrast, implies an obligation of the government to the people. Democracy maintains that each person's worth must be recognized both by other individuals and society as a whole, and no person should be limited for reasons such as race, religion, or gender. While not every race, nationality, or gender has realized full equality before the law over the course of the country's history, the United States has made great strides in the areas of civil liberties and civil rights to ensure that the ideal of full equality can be achieved.

What is political equality?

Closely tied to the concept of individual equality is the concept of political equality, in which each person has the right to participate in politics on equal terms. The political community, which began with America's forefathers—white, male property owners— now encompasses all races and genders. The Voting Rights Act of 1965 made racial discrimination in voting illegal and specifically sought to provide a remedy to the number of African Americans who were being kept from participating in the voting process due to various forms of racial discrimination in certain southern states. The ideal of political equality in America has come to be known by the phrase "one person, one vote," rooted in the concept that the right to participate in the voting process belongs to all.

11

How do the different eras of American government embody these fundamental values?

The three defining eras in the transformation of the American government are the years leading up to and including the Revolutionary War (1750s–1783), the Civil War period (1854–1865), and the FDR era (1933–1945). The Revolutionary period of American history was marked by the growing desire of the American colonists to break away from their mother country, England, and establish their independence. America became a new nation at the end of the Revolutionary War, giving birth to a new government based upon the principles of democracy, liberty, and equality. The principles of the Constitution and the portion of the Declaration of Independence that upholds "all men are created equal" were challenged during the Civil War era, when Northerners protested and went to war to end (among other things) the enslavement of blacks in the South. The concept of federalism was also threatened as Southerners demanded to run their states without the interference of the federal government and began to secede from the Union. The issues of basic human freedom and states' rights have never been so amplified as during this period in American history.

President Franklin D. Roosevelt is shown signing the 1935 Social Security Act. FDR put into effect a slew of social programs during the Great Depression.

The administration of Franklin D. Roosevelt and his Depression-era New Deal ushered in one of the most powerful economic forces of the twentieth century and challenged the concept of laissez-faire capitalism, that is, how much the government should interfere in the country's economics. With the passing of fifteen major bills into law, this period introduced large-scale federal oversight of the economy: it forced the development of bureaucratic procedures in business administration, revolutionized public finance, pioneered a mixed economy, and erected the welfare state. The economic philosophies and financial-management techniques that came out of the administration dominated American business life from 1945 to 1980. The era from 1980 to the present is commonly considered New Federalism, a political philosophy of devolution, or the transfer of certain powers from the United States federal government back to the states, that began with Richard Nixon and continued through the Obama Administration in varying degrees. In part, New Federalism involved the conversion of categorical grants into block grants, thereby giving state governments more power in spending.

When is government considered too big?

Opposition to "big government" has been a constant theme in American government, even predating the American Revolution. Americans tend to oppose big government—the large size and scope of government—in principle but support its benefits. When asked to choose among big government, big labor, and big business, 69 percent of Americans named big government as the biggest threat to the United States in the future, according to a 2015 Gallup poll.

POLITICAL IDEOLOGIES

What is a political ideology?

How Americans live in a democracy and resolve conflicts depends on their ideology: the ideas and beliefs an individual has about the role of government and its purpose, scope, and power. Traditionally, Americans have defined their personal political ideology as liberal or conservative and often frame their discussions of political ideology in these terms. Although the definitions have changed over the years, in their simplest form, a conservative generally believes that the best form of government is one that governs least and that a "hands-on" government only hinders individual and economic rights; a liberal tends to favor active government involvement in the economy and the creation and maintenance of social services.

What is individualism?

In the Declaration of Independence, Thomas Jefferson (1743–1826) stated that all individuals are endowed with certain inalienable, or fundamental, inalterable rights. The Founding Fathers placed great value on the individual in an American democracy and believed strongly in the concept of individualism, which dictates that the primary function of government is to enable the individual to achieve his or her highest potential, making the interests of the individual more important than those of the state. Since the early republic, individual freedom and the limits that have been placed on individual freedom have been at the heart of political debate, involving such topics as censorship, legalized abortion, homosexual rights, and affirmative action.

What is conservatism?

Conservatism, often referred to as mainstream conservatism, has at least two important aspects: "Political" conservatives generally support free-market economic principles and low taxes and tend to distrust federal, as opposed to state and local, government power. "Social" or "cultural" conservatives tend to stand for traditional values, such as those associated with family, church, and morality, and support government restrictions on personal behavior with the aim of upholding traditional values. Modern American political conservatism is widely perceived to support personal responsibility, Judeo-Christian religious and moral values, strong law enforcement and strong penalties for crimes, restraint in taxation and regulation of businesses, a strong military, and well-defended, protected borders with regulated immigration. Conservatives tend to oppose gun control laws, many social programs such as welfare and national health care (although many favor the country's mandatory, user-funded retirement benefits), and policies such as affirmative action and multilingual education, which they maintain are expressions of government favoritism of minority groups. The Republican Party is most closely associated with conservatism.

What is liberalism?

Modern American political liberalism is widely perceived to support affirmative action programs; abortion rights; government social programs such as welfare, national health care, unemployment benefits, and retirement programs; strong environmental regulations; trade unions and strong regulation of business; and animal rights. "Liberal" is the term given to those politicians or supporters who are "left" of center, favoring civil liberties and supporting the use of public resources to promote social change in a free-market society. "Political" liberals tend to favor greater federal power to remedy social inequities, while "cultural" liberals tend to support feminist causes, homosexual rights, and similar freedoms of personal choice and behavior. Of the two main political parties, the Democrats are considered to be more liberal.

What is neoconservatism?

In general, neoconservatives believe in the economic and political beliefs associated with classical liberalism of the early nineteenth century. Generally, classical liberalism maintains that unregulated free markets are the best means of allocating productive resources and distributing goods and services to society and that government intervention in society should be minimal. The philosophy of neoconservatism, made popular in the

1990s and early twenty-first century by the writings of *Wall Street Journal* columnist Irving Kristol and *Washington Post* columnist Charles Krauthammer, among others, includes the acceptance of an unregulated market economy; the belief in limited government, particularly with regard to its intervention in public policy; a general distrust toward the welfare state; and a commitment to individualism. While their positions continue to evolve, neoconservatives generally emphasize traditional values and institutions. Some hold positions consistent with New Deal liberalism, while others identify themselves with more mainstream conservatives. Many neoconservatives have been associated with the magazines *Commentary* and *The Public Interest*.

What is the difference between liberal and progressive?

Although opinions vary, the differences between liberals and progressives can be summarized as follows: Liberals tend to have higher incomes and education than progressives. They are more ethnically and culturally diverse than progressives and more concerned about a wider range of issues, including human rights, sexual equality, health care, public education, social services, immigration reform, poverty, international peace, environmentalism, gun control, voting rights, and prison reform.

Progressives are typically more religious than liberals and are distributed more evenly throughout the nation. Liberals are mostly clustered in a smaller number of urban and suburban communities. Progressives are more oriented toward economic issues and see income inequality as the greatest threat to the nation. They generally support collective bargaining, workers' rights, labor empowerment, progressive taxation, small business entrepreneurship, and domestic production. They oppose industrial mo-

How do libertarians differ from conservatives?

In general, libertarians emphasize limited government more than conservatives do and believe the sole legitimate purpose of government is the protection of property rights against force. According to James Kalb, a Yale-educated attorney who frequently writes on the subject of conservatism, because of this underlying philosophical difference, libertarians usually consider legal restrictions on such things as immigration, drug use, and prostitution to be illegitimate violations of personal liberty. Some, but not all, libertarians hold a position that might be described as economically right (that is, antisocialist) and culturally left (opposed to "cultural repressiveness," racism, sexism, and homophobia) and tend to attribute to state intervention the survival of things the cultural Left dislikes. In addition, libertarians tend to believe in rigid individualism and absolute and universally valid human rights, while conservatives are less likely to have that commitment, tending instead to understand rights within the context of particular societies and their norms.

15

nopolies, corporate consolidation, deregulation, money in politics, globalization, outsourcing, offshoring, and the dominance of big banks and multinational interests.

What is a moderate?

In general, a moderate supports democratically authored changes that are not excessive or extreme from either conservative or liberal viewpoints, tending to take a middle-of-the-road stand on many issues. Moderate conservatives tend to support prudent, cautious, traditionally aligned conservative changes in society, while moderate liberals tend to support broad-minded, tolerant, traditionally aligned liberal changes in society.

How have political ideologies changed?

According to the Pew Research Center, a nonpartisan think tank that informs the public about the issues, attitudes, and trends shaping America and the world, a decade ago, the public was less ideologically consistent than it is today. In 2004, only about one in ten Americans was uniformly liberal or conservative across most values. Today, the number who are ideologically consistent has doubled: 21 percent express either consistently liberal or conservative opinions across a range of issues from the size and scope of government to the environment and foreign policy. A 2014 survey found that, as ideological consistency has become more common, it has become increasingly aligned with partisanship. Looking at ten political values questions tracked since 1994, more Democrats now give uniformly liberal responses and more Republicans give uniformly conservative responses than at any point in the last twenty years.

Members of both parties have become more and more ideologically consistent. As a result, there has been less and less middle ground available for compromise. When the responses to ten questions are scaled together to create a measure of ideological consistency, the median (middle) Republican is now more conservative than nearly all Democrats (94%), and the median Democrat is more liberal than 92 percent of Republicans.

SHIFTING DEMOGRAPHICS AND POLITICAL IMPLICATIONS

How have ethnic and racial groups changed over time?

The United States is undergoing a historic demographic shift, with people of color expected to be a majority of the population by 2043. While Asians and Pacific Islanders had the fastest rate of growth during the 1980s and 1990s, the number of non-Hispanic Asians grew 179 percent over the period and reached 9.9 million. Nearly as many Asians as blacks were added to the population. Hispanics had the greatest numerical increase. Between 1980 and 1998, 15.6 million Hispanics (and just 14.8 million non-Hispanic whites) were added to the U.S. population, and today, they are the largest minority group in the United

During the 1980s and 1990s, the Asian American population exploded by 179 percent. While older Asian voters have tended to be conservative, the younger voters, who make up most of the increase, lean Democrat. Such demographic changes can have a significant effect on election results.

States. Likewise, the American Indian and Alaskan Native population has shown a remarkable increase since the 1960s, growing 255 percent between 1960 and 1990.

How are shifting demographics related to the electorate?

Many changes occurring throughout the population are never realized within the electorate. According to statistics from the Center of American Progress in Washington, D.C., for example, there is a large gap between the Latino share of the broader population—those eighteen years of age and older—and their share of the electorate. Since many Latinos are not U.S. citizens, they account for a larger share of the U.S. population than they do of the electorate.

Similarly, there is often a lag between broader population changes and those in the electorate. For example, in California, people of color became a majority of the population in 1999, but it was not until 2014 that enough U.S. citizens had aged into the electorate for people of color to make up a majority of all eligible voters in that state. Although demographic changes in the electorate do not fully track the demographic shifts in the population, there are nonetheless significant shifts occurring within the U.S. electorate. Each state's demographics are changing at different paces and are being driven by different racial or ethnic groups. In some states, voters of color are becoming a larger share of the electorate as a result of rapid growth within a specific racial or ethnic group, which may on its own be a rather small share of the overall electorate.

17

How do ethnicity and race relate to politics?

As people of color become an ever-larger share of states' electorates, the political implications for the Republican and Democratic parties come into even sharper focus: to win the presidency—as well as many U.S. Senate races—candidates must secure substantial support from voters of color. Although Democrats have historically received support from people of color, increased Republican support among voters of color is not unrealistic, particularly given the fact that, as recently as the 2004 presidential election, President George W. Bush received 44 percent of the Latino and Asian American vote and 11 percent of the African American vote nationally.

What does this mean for the future of the American political community?

Although people of color will not make up the majority of the U.S. population until 2043, the political implications of increased minority populations are already being felt in many states. By 2016, demographic shifts will be influential in states such as Florida, where voters of color are an increasingly significant share of the electorate, as well as in states such as Ohio, where elections are close and growth among voters of color is rapidly outpacing the growth of the non-Hispanic white electorate.

What can Americans do to influence their government?

Findings from several 2014 studies suggest that citizen participation in local communities through volunteerism and civic education is the best way to restore people's faith in the state and federal governments. More involvement by houses of worship, corporations, foundations, the media, public officials, and individuals would lead to increased activism and revitalized communities. Likewise, citizens who take personal responsibility for community issues by volunteering and making charitable contributions would feel more empowered. According to a report by the National Commission on Civic Renewal, "this idea—citizens freely working together—is at the heart of the American

Why is it important that Americans understand they can influence the government?

The main reason Americans need to know they can influence the government is that in a very real sense, Americans *are* the government. The Preamble to the Constitution opens with the statement "We the People of the United States...." Because the U.S. government is a constitutional democracy, created "of, by, and for the people," Americans have an inherent right to actively participate in their government. In fact, this clause regards "the People" as superior to any one ruler or governmental system. Additionally, the democratic form of government assumes that people are politically equal and, as equal persons, should all participate in the decision-making process.

Studies show that getting more involved in your community can make one feel empowered as a voter and encourage people to vote more often.

conception of civic liberty, through which citizens take responsibility for improving the condition of their lives. Civic liberty offers citizens the power to act, and it strengthens their conviction that they can make a difference." Another way that Americans can stay involved in the political process is to vote. Voting can provide people with a sense of purpose and empowerment because it is a direct, physical action that has a very specific outcome.

How can the average person get involved in government?

The average person can get involved in government by first educating him- or herself about current issues. This can be done by reading the newspaper daily, reading a weekly news magazine, watching the evening news or CNN, reading online media sites and blogs, or following a leading politician's or influencer's LinkedIn posts or Twitter feeds. In order to make a difference, a person needs to have a working understanding of government in America; indeed, a democratic system of government presupposes a knowledgeable, interested public body of citizens. After education, other very practical methods of involvement include volunteering at a local politician's office, working with voter registration drives, or registering to vote. Activities of a more political nature might include attending a local district or county meeting of a chosen political party, calling or emailing legislators to voice an opinion, and participating in nonviolent protest demonstrations or marches.

19

THE U.S. CONSTITUTION

THE COLONIAL BACKGROUND

Why did the Pilgrims leave their home for the unknown?

A group of people originally from England, the Pilgrims were known as Separatists—Protestants who separated from the Anglican Church of England to set up their own church. In 1609, they fled their home in Scrooby, England, and settled in Holland. Fearing their children would lose contact with their own culture and be assimilated into the Dutch culture, the group decided to voyage to America to establish their own community.

Under what conditions did the Pilgrims travel?

The Pilgrims were in all likelihood familiar with stories of the explorations in the New World and with the settlement in Virginia. Although they possessed neither adequate resources, nor patrons, nor a patent (a document granting the privilege to assume lands), they decided to travel to America. At this time, the Virginia Company was attempting to cure its financial ills by offering privileges and lands to "undertakers" who would set up private plantations. With the help of Sir Edwin Sandys, they secured a patent on June 19, 1619, and an unofficial assurance that the king would not harm them. Although the patent provided that they should settle within Anglican Virginia, they were to be allowed to live as a distinct body with their own government, subject only to the laws of the colony as a whole. They expected to obtain a grant of religious toleration. During the delay that ensued while the Pilgrims awaited royal approval of their grant, Thomas Weston, the leader of a group of London merchant adventurers, obtained a patent from the Virginia Company in the name of John Pierce, one of his associates. Approaching the Pilgrims in Leyden, he persuaded them to abandon their patent and join his group with the promise that the adventurers would supply the funds and handle the business end of the undertaking.

According to the agreement reached by the two parties, those persons going to the colony were to stand as equal partners with the London adventurers in the company. Three groups shared in the investment: seventy London adventurers who paid ten pounds sterling per share, planters who received one share each for their labor, and adventurer planters who were reckoned as having two shares each, one by purchase and a second by going to America. The adventurers in London were to exercise no civil authority over the planters. One hundred and one passengers departed from Plymouth, England, on September 16, 1620. The Pilgrims made up less than half the group. There were approximately thirty-five Pilgrims from Leyden, but of the sixty-six passengers recruited by the adventurers from London and Southampton, most were "strangers." Because the *Speedwell,* the ship in which the Pilgrims had come from Leyden, proved unseaworthy, all had to crowd aboard the *Mayflower* at Plymouth.

What was the Mayflower Compact?

Because the *Mayflower* passengers had traveled beyond the jurisdiction of the Virginia Company's patent, they needed to establish some form of legitimate government. On November 11, 1620, the Pilgrims drafted an agreement by which the adult male passengers aboard the *Mayflower* formed a body politic that was authorized to enact and enforce laws for the community. The men on the *Mayflower* signed the Mayflower Compact as

Signed in 1620 aboard the titular ship, the Mayflower Compact was the first agreement forming a government for the Plymouth Colony. There were forty-one signatories, who were all male because women and children could not vote.

a basis for their new civil government. The famous quote from this brief document, "We … solemnly and mutually in the presence of God, and one of another, covenant and combine ourselves together into a civil body," bound the settlers to create a representative government and abide by its laws.

Why was the Mayflower Compact not a constitution?

When the Pilgrims drafted the Mayflower Compact, it was in the form of a Separatist Church covenant. By its terms, the forty-one signatories (the adult male passengers aboard the *Mayflower*) formed a "Civill body politick," giving them the power to enact laws for the common good and obligating all to obey such laws. It provided the group of colonists with a basic form of government, but it was not a constitution since it did not outline the rules by which the government would operate or the limitations of the government's powers as a true constitution does. Furthermore, constitutions declare the liberties of individuals and government restraints in relation to these liberties. However, the Mayflower Compact was a landmark document in its own right since it provided a precedent for later voluntary democratic compacts that would establish a contractual relationship between the government and the governed.

How did the Pilgrims govern themselves?

Thirty-five more colonists arrived aboard the *Fortune,* putting a strain on already limited resources. Sicknesses such as pneumonia, tuberculosis, and scurvy claimed many lives, including that of Plymouth's first governor, John Carver (1576–1621). Furthermore, the merchants in the group challenged the religious purity of the settlement. Under a new patent secured from the Council of New England in June 1621, the lands of New Plymouth Colony were held in common by the Pilgrims and the merchants, but this communal system of agriculture proved unsuccessful, and in 1624 William Bradford (1590–1657), who had succeeded Carver as governor, granted each family its own parcel of land. The Wampanoag Indians, who had previously occupied the land settled by the Pilgrims, proved friendly and were helpful advisers in agricultural matters. In 1626, the Pilgrims bought out the merchants' shares and claimed the colony for themselves. Though they were inexperienced at government before arriving in America and had not been formally educated, the Pilgrims successfully governed themselves according to the Scriptures, and Plymouth Colony remained independent until 1691, when it became part of Massachusetts Bay Colony, founded by the Puritans.

EARLY COLONIAL GOVERNMENT

Who was John Locke, and why was he important?

English philosopher John Locke (1632–1704) challenged the concept of a king's divine right to rule and instead introduced the concept of the "social contract" of government.

Locke's central idea about government—that it can only exist with the consent of the people—had an enormous effect on the politics of the next century and sowed the seeds for the American Revolution. The American Declaration of Independence and the Constitution are based on principles set forth in Locke's *Two Treatises of Government,* wherein he proposes a theory for the origins and purpose of government based on natural law.

What is the concept of natural law?

Philosopher John Locke maintained that, because God had given each person his or her life, it was part of God's "natural law" that the individual was the only rightful owner of his life, that each had this right equally, and that the right was therefore inalienable. Locke argued that, before government existed, each person had sole responsibility for the defense of his or her own rights. For convenience and the better protection of their rights, people established societies with governments by consenting to a social contract. For Locke, it followed that the only legitimate reason a government had for existing was to preserve and protect rights. If the government violated individual rights, it destroyed the social contract, and this violation released the individual from any obligation and justified rebellion in order to establish a new social contract.

What was the concept of sovereignty that the colonists had been ruled under?

British kings under whom the colonists were ruled believed that the government was all-powerful and held supreme authority, or sovereignty, over the people. This ideology would hold the colonists until pre-Revolutionary War tensions ultimately forced them to challenge the rules of their mother country. The colonists would adopt a concept of popular sovereignty for their new government, giving the people the right to rule, or govern, themselves.

What ideas did the English colonists bring with them that would help shape the government of the United States?

Three cornerstones of English thought helped establish the government of the new land: government is ordered—that is, there is an inherent order, or hierarchy, in government; government is limited and not all-powerful; and government is representative, serving the will of the people and representing their voice.

What were the thirteen colonies, and how long did it take them to be established?

Each of the thirteen colonies was established separately, and for different reasons, over the course of 125 years. Just prior to the outbreak of the Revolutionary War, the thirteen colonies were: Virginia, founded in 1607 by the London Company; Massachusetts Bay Colony, founded in 1628 by the Puritans; New Hampshire, founded in 1629 by John Mason; Maryland, founded in 1634 by Lord Baltimore; Rhode Island, founded in 1636 by Roger Williams; Connecticut, founded in 1636 by emigrants from Massachusetts; Delaware, founded in 1638 by William Penn; North Carolina and South Carolina,

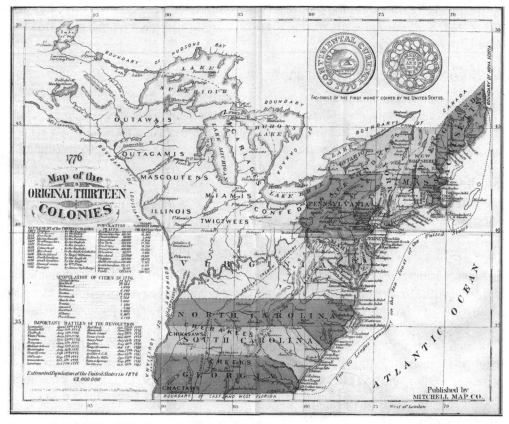

A map made in 1876 for the Centennial celebration shows the original thirteen colonies, as well as the largest cities before the Revolution and the battles of that war.

founded in 1663 by eight nobles; New York, founded in 1664 by the Duke of York; New Jersey, founded in 1664 by Lord John Berkeley and Sir George Carteret; Pennsylvania, founded in 1681 by William Penn; and Georgia, founded in 1732 by James Oglethorpe.

What did the charters have to do with classifying the colonies and establishing forms of government?

Charters not only granted the right to colonize, they determined the rules for establishing government in the colonies. The London Company, which established the colony of Virginia at Jamestown, was governed by a superior council in England with general powers, and this council directed a subordinate council in the colony that was required to govern according to the laws of England. The colonists had no share in their own government; rather, they were granted the liberties guaranteed to all Englishmen at the time, such as trial by jury and free speech. The company had the power to make and enforce laws for the colony as long as they were in concurrence with English law. Three types of colonial government were outlined in the charters: royal (or crown), charter

25

(also known as corporate), and proprietary (a form of chartered government). Regardless of their beginnings, at the start of the American Revolution, colonial governments were either royal or chartered.

Which colonies had bicameral chambers?

A legislative body that is bicameral consists of two chambers. The following colonies had bicameral legislatures: Connecticut, Rhode Island, Maryland, Delaware, Virginia, Massachusetts, New Hampshire, North Carolina, South Carolina, New York, and New Jersey. Today, the U.S. Congress is bicameral, consisting of a Senate and House of Representatives.

Which colonies had unicameral chambers?

A legislative body that is unicameral consists of one chamber. Only two colonies had unicameral legislatures: Pennsylvania and Georgia.

What types of local government did the colonies establish?

The colonies developed two leading types of local government, the New England town and the southern county. Towns arose in New England as the first colonists came in groups—either as congregations or those seeking religious freedom—wanting to live in close proximity. The rugged soil and harsh climate and the presence of Indians encouraged small-scale farming and tightly knit, compact communities. The southern colonies were settled under different circumstances by individual entrepreneurs who were met with a land and climate conducive to large-scale agriculture. The plantation system in that region necessitated a unit of local government larger than that in the North, and hence, the county was born.

A hybrid, called a county-town, emerged in the middle colonies. In all three cases, the units of local government had only as much power as the central government delegated to them. The New England town fostered a spirit of democracy, while the county tended to lean toward aristocratic government.

What was the New England Confederation?

In 1643, the Massachusetts Bay, Plymouth, New Haven, and Connecticut settlements formed the New England Federation, an early attempt at unity against the Native Americans. Meeting in Boston on May 29, 1643, the representatives "readily yielded each to other, in such things as tended to the common good" and drew up articles of confederation. When the last of the four general courts ratified them on September 8, 1643, the articles became binding. The United Colonies of New England, thereby established, encompassed all of the settlements along the coast and rivers from Long Island to New Hampshire. Rhode Island, which the Puritans considered anarchical, and Maine were not included. The United Colonies of New England did not consider themselves a nation but rather individual governments allied by a treaty.

As stated in the preamble to the articles, the purposes of the confederation were to preserve the purity of the Puritans' religion and allow worship free of interference, to promote cooperation, and to provide for defense. The articles themselves specified the duties and powers of the confederation's commissioners, the structure of the confederation, and the rules of procedure. Because there was no judicial authority over all the members, each colony could interpret the articles to suit its own needs.

The governing body of the confederation was to consist of two commissioners chosen annually from each colony. Approval of a matter required the votes of six commissioners, although only four could declare war in a state of emergency. Thus, the Massachusetts Bay Colony could not veto the wishes of the other three colonies. Each commissioner actually served as one of his colony's ambassadors. In matters of military preparation, declaration of war, and arbitration, the four colonies did surrender to the commissioners their individual power to act, yet, while the confederation in theory possessed vague executive and judicial powers, in actuality, it had only advisory powers in most areas. The articles specified that each colony's military obligation should be in proportion to its means and population. Each must send aid if one of the other three colonies should be invaded and must participate in all "just" wars. The commissioners were empowered to decide whether the confederation should wage an offensive war, and no colony could do so without their approval. Apart from military affairs, actual power rested with the general courts of the member colonies. The commissioners could not pass legislation binding on the general courts nor were they directly responsible to the people. They could neither levy taxes nor requisition supplies. Because the commissioners had no powers of enforcement, a colony that disagreed with a particular decision could simply nullify it by refusing to comply. To avoid conflict, the remaining colonies usually compromised.

Although the articles of confederation eventually died in 1684 when the danger of the native tribes had passed and tension among the settlements increased, the Board of Commissioners did perform numerous important services for the four participating colonies. It established various civil agreements of interest to all four colonies and arbitrated intercolonial disputes. Policies concerning the Indians and regulations governing runaway slaves and the extradition of criminals were also within its domain. In the judicial realm, the commissioners established uniform standards for probating wills and served as an admiralty court. Although serious flaws were inherent in the Confederation of the United Colonies of New England, it was to be the longest-lived interstate confederation in American history. The leadership that the confederation provided was essential to the existence of the colonies in their early years. It concentrated the colonies' resources in military emergencies and protected the three weaker colonies from encroachment by the Massachusetts Bay Colony. Most important of all, it preserved the peace in New England.

What was the spirit of the colonies as they grew?

As the colonies started to flourish and grow, a growing spirit of independence emerged. Although each colony was separately controlled by the king of England under English law, the colonies developed a large measure of self-government. Over the century and a half that followed the first settlement at Jamestown, Virginia, each colonial legislature assumed its own broad lawmaking powers. By the mid-1700s, the relationship between

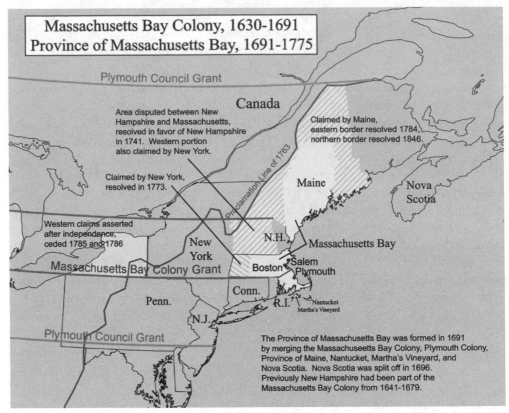

The following labels appear on the map:

Massachusetts Bay Colony, 1630-1691
Province of Massachusetts Bay, 1691-1775

Plymouth Council Grant

Canada

Area disputed between New Hampshire and Massachusetts, resolved in favor of New Hampshire in 1741. Western portion also claimed by New York.

Claimed by Maine, eastern border resolved 1784, northern border resolved 1846.

Claimed by New York, resolved in 1773.

Proclamation Line of 1763

Maine

Nova Scotia

Western claims asserted after independence, ceded 1785 and 1786

New York

N.H.

Massachusetts Bay

Massachusetts Bay Colony Grant

Boston   Salem
Plymouth

Penn.

Conn.

R.I.   Nantucket
Martha's Vineyard

N.J.

Plymouth Council Grant

The Province of Massachusetts Bay was formed in 1691 by merging the Massachuseetts Bay Colony, Plymouth Colony, Province of Maine, Nantucket, Martha's Vineyard, and Nova Scotia. Nova Scotia was split off in 1696. Previously New Hampshire had been part of the Massachusetts Bay Colony from 1641-1679.

A map showing the Massachusetts Bay Colony and how borders changed due to wars and treaties. Originally, the borders continued west throughout the continent, but this changed after the Seven Years' War with France and King George's establishment of the Proclamation Line of 1763. Colonies in the early eighteenth century had governments that functioned independently of England in many ways.

England and the colonies had become federal; that is, a central government in London was responsible for the colony's defense and foreign affairs. The mother country also provided the colonies with a uniform monetary and credit system as well as a common market for colonial trade. Beyond this, however, the colonies could rule independently, and little money was taken from them in direct taxes to pay for the central government overseas. The few trade regulations that Parliament set were disregarded by the colonies.

THE ROAD TO REVOLUTION

How did the relationship between the colonies and Great Britain change during the pre-Revolutionary period?

In the years preceding the American Revolution, English ministers and members of Parliament often treated the colonists with disrespect. England regarded the Americans as its citizens under their traditional imperialistic system, yet refused to grant them rights enjoyed by their countrymen in Britain. In some cases, England passed legislation that had a significant impact on millions of colonists without making the least inquiry into its reception in America. In other instances, England's lawmakers simply ignored the complaints of Americans, disregarding cries for compromise or reconciliation and expressing outrage when the colonies subsequently balked.

Meanwhile, in America the English colonists had become both confident of their own abilities and disillusioned with the motivations of their mother country. By the mid-1700s, the pioneers of the New World felt that they had carved a viable and vibrant society out of a dangerous wilderness. America, the colonists declared, was a place where one's destiny was shaped by talent and perseverance rather than bloodlines. Life on the edge of the civilized world had brought about changes in the colonists' attitudes and outlook, fostering self-sufficiency and autonomy. A tough brand of independence took root in American soil, and as the years passed, the colonists felt less and less inclined to heed the words of a domineering foreign empire. The tenuous relationship of royal authority and colonial autonomy became stretched over the period between 1763 and 1776, finally resulting in the Revolutionary War.

What were the main conflicts that led up to the American Revolution?

The American colonies' relationship with England, which had grown increasingly strained during the first half of the eighteenth century, continued to deteriorate during the 1750s and 1760s. American resentment of English trade restrictions and taxation was exacerbated by Parliament's refusal to grant the colonies a representative voice in the British Empire. By the early 1770s, the anger of the independent-minded colonists, who had forged productive lives for themselves out of the American wilderness, was beginning to crest.

The Townshend Acts (a new set of levies passed in 1767), the Boston Massacre of colonists by British troops (1770), the destruction of the British revenue cutter HMS *Gaspee* by American smugglers (1772), the Boston Tea Party protest (1773), and the Intolerable Acts (a set of 1774 laws which included the closing of Boston Harbor and severely limited self-governance in Massachusetts) were major events that contributed to the animosity between the two sides, and in September 1774, the First Continental Congress convened to discuss the colonies' options. Observers on both sides of the Atlantic warned that revolution could well result if the complaints of the colonies were not addressed. But England proved unwilling to change its methods of governance, and America subsequently declared its independence. From 1775 to 1783, British troops and the colonists' Continental Army battled for control of the American colonies in the Revolutionary War.

What were the Townshend Acts?

The Townshend Acts, named after Charles Townshend, the British colonial minister who enacted them, were a series of revenue laws imposed on the colonies by Parliament. Seizing upon Benjamin Franklin's statement preceding the Stamp Act's repeal to the effect that Americans opposed on principle only internal taxes, Townshend declared that if the colonists adhered to such a distinction, they should be saddled with external duties on tea, lead, paper, paints, and glass. The danger to Americans in the subsequent Revenue Act of 1767 containing these proposals was not in the sums of money colonists would pay. The danger rather was that Parliament was persisting in its efforts to destroy the colonists' rights, not only by taxing them without their consent but also by a provision in the act stating that part of the amount collected was to be used to pay the salaries of judges and governors in America, thus making them independent of the financial jurisdiction of the colonial assemblies.

The assemblies believed themselves threatened on still another front by the Quartering Act of 1765. When barracks were unavailable, British troops in the colonies were to be lodged in taverns and other public houses at the expense of the provincial authorities. The colonists felt that Parliament was taxing Americans indirectly by ordering their assemblies to levy monies for the upkeep of royal regiments. Although the American legislatures after 1765 usually provided for the army's needs, they were careful to maintain their constitutional integrity by avoiding precise compliance with the letter of the law. But when New York (whose location made it the colony most frequently called upon for support) enacted a measure providing for the housing of troops that was deemed inadequate by the military, Parliament suspended the colony's legislature until it bowed to the letter of the British Quartering Act. New York did not back down, nor

Boston's Old State House (from which the British governed Massachusetts until the Revolutionary War) still stands today. It was in front of this building that the Boston Massacre occurred in 1770.

did the other assemblies, and when a compromise on military appropriations for New York was reached with local leaders, the ministry secured a lifting of the ban, but not before Americans realized that a dangerous precedent had been set in temporarily depriving subjects of the British Empire of their political representation.

Additionally, Townshend brought about a reorganization of the customs service in America to guarantee collections of the new taxes as well as to achieve greater compliance with the older Navigation Acts of the mid-seventeenth century. Previously controlled from Great Britain, customs officers in the colonies were now under a special board sitting in Boston; they would predictably be zealous in the handling of their assignment for a third of all fines received in the Vice Admiralty courts went to the customs men. Additional courts were established the following year, and many merchants faced charges of violating the exceedingly complicated provisions of the Sugar Act of 1764.

Although these various British measures prompted a less violent reaction in the colonies than the Stamp Act of 1765, they collectively represented an even larger threat to American rights. The point was brought home when, in response to the customs collectors' appeal for protection, the secretary of state for the colonies, the Earl of Hillsborough (Wills Hill), ordered General Thomas Gage, the British commander in chief in North America, to station regular troops in Boston. In 1770, Parliament repealed all the Townshend duties except the one on tea, a symbol of Parliament's authority to tax.

What was the Boston Massacre?

As new laws were passed by Great Britain in order to keep the colonists under the royal thumb, colonists began to show their resentment and opposition by disregarding the laws altogether. Mob violence was commonplace at several colonial ports, and colonists supported a boycott on English goods. Finally, on March 5, 1770, British troops in Boston fired on a crowd that had assembled, killing five men, in an event history will forever call the Boston Massacre. The Boston Massacre may have been a misnomer, the result of extreme harassment of the British redcoats, and triggered, according to defender John Adams, by Crispus Attucks, an escaped slave who was the first to die and "to whose mad behavior, in all probability, the dreadful carnage of that night is chiefly to be ascribed." The result of the attack caused Americans to wonder if their respective colonies would be the next to have a standing army in their midst—one seemingly intent on destroying their liberties not only by its presence but through violent means.

In the wake of the Boston Massacre, it was not the townspeople who had provoked the riot who had to stand trial but the British soldiers who had fired their weapons in self-defense. Though the soldiers were acquitted, lawyer Samuel Adams made so much of the event that he was able to force Governor William Hutchinson (1711–1780) to withdraw all six hundred British troops from the city of Boston and keep them in barracks at Castle William. The event and subsequent removal of soldiers quieted the city, and the repeal of the Townshend Acts, along with the reinstatement of the dissolved assemblies, brought a period of relative peace in the colonies from 1770 to 1772.

What was the burning of the *Gaspee?*

On June 9, 1772, the HMS *Gaspee,* a British warship, was docked at Providence, Rhode Island, while pursuing a merchant ship suspected of smuggling. The next night, eight boatloads of men, led by the wealthy Providence merchant John Brown, boarded the ship, wounded its commander, Lieutenant William Dudingston, and burned the ship in retaliation against Dudingston's harassment of local farmers and fishermen in his mission to put an end to smuggling in Rhode Island. When England threatened to revoke Rhode Island's charter if a reasonable explanation for the event couldn't be provided, Rhode Island half-heartedly apologized, ending the incident.

What was the Tea Act of 1773?

On May 10, 1773, Parliament passed the Tea Act, which lightened duties on tea imported into Britain to give relief to the East India Company, which had seven years' supply in warehouses on the Thames River

An 1883 issue of *Harper's* magazine included this illustration of the burning of the *Gaspee* in 1772 by rebellious Americans upset over the Navigation Acts.

and was being strained by storage charges. However, the act permitted tea to be shipped at full duty to the American colonies and to be sold directly to retailers, eliminating colonial middlemen and undercutting their prices. The passage of the Tea Act coincided with Parliament's passage of a Regulating Act, which was an effort to bring the East India Company under government control.

Was the Boston Tea Party really a party?

Slightly disguised as Mohawk Indians, members of the Sons of Liberty boarded ships in Boston Harbor in December 1773 in reaction to the tax Britain had imposed on tea. In protest, they dumped a shipload of tea (23,000 pounds) belonging to the East India Company into Boston Harbor. The origins of the famous Tea Party—which was really outright defiance of taxation and not at all celebratory—are found in Parliament's repeal, in 1770, of all the external taxes in the controversial Townshend Revenue Act, except the tax on tea, which was to remain principally as a symbol of the mother country's right to tax the colonists.

How did England react to the Boston Tea Party?

Ironically, British politicians had acted not with the purpose of disciplining the Americans but with the intention of boosting the sagging fortunes of the giant East India

Company. After unsuccessful attempts to help the ailing corporation with huge investments in India, the prime minister of Great Britain, Frederick North, Earl of Guilford (1732–1792), secured passage of the Tea Act, which for the first time allowed the East India Company to sell tea directly to America and to do so through its own agents; previously, it had sold its product to English wholesale merchants, the tea then passing into the hands of American wholesalers and retailers. By depriving the English and American middlemen of their former profits and by adding a provision eliminating English duties on tea exported to the New World possessions, the company hoped to undersell Dutch-smuggled leaves in America, even though the provincials would still have to pay the remaining Townshend tax of three pence on each pound.

Everywhere in North America, North's move met stiff resistance. Merchants accused the ministry of giving the East India Company and its agents a monopoly on the local tea market that would be followed in time by other monopolies in American trade. More frightening to Americans was their vulnerability; they were vulnerable already since the taxed herb had been purchased in America after 1770. Now, if they consumed even more of the dutied drink, they would implicitly admit the authority of Parliament to tax them. In fact, they saw in Lord North's efforts a cynical attempt to get them to "barter liberty for luxury." Consignees charged with collecting the tax in New York, Philadelphia, and Charleston, like the stamp tax collectors before them, were persuaded to resign their commissions. The outcome was different in Boston, where Governor Hutchinson supported the consignees and refused to let the tea ships return to England without first unloading their cargo.

When the colonists performed the task of "unloading," Parliament's response was one of unparalleled severity. It passed the Coercive Acts—otherwise known as the In-

A 1789 depiction by artist W. D. Cooper shows the Boston Tea Party of 1773 in which Americans, some dressed as Indians, destroyed a shipment of tea from the East India Company to protest the Tea Act.

tolerable Acts—in order to bring rebellious Massachusetts under control by closing the Port of Boston; altering the structure of government in the colony; allowing British officials and soldiers accused of capital offenses to be tried in England or, to avoid a hostile local jury, in a colony other than the one where the offense had occurred; and providing for the quartering of troops again in the town of Boston. Massachusetts and the other twelve colonies did not accept this verdict as it struck at the foundations of self-government more than any other of Parliament's actions.

What were the Intolerable Acts of 1774?

The Intolerable Acts, also known as the Coercive Acts, were five laws passed by the British Parliament early in 1774. Intended to assert British authority in the Massachusetts colony, the measures were seen as punishment for the Boston Tea Party of December 1773. In brief, the laws mandated the following: closure of the Port of Boston until the tea was paid for (the Port Bill), an English trial for any British officer or soldier who was charged with murder in the colonies, the change in the charter of Massachusetts such that the colonial council had to be appointed by the British and town meetings could not be held without the (British-appointed) governor's permission, the requirement that the colonists house and feed British soldiers, and the extension of the province of Quebec southward to the Ohio River. A separate Quebec Act set up an undemocratic government in that expanded colony.

Closing the Boston port and quartering troops in private households were unprecedented actions, and colonial charters had never been revoked outright—only annulled through quo warranto judicial proceedings. While the British intention was to bring the Massachusetts colony under control (and actually, the fifth act was not intended to have any punitive effect on the colony), the result was instead to unite all the colonies in opposition to British rule. The acts are thus seen as the major precursor to the American Revolution.

Why was Samuel Adams called the Father of the American Revolution?

The radicals' most effective leader was Samuel Adams (1722–1803) of Massachusetts, who earned the title "Father of the American Revolution" (or "Father of Independence") for his spirit, determination, and leadership qualities. Although he is known primarily for his active role in opposing the Stamp Act and the Townshend Acts and for orchestrating the Boston Tea Party, Adams' influence extended far beyond his role in aggravating the loyalists. From the time he graduated from Harvard College in 1740, Adams toiled tirelessly for a single cause: independence. Adams was always a public servant in some capacity—inspector of chimneys, tax collector, and moderator of town meetings. A shrewd politician, he had the primary goal of freeing people from their awe of social and political superiors, making them aware of their own power as individuals, and rallying them to action. As a motivator of the people toward independence, he published dozens of articles in newspapers and made speeches in town meetings, instigating resolutions that appealed to the colonists' democratic impulses.

By the time of the battles of Lexington and Concord in 1775, Adams' career as a propagandist and agitator had peaked. However, Adams continued to stay active in politics, and at the First and Second Continental congresses, he represented Massachusetts by signing the Declaration of Independence, espousing immediate political separation from Britain, and recommending the formation of state governments and a confederation among the new states. He supported George Washington for commander in chief of the Continental Army and helped draft the Articles of Confederation, America's first attempt at government.

What types of political writing preceded the Revolution?

In 1767, the Philadelphia lawyer John Dickinson (1732–1808) published the first installments of *Letters from a Farmer in Pennsylvania*. Dickinson had drafted the resolutions and grievances of the Stamp Act Congress two years earlier as a member of that body, and his letters on the nonimportation and nonexportation agreements continued to appear through much of 1768, winning him wide popularity in the colonies. Other writers joined the battle, most notably Thomas Jefferson (1743–1826), who expressed the thinking of many of his countrymen in 1774. His pamphlet *Summary View* referred to the king as the "chief magistrate" of the empire and denied the authority of Parliament to legislate for the colonies in any case whatsoever. In addition, Samuel Adams published his famous "circular letters," arguing that Parliament did not have unlimited power to overrule the will of popular assemblies in the colonies.

Most students of the pre-Revolutionary era are familiar with Thomas Paine (1737–1809), whose *Common Sense* is heralded as the most popular pre-Revolutionary pamphlet, ever. Published anonymously by Paine in January 1776, *Common Sense* was an instant best seller, with 120,000 copies sold within three months of its distribution. Often called "the book that started the American Revolution," Paine's political pamphlet rallied the hearts of revolutionaries by placing blame for the suffering of the colonies on the reigning British monarch, George III. It called for an immediate declaration of independence, noting that it was the moral obligation of America to break free from its mother country. Not long after publication, the spirit of Paine's argument found resonance in the Declaration of Independence. The pamphlet made Paine internationally famous, and he continued to inspire the patriots during the Revolutionary War with a series of pamphlets titled *The American Crisis*.

When was the First Continental Congress convened?

In response to the Intolerable Acts, the Massachusetts and Virginia assemblies called together a meeting of the colonies. The First Continental Congress, composed of fifty-six delegates from twelve of the thirteen colonies (Georgia was not represented), met in Philadelphia on September 5, 1774. For almost two months, the Congress met to discuss the current situation with Great Britain and set a course of action. It was in this meeting that two major proposals were made: a general boycott of English goods and the organizing of a militia.

Before adjourning on October 26, Congress dispatched the Declaration of Rights: a series of declarations and addresses to the king, to the people of Great Britain, and to the people of America. The delegates called for a return to the relationship the colonies had enjoyed with the mother country in the years prior to 1763 and asked for the repeal or withdrawal of policies and laws, beginning with the decision to keep an army in America and concluding with the Coercive Acts. In Great Britain, the Congress's appeals fell largely on deaf ears. As early as November 18, 1774, King George III informed his prime minister, Lord Frederick North (Earl of Guilford), that "the New England governments are in a state of rebellion, blows must decide whether they are to be subject to this country or independent." The meeting provided for another intercolonial meeting the following spring, and over the course of the next few months, all the colonial legislatures (including Georgia's) supported the actions of the First Continental Congress.

Is it true that the First Continental Congress was made up of conservatives and radicals?

Yes. From the outset of the Congress, the delegates' main objective was to review their relationship with Great Britain. Since Parliament had refused to recognize the colonists' repeated attempts to distinguish between taxation and legislation regulating trade for the benefit of the empire but not for revenue, many Americans felt they had no choice but to conclude that Parliament should have no control over them at all. Men like Thomas Jefferson, who referred to the king as the "chief magistrate" of the empire and denied the authority of Parliament to legislate for the colonies in any case whatsoever, were called radicals. Also known as Patriots, or Whigs, they urged a united resistance to the acts of Parliament. Some of the congressmen, however, were reluctant to reject the word of Parliament completely and instead urged compromise and reconciliation with the mother country. They were generally termed conservatives, or Tories. Extreme conservatives would later become active supporters of England during the Revolutionary War and be known as Loyalists because they retained their allegiance to England. Although the result was a compromise resolution stating that by consent, not by right, Parliament might regulate commerce in the interest of all, these two groups were increasingly at odds with one another.

The First Continental Congress was held in this building, Carpenters' Hall, in Philadelphia. It is now part of Independence National Historic Park.

Who were the Patriots?

Patriots were those revolutionists who supported an independent America, free of

British rule. They would go to war for their convictions and called themselves Patriots because of their love for their country. With two million people who hailed freedom as their cause, they were the party in the majority, although little military training, lack of a navy, and minimal canons and gunpowder contributed to their weaknesses as an army. The patriots that fill the history books include General George Washington, commander of the Continental Army; James Madison, a member of the Virginia legislature and Continental Congress; John Adams, a delegate to the Continental Congress; Samuel Adams, a Boston tax collector, member of the Massachusetts legislature, and delegate to the First and Second Continental congresses; Benjamin Franklin, a publisher, printer, inventor, and deputy postmaster general for the colonies; Patrick Henry, a Virginia lawyer and orator; John Paul Jones, an American naval officer; Thomas Paine, a political philosopher and author of *Common Sense*; and Paul Revere, a silversmith and engraver who took part in the Boston Tea Party.

Lesser-known Patriots include Mary McCauley, otherwise known as Molly Pitcher, for carrying water to wounded soldiers during the Revolutionary War; James Lafayette, an African American double agent and Revolutionary War hero; and Abigail Adams, a writer and the wife of John Adams, who would become the second president of the United States.

Who were the Loyalists?

Loyalists, or Tories, as their adversaries called them, were those American men and women who supported Great Britain and its colonial rule of America. Loyalists believed that independence would give rise to mob rule and result in the loss of economic benefits derived from membership in the British mercantile system. The majority of Loyalists were small farmers, artisans, and shopkeepers. In addition, British officials, wealthy merchants, and Anglican ministers, especially in Puritan New England, tended to remain loyal to the Crown. By mid-1775, Loyalists who openly opposed the Patriots and supported Britain were no longer tolerated in the colonies and exiled.

Approximately 19,000 Loyalists, armed and supplied by the British, fought in the American Revolution. They included African American slaves, who were promised freedom if they fought for the British; Native Americans, who believed the British would not infringe upon their land; and other men and women, generally in the southern colonies, who felt the colonists were reactionary and wild. Well-known Loyalists William Howe, commander of the British Army during the Revolution, whose victories included the Battle of Bunker Hill (1775), the capture of New York City (1776), and the Battle of Brandywine (1777); General Thomas Gage, an English general and the last royal governor of Massachusetts; and Lord Charles Cornwallis, a major general responsible for driving General Washington out of New Jersey but eventually defeated at Yorktown by French and American armies. Other Loyalists, who eventually left America after the American Revolution, include William Franklin, the son of Benjamin, and John Singleton Copley, the greatest American painter of the period.

When did the Second Continental Congress convene?

After fighting broke out at Lexington and Concord in April 1775, the colonies again sent representatives to Philadelphia, convening the Second Continental Congress on May 10, 1775. Delegates—including George Washington, Thomas Jefferson, Benjamin Franklin, and John Hancock as president—organized and prepared for the fight, creating the Continental Army and naming Washington as its commander in chief. With armed conflict already under way, the Congress nevertheless moved slowly toward proclaiming independence from Britain. On July 10, two days after issuing a declaration to take up arms, the Congress made another appeal to King George III, hoping to settle the matter without further conflict. The Congress adjourned on August 2, 1775, with the legislators agreeing to reconvene six weeks later.

What was the role of the Second Continental Congress once the Revolution began?

When the Second Continental Congress convened in May 1775, its goals included establishing a national army and stopping the colonies from attempting to make separate reconciliation agreements with England. With small battles continuing and news coming in of the battle at Bunker Hill, the Congress encouraged the separate colonies to organize their own militias. The Congress also put George Washington at the head of a Patriot army and ordered American troops to march north into Canada by autumn. The Congress voted to print paper money to help pay for this army, to establish a post office, and to send commissioners to negotiate with Indians. In July 1775, the Congress sent the Olive Branch Petition to Britain in an attempt to mend the divide between the colonies and the British government. The Congress was no longer a temporary council

The Second Continental Congress was held in 1776 and took the important step of adopting the Declaration of Independence.

of Americans articulating constitutional doctrines; it was the central government of a people at war. The attempt at reconciliation with the king failed, and the following summer, the Second Continental Congress took its most famous action when it approved the Declaration of Independence, breaking off all ties with Great Britain.

Why was the Second Continental Congress so important to the foundations of government?

In essence, the Second Continental Congress became America's first government. Although it had no constitutional base and was denounced by Great Britain, it was supported by the people and fueled by public opinion. It functioned as the first government for five years—from the adoption of the Declaration of Independence in July 1776 until the Articles of Confederation went into effect on March 1, 1781. In that time period, it fought the Revolutionary War, raised armies and a navy, made treaties with foreign countries, and in general performed all the functions of a government. During this time, the unicameral Congress exercised both legislative and executive powers. Each colony—and later state—had one vote in legislative issues, and executive duties were allocated to a committee of delegates.

How did the American Revolution end?

The conflict raged on through the end of the 1770s and into the 1780s, but in October 1781 the war for independence finally came to a close. The defeat of General Charles Cornwallis (1738–1805) and his British troops at Yorktown, Virginia, largely ended the fighting, although small skirmishes continued for two more years. Weary of its war with the rebellious colonies and aware of threats from other European nations at home, England decided to make peace with America, even at the price of conceding American independence. In 1783, after months of negotiation with English, French, and Spanish representatives, an agreement was reached, and the Treaty of Paris formally recognized America as an independent nation.

How did the American Revolution constitute the birth of a new nation?

By spring 1776, a spirit of independence was mounting in America. Various military successes and the acts of the Continental Congress inspired leaders, and after the Virginia delegate Richard Henry Lee (1732–1794) proposed that the states should be independent, triggering the appointment of a committee to write a formal declaration of independence, it wasn't long before the Declaration of Independence was approved on July 4, 1776. This document broke all ties with England and officially declared the thirteen colonies to be thirteen united states, giving birth to a new nation.

What significance does the American Revolution have today?

Twenty-first-century Americans living under a free government owe a lot to the American Revolution, which was fought for many of the freedoms people sometimes take for

39

granted today. These include the right to elect a head of government who can only act with the consent of the people; the right to elect public officials who must obey the law just like other Americans; and the civil rights of free speech, free religion, a fair trial, and justice for all men and women, regardless of position in life.

How was the Declaration of Independence key to the formation of a new government?

The Declaration of Independence, formally adopted on July 4, 1776, by the Continental Congress, announced the birth of a new nation and set forth a philosophy of human freedom that would become a dynamic force throughout the world. The preamble borrows from English Enlightenment political philosophy, specifically John Locke's *Second Treatise of Government,* when it justifies the people's right

One of history's most famous documents, the Declaration of Independence, is unique for the ideology behind it. Not only was it a statement of breaking away from the mother country, but it also set forth a philosophy of human freedom that was unprecedented.

to overthrow a government that denies them their natural rights: "We hold these truths to be self-evident, that all men are created equal, that they are endowed by their Creator with certain unalienable Rights, that among these are Life, Liberty and the pursuit of Happiness. That to secure these rights, Governments are instituted among Men, deriving their just powers from the consent of the governed, that whenever any Form of Government becomes destructive of these ends, it is the Right of the People to alter or to abolish it, and to institute a new Government, laying its foundation on such principles, and organizing its powers in such form, as to them shall seem most likely to effect their Safety and Happiness."

Here, Thomas Jefferson linked Locke's principles directly to the situation in the colonies. To fight for American independence was to fight for a government based on popular consent in place of a government rule by an authoritarian king—a government that could secure natural rights to life, liberty, and the pursuit of happiness. The body of the Declaration lists the colonists' grievances against the king of England and, for the first time, officially employs the phrase "United States of America," uniting the thirteen colonies into thirteen united states that from this point in history would function under one nation.

THE FIRST STATE GOVERNMENTS

Why did the states develop their own constitutions?

After the outbreak of the Revolutionary War, when the New Hampshire and South Carolina provincial congresses asked Congress for advice on how to govern, Congress responded by urging each colony to establish its own government, stating that each should have "full and free representation of the people" and "establish such a form of Government, as in their Judgment will best produce the happiness of the People." In each colony, the provincial congress named itself the House of Representatives, declared the office of governor vacant, and continued governing. By the end of 1775, royal authority had collapsed in most of the American colonies. In response, each state except Connecticut and Rhode Island, who simply eliminated the references to the monarch in their colonial charters, drew up new plans of government.

What were the main features of the first state constitutions?

Most of the new constitutions of 1776 and 1777 created systems that looked a lot like the old charter governments, although the governor was almost completely under the assembly's control. He would be chosen by the assembly or by the people and would not have power to veto the assembly's actions. Virginia, which drew up the first constitution in June 1776, began its constitution with a declaration of rights, a model other states followed. Such declarations displayed the states' belief that the purpose of government was to secure rights to its citizens. Pennsylvania created a unique government, with a single-house legislature chosen every year by all adult male taxpayers, making the legislature the most representative body in the world. Although the first state constitutions differed, they shared several common features: each was based upon popular sovereignty, meaning that the government could only rule with the consent of the governed; each upheld a limited government, with many restrictions; seven constitutions contained a bill of rights outlining "inalienable rights" for the people; and there was a separation of powers, whereby government authority was divided among executive, legislative, and judicial branches.

Which seven state constitutions contained a bill of rights?

The constitutions of Delaware, Maryland, Massachusetts, New Hampshire, North Carolina, Pennsylvania, and Virginia all contained a bill of rights.

How were the state constitutional conventions formed?

When the Massachusetts legislature submitted a constitution to the people of the state in 1778, the people rejected it because the legislature did not have the power to write a constitution. The idea emerged that a constitution could not be written by a legislature but had to originate from a special convention that the people had chosen specifically to write a constitution. This convention would represent the sovereign power of the people and could create a fundamental law delegating power to the legislature that the constitution created. New Hampshire held the first constitutional convention in June 1778, although the constitution this convention submitted to the people was rejected. After 1778, states used conventions, rather than legislatures, to draw up their fundamental laws.

What were the Articles of Confederation?

Although each state created a new government, the states were also members of a union, the United States of America. As the United States, they formed treaties with other nations, maintained General George Washington's army, issued paper money, and borrowed money to pay for the war. In the weeks after independence was declared, John Dickinson (1732–1808) began drafting a plan of union, and in autumn 1777 Congress submitted this plan to the states. This early agreement was not a constitution but rather an "agreement to cooperate" that attempted to unite the thirteen original states.

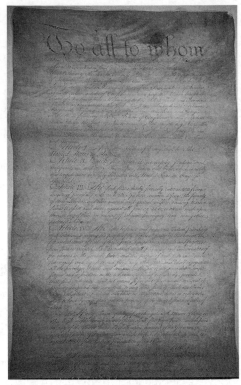

The Articles of Confederation, the first attempt at a constitution, were ratified in 1777 and came into force in 1781. The document's main flaw was that the central government it formed was too weak.

In November 1777, Congress voted its approval of a constitution for the United States—the Articles of Confederation—and submitted it to the states to accept or reject. Under the articles, Congress continued as the only branch of the central government. Each state could choose no fewer than two and no more than seven delegates to Congress. In addition, each state could have only one vote in Congress. A simple majority of states assembled decided issues, except for specified matters that required the consent of nine (out of thirteen). Each state alone could tax itself or regulate its commerce, although each had to contribute its share of money to the upkeep of the Confederation. Each state claiming territory in the trans-Appalachian region was allowed to keep its possessions instead of turning them over to the United States. Individually, the states were to retain their "sovereignty, freedom and independence" not specifically granted by Congress. In turn, Congress's authority covered making war and peace, making military and naval appointments, requisitioning men and money from the states, sending and receiving ambassadors, negotiating treaties and alliances, conducting Indian relations, managing postal affairs, coining money, deciding weights and measures, and settling disputes between states. Although Congress approved the articles in 1777, they were not ratified by all of the states until 1781. The articles served as the nation's basic charter of government until the first government under the Constitution of the United States was formed in 1789.

What type of government did the Articles of Confederation create?

This first government was known as a confederation or confederacy because the national government derived all of its powers directly from the states. Congress was denied power to raise taxes or regulate commerce, and many of the powers it was authorized to exercise required the approval of a minimum of nine states (out of thirteen), thereby handicapping its ability to do business.

How did the states attempt to remedy these weaknesses?

With the central government unable to enforce any regulations on the states, the states argued among themselves and became increasingly suspicious of one another's activities, taxing each other's goods, banning one another's trade, and printing their own money. Economic instability spread throughout the states, prices of goods soared, and sound credit disappeared. The states refused to support the central government, and several of them made agreements with foreign countries, even though the articles forbade it. Most of the states organized their own militias. In 1785 and 1786, some states began to discuss ways to strengthen the national government, with Maryland and Virginia leading the way in a meeting held in Alexandria, Virginia, to address their trade issues.

What were the shortcomings of the Articles of Confederation?

There were many shortcomings in the Articles of Confederation, which according to its own words granted the Continental Congress limited powers and allowed each state to retain its sovereignty. First, Congress had no direct authority over citizens of the United States but rather had to work through the states; as such, it could not pass laws or levy taxes that would allow it to carry out its responsibilities of defending the nation. Second, Congress could not regulate trade between the states or with other nations. Third, Congress could not stop the states from issuing their own currency, and as a result, the country was inundated with various currencies. Fourth, because there was no executive branch, Congress was weighed down with responsibility for all administrative duties. And finally, because there was no judiciary system in place, the national government had to trust the state courts to enforce national laws and settle interstate disputes. The articles' greatest weakness, however, was its failure to create a strong central government. Although the states submitted to the national government's authority briefly during the war, once the war was over, each state resumed its sovereignty and was unwilling to give up its rights—including the power to tax—to a fledgling national government.

How did the Articles of Confederation compare with previous attempts at creating a union?

All delegates to the Continental Congress understood the importance of unity, and thus, many attempts at creating a union preceded the Articles of Confederation. In 1754, when France threatened the colonies, Benjamin Franklin proposed a plan of union that called for the colonies to unite under a general council, with a governor appointed by the king. In 1774 Joseph Galloway (1731–1803) proposed a similar plan of union, but by this time, delegates from Massachusetts were not willing to support any concessions to British power. Galloway's plan was struck from the record, and he would remain loyal to the king, while his colleagues in Congress drifted toward independence. In the sum-

Joseph Galloway, a Pennsylvanian delegate to the Continental Congress, proposed a Plan of Union that would have kept some political ties to England.

mer of 1775, Franklin proposed another plan of union, with Congress serving as a governing body for the colonies. Silas Deane of Connecticut proposed a similar plan, but Congress was consumed with other problems and did not seriously consider either plan.

How did the Articles of Confederation lay the groundwork for the U.S. Constitution?

Dissatisfaction with the Articles of Confederation was aggravated by the hardships of a postwar depression, and in 1787—the same year that Congress passed the Northwest Ordinance, providing for the establishment of new territories and states on the frontier—a convention assembled in Philadelphia to revise the articles. The convention adopted an altogether new constitution, the present Constitution of the United States, which greatly increased the powers of the central government at the expense of the states. This document was ratified by the states on the understanding that it would be amended to include a bill of rights guaranteeing certain fundamental freedoms. These freedoms—including the rights of free speech, press, and assembly, freedom from unreasonable search and seizure, and the right to a speedy and public trial by an impartial jury—are assured by the first ten amendments to the Constitution, adopted on December 5, 1791, and officially known as the Bill of Rights.

THE CONSTITUTIONAL CONVENTION

What was the Constitutional Convention, and when did it convene?

Beginning on May 25, 1785, and running for approximately five months, the Constitutional Convention consisted of an assembly of delegates who convened in Philadelphia at Independence Hall. They initially met to discuss revisions to the Articles of Confederation but soon abandoned the revision in order to create a new constitution that would allow for a strong federal government.

Who attended the Constitutional Convention?

Every state except Rhode Island sent delegates, although the delegates were in attendance at varying times. In all, seventy-four men were appointed as delegates, fifty-five attended at one time or another, and approximately forty were responsible for the hands-on work of developing a constitution. The delegates were the elite of the American republic: lawyers, merchants, physicians, planters, and at least nineteen slaveowners. Twenty-six were college educated, thirty-four were lawyers or had studied law, three were physicians, approximately forty had served as legislators, thirteen had held state offices, and as many as twenty had helped write state constitutions. Because of the unique gifts of this assembly, Thomas Jefferson referred to them as an "assembly of demigods."

The most active delegates in favor of establishing a stronger federal government were James Madison and George Mason from Virginia, James Wilson and Gouverneur Morris from Pennsylvania, John Dickinson from Delaware, John Rutledge and Charles Pinckney from South Carolina, and Oliver Ellsworth from Connecticut. The more active and important leaders who preferred to amend the Articles of Confederation were Roger Sherman from Connecticut, William Paterson from New Jersey, Elbridge Gerry from Massachusetts, and Luther Martin from Maryland. George Washington was appointed president of the convention. Leaders who did not attend include Richard Henry Lee, Patrick Henry, Thomas Jefferson, John Adams, Samuel Adams, and John Hancock.

Who were the oldest and youngest members of the Constitutional Convention?

Benjamin Franklin of Pennsylvania was eighty-one years old at the time, and Jonathan Dayton of New Jersey was twenty-six.

Were there any special rules that governed the convention?

At the second session, held on May 28, the delegates adopted several rules regarding how they were to conduct business. They agreed that a majority of the states would be necessary in order to move forward on any issue; each state would have one vote, and a majority of votes would carry any given proposal. To protect the interests of each state and avoid public pressure, the Constitutional Convention also adopted a pact of secrecy.

What was the Virginia Plan?

Edmund Randolph (1753–1813) submitted the Virginia Plan, representing the ideas of James Madison and the interests of the large states, to the Constitutional Convention on May 29, 1787. The plan called for a new government with greatly expanded powers to be exercised by three separate branches: legislative, executive, and judicial. It called for a bicameral, or two-house, national legislature, with representation based on population or financial contribution to the central government. The people would elect the members of the lower house, or House of Representatives, who would then elect the members of the upper house, or Senate. The national legislature would, in turn, choose a national executive. The Virginia Plan also provided for a national judiciary and granted the national legislature the power to veto any law passed by the states that was in conflict with national law. Since the states varied in size and wealth, a number of delegates thought the Virginia Plan was biased toward the large states and quickly developed a counterproposal.

What was the New Jersey Plan?

William Paterson (1745–1806) of New Jersey, representing the small states, presented his alternative plan on June 15, 1787. The New Jersey Plan suggested giving Congress more power over commerce and revenue but keeping equal state representation in the legislature, regardless of population. It also called for a federal executive branch of more than one person who was chosen by Congress but could be recalled at the motion of a

William Paterson (left), who would later serve as governor of New Jersey, proposed the New Jersey Plan, which gave states equal representation regardless of population. Edmund Randolph (right), who would go on to be U.S. attorney general and a governor of Virginia, proposed the Virginia Plan, which gave more power to states with higher populations and that made more financial contributions to the federal government.

majority of state governors. As the various plans were discussed, central to the debate was how the states would be represented in Congress.

What agreements were reached at the Constitutional Convention?

The delegates believed in the concept of a balance of power in politics, which was supported by colonial experience and reinforced by the familiar writings of John Locke. These influences led to the conviction that three equal and coordinating branches of government should be established—legislative, executive, and judicial—so that no one entity could ever gain complete control. The delegates agreed that, like the colonial legislatures and the British Parliament, the legislative branch should consist of two houses. However, along with this initial agreement, much debate and compromise took place, and generally, three main compromises are known to have shaped the Constitutional Convention: the compromise between large and small states over their representation in Congress, known as the Connecticut Compromise; the compromise between the North and the South over how slaves would be counted for taxation and representation, determined by the Three-Fifths Compromise; and the compromise between the North and the South over the regulation and taxation of commerce, known as the Commerce and Slave Trade Compromise.

What was the Connecticut Compromise?

The outcome of the debate between the Virginia and New Jersey plans was the Connecticut Compromise, also known as the Great Compromise. It called for the formation of a bicameral legislature, or two houses of Congress, in order to satisfy both the big and small states. It called for the representatives in the first branch of Congress, or the House of Representatives, to be apportioned according to the state's population. However, in the second branch, or Senate, each state would have an equal vote regardless of the size of its population. Although the plan was not immediately accepted, the delegates preferred the arrangement to the breakup of the union and finally agreed to the Connecticut Compromise.

What was the Three-Fifths Compromise?

Once the Connecticut Compromise decided that the seats in the House would be based on state population, the delegates argued over whether slaves should be counted in the populations of the southern states. Because their numbers were significant—with ninety percent of all slaves residing in Georgia, North Carolina, South Carolina, Maryland, and Virginia—most delegates from the slaveholding states argued that their numbers be factored in. The North, however, disagreed. The result was the Three-Fifths Compromise, which determined that "three-fifths of all other persons" would be counted; in other words, five slaves would instead be counted as three. This formula was also used to calculate the amount of money raised in each state by any direct tax levied by Congress.

What was the Commerce and Slave Trade Compromise?

Although convention delegates agreed that Congress had the power to regulate interstate and foreign trade, many southerners feared that Congress would side with the commercial interests of the northern states, interfere with its slave trade, and try to pay for government out of the export duties of the South's biggest crop, tobacco. The Commerce and Slave Trade Compromise addressed the South's concerns, denying Congress the power to tax the export goods of any states and initiating a hands-off policy whereby it was denied the power to act on the slave trade for at least twenty years.

How did the framers of the Constitution reconcile their interests and principles?

The men who met at the Constitutional Convention were willing to make many compromises in order to reach their goal of a strong national government. Although there were arguments, and even shouting matches, over some of the most heated issues, the men pressed on, and when the issue of how the states should be represented in Congress arose, Benjamin Franklin suggested forming a separate committee—consisting of one member from each state—to debate the issue. *Compromise* is the word that comes up repeatedly in historians' summaries of the Constitutional Convention. In *The Morning of America,* historian Darrett Rutman wrote, "The extraordinary feature of the Philadelphia convention was that the delegates could surmount their fears and prejudices, hammering out one practical compromise after another in the interest of a 'more perfect union.'"

Who earned the title Father of the Constitution?

James Madison (1751–1836) of Virginia earned the title of Father of the Constitution for his contributions as a political theorist and practical politician. In the month before the Constitutional Convention opened, Madison pored over historical texts and drew on his legislative experience to analyze the pitfalls of the U.S. government under the Articles of Confederation. In Madison's view, the state constitutions, which existed to protect the people from their rulers, actually contributed to a breakdown of social order because those in power used majority rule to pass laws to protect their private interests. For example, Rhode Island passed paper money laws that helped farmers and hurt their creditors, and Maryland and New York passed navigation laws that favored their commercial interests over the interests of other states or the United States as a whole. To end this self-interest, Madison advocated the establishment of a large national republic whose legislators would act in the best interests of all the people, thus initiating the formation of the new government as established by the Constitution.

James Madison, who was the fourth U.S. president, is remembered as the Father of the Constitution for his contributions as a political theorist.

What is meant by the term "constitution"?

A constitution embodies the fundamental principles of a government. The U.S. Constitution, adopted by the sovereign power—the people—is amendable by that power only. All laws, executive actions, and judicial decisions must conform to the Constitution as it is the creator of the powers exercised by the departments of government. Because no law may be passed that contradicts its principles, and no person or government is exempt from following it, it has earned its title as the "supreme law of the land."

Who actually wrote the Constitution?

In none of the records of the Constitutional Convention is the literary authorship of any part of the Constitution definitely established. The framers of the Constitution debated proposed plans until July 24, 1787, when a Committee of Detail was appointed, consisting of John Rutledge of South Carolina, Edmund Randolph of Virginia, Nathaniel Gorham of Massachusetts, Oliver Ellsworth of Connecticut, and James Wilson of Pennsylvania. On August 6, these men submitted a draft that included a preamble, twenty-three articles, and fifty-seven sections. Debate continued until September 8, when a new Committee of Style was named to revise the draft, including William Samuel Johnson of Connecticut, Alexander Hamilton of New York, Gouverneur Morris of Pennsylvania, James Madison of Virginia, and Rufus King of Massachusetts, who submitted the final draft on September 12. Historians generally attribute the literary form of the Constitution to Morris, based on Morris' own claim and Madison's papers.

Who signed the Constitution?

On September 17, 1787, after sixteen weeks of deliberation, the finished Constitution was signed by thirty-nine of the forty-two delegates present, including such historical notables as George Washington, James Madison, Alexander Hamilton, and Benjamin Franklin. Famous dissenters include Edmund Randolph, George Mason, and Luther Martin.

PRINCIPLES OF THE CONSTITUTION

What are the basic principles of the Constitution?

The final version of the Constitution, approved on September 17, 1787, established a federal democratic republic with an indivisible union of sovereign states. It is a democracy because people govern themselves, representative because people choose elected officials by free and secret ballot, and a republic because the government derives its power from the people. This model of government is based upon the idea of popular sovereignty, which upholds that the people are the only source of government's power. Furthermore, the government's power is limited because it can only do the things that people have authorized the government to do. The Constitution established a federal government with broad powers that were equally divided among the three branches, firmly establishing the principle of balanced government with a separation of powers and a system of checks and balances. Although powerful, the federal republic was created to uphold liberty, guaranteed because a division of power between the federal and state governments, known as federalism, would prevent one government entity from assuming too much power.

Specifically, Article I, Section 8 gives Congress far-reaching control over domestic, economic, and foreign affairs in addition to the power to make all laws necessary for executing its powers. The Constitution also contains a long list of powers that are forbidden to the states. The president has widespread authority over the military, foreign policy, and appointments to office. The courts have the power of judicial review: the authority to decide whether the government's actions are constitutional. After the Constitution was written, in time, the Supreme Court assumed the power of reviewing the constitutionality of state laws that had been denied to Congress.

Why was a democracy chosen?

Although the word "democracy" is not found in the Declaration of Independence or the Constitution and the Founding Fathers preferred the word "republic," the framers of the

Ratified in 1787, the U.S. Constitution established a federal democratic republic. It is important to note that this established the country not as a democracy but as a republic. A democracy means that a majority rules over everyone else, no matter the majority's will; in a republic, certain rights are protected for all citizens and cannot be taken away even if a majority wants to.

Constitution chose democracy as both a way and form of government and a political mindset because they wanted a government ruled by the people. The characteristics of the nation's constitutional democracy are everything the Founding Fathers felt would allow for the most effective and successful nation—a recognition of every person's fundamental worth (the widest degree of individual freedom), equality of opportunity, a belief in majority rule, and an upholding of minority rights—all functioning under the banner of popular consent and within a system of interdependent political structures.

Did the framers of the Constitution place equal weight on the concepts of liberty, equality, and democracy?

No. The Preamble to the Constitution states that the purpose of the federal government is to "establish Justice, insure domestic Tranquility, provide for the common defence, promote the general Welfare, and secure the Blessings of Liberty to ourselves and our Posterity." Although the framers had a high regard for the concept of freedom of each individual and the "Blessings of Liberty" as a nation, they failed to include clauses that protected the liberties of the people. These would not be added until the passage of the Bill of Rights, the first ten amendments to the Constitution, which guarantee civil liberties. And although respect for the individual—as a unique entity to be valued—is the basis of popular rule in a democracy, not all men and women (or rich and poor or black and white people, for that matter) were treated equally in the early republic. The Constitution itself discounted slaves as citizens and counted five slaves for every three free white men in each state's representation in Congress. The principles of democracy probably hold the greatest weight in the Constitution, since the word covers a breadth of values, political processes, and political structures that this key document guarantees.

Why was a three-branch model chosen?

Although the framers of the Constitution intended to create a stronger central government for the fledgling United States, they also wanted to limit the powers of the government. A three-branch model—the legislative branch (Congress), the executive branch (the president), and the judicial branch (the courts)—distributes the power of the national government among these three authorities, ensuring that not all power is consolidated in one place.

What did the Founding Fathers mean by a "separation of powers"?

In 1787, Founding Father Thomas Jefferson wrote to John Adams: "The first principle of a good government is certainly a distribution of its powers into executive, judiciary, and legislative, and a subdivision of the latter into two or three branches." Jefferson's words express one of the core principles of American government: its separate but shared power structure. Three separate and independent branches—the executive, the legislative, and the judicial—function together as the national government. Each branch has its own set of powers and responsibilities, although there is an intentional overlap of

51

some powers. The framers of the Constitution believed that this separation of powers would protect individuals' liberties and prevent the government from abusing its power. The separation of powers is enforced by a system of checks and balances.

What does "checks and balances" mean?

Although each branch has its own authority, they are not completely separate or independent of one another. Instead, they are threaded together by a system of "checks and balances" that subjects each branch to a number of constitutional checks, or restraints, by the other branches. The system of checks and balances was designed by the Founding Fathers to prevent a concentration of power in any one branch and to protect the rights and liberties of citizens. For example, the president can veto bills approved by Congress, and the president nominates individuals to serve in the federal judiciary; the Supreme Court can declare a law enacted by Congress or an action by the president unconstitutional; and Congress can impeach the president and federal court justices and judges.

A portrait of Thomas Jefferson painted by Mather Brown in 1786. Jefferson was one of several Founding Fathers who believed in the division of governmental powers that resulted in the three-branch model used in the United States.

Did the states or the people ratify the Constitution?

The states. Before the Constitution could take effect, it had to be ratified by specially elected conventions in at least nine of the thirteen states. Although the Constitution was debated, by June 21, 1788, more than the required nine states had ratified the document in the following order: Delaware, Pennsylvania, New Jersey, Georgia, Connecticut, Massachusetts, Maryland, South Carolina, New Hampshire, Virginia, and New York. After George Washington was inaugurated president of the United States, North Carolina and Rhode Island ratified.

What is the most widely quoted phrase from the Preamble to the Constitution?

The opening lines of the Preamble to the Constitution, beginning with "We the People," are the most oft quoted by students and scholars alike. Unlike the Articles of Confederation, which spoke to the states and had their best interests in mind, these words of the preamble directly link the Constitution to the people of the United States of America.

What is an expressed power?

In order to further guarantee the limits of the new national government, the Constitution grants expressed powers: those powers expressly stated in the Constitution. Also called enumerated powers, most expressed powers are found in Article I, Section 8, where the Constitution expressly gives twenty-seven powers to Congress, including the power of taxation, coining money, regulating foreign and interstate commerce, and declaring war.

What is an implied power?

Implied powers, on the other hand, are those powers not expressly stated in the Constitution but reasonably implied by the expressed powers. Implied powers are granted by the Necessary and Proper Clause, found in Article I, Section 8. Examples of implied powers include Congress's regulation of labor-management agreements, the prohibition of racial discrimination in public places, and the building of an interstate highway system. Although these powers are very diverse, Congress acted on its authority under one expressed power—the power to regulate foreign and interstate commerce—to initiate actions such as these.

What is an inherent power?

An inherent power is any power that belongs to the national government simply because it is the national government of a sovereign state, the United States of America. The Constitution does not expressly provide for inherent powers, but they include the powers that national governments have historically held, including the power to regulate immigration, the power to acquire land, and the power to protect government land against rebellion or war.

Is the Constitution a rigid or flexible document?

Both. Many historians use the term "rigid" to describe the Constitution because the provisions are in a written document that cannot be legally changed with the same ease and in the same manner as ordinary laws. The British Constitution, on the other hand, has been called "flexible" because it is an unwritten document that can be changed

What is the Elastic Clause?

Because the framers wanted to create a dynamic government, they included the Necessary and Proper Clause, also known as the Elastic Clause, in Article I, Section 8 of the Constitution. Meant to empower rather than limit government, it gives Congress the authority to pass all laws "necessary and proper" to carry out the enumerated powers outlined in the Constitution.

overnight by an act of Parliament. However, many scholars have pointed out that the Constitution is rigid—in that, as the supreme law of the land, it must be followed—yet flexible enough to allow for changes through a formal amendment and ratification process. Indeed, the Founding Fathers included a provision in the Constitution for amending the document when social, economic, or political conditions demanded it. Twenty-seven amendments have been added since the original Constitution was ratified, and this flexibility has proven to be one of the Constitution's greatest strengths. Without such flexibility, it is inconceivable that a document drafted more than two hundred years ago could effectively serve the needs of 260 million people and the thousands of multilevel governmental units in the United States today.

AMENDING THE CONSTITUTION

What is an amendment?

The process of constitutional change and growth comes through the Constitution's own amendment—literally, a change or addition to its written words that then becomes part of the Constitution itself.

How is the Constitution amended?

Under Article V of the Constitution, there are two ways to propose amendments to the Constitution: two-thirds of both houses of Congress vote to propose an amendment, or two-thirds of the state legislatures ask Congress to call a national convention to propose amendments. The latter method has not yet been used.

What does the term "ratification" mean?

The ratification of a document is its formal approval. It is the final consent to a constitution, constitutional amendment, or treaty. The Constitution was ratified by nine of thirteen states before it was legally adopted, and likewise, each amendment must be ratified by three-fourths of the states before it can be added to the Constitution.

How is an amendment ratified?

Article V of the Constitution outlines the two ways for amendments to be ratified by the states. An amendment must be approved either by three-fourths of the state legislatures or by ratifying conventions in three-fourths of the states. The latter method was used only once: to ratify the Twenty-first Amendment, which repealed Prohibition.

How many amendments have been made to the Constitution?

Since 1789, Congress has proposed more than ten thousand joint resolutions calling for amendments to the Constitution. Of these thousands, only thirty-three have been sent to the states, and only twenty-seven have been ratified.

Is there a specified time limit for the ratification process?

Legally, no. In 1917, when Congress proposed the Eighteenth Amendment to the Constitution, it set a seven-year deadline for the ratification process. Since that time, it has set a similar deadline for the ratification of every amendment proposed, with the exception of the Nineteenth Amendment. In the case of *Dillon v. Gloss* (1921), the Supreme Court upheld that Congress can place "a reasonable time limit" on the ratification process, but there has been no legal determination of just how long a reasonable time limit is. Indeed, a handful of would-be amendments were never added to the Constitution be-

The Bill of Rights contains the first ten amendments of the Constitution. Since then, only seventeen more amendments have been added.

cause they fell short of meeting their deadlines. In the twentieth century these include a 1924 amendment that would have authorized Congress to regulate child labor; the 1972 Equal Rights Amendment, which fell three states short of ratification when it finally died in 1982; and a 1978 amendment to give the District of Columbia seats in Congress, which lost steam in 1985.

What are the amendments, and what changes did they make?

The most famous are the first ten amendments to the Constitution, known as the Bill of Rights. Added in 1791, the Bill of Rights guarantees people's basic freedom of expression and belief. Other amendments include the Thirteenth Amendment, which prohibits slavery, added in 1865; the Fourteenth Amendment, which guarantees citizenship, due process, and equal protection under law, added in 1868; the Nineteenth Amendment, which gives women the right to vote, added in 1920; and the Twenty-second Amendment, which limits presidential tenure, added in 1951.

What was the longest period during which no amendment was added to the Constitution?

Sixty-one years, from 1804 to 1865, is the longest stretch of years between constitutional amendments (in this case, the Twelfth and Thirteenth amendments).

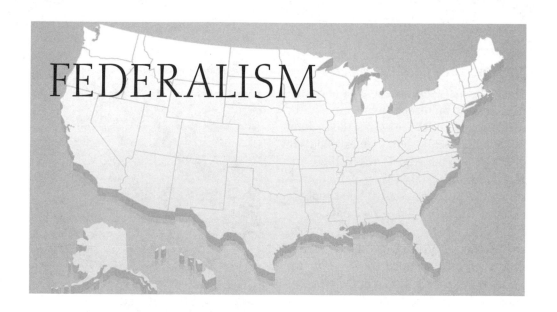

FEDERALISM

FEDERALISM AND ITS CONSTITUTIONAL BASIS

Who were the Federalists and the Anti-Federalists, and how did they differ?

Proponents of the Constitution adopted the name Federalists, taking the name from their opponents, known as Anti-Federalists, who claimed that the confederation of states under the Articles of Confederation was a true federal government. Federalist leaders included men like James Madison, Alexander Hamilton, and John Jay, who together wrote a series of eighty-five newspaper essays collected in a book called *The Federalist* (1788), as well as George Washington and Benjamin Franklin. As nationally known figures, they used their prestige and political finesse to organize support for the Constitution. They attracted merchants, lawyers, planters, and other elites but also artisans, shopkeepers, farmers, and other members of the middle classes whose livelihoods would benefit from stronger national economic control.

On the other hand, most Anti-Federalists were not prominent national leaders, but they vehemently opposed the Constitution for various reasons. Some were opposed to Congress's taxation power, others disliked the president's sweeping authority, and still others objected to the omission of a Bill of Rights to protect individual liberties. In general, however, the Anti-Federalists, many of whom were small farmers, feared that the Constitution created a national government that would be dominated by aristocrats, whose nearly limitless power would deprive ordinary people of their independence. Prominent Anti-Federalists included Patrick Henry, Richard Henry Lee, George Mason, and Samuel Adams.

What are *The Federalist Papers?*

The Federalist Papers are a series of eighty-five essays published anonymously by Alexander Hamilton (c. 1756–1804), John Jay (1745–1829), and James Madison (1751–1836) between October 1787 and May 1788 urging ratification of the Constitution. Because the Constitution sought to increase the power of the national government at the expense of the state governments, the national debate over ratification began almost immediately after the Philadelphia Convention sent the proposed constitution to Congress on September 10, 1787, and its contents became known. Late in September, the *New York Independent Journal* began printing a series of Anti-Federalist essays by "Cato" (who was possibly New York's powerful governor, George Clinton). In order to refute these and other Anti-Federalist tracts, Alexander Hamilton and John Jay, two of New York's most prominent Federalists, agreed to write a series of newspaper essays under the name "Publius." The first (*Federalist* No. 1), written by Hamilton, appeared in the *New York Independent Journal* on October 27, and in

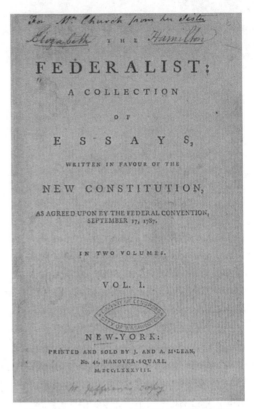

Published between 1787 and 1788, *The Federalist Papers* comprised essays by John Jay, Alexander Hamilton, and James Madison that argued for ratification of the Constitution.

it, Hamilton outlined the purpose of the entire series. The essays would explain the necessity of the union for "political prosperity," the "insufficiency of the present Confederation to preserve that Union," and the need for a more "energetic" government than that which existed under the Articles of Confederation. John Jay wrote the next four installments before ill health forced him to quit. In November, James Madison, who was in New York representing Virginia in Congress, took Jay's place, and between them, Madison and Hamilton produced all but one of the remaining eighty essays; Jay wrote No. 64.

Which is the most famous of all the *Federalist* essays?

Scholars generally agree that James Madison's first contribution to the series, *Federalist* No. 10, is the most famous of all the essays. In it, Madison discussed the origins of parties, or "factions," as he called them, and argued that they sprang inevitably from "the unequal distribution of property." Some Anti-Federalists argued that the nation was much too large and diverse to be governed effectively by a powerful central government without sacrificing people's liberties and freedoms in the process, but in *Federalist* No.

10, Madison used his ideas about factions to reverse their argument. The nation's size, he wrote, and the great variety of its people and their interests were sources of strength, not weakness. There were so many different groups, so many different interests that would be represented in the new government, that no one faction, no one group, could ever capture control of the national government. Far from inviting tyranny, he argued, the nation's size and diversity, when coupled with the federal republican form of government proposed by the Constitution, would provide a strong check against tyranny.

What is the significance of *The Federalist Papers* today?

Although the effectiveness of *The Federalist Papers* as political tracts in 1788 has been debated, historians consider the essays important keys to understanding the intentions of the members of the Philadelphia Convention. Historians, scholars, students, and Supreme Court justices alike have studied the papers as a guide to the framers' mindset, in spite of the fact that one author (John Jay) did not attend the Philadelphia Convention, another (Alexander Hamilton) played a very small role there and was himself dissatisfied with the Constitution, and the third (James Madison) came to have serious doubts about the meaning of the Constitution and the kind of government it created within a few years after he wrote his essays for *The Federalist*.

The essays have been brought into many public political debates since they were written, particularly during times of constitutional crisis, such as the states' rights debates that preceded the Civil War, the discussion over the constitutionality of President Franklin D. Roosevelt's New Deal policies, and the debate over states' rights and civil liberties in the 1950s. Apart from its partisan political value, many historians and political scientists consider *The Federalist* to be the best existing defense of federal republicanism in general and of the American Constitution in particular. Few would disagree that it is among the foremost works of political science produced in the United States.

What is federalism?

In its simplest definition, federalism is a form of government in which a written constitution divides governmental powers between a central government and several regional governments. In the United States, federalism is the constitutional arrangement that divides sovereignty, or governmental authority, between the national and state governments, each of which enforces its own laws directly on its citizens. Neither side can change this division of power or amend the Constitution without the consent of the other. Nearly 40 percent of the world's people live under federalist governments, including Canada, Switzerland, Australia, and Mexico.

Can the words "federal system" be found in the Constitution?

No. The term "federal system" does not appear in the Constitution, nor is it possible to find a systematic division of government authority between the national and state governments in that document. Rather, the Constitution clearly outlines different types of powers:

(1) powers of the national government;

(2) powers of the states; and

(3) prohibited powers.

The Constitution also makes it clear that if a state or local law conflicts with a national law, the national law will prevail.

How does the U.S. Constitution allow for federalism?

Under the Constitution, both the nation and the fifty states pass laws, impose taxes, have their own budgets, and run their own courts. Neither side gets its power from the other—both get their power directly from the people—and both are subject to the Constitution as the only legal source of authority for both the states and the nation. The Tenth Amendment outlines this division of powers, which in essence produces a dual system of government. By providing for two basic levels of government, the Constitution allows both the states and the national government to govern the same people and the same territory simultaneously.

What is a unitary system?

The alternative to federalism is a unitary system of government, which favors a centralized government that holds all the power. Rather than a division of powers among

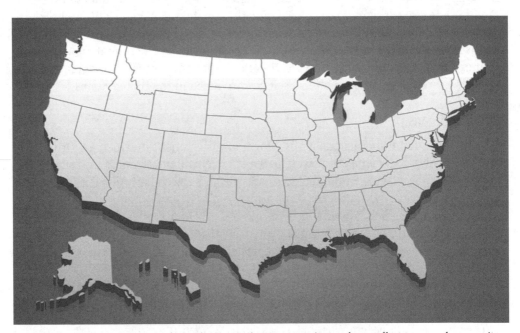

Federalism in the United States works by allowing each state to pass its own laws, collect taxes, and manage its own budget. Meanwhile, the federal government can do the same, setting up a dual government for each citizen, in essence.

entities, the central government retains all authority and as such determines, at its sole discretion, which powers it will delegate or take away. Examples of unitary governments include Great Britain, France, Israel, and the Philippines.

How does the concept of federalism limit the national government's power?

Because the concept of federalism allows for a division of powers between the national government and the states, it prevents the national government from becoming all-powerful. The concept of federalism creates a dual system of government, in which two sovereigns, each with its own sphere of authority, operate over a nation simultaneously. The Tenth Amendment gives a large sphere of power to the states, in which they can exercise all the powers reserved to them as well as those that the Constitution does not expressly forbid. The national government does not enjoy that luxury: as a government of delegated powers, it can only exercise the powers that the Constitution specifically grants.

What powers are delegated to the national government, and which are reserved by the states?

The powers delegated to the national government include printing money, regulating interstate and international trade, making treaties and conducting foreign policy, declaring war, providing an army and navy, establishing post offices, and making any laws necessary and proper to carry out these powers. The states enjoy certain powers reserved to them within the federal system, including issuing licenses, regulating intrastate businesses, conducting elections, establishing local governments, ratifying amendments to the Constitution, taking measures for public health and safety, and exercising powers the Constitution does not delegate to the national government or prohibit to the states.

Political scientists have noted that the sharing of power between the national government and state governments allows citizens to enjoy the benefits of both diversity and unity. For example, the national government has the authority to set up a uniform currency system, which benefits interstate travelers and relieves the states of having to regulate their own currency. However, issues like the death penalty have been left up to the individual states, allowing each state to live by its own philosophy according to its individual needs.

What powers are shared by both the national government and the states?

The national government and the state governments share many powers. For example, both can collect taxes, build roads, borrow money, establish courts, make and enforce laws, charter banks and corporations, spend money for the general welfare, and acquire private property for public purposes with just compensation.

What powers are denied to national and state governments?

Under the Constitution, the national government may not violate the Bill of Rights, impose export taxes among states, use money from the treasury without the passage and approval of an appropriations bill, or change state boundaries. State governments may not enter into treaties with other countries, print money, tax imports or exports, impair contractual obligations, or suspend a person's rights without due process. In addition, neither the national government nor state governments may grant titles of nobility; permit slavery (as established by the Thirteenth Amendment); deny citizens the right to vote due to race, color, or previous servitude (as established by the Fifteenth Amendment); or deny citizens the right to vote because of gender (as established by the Nineteenth Amendment).

What is meant by "dual federalism," and what was its role in the nation's early history?

Although state governments have their own constitutions, the laws made in individual states must not conflict with the Constitution. During the first one hundred years of United States history, the states did most of the governing that directly affected the people, while the national government mainly concentrated on foreign affairs. This two-

The U.S. Civil War led to important changes in the balance between federal and state powers in America, starting with amendments determining voting rights for citizens, including those regarding race.

layer system of government, where each level of government controls its own sphere, is known as dual federalism. Under this system, sometimes called the traditional system because it functioned from 1789 to 1937, the national government retained less power than the state governments and had little effect on state economics other than promoting interstate commerce. The emphasis of the national government's programs was on internal improvements, disposal of public lands, tariffs, and maintaining a national currency, while the state legislatures controlled all property laws (including slavery), commerce laws, insurance laws, education laws, and local government and civil service laws, to name a few.

During this time, a divide began to form between the two entities over the issue of who had sovereignty, culminating in the Civil War. After the war, a series of constitutional amendments were passed that outlined the federal government's control over social and economic policy and the protection of the civil rights of citizens. Known as Civil War Amendments, these included the Thirteenth Amendment, which prohibited slavery; the Fourteenth Amendment, which defined citizenship and guaranteed due process under the law; and the Fifteenth Amendment, which maintained that a person could not be denied the right to vote based on race. Dual federalism continued after 1860, but the power of the federal government began to strengthen. However, full national expansions into local and intrastate matters would not come about until the 1930s.

What role did *McCulloch v. Maryland* play in the concept of dual federalism?

Dual federalism reigned in America despite landmark Supreme Court cases that ruled for a pro-national interpretation of the Constitution. *McCulloch v. Maryland* (1819) was the premiere case favoring national authority over the economy. The Supreme Court ruled that the national government held authority over the states, as implied from the powers delegated to Congress by the Constitution, specifically Article I, Section 8, which gives Congress the power to "regulate commerce with foreign nations, and among the several States and with the Indian tribes." While the case involved the question of whether Congress had the right to charter a national bank (an explicit power not written in Article I, Section 8), the Supreme Court ruled that such power could be implied from others that were expressly delegated to Congress, specifically the powers "to lay and collect taxes; to borrow money; to regulate commerce; to declare and conduct a war."

What role did *Gibbons v. Ogden* play in the concept of dual federalism?

The Supreme Court's decision in the 1824 case *Gibbons v. Ogden* reasserted the federal government's authority over the states and strengthened the concept of dual federalism. Aaron Ogden had a monopoly on steamship navigation from the state of New York. When Thomas Gibbons began operating his steamship in New York waterways, Ogden sued. The Court found that New York State did not have the right to issue a monopoly to Ogden because only the national government has the power to regulate interstate commerce. Chief Justice John Marshall referred to the U.S. Constitution's commerce clause, which gives Congress the authority to regulate interstate commerce, as justification for his decision. This included the power to regulate not just trade but also navigation as well as intrastate activities that affect interstate commerce.

Why did the balance of responsibility shift to national government in the 1930s?

During the first 150 years of the nation's history, the concept of dual federalism specifically limited the power of the national government over the economy. The Supreme Court's definition of interstate commerce was so restrictive that the federal government could only pass legislation that applied to the transfer of goods over state lines; intrastate (within state) commerce was left to the states. This type of federalism, with strong state control and a weak national government, succeeded until 1937, when the Supreme Court redefined the concept of interstate commerce to allow the national government to regulate a state's economic conditions. In addition, the Great Depression of the 1930s brought an end to dual federalism as states were unable to cope with the nation's economic upheaval. Instead, President Franklin D. Roosevelt's New Deal brought about a system of cooperative federalism. Instead of assigning specific functions to each level of government, Roosevelt encouraged the national, state, and local governments to work together on specific programs. Since this time, the United States has moved further and further away from state individualism and toward a greater national uniformity in state laws and citizens' rights.

What is meant by "cooperative federalism"?

The concept of dual federalism evolved into cooperative federalism, whereby intergovernmental cooperation has blurred the lines between the responsibilities of state and national governments. A result of the New Deal era, cooperative federalism encourages states and local governments to comply with national goals. This encouragement is fostered primarily through grants-in-aid, in which Congress gives grant money to local and state governments on the condition that the money be used for a particular congressional goal. In recent years, the federal government has assumed increasing responsibility in matters such as health, education, welfare, transportation, and housing and urban development. However, federal programs are usually adopted on the basis of cooperation between state and federal entities rather than as an imposition by one or more federal bureaucracies.

President Franklin D. Roosevelt's New Deal ushered in an era of cooperative federalism, in which states were urged to contribute to national goals.

What is the concept of New Federalism?

Since the mid-1970s, cooperative federalism has turned into a type of regulated federalism, in which the national government regulates, or controls, the states by withholding monetary aid unless the states meet specific obligations outlined by Congress. In rebuttal, the states have fought for more authority, calling their concept New Federalism. Presidents Richard Nixon, Ronald Reagan, and George H. W. Bush supported New Federalism because they advocated a reversal of the trend toward nationalization, instead calling for a return of fiscal resources and management responsibilities to the states in the form of large block grants and revenue-sharing programs.

How do changes in federalism over the years reflect different interpretations of democracy?

Advocates of a strong centralized government maintain that a strong federal role in setting standards for the nation is more democratic. A reduction in national standards only increases state-to-state discrepancies, as seen during America's first 150 years. A true constitutional government maintains the division of powers mandated by federalism and specified by Americans as a condition of their consent to be governed. Additionally, advocates maintain that the expansion of the national government's power was not at the states' expense, nor has it left the states powerless, as the states continue to make most of the fundamental laws in their domain and ultimately have the responsibility of implementing federal programs such as welfare and public assistance.

Advocates for more state power argue that increased state power is more democratic because it puts the power into the hands of the people at a local level, ensuring the Founding Fathers' intent that no single branch of government—be it executive, legislative, or judicial—gain a tyrannical use of power. They argue that the federal government's excessive involvement in state matters takes the decision-making ability out of the domain of the elected officials who are closest to the people they govern and instead puts it into the domain of Washington bureaucrats. The Founding Fathers established constitutional guarantees to safeguard against the abuse of centralized power, and advocates of state power maintain that regulated federalism—which more or less "bribes" states into following congressional agendas by threatening to withhold aid—is an embodiment of that abuse.

STATE RIGHTS AND BUDGETS

What is a state?

A state is a body of people, occupying a specific geographic location, that organize into a political unit. States can also be smaller geographic and political units that make up a larger state. In U.S. politics, "state" is generally used to refer to one of the fifty states that make up the Union, but in international politics, nations and governments are often called states.

How is state government organized?

Like the national government, state governments have three branches: the executive, legislative, and judicial. Each branch functions and works a lot like its national counterpart. The chief executive of a state is the governor, who is elected by popular vote, typically for a four-year term (although New Hampshire and Vermont have two-year terms). Except for Nebraska, which has a legislature with a single house, all states have bicameral (two-house) legislatures, with the upper house usually called the Senate and the lower house called the House of Representatives, the House of Delegates, or the General Assembly. In most states, senators are elected to four-year terms, and members of the lower house serve two-year terms. The sizes of these two houses vary. Typically, the upper house consists of between 30 and 50 members, and the lower house is made up of between 100 and 150 members. Minnesota has the largest upper house, with 67 members, and New Hampshire has the largest lower house, with almost 400 members—at least quadruple the number of most states.

Does every state have a constitution?

Yes. The states had constitutions years before the U.S. Constitution was written. Since the Declaration of Independence, states have written a total of approximately 150 constitutions, with several states writing new ones frequently. State constitutions tend to be an average of four times longer than the national one, and they also are more specific. As a result, they often are heavily amended.

The constitutions of the various states differ from one another, but they generally follow a structure similar to that of the federal Constitution. Each includes a statement of the rights of the people, often called the Bill of Rights, and a plan for organizing the government. Each state constitution grants the final authority to the people of the state; sets standards, principles, and limitations for governing the state; and details the operation of businesses, banks, public utilities, and charitable institutions within the state. Although a state's constitution is above all other state and local laws within that state, it is subordinate to the U.S. Constitution. In addition, no state can make any law that conflicts in any way with federal law or the state's constitution.

What does state government do?

The U.S. Constitution reserves to the states all those powers not expressly delegated to the national government and not specifically denied to the states. They include the power to maintain state militias (the National Guard), regulate intrastate commerce, establish and operate state court systems, levy taxes, and borrow money. In everyday practice, the duties of state government vary from state to state, and they are innumerable. One of the state's primary roles includes the education of its residents through the establishment of primary and secondary public school systems and colleges and universities. State government is also responsible for promoting people's health and welfare, which it achieves by establishing hospitals, immunization programs, outreaches to the

One power granted states is to have their own militias (National Guard), such as these troopers from the Missouri National Guard.

needy and homeless, low-income housing, and antipollution laws. State government plays a role in public safety by creating and maintaining a police force and a corrections system. Conservation efforts, recreational use of public lands, building and maintaining roads and highway systems, regulating business and commerce, and instituting consumer protection laws are just a handful of the services a state government provides to ensure the overall well-being of its territory and residents. In order to carry out this business, state governments establish local governments and administrative bodies at various levels.

What is meant by "fiscal federalism"?

"Fiscal federalism" is the term given to a system of financial transfers between federal, state, and local governments for policy initiatives. Political scientists often describe it as leveraged federal money—grants and matching payments provided in exchange for state commitments. For an education grant, for example, a state might commit to employing a certain number of teacher assistants, or for infrastructure, to producing a certain amount of energy using alternative resources. The long-term costs of maintaining those kinds of projects can often be more expensive than the original amount of federal funding promised.

How do states produce their budgets?

State budget procedures—the way states produce their budgets—vary in America's state and territorial legislatures. Important structural differences include the nature of a state

67

requirement to balance the budget, an annual or biennial budget cycle, the governor's authority to revise an enacted budget, and whether earmarked or federal funds are subject to a state's appropriations process. The most important political difference among states is the balance between legislative and executive authority in composing the budget. A governor's line-item vetoes are one element in legislative and executive balance, but tradition and partisanship often play equally decisive roles. Just as with the federal government, a state's executive or legislative branch can dominate the budget process.

For state policy makers, each state's balanced-budget requirement largely applies to the state's operating budget. In most states, that is also called the general fund budget, into which most state tax revenues are deposited and from which most appropriations are made. A few states also have an education fund that receives tax revenues, is appropriated, and is subject to balance requirements just like the general fund.

Generally speaking, grants and reimbursements from the federal government make up most of a state's nongeneral fund. Balancing these revenues with expenditures is not a factor, since states can spend only as much as they receive. State nongeneral fund expenditures from state sources tend to be revenues legally designated, or "earmarked," for specific purposes and controlled by their availability.

STATE AND LOCAL GOVERNMENT

What is the role of the governor?

As the main executive officer of a state, the governor is responsible for the well-being of his or her state. The details of this job include numerous hands-on administrative tasks and leadership duties. The governor's executive powers include the appointment and removal of state officials, the supervision of thousands of executive-branch employees, the formulation of the state budget, and the leadership of the state militia as its commander in chief. Legislative powers include the power to recommend legislation, to call special sessions of the legislature, and to veto measures passed by the legislature. In forty-three states, governors have the power of an item veto, meaning that he or she can veto several components of a bill without rejecting it altogether. The governor's judicial powers are relegated to the realm of clemency. They include the power to pardon a criminal; the power to reduce a criminal's sentence; the power to reprieve, or postpone, the execution of a sentence; and the power to parole a prisoner.

What are the qualifications for governorship?

Each state dictates its own qualifications for governor. However, they generally include being an American citizen, reaching a certain age (usually twenty-five or thirty), and being a resident of the state in which the candidate is running for office. Informal qualifications that come into play include a person's race, sex, name familiarity, party membership, government experience, media personality, political savvy, and perspective on state issues. All states elect their governors to four-year terms, with the exception of New Hampshire and Vermont, which have two-year terms. Most states have a term limit of two terms. More than half the states put limits on the number of times an individual may be elected.

Who are the women governors currently serving?

Of the more than three thousand people who have served as governor, thirty-seven women (twenty-two Democrats and fifteen Republicans) have served as governor in twenty-seven states. In addition, one woman has served as governor in Puerto Rico. Arizona is the first state where a woman succeeded another woman as governor and the first state to have had four women governors. Of the thirty-seven women governors, twenty-five were first elected in their own right,

The first woman to hold the office of state governor was Nellie Tayloe Ross, who assumed the office in Wyoming in 1925 when her husband died. She served for two years. Later, from 1933 to 1953, she was director of the U.S. Mint.

three replaced their husbands, and nine became governor by constitutional succession, four of whom subsequently won full terms. The record number of women serving simultaneously, achieved in 2004 and again in 2007, is nine. As of early 2017, women run four states: Susana Martinez of New Mexico, a Republican; Mary Fallin of Oklahoma, a Republican; Kate Brown of Oregon, a Democrat; and Gina Raimondo of Rhode Island, a Democrat.

Which states held gubernatorial elections in 2016?

Twelve states held gubernatorial elections in 2016: Delaware, Indiana, Missouri, Montana, New Hampshire, North Carolina, North Dakota, Oregon, Utah, Vermont, Washington, and West Virginia. Five of those races featured incumbents, with four successfully defending their seats: Steve Bullock (D-MT), Kate Brown (D-OR), Gary Herbert (R-UT), and Jay Inslee (D-WA). The fifth, Pat McCrory (R-NC), narrowly lost to Democratic challenger Roy Cooper, the only seat Democrats picked up in 2016.

In the open races, Republicans picked up seats formerly held by Democrats in three states—Montana, New Hampshire, and Vermont—and retained seats in Indiana and North Dakota. Democrats did not pick up any open seats formerly held by Republicans but did defend seats in Delaware and West Virginia. As a result, Republicans picked up a net of two seats in this election, expanding their already historic lead among the nation's governorships: as of 2017, there are thirty-three Republican governors, sixteen Democrats, and one independent. This is the most governorships held at one time by either party since 1984, when the Democrats held thirty-four seats.

How are state and city governments related?

State and local (city and town) governments work together to implement and carry out functions important to everyday life, including planning and funding roadways, funding and running public schools, providing water, organizing police and fire services, establishing zoning regulations, licensing professions, and arranging elections. State and local governments have never been totally separate entities because they cooperate on services ranging from welfare to transportation and because they serve the same residents. However, the state government has the final decision when it comes to local functions. For example, a state government can abolish a local government, merge it with other entities, or give it additional authority. Local authority comes from specific state constitutional provisions or from acts of the state legislature.

How is city government organized?

According to the U.S. Bureau of the Census, there are almost 88,000 local governmental units in the United States, including cities, counties, municipalities, townships, school districts, and special districts. Because at least 80 percent of America's citizens live in towns or cities, city governments play an important role in the overall context of American life and government. The city directly serves the needs of the people, providing everything from police and fire protection to sanitary codes, health regulations, education, public transportation, and housing. Although city governments are chartered by states, and their charters detail the objectives and powers of the municipal government, in many ways, they operate independently from the states. For most big cities, however, cooperation with both state and federal organizations is essential to meeting the needs of their residents. Almost all cities have some kind of central council, elected by the voters, and an executive officer, assisted by various department heads, to manage the city's affairs. Typically, there are three general types of city government: the mayor-council, the commission, and the council-manager, although many cities have developed hybrids of these offices.

What are the types of local government in the U.S. today?

There are two types of local government in the U.S. today: territorial and corporate. Territorial governments have jurisdiction over certain geographic areas. Some county governments and local school districts are examples of these. Corporate governments are based on charters granted to cities, towns, or villages by the state government. City charters are like constitutions, although their jurisdiction is at a local level. The state authorizes and approves these charters, which must conform to state law.

Some corporate governments have received various degrees of what is called home rule, which enables them to change their structures and pass laws with which the state government cannot interfere. However, changes and laws made under home rule cannot conflict with state law. In most instances, state legislatures allow cities to adapt state laws to local circumstances, but cities are ultimately bound by the state authority that created them. As a result, states delegate power to local bodies, and their relations are much more hierarchical than the relations between state governments and the federal government.

What is the role of a mayor?

The mayor-council is the oldest form of city government in the United States. Its structure is similar to that of the state and national governments, with an executive branch headed by an elected mayor and a legislative branch consisting of an elected council that represents the various neighborhoods. The mayor appoints heads of city departments and other officials, sometimes with the approval of the council. He or she has the power to veto city laws, called ordinances, and often is responsible for preparing the city's budget. The council passes city ordinances, sets the tax rate on property, and apportions money among the various city departments.

How is county government set up?

The county is a subdivision of the state and is usually made up of two or more townships and several villages. New York City is so large that it is divided into five separate boroughs, each a county in its own right: the Bronx, Manhattan, Brooklyn, Queens, and Staten Island. However, most counties serve populations of fewer than fifty thousand residents. In most counties across America, one town or city is designated as the county seat, and this is where the government offices are located and where the board of commissioners or supervisors meets. In small counties, the county as a whole chooses the board; in the larger ones, supervisors represent separate districts or townships. The board levies taxes, borrows and appropriates money, sets the salaries of county employees, supervises elections, builds and maintains highways and bridges, and administers national, state, and county welfare programs.

New York City is so large and highly populated that it is managed under five separate boroughs.

How is the government of a town set up?

Thousands of municipal jurisdictions are too small to qualify as city governments, and so these governments are chartered as towns and villages. They deal with strictly local needs, including paving and lighting the streets, ensuring water supply, providing police and fire protection, establishing local health regulations, arranging for garbage, sewage, and other waste disposal, collecting local taxes to support government operations, and, in cooperation with the state and county, directly administering the local school system. The government is usually run by an elected board or council, which might be called the town or village council, board of selectmen, board of supervisors, or board of commissioners. The board may have a chairperson or president who functions as chief executive officer, or there may be an elected mayor. Government employees often include a clerk, treasurer, police and fire officers, and health and welfare workers.

What is a town meeting?

The town meeting is one aspect of local government that still exists today, although it was created in the early years of the republic. At least once a year, the registered voters of the town meet in open session to elect officers, debate local issues, and pass laws for operating the government. As a body, they decide on road construction and repair, construction of public buildings and facilities, tax rates, and the town budget. Having existed for more than two centuries, the town meeting is often called the purest form of direct democracy because governmental power is not delegated but rather exercised directly by the people: communities coming together to debate issues, build consensuses, and vote. As opposed to state and federal legislatures, where citizens elect someone to represent them, each citizen represents him- or herself at a town meeting. However, town meetings cannot be found in every area of the country; they are mostly conducted in the small towns of New England, where the first colonies were established.

When was the first town meeting?

American history's earliest recorded town meeting was held in 1633 in Dorchester, Massachusetts, and established meetings as a system of town government. The town records from October 8, 1633, declare that "for the general good and well ordering of the affayres of the Plantation there shall be every Mooneday … a generall meeting of the inhabitants of the Plantation at the meeting-house there to settle (and sett downe) such orders as may tend to the generall good as aforesayd; and every man to be bound thereby, without gaynesaying or resistance."

THE U.S. CONGRESS

THE NATURE AND FUNCTIONS OF CONGRESS

What is Congress?

The Congress of the United States is the legislative (lawmaking) and oversight (government policy review) body of the country's national government. The U.S. Congress consists of two houses: the Senate and the House of Representatives. A member of the Senate is referred to as a senator, and a member of the House of Representatives is called a representative or a congressman or congresswoman. The term "member of Congress" is also used to refer to a representative.

How is Congress divided and why?

As part of the government's overall system of checks and balances, Article I of the Constitution grants all legislative powers of the federal government to a Congress divided into two chambers: a Senate and a House of Representatives. In the early republic, senators were not elected by direct vote of the people but chosen by state legislatures and viewed as representatives of their home states. Their primary duty was to ensure that their states were treated equally in all legislation. The delegates to the Constitutional Convention reasoned that if two separate groups—one representing state governments and one representing the people—must both approve every proposed law, there would be little danger of Congress passing legislation hurriedly or aimlessly. One house could always check the other, just as in the British Parliament. The Seventeenth Amendment established direct election of the Senate by the people, although it did not substantially alter this balance of power between the two houses.

What is meant by the term "bicameralism"?

"Bicameralism" is the name given to a legislative system made up of two separate chambers, usually called the upper house and the lower house, each serving as a check on the other's power. In most cases, the members of each chamber are elected on a different basis. For example, in the U.S. Congress, two senators are elected from each of the fifty states, whereas the number of House members assigned to each state varies according to the state's population. Examples of bicameral legislatures include the Australian Parliament, the Parliament of Great Britain, the Russian Federal Assembly, the South African Parliament, and the National Congress of Chile.

Are the terms "Congress" and "legislative branch" interchangeable?

No. Although people often use these two terms interchangeably, Congress is actually a part of the larger legislative branch of the federal government. In addition to Congress—the House of Representatives and the Senate—the legislative branch includes the Architect of the Capitol, the Government Printing Office (GPO), the Library of Congress, and the legislative support agencies. The architect's main duties involve the construction, maintenance, and renovation of the Capitol Building as well as the congressional office buildings and other structures in the Capitol complex, such as the Library of Congress buildings. The GPO publishes the Congressional Record, congressional committee hearings and reports, and other congressional documents as well as many executive-branch

The Capitol Building in Washington, D.C., houses the U.S. Congress, the legislative (lawmaking) branch of government that is composed of the Senate and House of Representatives.

publications. In addition to providing library services, research, and analysis to Congress, the Library of Congress is also the national library. It houses premier national book, map, and manuscript collections, serves a major role assisting local libraries in book cataloging and other services, and supervises the implementation of U.S. copyright laws. In addition, three support agencies—the Congressional Budget Office, the Congressional Research Service in the Library of Congress, and the General Accounting Office—directly assist Congress in the performance of its duties.

What is the first and foremost characteristic of Congress?

The U.S. Congress is known primarily as the nation's lawmaking body. However, in order to make laws and carry out other responsibilities as the "first branch of government" in a democracy like the United States, several inherent features are necessary. Norman J. Ornstein, author of *The Role of the Legislature in Western Democracies,* outlines several of these characteristics. The first and foremost characteristic of Congress is its intrinsic link to the nation's citizens, otherwise known as representation. As John Stuart Mill wrote in 1862, in a representative democracy, the legislature acts as the eyes, ears, and voice of the people: "[T]he proper office of a representative assembly is to watch and control the government: to throw the light of publicity on its acts; to compel a full exposition and justification of all of them which any one considers questionable; to censure them if found condemnable...." The U.S. Congress represents a permanent and independent link between the public and the government. Through elections, petitions, lobbying, and participation in political parties and interest groups, citizens can express their will and affect the outcomes of the legislative process.

Besides representing the public will, what are some other distinguishing features of the U.S. Congress?

In addition to representing the public will, Congress has other distinguishing features. For instance, it has a system of collective decision making. A large group of individuals come together, at least in theory, as equals. While some members may assume leadership positions or special responsibilities, each member's vote is weighed equally. In addition, Congress adopts policies and makes laws through the process of deliberation, and its decisions do not need to proceed from the rule of law or specific legal precedents, making Congress very different from the courts. Congress also performs a unique educational role. Individual legislators simplify complicated issues and define policy choices. They use their resources and expertise to filter information from many sources and to resolve conflicting ideological positions, ultimately presenting their constituents with clear-cut options. This educational function has become increasingly important as society has become more complex, the scope of government activity has become more extensive, and the public has gained increased access to legislative proceedings, particularly via television and the Internet. Another defining characteristic of Congress is the dual role of legislators. On the one hand, Congress makes laws that affect the entire nation and are presumably intended to be for the entire nation's well-being. On the other hand, its individual members, the legislators, have a duty to represent the interests of their individual constituencies—a tension unique to a representative government, like the United States, that has districts.

How do the House of Representatives and the Senate represent the people?

Of the two chambers of Congress, the House of Representatives is the one considered closest to the electorate. Because members run for reelection every two years, representatives come to know their constituents well. They are more likely to reflect accurately the views of the local citizenry, advocate the needs of their districts, and be alert to changes in popular opinion. However, the Constitution's framers believed that these same characteristics might lead to a short-term view of what constitutes good public policy. For that reason, the Senate was constructed to protect against the popular sentiment of the day. Senators hold longer terms than representatives, running for election every six years. Moreover, the Senate is a continuing body, meaning that only one-third of its membership runs for reelection at any one time. This continuity and the longer term are meant to enable senators to resist the pressure of popular opinion and to serve as a restraint on House action. The framers expected senators to be older, wiser, and more deliberative than representatives and thus able to offer a long-term perspective on what makes beneficial and substantial public policy.

What are the enumerated powers of Congress?

Article I, Section 1 of the Constitution grants "all legislative powers" to Congress. The authority to make laws is regarded as Congress's most important power. Article I, Section 8 of the Constitution empowers Congress to perform a host of specific duties, known as Congress's enumerated, or express, powers. These are the power to levy taxes, collect revenue, pay debts, and provide for the general welfare; the power to borrow money; the power to regulate interstate and foreign commerce; the power to establish uniform rules of naturalization and bankruptcy; the power to coin money and regulate its value; the power to punish counterfeiters; the power to establish a postal system; the power to enact patent and copyright laws; the power to establish federal courts inferior to the Supreme Court; the power to declare war; the power to provide for the armed forces; the power to impeach and try federal officers; and the exclusive legislative power over the District of Columbia. Congress is also given the power to enact such laws as may be "necessary and proper" to implement its mandate in Article I. The power to enact laws is also contained in certain amendments to the Constitution. In addition, Article II, Section 2 grants the Senate the power to consent to the ratification of treaties and confirm the nomination of public officials. While a few of the powers outlined in Article I are outdated (such as the power to punish piracy), they nevertheless remain in effect.

What is the Necessary and Proper clause?

Article I, Section 8 of the Constitution grants Congress the authority to "make all Laws which shall be necessary and proper for carrying into Execution the foregoing powers, and all other powers vested by this Constitution in the government of the United States." This clause, when coupled with one or more of the specific enumerated powers outlined in Article I, Section 8, allows Congress to increase the scope of its authority and undertake responsibilities that are known as its implied powers. For example, the explicit power to tax and provide (spend) for the general welfare is implied to mean that Congress has the power to spend tax money for highways, public school aid, and Social Security—none of which are explicitly mentioned in the Constitution. Congress is also expressly given the power to raise an army; this express power assumes the implied power of specifying regulations concerning who can join the army. The Necessary and Proper Clause is also known as the Elastic Clause because it has been expansively stretched and interpreted by the Supreme Court to fit almost any circumstance.

An expressly given power of Congress is to raise an army; implied in this power is the ability to determine who can be in the military. Women, for example, were not allowed to join the army until World War I, and it was only much more recently (2015) that they could serve on the front lines.

What are Congress's implied powers?

Congress's implied powers are justified by the Necessary and Proper Clause of the Constitution, which grants Congress far-reaching powers to do its job. When discussing the scope of Congress's implied powers, scholars note several landmark Supreme Court cases. In *McCulloch v. Maryland* (1819), the Supreme Court ruled that the Necessary and Proper Clause gave Congress the power to create a national bank (an implied power) as an aid to carrying out its enumerated borrowing and taxing powers. *U.S. v. Gettysburg Electric Railway Co.* (1896) considered whether Congress had the power to condemn a railroad's land in what was to be Gettysburg National Military Park and found that the power to condemn the railroad's land was implied by the enumerated powers of Congress to declare war and equip armies because creation of the park strengthens the motives of the citizen to defend "the institutions of his country." A highly guarded implied power that is almost always mentioned when discussing Congress is its oversight function.

What are the limits to congressional authority?

The Tenth Amendment to the Constitution sets definite limits on congressional authority by providing that powers not delegated to the national government are reserved to the states or to the people. In addition, the Constitution specifically forbids certain acts by Congress. Congress may not suspend the writ of *habeas corpus*—a requirement that those accused of crimes be brought before a judge or court to review the charges

77

against them before being imprisoned—except as necessary in time of rebellion or invasion. In addition, Congress may not pass laws that condemn people for crimes or unlawful acts without a trial, pass any law that retroactively makes a specific act a crime, levy direct taxes on citizens except on the basis of a census already taken, tax exports from any one state, provide specially favorable treatment in commerce or taxation to the seaports of any state or to the vessels using them, or authorize any titles of nobility.

What are the two executive powers the Constitution gives to the Senate?

While the Constitution assigns the House and Senate equal responsibility for such tasks as declaring war, assessing taxes, and making all laws necessary for the operation of the government, the Senate holds exclusive authority to advise and consent on treaties and to review and approve or reject presidential appointees to executive and judicial posts. These two areas of authority are called the Senate's executive powers, or executive business, because they come from the president. From its earliest years, the Senate has zealously guarded these powers. In its history, the Senate has rejected only 12 of 159 Supreme Court appointments and only 9 of more than 700 cabinet appointees. The Senate has rejected relatively few of the hundreds of treaties it has considered.

Does the House have any exclusive powers?

Yes. Article I, Section 7 gives special, exclusive powers to the House of Representatives. The constitutional provision that "all Bills for raising Revenue shall originate in the House of Representatives" is an adaptation of an earlier English practice. It was based on the principle that the national purse strings should be controlled by a body directly responsible to the people. Therefore, when the Constitution was written, the authority to initiate revenue legislation was vested in the House of Representatives, where the members are subject to direct election every two years. However, the Constitution also guarantees the Senate's power to "propose or concur with Amendments as on other Bills." In addition to this exclusive power, only the House holds the power of impeachment; that is, the authority to charge the president, vice president, or other civil officers with "Treason, Bribery, or other high Crimes and Misdemeanors." Besides initiating the impeachment process, only the House can pass articles of impeachment.

What are Congress's war powers?

The Constitution states that the president is the commander in chief of the U.S. Army, Navy, and, when it is called into federal service, the National Guard. Historically, presidents have used this authority to commit U.S. troops without a formal declaration of war. However, Article I, Section 8 of the Constitution reserves to Congress the power to raise and support the armed forces as well as the sole authority to declare war. These competing powers have been the source of controversy between the legislative and executive branches over warmaking. In 1973, Congress enacted the controversial War Powers Resolution, which limits the president's authority to use the armed forces without specific congressional authorization in an attempt to increase and clarify Congress's control over the use of the military. In addition, the

President Franklin D. Roosevelt is shown here signing a declaration of war against Germany in 1941. Congress must approve such declarations, but the commander in chief is also allowed to take military action without declaring war.

armed forces operate under the doctrine of civilian control, which means that only the president or statutory deputies (the secretary and deputy secretary of defense) can order the use of force. The chain of command is structured to ensure that the military cannot undertake actions without the approval or knowledge of the people of the United States.

What role does the Congress play in the procedure for committing America's military forces to war?

The Constitution provides Congress with the authority to declare war. This has occurred on only five occasions since 1789, the most recent being World War II. However, the president, as commander in chief, has implied powers to commit the nation's military forces—something that has occurred on more than two hundred occasions in U.S. history. Moreover, Congress may authorize the use of the military in specific cases through public law. The 1973 War Powers Resolution tried to clarify these respective roles of the president and Congress in cases involving the use of armed forces without a declaration of war. The president is expected to consult with Congress before using the armed forces "in every possible instance" and is required to report to Congress within forty-eight hours of introducing troops. According to the resolution, the use of the armed forces is to be terminated within sixty days, with a possible thirty-day extension by the president, unless Congress acts during that time to declare war, enacts a specific authorization for use of the armed forces, extends the sixty-to-ninety-day period, or is physically unable to meet as a result of an attack on the United States.

What is Congress's oversight function?

Congressional oversight, or Congress's "watchful care" role, is one of the most effective jobs that Congress has adopted to influence the executive branch. It applies to cabinet departments, executive agencies, regulatory commissions, and the presidency. Congressional oversight of policy implementation and administration takes a variety of forms and utilizes various techniques. These range from specialized investigations by select committees to the use of extra-congressional mechanisms, such as offices of inspector general and study commissions. Because of its "watchdog" nature, the oversight power of Congress has helped to force officials out of office, change policies, and provide new statutory controls over the executive. Oversight is an integral part of the system of checks and balances between the legislative and executive branches and as such is supported by a variety of authorities: the U.S. Constitution, public law, and chamber and committee rules.

How is Congress's oversight function exercised?

Although Congress's oversight function takes many forms, it is primarily exercised through committee inquiries and hearings, formal consultations with and reports from the president, Senate advice and consent for presidential nominations and treaties, House impeachment proceedings and subsequent Senate trials, and House and Senate proceedings under the Twenty-fifth Amendment in the event that the president becomes disabled or the office of the vice president becomes vacant. In addition, the oversight function covers informal meetings between legislators and executive officials, congressional membership on government commissions, and studies by congressional committees and support agencies such as the Congressional Budget Office, the General Accounting Office, and the Office of Technology Assessment.

What are Congress's powers of investigation?

One of the most important nonlegislative functions of Congress is the power to investigate. This power is usually delegated to committees—either to the standing committees, to special committees set up for a specific purpose, or to joint committees composed of members of both houses. Investigations are conducted to gather information on the need for future legislation, to test the effectiveness of laws already passed, to inquire into the qualifications and performance of members and officials of the other branches, and, on rare occasions, to lay the groundwork for impeachment proceedings. Frequently, committees call on outside experts to assist in conducting investigative hearings and to make detailed studies of issues.

What are the powers associated with Congress's investigative power?

The investigative power has certain associated powers. One is the power to publicize investigations and their results. Most committee hearings are open to the public and are widely reported in the mass media. Congressional investigations thus represent one important tool available to lawmakers to inform the citizenry and pique public interest in national issues. Congressional committees also have the power to compel testimony from unwilling witnesses, to cite witnesses who refuse to testify for contempt of Congress, and to cite those who give false testimony for perjury.

What role does Congress play in the impeachment process?

The president, vice president, and all civil officers of the United States are subject to impeachment, and their conviction results in automatic removal from office. Under the Constitution, the House of Representatives has the power to impeach a government official, in effect serving as prosecutor. The Senate then holds the impeachment trial, serving as jury and judge, except for the impeachment of a president, when the chief justice presides. Once the Senate votes to convict, there is no appeal. Congress's impeachment power is often considered its most serious power. Congress is so conscious of this that impeachment proceedings have been initiated in the House only sixty-two times since 1789. Only seventeen federal officers have been impeached: two presidents, one cabinet officer, one senator, and thirteen federal judges. Sixteen cases have reached the Senate.

Americans began calling for the impeachment of President Donald Trump before he even finished his first few months in office, but it takes a majority vote in the House of Representatives to actually take a president, vice president, or other civil officer to trial.

Of these, two were dismissed before trial because the individuals had left office, seven ended in acquittal, and seven in conviction. Each of the seven Senate convictions involved a federal judge.

What role does Congress play in a contested presidential election?

In the case of a contested presidential election, the Constitution grants Congress two roles: to officially count the ballots and announce the results of the electoral college votes for president and vice president and to elect the president and vice president if the electoral college fails to do so. The electoral college ballots for the November 2000 election were counted officially in a joint session of the U.S. Congress held on January 6, 2001. Had no majority materialized behind one candidate, the House and Senate would have then, pursuant to the Constitution, proceeded immediately to an election for president and vice president, known formally as a contingent election.

According to the Twelfth Amendment, in a contingent election, the House is instructed to vote state by state, with each state receiving one vote. A majority of the fifty states is needed to win the presidency, or twenty-six votes. The Constitution is silent on how each state is to determine its one vote. Most likely, the representatives of each state would meet first to take a straw poll within their delegation. In the seven states that have only one representative, that member would make the decision for his or her state. In the Senate, the Constitution authorizes the vote to be taken member by member, with a majority of fifty-one votes needed to win the vice presidency. In the case of a tie, the president of the Senate (the current vice president of the United States) would break the tie.

What is Congress's scope of authority over the independent agencies?

Independent agencies—that is, all federal administrative agencies not under the executive departments or under the direct, immediate authority of the president—include regulatory commissions, government corporations such as the U.S. Postal Service, and a wide variety of boards and foundations. Their commissioners, directors, and governors are appointed by the president and confirmed by the Senate. In addition to confirming the president's selections, independent regulatory commissions have long been established by Congress—beginning in the 1880s with the now defunct Interstate Commerce Commission—to regulate some aspect of the U.S. economy. These include the Securities and Exchange Commission, the Federal Communications Commission, the Federal Trade Commission, and the Nuclear Regulatory Commission. Such agencies are subject to the laws Congress generates and the president signs. In addition, almost all the independent regulatory commissions rely on government funding as determined by Congress. Finally, they are subject to periodic authorization and appropriations hearings in Congress, where their activities and operations are reviewed.

HOUSE–SENATE DIFFERENCES AND CONGRESSIONAL PRIVILEGES

What are the characteristics of the 115th Congress?

Historically, members of the Senate and House of Representatives are atypical citizens in that they are older than most Americans, disproportionately white, male, and trained in high-status occupations. Lawyers are the largest occupational group among congresspersons, although the proportion of lawyers in the House is lower now than it was in the past. The 115th Congress, which convened in January 2017, is unique in that it is the most racially diverse in history. Most of the racial, gender, and religious diversity is represented by Democratic lawmakers in the House and Senate, even though the party is a minority of both chambers. The Congress is overwhelmingly white and male compared to the overall population.

How much money do members of Congress make?

Compared with the average American, members of Congress are well paid. As of January 2017, each senator and representative receives an annual salary of $174,000. The House and Senate majority and minority leaders earn more, $193,400. The Speaker of the House earns $223,500. In addition to their base pay, members of Congress receive yearly allowances to maintain an office and compensate a full staff. House members are allotted more than $900,000 to pay up to eighteen employees, along with another $250,000 to cover their office expenses. Several items are classified as office expenses, including travel, so members do not have to pay for transportation between home and Washington, D.C. For senators, the allotments are even higher, averaging more than $3 million per year. Along with these perks, members are also given free office space in Washington as well as in their home states, with additional funds to purchase furniture.

What are franking privileges?

For more than two hundred years, members of Congress have sent mass mailings to their constituents without paying postage. The communications are presented to the Franking Commission beforehand, and, if approved, the federal government reimburses the U.S. Postal Service for the expense of mailing them. Although the purpose of the privilege is to keep citizens informed, franking privileges provide incumbent Congress members with an advantage during elections because their mail can be used as a campaign tool. Even though the mailings are not allowed to include specific campaign information, they *can* highlight the accomplishments of the Congress member, thus providing a significant financial advantage over an opponent who must pay for postage.

What are some of the perks and privileges members of Congress receive?

In addition to the power to shape policy and public discourse, legislators receive high salaries, strong health care and retirement benefits, and annual cost-of-living increases. Members of Congress are also permitted to deduct $3,000 in living expenses from their yearly federal income tax to cover the cost of living away from their home district or state.

Are members of Congress privileged from arrest?

To some extent, yes. Article I, Section 6 of the Constitution states that senators and representatives "shall in all Cases, except Treason, Felony, and Breach of the Peace, be privileged from Arrest during their Attendance at the Session of their respective Houses, and in going to and returning from the same." The phrase "Treason,

Members of Congress are immune from arrest in many cases, except when it is a serious matter of treason, breach of peace, or a felony, which are all indictable crimes.

Felony, and Breach of the Peace" has been interpreted to mean all indictable crimes, and the Supreme Court has held that the privilege against arrest does not apply in criminal cases.

CONGRESSIONAL ELECTIONS AND APPORTIONMENT

What is the makeup of the 115th Congress?

The 115th Congress, sworn in on January 3, 2017, is made up of the following: In the House of Representatives, there are 237 Republicans, 193 Democrats, and 0 independents. In the Senate, there are 52 Republicans and 48 Democrats. The average age of representatives was fifty-seven; of senators, sixty-one. A substantial majority of members in both houses are college educated, and the dominant profession is law, followed by business. Protestants make up the majority religious affiliation. One hundred and eight women serve in this Congress as well as a substantial number of people of color: thirty-eight Hispanics, forty-nine African Americans, and fifteen members of Asian or Native Hawaiian/Pacific Islander descent.

How many women serve in the 115th Congress?

The number of women remains at a total of 108 members, or 19 percent, far less than the overall American population, which is 50 percent female. Female representation in the House has dropped slightly from eighty-four to eighty-three as a result of eleven retirements. A record number of twenty-one women serve in the Senate, however. The number of women of color has also increased, with some female firsts: Senator Mazie Hirono, a Democrat from Hawaii, was only the second minority woman ever to serve in the Senate. Democrats Tammy Duckworth from Illinois, Kamala Harris from California, and

As the House minority leader, California Democrat Nancy Pelosi is the highest-ranking congresswoman in the 115th U.S. Congress. There are 108 women in Congress as of 2017.

Catherine Cortez Masto from Nevada join her. Harris, whose father is from Jamaica and mother is from India, is the second black woman to serve in the Senate and the first woman of South Asian descent.

What is the breakdown of African Americans serving in the 115th Congress?

The new Congress has a record number of black lawmakers, increasing from forty-six to forty-nine. That number includes three Republicans: Senator Tim Scott of South Carolina and representatives Mia Love of Utah and Will Hurd of Texas. Lisa Blunt Rochester is the first African American and first woman to represent Delaware in Congress. In Florida, former Orlando Police Chief Val Demings is also the first woman and first African American to represent her district.

What is the breakdown of Hispanics serving in the 115th Congress?

Thirty-four Hispanics serve in the House, while the Senate has four Hispanic members. Seven Hispanic Democrats won election to the House for the first time during this Congress: Nanette Barragán (California), Salud Carbajal (California), Lou Correa (California), Adriano Espaillat (New York), Ruben Kihuen (Nevada), Darren Soto (Florida), and Vicente González (Texas). Cortez Masto is the first Latina to serve in the Senate. In the House, Espaillat, who replaced retiring Representative Charles Rangel, a Democrat from New York, is the first Dominican American elected to Congress.

Can anyone run for Senate?

Article I, Section 3 of the Constitution outlines the qualifications for members of the Senate. A senator must meet a higher level of qualifications than a representative. In order to run for office, a senator must be at least thirty years old, must have been a citizen of the United States for at least nine years, and must be an inhabitant of the state from which he or she is elected. Although most senator-elects are residents of their states and often longtime participants in their communities, under the inhabitant qualification, it is not mandatory that a senator have lived in a state for any set length of time.

What is the breakdown of Asian Americans in the 115th Congress?

Fifteen members of the 115th Congress were of Asian or Native Hawaiian/Pacific Islander descent.

How many senators are there?

Article I of the Constitution states that the Senate "shall be composed of two senators from each State," making the Senate smaller than the House of Representatives. By the end of the First Congress in 1790, the Senate had only twenty-six members. The size of the Senate has grown along with the country, and today, one hundred senators represent the fifty states.

What is equal representation?

Unlike members of the House of Representatives, U.S. senators do not have congressional districts. Rather, senators represent an entire state. Each state has two senators, thus giving each state equal representation in Congress.

How are senators elected?

Originally, the Constitution provided that state legislatures would elect senators, but in 1913, the Seventeenth Amendment established direct election of senators by "the people." Since that time, voters in each state have cast their ballots for their senator of choice in the regularly scheduled November elections.

How long is a senator's term of office?

Under the Constitution, each state is entitled to two senators, each serving a six-year term. Senate terms are staggered, and the Senate is a continuous body, which means that approximately one-third of the total membership of the Senate is elected every two years. This ensures that all senators will not be up for reelection at the same time. The continuity of the office and the longer term (as compared to that of representatives) were established by the Founding Fathers to ensure that senators would be better able to resist the pressures of the popular culture and restrain the House, a body often subject to public whim. However, because of the Constitution's fundamental principle of representative democracy—that the people should choose who governs them—there are no term limits for members of Congress. According to statistics of the 107th Congress, the average length of service in the Senate is eleven and a half years.

Has Congress ever considered term limits for its members?

Yes. Overall, the general public supports limiting the terms of senators and representatives. A 2016 poll by the Tarrance Group showed that 84 percent of Americans favor term limits, and these limits are supported in all regions of the United States and by both sexes as well as by blacks and Hispanics. Proponents of term limits say that careerism is the dominant motive of most legislators. By removing that motive, they argue, term limits would make Congress less swayed by public opinion and more deliberative. In addition, long-term congressional incumbency tends to distort representation. By becoming overly comfortable with the federal government and insulated from the public, members are more likely to develop interests in conflict with those of their constituents. Term limits therefore would work to keep elected officials more in touch with voters. Frequent rotation of elected officials would help ensure continuous energy and innovative thinking. Despite public support, in May 1995, the Supreme Court ruled in *U.S. Term Limits v. Thornton* that state-imposed term limits on federal lawmakers are unconstitutional. A constitutional amendment would be required to impose a limit on the number of times a member of Congress can run for reelection. When the Senate debated such an amendment in April 1996, it fell far short of the two-thirds support needed to send it to the states for ratification. The amendment, if passed, would have provided for a uniform term limit of twelve years for both representatives and senators.

How did Hillary Rodham Clinton run for the Senate in New York, a state in which she had never lived?

The Constitution requires that a prospective senator be a resident of the state when elected. Hillary Clinton (1947–), wife of President Bill Clinton and who would later serve as secretary of state under President Barack Obama, only needed to establish a

Although Secretary of State Hillary Clinton was not from the state of New York, all she had to do was establish a residence there in order to run for the office of senator in 2000.

87

residence in New York State at any time prior to election day to meet the constitutional requirement, and she did so when she purchased a home in Chappaqua. However, this issue of residency did not pass under the radar of the voting public, who questioned the length of Clinton's residency in the state, whether the residency was real or merely technical, and her overall familiarity with the Big Apple and its environs. Nevertheless, the voters of New York ultimately elected her. This wasn't the first time New York elected a "new" senator, having voted in Daniel P. Moynihan (in 1977) and Robert F. Kennedy (in 1965), both of whom moved to New York only a short time before running for office.

How are vacancies due to death, resignation, or expulsion filled?

When a vacancy occurs in the Senate for any reason, the Seventeenth Amendment directs the governor of the state to call an election to fill such vacancy and authorizes the legislature to make provision for an immediate appointment pending such election. Among the states, only Arizona does not allow the governor to make interim appointments and instead requires a special election to fill any Senate vacancy. Prevailing practice in the states is that a special election to fill the vacancy is held at the time of the next statewide general election.

How did the drafters of the Constitution originally envision the role of the Senate?

Those who wrote the Constitution created the Senate as a safeguard for the rights of states and minority opinion in a system of government designed to allocate greater power at the national level. They modeled the Senate on colonial governors' councils and on the state senates that had evolved from them. The framers intended the Senate to be an independent body of responsible citizens who would share power with the president and the House of Representatives. In defining this position, James Madison explained that the Senate's role was "first to protect the people against their rulers [and] secondly to protect the people against the transient impressions into which they themselves might be led."

To balance power between the large and small states, the Constitution's drafters agreed that states would be represented equally in the Senate and in proportion to their populations in the House. To further preserve the authority of individual states, they provided that state legislatures would elect senators. To guarantee senators' independence from short-term political pressures, the framers assigned them a six-year term, three times as long as that of the popularly elected House members. Responding to fears that a six-year Senate term would produce an aristocracy far from the will of the people, the framers specified that one-third of the terms would expire every two years, thus combining the principles of continuity and rotation in office. In the early weeks of the Constitutional Convention, the participants had tentatively decided to give the Senate sole power to make treaties and to appoint federal judges and ambassadors. As the convention drew to a close, however, they agreed to divide these powers between the Senate and the president. The framers determined that the ratification of a treaty would require a two-thirds vote so that certain states could not unite against others, by a simple majority vote, for commercial or economic gain. In dealing with nominations, senators, as statewide officials, would be uniquely qualified to identify suitable candidates for federal judicial posts and would confirm them, along with cabinet secretaries and other key federal officials, by a simple majority vote.

What two major changes were made to the Senate in the twentieth century?

The first major change occurred in 1913, when, due to a Republican Party split, the Democrats took control of the Senate and established the position of majority floor leader. They established this position to push through the party's legislative agenda. Within a decade, the post of party floor leader had begun to achieve the influence in conducting the Senate's business that it has today. A second major change in the Senate's structure occurred in 1913 with the ratification of the Constitution's Seventeenth Amendment, which provides for the direct popular election of senators. While the selection of senators by state legislatures had worked reasonably well for the Senate's first half century, eventually, deadlocks began to occur between the upper and lower houses of those bodies. This delayed state legislative business and deprived states of their full Senate representation. By the start of the twentieth century, direct popular election of senators had become a major objective for reformers who sought to remove control of government from the influence of special interests and corrupt state legislators. The amendment marked the only structural modification of the framers' original design of the Senate.

Who is the president of the Senate, and what is his or her role?

Article I, Section 3 of the Constitution provides that "the Vice President of the United States shall be the President of the Senate." In this role, the vice president presides over the Senate, makes parliamentary rulings (which may be overturned by a majority vote of the Senate), and may cast tie-breaking votes. In the early republic, vice presidents presided on a regular basis, but in recent years, they have been present in the chair only when a close vote is anticipated, during major debates, or on important ceremonial occasions, such as the swearing in of newly elected senators or during joint sessions of Congress. In the absence of the vice president, the Senate elects a president pro tempore (meaning president "for the time being") to preside. In recent decades it has become traditional for this post to go to the senior senator from the majority party. The president pro

The Constitution indicates that the vice president will also serve as president of the Senate. As of 2017, Vice President Mike Pence holds that role.

89

tempore assigns other members of the majority party to preside by rotation during each day's proceedings. These senators and the president pro tempore retain their rights to vote on all issues before the body and to debate when they are not presiding.

Do senators have individual seats assigned to them?

Yes. The individual seats in the Senate are numbered and assigned on request of senators in order of their seniority. Democrats occupy the west side of the chamber on the vice president's right; Republicans sit across the main aisle to the vice president's left. There is no set rule for the seating of independents. By custom, the majority and minority leaders occupy the front-row seats on either side of the aisle, and the majority and minority whips occupy the seats immediately next to their party's leader.

Do the terms "senior senator" and "junior senator" apply to age or service?

The words "senior" or "junior," as applied to the two senators from a state, refer to their length of continuous service in the Senate and not to their ages. Thus, a senior senator may be younger in age than the junior senator from the same state.

Who are some "first" women of Congress?

The first woman to serve in the Senate was eighty-eight-year-old Rebecca Latimer Felton (1835–1930) of Georgia. Appointed to fill a vacancy in a symbolic concession to the women's suffrage movement, Felton served for just twenty-four hours, from noon on November 21 to noon on November 22, 1922. Because of her short term, she is very rarely mentioned as the first woman senator. Credit usually goes to Hattie Caraway, who was the first woman elected to the Senate. Although Caraway was first appointed to fill the vacancy caused by the death of her husband, Senator Thaddeus Caraway, she later won a special election in 1932. She ran for reelection and won several times, ending her tenure in January 1945. The first woman to chair a Senate standing committee, Caraway also takes credit as the first woman to preside over the Senate.

The first female member of the House of Representatives was Jeannette Rankin, a representative from Montana who served from 1917 to 1919. The first black woman elected to the House of Representatives was Shirley Chisholm in 1968. In 1972 she ran in the presidential primaries on the Democratic ticket. Although Chisholm entered a substantial number of primaries, she only received 7 percent of the vote. She continued to serve as a representative until January 1983. Carol Moseley-Braun of Illinois was the first African American woman senator, a post she held for one term, from 1993 to 1999, before becoming the U.S. ambassador to New Zealand.

Who was the first African American to serve in Congress?

Hiram R. Revels (1827–1901), an African American born to free parents in 1827, was elected as a Republican to the Senate in 1870, after the Senate resolved a challenge to his credentials. A few members attempted to block his seat, arguing that Revels had not been a U.S. citizen for the nine years required of all senators. His supporters argued that, although black Americans had only become citizens with the passage of the 1866 Civil Rights Act—just four years earlier—Revels had been a voter many years earlier in Ohio and was therefore a citizen. He served as a senator for his state, Mississippi, until March 1871. Also in 1870, fellow Republican Joseph H. Rainey became the first black member of the U.S. House of Representatives.

In the latter half of the 1900s, African Americans in Congress achieved several significant milestones. In 1966 Edward Brooke of Massachusetts became the first African American senator of the century. And in 1969, Shirley Chisholm (1924–

The first African American elected to the U.S. Congress was Hiram R. Revels, a senator from Mississippi.

2005) became the first black woman in U.S. history to sit in the House of Representatives. In 1993, Carol Moseley-Brown became the first African American senator, only the second black senator since the Reconstruction era.

Who was the first Native American to serve in Congress?

In 1907, Charles Curtis of Kansas became the first American Indian to become a U.S. senator. He was also the first to serve as Senate majority leader. In addition to being a first, Curtis holds the record for the senator who served on the most subcommittees at one time. He resigned from the Senate in March 1929 to become President Herbert Hoover's vice president, thus becoming the first and only Native American vice president.

Can anyone run for the House?

Article I, Section 2 of the Constitution outlines the qualifications for members of the House of Representatives. A member of the House must be at least twenty-five years of age when entering office, must have been a U.S. citizen for at least seven years, and must be a resident of the state in which the election was held.

How are House members nominated and elected?

In most states, House candidates of major political parties are nominated by primary election. Some states also provide for a party convention or committee recommendation in conjunction with a primary. In many states, no primary election is held for a particular office if the candidate is unopposed for nomination. In most states, minor-party candidates are nominated according to individual party rules and procedures. Independent candidates are nominated by self-declaration.

Major party candidates are given automatic ballot access in all states, while minor-party and independent candidates must meet various state requirements, such as a certain number of petition signatures of registered voters, in order to be placed on the general-election ballot. Representatives are elected by plurality vote in the congressional district in which they are candidates. The only major exception to this rule in federal general elections is found in the District of Columbia, which requires that a candidate receive a majority of popular votes in order to be elected as its delegate to the House. In the event that no candidate receives the requisite majority, a runoff election is scheduled. In addition, Louisiana requires that all candidates compete in an all-party primary election. Under this arrangement, a candidate who receives a majority of votes is declared the winner, and the general election is canceled for that office.

How long is a representative's term of office?

The Constitution entitles each state to at least one representative, who serves a two-year term. According to the statistics of the 114th Congress, the average length of service in the House is nine years.

How are vacancies due to death, resignation, or expulsion filled?

Article II, Section 2 of the Constitution requires that all vacancies in the House of Representatives be filled by election. All states require special elections to fill any House seat that becomes vacant during the first session of a Congress. Procedures governing vacancies occurring during the second session of a Congress differ from state to state and are largely dependent on the amount of time intervening between the opening of the vacancy and the next general election.

What is the size of the House of Representatives?

The membership of the House of Representatives is fixed by law at 435 members representing the fifty states. In addition to the 435 representatives, there is one delegate each for the District of Columbia, the Virgin Islands, Guam, and American Samoa. Each delegate is elected for a two-year term. In addition, there is a resident commissioner from Puerto Rico who is elected for a four-year term. The delegates and the resident commissioner can sponsor legislation and vote in committees but not in the House chamber.

How is the size of the House determined?

According to the Constitution, each state is entitled to at least one representative. Additional House seats are apportioned (distributed) on the basis of state population. Population figures used for apportionment are determined on the basis of each ten-year census. Following the 2010 census, the average district size was 710,767 people. In order to minimize the differences in district populations among the states, since 1941, Congress has used the method of "equal proportions" to calculate actual apportionment. Based on the 2010 census apportionment, the state with the largest average district size is Montana (994,416), and the state with the smallest average district size is Rhode Island (527,624).

Which states have the most representatives in Congress?

Because the number of representatives per state is based on a state's population, those states with the largest populations have the most representatives. The ten biggest states with the most representatives are California (53 members), Texas (36), New York (27), Florida (27), Pennsylvania (18), Illinois (18), Ohio (16), Michigan (14), North Carolina (13), and New Jersey (12).

What is redistricting?

Every ten years, following the U.S. Census, political district boundaries are adjusted to take into account population changes that have occurred over the preceding decade, a process known as redistricting. Districts are redrawn so that they are as equal in population as possible. Redistricting committees at the state and county level develop proposed plans and changes in district boundaries. These new district plans are passed by both houses of the legislature at the state level and the board of supervisors at the county level. The governor then signs legislation for the new district lines to become effective.

Do the federal government or the states define the congressional districts?

Congress fixes the size of the House of Representatives as well as the procedure for apportioning the number of representatives among the states, and the states proceed from there. State legislatures pass laws defining the physical boundaries of congressional districts within certain constraints established by Congress and the Supreme Court (through reapportionment and redistricting rulings). Each state is apportioned its number of representatives by means of the Department of Commerce's decennial census.

In the early years of the republic, most states elected their representatives at large. The practice of dividing a state into districts, however, was soon instituted. Congress later required that representatives be elected from "districts composed of a contiguous and compact territory," but this requirement is no longer in federal law. The redistricting process has always been provided for by state law, but Congress can choose to exercise greater authority over redistricting. In 1967, for example, by law, Congress prohibited at-large elections of representatives in all states entitled to more than one representative. Today, all states with more than one representative must elect their representatives from single-member districts.

What is gerrymandering?

The term "gerrymandering" means the drawing of district lines in order to maximize the electoral advantage of a political party or faction. The term was first used in 1812, when Elbridge Gerry (1744–1814) was the governor of Massachusetts, to characterize the state's redistricting plan. Gerry persuaded the state legislature to create a district in order to favor the election of a fellow Republican. Because of the district's unique shape, one critic reportedly observed, "That looks like a salamander!" to which another observer quipped, "That's not a salamander, that's a gerrymander." Since that incident, "gerrymandering" has become a common term in popular political discussions.

The name "gerrymandering" came from an 1812 newspaper cartoon that poked fun at how a district was drawn in Massachusetts to specifically help Governor Elbridge Gerry win office. Because some said the outline looked like a salamander, a portmanteau of Gerry and salamander became gerrymander, which now refers to any district with ridiculous borders made to help someone or some party win an election.

Can members of Congress be removed from office or disciplined for misconduct?

Yes. The Constitution states that "Each House shall be the Judge of the … Qualifications of its own Members … [and may] punish its Members for disorderly Behaviour, and with the Concurrence of two thirds, expel a Member." Thus, disciplinary actions taken against a member are a matter of concern for that house alone. Each chamber has established a committee charged with reviewing allegations of misconduct against its members: the House Committee on Standards of Official Conduct and the Senate Ethics Committee. The rules of the House and Senate also contain a Code of Official Conduct. The ethics committees review charges against a member filed by another member or by a private citizen.

What generally happens when members of Congress act inappropriately?

The expulsion of a member is the most severe form of discipline the House or Senate can impose. According to the Constitution, this action requires an affirmative vote of two-thirds of the members of the chamber voting, a quorum being present. Alternatively, the House may vote to censure a member for misconduct. Censuring requires only a majority vote, and, under party rules in the House, a censured member automatically loses any committee or party leadership positions held during that Congress. In the Senate, the terms "censure" and "denunciation" are used almost interchangeably for violations of this magnitude. A less severe form of disciplinary action is a "reprimand," again imposed by either chamber by a simple majority vote. Typically, reprimands are reserved for ethical violations that are minor or appear to be unintentional on the part of the member. Additionally, members of Congress are subject to prosecution for treason, felony, or breach of the peace. Generally, a member who has been indicted for a felony must take a leave of absence from any party or committee leadership position for as long as the charges are pending. Usually, the House or Senate will not initiate internal disciplinary action until the criminal proceedings against the member have been completed. In July 2002, Representative James Traficant ([D-OH] 1941–2014) became only the fifth member in history to be expelled from the House after his conviction on charges of racketeering, bribery, and tax evasion.

How do members of Congress differ from delegates and resident commissioners?

The post of delegate was established by ordinance of the Continental Congress and confirmed by a law of Congress. From the time of the early republic, the House of Representatives has admitted delegates from territories or districts organized by law. Delegates and resident commissioners may participate in House debate, but they are not permitted to vote on the floor. All serve on committees of the House and have powers and privileges equal to other committee members, including the right to vote in committee.

Do members of Congress ever change their party affiliation?

During the nineteenth century, as political parties evolved, members of Congress often changed parties or helped create new parties. However, twentieth- and twenty-first-century members of Congress—Republicans, Democrats, and independents alike—have rarely changed their party affiliation. The most publicized recent example is James Jeffords (1934–2014), a senator from Vermont. Jeffords, who had served twenty-six years in Congress before making a switch, left the Republican Party in June 2001 to become an independent. At the beginning of 2001, the Senate was equally divided between Democrats and Republicans. Jeffords' switch threw the Senate—however marginally—to the control of the Democrats, thus changing the balance of the entire legislative body. Jeffords cited his desire to bring balance to the Senate's deliberative process (indeed the legislative agenda overall) as his primary reason for switching parties.

One of the longest-serving U.S. senators in history (over forty-seven years), Strom Thurmond was a South Carolina Democrat until his party supported the 1964 Civil Rights Act. He became a Dixiecrat and then a Republican.

Along with Jeffords, Republican senator Strom Thurmond (1902–2003) from South Carolina is cited in this category. A

95

member of the Republican Party since 1964, Thurmond began his career as a Democrat. However, when the Democratic Party adopted a strong civil rights policy for its 1948 campaign, Thurmond ran for president on the States' Rights (Dixiecrat) ticket, receiving thirty-nine electoral votes, the third-largest independent electoral vote in U.S. history. He then switched back to the Democratic Party in 1956, where he stayed until 1964. Other notables include Richard Shelby (1934–) of Alabama, who made the switch from Democrat to Republican in 1994; Ben Nighthorse Campbell (1933–) of Colorado, who made the switch from Democrat to Republican in 1995; and Bob Smith (1941–) of New Hampshire, who went from Republican to Independent to Republican again in 1999.

HOW CONGRESS IS ORGANIZED

What are the duties of members of Congress?

While Article I of the Constitution outlines the powers of Congress and the qualifications necessary for election, there is no guidance on the specific duties that each individual member must perform on a daily basis. However, the following duties are typical: First, each member is responsible for local representation, meaning that members advocate in Washington on behalf of the economic needs and political interests of their local district or state. Members analyze proposed legislation, keep in touch with local opinion leaders, and read and answer their mail and phone calls. Related to this are their office-management duties, which involve managing a staff of up to twenty-two people for House members and an average of thirty-eight for senators. Each member is also responsible for constituency service, meaning that members alert their constituents to federal government actions and programs and respond to requests for information about federal activities. Members provide their constituents with help in obtaining federal benefits and grants and seek federal funds for local projects and programs. Members are also involved in national policy making, negotiating with their colleagues to reconcile various regional interests in order to create one national policy. Members meet to exchange views and information with officials from the executive branch, lobbyists, representatives of the business community, professionals, and academics. They analyze proposed legislation to determine its national implications. In addition, all members must stay involved in their committee work, which means developing expertise in the subject matter of their respective committee assignments. On average, a House member serves on two committees, and a senator serves on four. Members attend committee meetings and take testimony or mark up legislation, prepare amendments to bills under committee consideration, and vote on motions, amendments, and decisions on whether or not to report a bill out of committee to the floor.

Members must stay on top of their oversight and investigation responsibilities, supervising the activities of government agencies and reviewing the expenditures and implementation of government programs. Members respond to scandals and crises through their work on investigatory panels. Their work on the floor involves participating in floor debate, proposing amendments to bills in debate, casting floor votes on legislation, and preparing and delivering floor statements during legislative debates. Congressional leadership responsibilities include persuading fellow members to vote with their party, heading discussions with their party caucus to arrive at a common position on various issues, and negotiating agreements with the other party on when and how to consider specific bills on the floor. In addition, leaders negotiate with the president of the United States on legislation. Members play a public role, speaking on behalf of their party to the press, educating the public via meetings and public appearances, and serving as a role model for public service, civic responsibility, and voter participation. Along with all of this, members of Congress must keep an eye toward the future, organizing and maintaining a campaign for reelection to office.

How many people does it take to do the work of Congress?

The U.S. Congress comprises the House of Representatives and the Senate—all told, some 540 people. The Congress unites more than 400 representatives of the people, 100 senators from fifty states, and 5 delegates from the territories of the United States—an assembly of 540 to make the laws that govern the nation and carry out other powers and duties. In addition to this core group, more than eighteen thousand staff members serve individual members and committees.

What are the terms and sessions of Congress?

A given Congress begins at noon, January 3, of each odd-numbered year following a general election, unless a different day is designated by law. A Congress lasts for two years, with each year normally constituting a separate session. The Legislative Reorganization Act of 1970 requires Congress to adjourn *sine die* ("without a specified day") no later than July 31 of each year unless there is a declared war or unless Congress otherwise provides. In odd-numbered years, Congress must take an August recess if it doesn't adjourn by July 31. Neither the House nor the Senate may adjourn for more than three days (excluding Saturdays, Sundays, and holidays) without the agreement of the other chamber. It has also become a common practice for Congress to adjourn after making provision for the House and Senate leaders to summon Congress back into session in emergency circumstances. Similarly, the president has constitutional authority to summon the Congress for a special session when necessary.

What are joint sessions and joint meetings?

Joint sessions and joint meetings are the two primary ways that a Congress convenes. Congress holds joint sessions to receive addresses from the president, such as the State of the Union and other addresses, and to count electoral ballots for president and vice president. Congress also holds joint meetings to receive addresses from foreign heads of state or heads of governments or from distinguished American citizens. Of the two types of gatherings, the joint session is the more formal and typically occurs upon adoption of a concurrent resolution passed by both houses of Congress. A joint meeting, however, typically occurs when each of the two houses adopts a unanimous agreement to recess in order to meet with the other. Since 1809, the practice has been to hold joint sessions and joint meetings in the Hall of the House of Representatives, the larger of the two chambers. Except for the first inauguration in 1789, when Congress convened in joint session to inaugurate President George Washington, these special occasions have occurred outside of the regular legislative calendars. Occasionally one chamber will convene a legislative session prior to attending the ceremony, but unless both do so and subsequently adjourn to attend the ceremony, the inauguration is not a joint session.

What are party leaders?

The political parties in the House and Senate, namely Republicans and Democrats, elect leaders to represent them on the floor, to advocate their policies and viewpoints, to coordinate their legislative efforts, and to help determine the schedule of legislative business. The leaders serve as spokespersons for their parties and for the House and Senate as a whole. Since the framers of the Constitution did not anticipate political parties, these leadership posts are not defined in the Constitution but have evolved over time. The House, with its larger membership, required majority and minority leaders in the nineteenth century to expedite legislative business and to keep its parties united. The Senate did not formally designate party floor leaders until the 1920s, although several caucus chairs and committee chairs had previously performed similar duties.

In both houses, the parties also elect assistant leaders, or "whips." The majority leader is elected by the majority-party conference (or caucus) and the minority leader by the minority-party conference. Third parties rarely have enough members to warrant an elected leadership, and independents generally join one of the larger party organizations to receive committee assignments.

Are the majority leaders elected by their respective houses of Congress?

No. Rather, members of the majority party in the House, meeting in caucus or conference, select the majority leader. In a similar meeting, the minority-party members select their minority leader. In the Senate, the majority and minority parties also hold separate meetings to elect their leaders.

What do the House majority and minority leaders do?

Since the nineteenth century, the House of Representatives has chosen majority and minority leaders to expedite legislative busi-

Senator Mitch McConnell (R-SC) became the majority leader in 2015, when his party grabbed the majority of Senate.

ness and to keep their parties united. These leaders are elected every two years in secret balloting of the party caucus or conference. The role of the majority leader has been defined by history and tradition. This officer is charged with scheduling legislation for floor consideration; planning the daily, weekly, and annual legislative agendas; consulting with members to gauge party sentiment; and, in general, working to advance the goals of the majority party. The minority leader serves as floor leader of the "loyal opposition" and is the minority counterpart to the Speaker of the House. Although many of the basic leadership responsibilities of the minority and majority leaders are similar, the minority leader speaks for the minority party and its policies and works to protect the minority's rights.

What does the speaker of the House do?

Article I, Section 2 of the Constitution states: "The House of Representatives shall chuse [sic] their speaker and other Officers." The speaker acts as leader of the House and combines several roles: the institutional role of presiding officer and administrative head of the House, the partisan role of leader of the majority party in the House, and the representative role of an elected member of the House. The speaker appoints chairs to preside over the Committee of the Whole, appoints all special or select committees, appoints conference committees, has the power of recognition of members to speak, and makes many important rulings and decisions in the House. The speaker may vote but usually does not, except in case of a tie. The speaker and the majority leader determine the legislative agenda for the House and often confer with the president of the United States and with the Senate leadership. In addition to these roles, the speaker of the House is second in line to succeed the president.

Who held the position of speaker of the House for the longest period of time?

Sam Rayburn (1882–1961) of Texas, who was a member of the House for more than 48 years, served as Speaker for 17 years and 2 months. However, the record for longest continuous service as Speaker is held by Thomas P. "Tip" O'Neill of Massachusetts, who served consecutively for 10 years, surpassing other long-serving contenders, such as John McCormack (8 years, 11 months), Champ Clark (7 years, 10 months), and Joseph G. Cannon (7 years, 3 months).

Who are the officers of the House, and how are they chosen?

Elected officers include the Speaker of the House, clerk (the chief legislative officer of

Sam Rayburn (D-TX) filled the office of speaker of the House longer than anyone to date (fifteen nonconsecutive years during the 1940s and 1950s).

99

the House), sergeant at arms (who is responsible for maintaining order on the floor and in the galleries when the House is in session), chief administrative officer (CAO, the principal House officer responsible for the financial management of House accounts), and chaplain (who opens each daily House session with a prayer and provides pastoral services to House members, their families, and staff). These officers are the House's principal managers of essential legislative, financial, administrative, and security functions. Their duties are outlined in House rules and in statutes. Because the Constitution says that the House "shall chuse [sic] their Speaker and other officers," the members vote on who will be officers as they do on any other question, except that in most cases, it is strictly a party vote. Republicans and Democrats both meet before the House organizes for a new Congress and choose a slate of officers. These two slates are presented at the first session of the House, and the majority-party slate can be expected to be selected. Traditionally, the majority party's nominee for chaplain is not contested.

Another officer, the inspector general, is appointed jointly by the Speaker, majority leader, and minority leader. The inspector general is the chief investigative officer of the House, whose office conducts periodic audits of House financial and administrative offices and operations. In addition, there is a general counsel, the chief legal advisor to the House, who is appointed by the Speaker in consultation with a bipartisan legal advisory group, which includes the majority and minority leaders. Finally, the historian preserves the historical records of the House and its members, encourages historical research on the House, and does original research and writing on the history of the House. The historian is appointed by the Speaker.

Do members of the House have individual seats on the chamber floor?

Representatives had individual seats until the 63rd Congress (1913), but now members may sit where they choose. Democrats occupy the east side of the chamber, on the Speaker's right; Republicans sit across the main aisle, on the Speaker's left. Two tables each on the Democratic and Republican sides of the aisle are reserved for committee leaders during debate on a bill reported from their committee as well as for party leaders.

What is a party caucus or party conference?

A party caucus or conference is the name given to a meeting of all party members in the House or Senate, whether regular or specially called. The term "caucus" or "conference" can also mean the organization of all party members in the House or Senate. House Democrats refer to their organization as a "caucus." House and Senate Republicans and Senate Democrats call their three organizations "conferences." The caucus or conference officially elects party floor leaders and whips and nominates each party's candidates for the Speakership or president pro tempore and other offices in the House or Senate.

The chairs of party conferences and other subordinate party leaders are elected by vote of the conference or caucus at the beginning of each Congress. Regular caucus or conference meetings provide a forum in which party leaders and members can discuss party policy, pending legislative issues, and other matters of mutual concern. The party caucus or conference traditionally establishes party committees with specialized functions. The caucus or conference may also decide to appoint task forces to do research on a new policy proposal or to assist the formal leadership in developing a party position on important legislation. Traditionally, these task forces are disbanded once their work is complete.

What is a committee?

A committee is a panel of members elected or appointed to perform some service or function for its parent body. Committees are essential to the effective operation of legislative bodies. As "little legislatures," committees monitor ongoing government operations, identify issues suitable for legislative review, gather and evaluate information, and recommend courses of action to their house or to Congress. Congress has four types of committees: standing, special or select, joint, and, in the House, a Committee of the Whole. Except for the Committee of the Whole, committees conduct investigations, make studies, issue reports and recommendations, and, in the case of standing committees, review and prepare measures on their assigned subjects for action by their respective houses. Most committees divide their work among several subcommittees or, in some cases, task forces, but only the full committee may submit reports or measures to its house or to Congress. With rare exceptions, the majority party in a house holds a majority of the seats on its committees, and their chairs are also from that party.

The Senate Armed Services Committee meets in this 2007 photograph. Committees are like little legislators that are tasked to manage certain aspects of government.

What is a subcommittee?

Most committees form subcommittees with legislative authority to consider and report bills on particular issues within the range of authority of the full committee. Committees may assign their subcommittees such specific tasks as the initial consideration of measures and oversight of laws and programs in their areas. Subcommittees are responsible to and work with guidelines established by their parent committees. Consequently, their number, independence, and autonomy vary among committees.

What are party committees?

The party caucus or conference traditionally establishes party committees with specialized functions. Party committees generally nominate party members to serve on the various committees of the House or Senate, subject to approval by the caucus or conference. Policy committees generally discuss party positions on pending legislation. Steering committees generally plan the schedule of chamber action on pending legislation. Research committees conduct studies on broad policy questions, generally before committees of the House or Senate begin action on legislation. Campaign committees provide research and strategy assistance to party candidates for election to the House or Senate. The chairs of party committees are generally elected by their respective party caucus or conference; the exception is the House Democratic Steering Committee, which is chaired by the Speaker of the House when the Democrats are in the majority or by the Democratic floor leader when the Democrats are in the minority.

What are congressional standing committees, and why are they necessary?

Standing committees are permanent panels made up of members of a chamber. Each panel has authority over measures and laws in certain areas of public policy, such as health, education, energy, the environment, foreign affairs, and agriculture. Each chamber has its own standing committees, which allows it to consider many issues at the same time. Each committee selects, from the measures it receives during each Congress, a relatively small number (approximately 10 percent) that merit committee review and subsequent consideration by the full chamber. Because of the small size of committees—and the often lengthy service of members on the same panel—committees provide an effective means of managing Congress's enormous workload and gaining expertise in the range of complex subjects with which the federal government deals.

Have there always been standing committees?

Yes. Although Congress has used standing committees since its earliest days, it did not predominantly rely on them during its first quarter century. In these early years, legislative proposals were considered initially by all members of one chamber in plenary session; afterward, each proposal was referred to a temporary, ad hoc committee responsible for working out a proposal's details and making any technical changes. As the amount of legislative proposals increased, especially in certain subject areas, permanent committees replaced temporary ones for more expeditious screening and processing of legislation before its consideration by an entire chamber.

What are the standing committees of the House?

In the 115th Congress, the following standing committees were named:

- Agriculture
- Appropriations
- Armed Services
- Budget
- Education and the Workforce
- Energy and Commerce
- Ethics
- Financial Services
- Foreign Affairs
- Homeland Security
- House Administration
- Judiciary
- Natural Resources
- Oversight and Government Reform
- Rules
- Science, Space, and Technology
- Small Business
- Transportation and Infrastructure
- Veterans' Affairs
- Ways and Means

What are the standing committees of the Senate?

In the 115th Congress, the following standing committees were named:

- Agriculture, Nutrition, and Forestry
- Appropriations
- Armed Services
- Banking, Housing, and Urban Affairs
- Budget
- Commerce, Science, and Transportation

Speaker of the House Paul Ryan (R-WI) takes the podium at a House Budget Committee meeting. Budget committees, as one can imagine, are one of the more important legislative groups.

- Energy and Natural Resources
- Environment and Public Works
- Finance
- Foreign Relations
- Health, Education, Labor, and Pensions
- Homeland Security and Governmental Affairs
- Judiciary
- Rules and Administration
- Small Business and Entrepreneurship
- Veterans' Affairs

Who sits on standing committees, and how are they selected?

Before members are assigned to committees, each committee's size and the proportion of Democrats to Republicans must be decided by each chamber's party leaders. The total number of committee slots allotted to each party is approximately the same as the ratio between majority-party and minority-party members in the full chamber. Members are then assigned to committees in a three-step process, in which the first step is the most critical and decisive. Each of the two principal parties in the House and Senate is responsible for assigning its members to committees, and, at the first stage, each party uses a committee on committees to make the initial recommendations for assignments. At the beginning of a new Congress, members express their assignment preferences to the appropriate committee on committees; most incumbents prefer to remain on the same committees in order to retain their committee seniority and build upon their expertise. These committees on committees then match preferences with committee slots, following certain guidelines designed in part to distribute assignments fairly. They then prepare and approve an assignment slate for each committee and submit all slates to the appropriate full-party conference for approval. Approval at this second stage often is granted easily, but the conferences have procedures for disapproving recommended members and nominating others instead. Finally, at the third stage, each committee submits its slate to the pertinent full chamber for approval, which is generally granted.

Who is the committee chair, and what does his or her selection have to do with "seniority rule"?

Generally, it has been the custom for the member who has served longest on the majority side of a committee to become its chair or, if on the minority side, its ranking member. Members are ranked from the chair or ranking member down, according to length of service on the committee. Modifications—including party practices, term limits on chairmanships, and limits on the number of committees and subcommittees chaired—have caused the seniority rule to be less rigidly followed in recent congresses. Nevertheless, length of service on a committee remains the predominant criterion for

choosing its chair and ranking member.

In both chambers, nominees for committee chair are subject to public votes, first in meetings of their party colleagues (in conference or caucus), then in the full chamber. Members who interrupt their service in a chamber but subsequently return to Congress, start again at the bottom of a committee list. Returning members outrank other new members who have no prior service. New members also earn seniority over other newly elected members by having prior service in the other legislative chamber. In cases where two members have served an equal time in a chamber, prior service as a state governor or state legislator also may contribute to the determination of seniority.

What are joint committees, and how are they established?

Joint committees are those committees that have members from both the House and Senate, generally with the chairmanship rotating between the most senior majority-party senator and representative. In general, select committees do not have legislative power to consider and report legislation to the full chambers. These committees can be created by statute or by joint or concurrent resolution, although all existing ones have been established by statute. Congress now has four permanent or long-term joint committees, the oldest being the Joint Committee on the Library, which dates from 1800. The other three are the Joint Economic Committee, the Joint Committee on Printing, and the Joint Committee on Taxation. In addition, Congress sometimes establishes temporary joint committees for particular purposes, such as the Joint Congressional Committee on Inaugural Ceremonies, which is formed every four years to handle the organizational and financial responsibilities for the inauguration of the president and vice president of the United States.

What is the House Committee of the Whole?

The Committee of the Whole House on the State of the Union (or Committee of the Whole) is a hybrid form of the House itself. Technically, it is a committee of the House on which all representatives serve that meets in the House chamber. However, it is governed by different procedural rules than other House meetings. This concept of the

---

What is a select committee?

The House and Senate select committees usually meet for limited time periods and for limited purposes. Although there are exceptions, most are not given legislative power—that is, the authority to consider and report legislation to the full chamber. After completing its purpose, such as investigating a government activity and making a related report, the select committee disbands. Recently, however, the chambers have allowed select committees to continue to exist over extended periods of time. Some, such as the House and Senate Select Committees on Intelligence, have been granted legislative authority.

"grand committee" has been carefully developed from the early days of the House and in modern practice gives the House a more expeditious means of considering the complex and often controversial legislation referred to it.

Historically, it was devised by the English House of Commons to give them the ability to debate privately and not have their votes committed to record. The Committee of the Whole in the U.S. House permitted recorded votes beginning in January 1971. The House resolves itself into a new Committee of the Whole for the consideration of each bill. A specific Committee of the Whole is dissolved when it "rises and reports with a recommendation" to the House. When the Committee rises after not having resolved the matter committed to it, that bill is carried on the calendar as "unfinished business of the Committee of the Whole" until consideration has been completed. When a bill or resolution is considered in the Committee of the Whole, there first is a period of time, usually one hour, for general debate on the merits of the bill or resolution. If enforced, a quorum (a group considered complete enough to conduct business) in the Committee of the Whole is a hundred members (whereas 218 are required in the House to conduct business). After general debate, members may offer amendments, with each speech for or against an amendment being limited to five minutes. If a recorded vote is desired on any amendment, the call for the vote must be seconded by twenty-five members (whereas forty-four or more are required in the House). When the amending process is completed, the Committee of the Whole "rises" and reports its actions to the House through the Speaker. The House then votes on whether or not to adopt the amendments recommended by the Committee of the Whole and then votes on final passage of the measure as amended. The Senate stopped using the Committee of the Whole as a parliamentary forum for debate in 1986.

What is the role of the House Rules Committee?

The House Rules Committee makes recommendations to the House on possible changes in the standing rules of the House as well as the order of business on the House floor. The committee affects the order of business by reporting resolutions that make it possible for the House to begin acting on a bill that is on the House or Union calendar. These resolutions are known as special rules or simply as rules. Each special rule may also propose a set of ground rules for debating and amending a particular bill that is different from the normal rules for considering legislation. For example, a special rule may impose limitations on the amendments that members can propose to a bill, or it may allow an amendment to be proposed even though it violates a standing rule of the House. The House as a whole decides by majority vote whether to accept, reject, or modify each special rule that the Rules Committee proposes. The Senate Committee on Rules and Administration also considers possible changes in the standing rules of the Senate, but it doesn't determine the order of business on the Senate floor. In addition, the Senate committee reports on resolutions to fund the work of all the Senate committees. In the House, this responsibility belongs to the Committee on House Administration.

LAWMAKING AND BUDGETING

How does the legislative perspective differ in the Senate and the House?

The power to legislate is vested in a Congress with two distinct bodies, the Senate and the House of Representatives. While the concurrence of both houses is required to enact a law, each chamber has a distinct mission, different rules of procedure, and unique traditions. The Congress does not act as one homogeneous unit; rather, conflict is inherent in this bicameral legislature. Conflict primarily arises in the passage of a bill into law, where it is easier to block a bill's passage than to pass it. In recent congresses, not even 6 percent of all bills have become law.

In the lawmaking process, the House is meant to reflect the wishes of the majority of Americans. The Senate, on the other hand, is meant to force the debate necessary to thoroughly examine popular opinion. In short, the House is more centralized and organized than the Senate, and the Senate is more deliberative. Because deliberation involves delaying the passage of proposals until adequate discussion has taken place, the Senate's rules and traditions give advantages to the minority—such as unlimited debate—in an effort to stop the majority from acting too swiftly. The opposite is true of the House: its rules and traditions favor the majority to ensure that the people's views prevail and that no minority obstructs them. Furthermore, the rules give House leaders more control over the legislative process and allow House members to specialize in legislative areas; the rules of the Senate, on the other hand, limit their power and discourage specialization. Finally, due to factors such as their length of terms and the constituencies they serve, members of the House serve local interests with specific legislative agendas, while senators serve larger, more diverse constituencies. Senators have the added benefit of considering new ideas and ways of uniting various interests and thus serve as the agents for interests organized on a statewide or national basis.

What are the four forms of legislation introduced in Congress?

Congressional legislation takes one of the following four forms: the bill, the joint resolution, the concurrent resolution, and the simple resolution. A bill is the form used for most legislation, whether permanent or temporary, general or special, public or private. Bills are presented to the president of the United States for action when approved in identical form by both the House of Representatives and the Senate. Like a bill, joint resolutions may originate either in the House of Representatives or in the Senate. There is little practical difference between a bill and a joint resolution. Both are subject to the same procedure, and joint resolutions become law in the same manner as bills. The only exception to this is a joint resolution proposing an amendment to the Constitution. On approval of such a resolution by two-thirds of both the House and Senate, it is not presented to the president for approval. Rather, it is sent directly to the administrator of general services for submission to the individual states for ratification. Matters affecting the operations of both the House of Representatives and Senate are usually initiated by means of concurrent resolutions. Instead of being presented to the president for signature, on approval by both the House of Representatives and Senate, they are signed by the clerk of the House and the secretary of the Senate. A matter concerning the operation of either the House of Representatives or Senate alone is initiated by a simple resolution. Like concurrent resolutions, they are not presented to the president for action.

How many amendments to the Constitution have there been over time?

Because the requirements for amending the Constitution are so stringent, it is not often done. Since 1789, over ten thousand amendments have been proposed in Congress. Of those, only thirty-three were sent to the states for ratification, and only twenty-seven were ultimately ratified. Examples of recent amendments that received much congressional attention but failed to survive the process include the Flag Desecration Amendment, the Balanced Budget Amendment, the Equal Rights Amendment, a Term Limits Amendment, and a School Prayer Amendment.

What is a quorum?

A quorum is the number of senators or representatives that must be present to do business. The Constitution requires a simple majority of senators (fifty-one) for a quorum. Often, fewer senators are actually present on the floor, but the Senate presumes that a quorum is present unless the contrary is shown by a roll call vote or quorum call. Likewise, in the House of Representatives, a quorum is a simple majority of the members. When there are no vacancies in the membership, a quorum is 218. When one or more seats are vacant because of deaths or resignations, the quorum is reduced accordingly. Because of members' other duties, a quorum often is not actually present on the House floor, but any member may insist that a quorum be present. If the Speaker agrees, a series of bells ring on the House side of the Capitol and in the House office buildings to alert members to come to the chamber and record their presence.

What is a whip?

The Democratic and Republican whips assist the Democratic and Republican leadership, respectively, in managing the party's legislative program on the House and Senate floor. The whip keeps track of all legislation and ensures that all party members are present when important measures are to be voted on. When a vote appears to be close, the whips contact absent members of their party and advise them of the vote. The authority of the whips over party members is informal; in Congress, a member may vote against the position supported by a majority of the member's party colleagues because of personal opposition or because of opposition within his or her constituency. In most cases, parties take no disciplinary action against colleagues who vote against the party position. The majority and minority whips in the House and Senate are elected

In the 115th Congress, Steve Scalise (R-LA) serves as majority whip. The whip is the assistant to the party's majority leader.

by party members in their respective chambers. Because of the large number of representatives, the House majority and minority whips appoint deputy whips to assist them in their activities.

How is a bill introduced?

In both the House and Senate, any number of members may join in introducing a single bill or resolution. The first member listed is the sponsor of the bill, and all members' names following the sponsor's are the bill's cosponsors. When introduced, a bill is referred to the committee or committees that have authority over the subject with which the bill is concerned. Under the standing rules of the House and Senate, bills are referred by the Speaker of the House and by the presiding officer in the Senate. In practice, the House and Senate parliamentarians act for these officials and refer the vast majority of bills.

How does a bill become a law?

Every year, Congress considers hundreds of legislative proposals. For every bill that is proposed, there is a series of steps it must go through before it becomes law. To begin with, a bill must pass both bodies of Congress in the same form before it can be presented to the president of the United States for signature into law. The process begins when a representative has an idea for a new law. He or she becomes the sponsor of that bill and introduces it by giving it to the clerk of the House or by placing it in a box, called the "hopper." The clerk assigns a legislative number to the bill, with the initials "H.R." for bills introduced in the House and "S." for bills introduced in the Senate. The Government Printing Office (GPO) then prints the bill and distributes copies to each representative for his or her review.

The bill is then referred by the Speaker to one or more of the twenty-two standing committees of the House. The standing committee, or often a subcommittee, studies the bill and hears testimony from experts and people interested in the bill, including lobbyists, interest groups, and members of the academic and business communities. After hearing an array of opinions, the committee may decide to release the bill with a recommendation to pass it, revise the bill and release it, or lay it aside so that the House cannot vote on it. Releasing the bill is called "reporting it out," while laying it aside is called "tabling." If the bill is released, it then goes on a calendar, or list, of bills awaiting action. At this point, the House Rules Committee may call for the bill to be voted on quickly, limit the debate, or limit or prohibit amendments. Undisputed bills may be passed by unanimous consent or by a two-thirds vote if members agree to suspend the rules.

The bill then goes to the floor of the House for consideration, which begins with a complete reading of the bill. There is a time allotted for general debate on the bill, and there is a time allotted for amending the bill, one part at a time, under a rule that limits speeches on amendments to five minutes each. A third reading (of the title only) occurs after any amendments have been added. If the bill passes by simple majority (218 of 435), the bill moves to the Senate.

In order to be introduced in the Senate, a senator must be recognized as the presiding officer and announce the introduction of the bill. Just as in the House, the bill is assigned to one of the Senate's sixteen standing committees by the presiding officer; the Senate committee studies and either releases or tables the bill. Once released, the bill goes to the Senate floor for consideration. When the Senate considers the bill, members can debate it indefinitely. When there is no more debate, the bill is voted on. A simple majority (51 of 100) passes the bill.

The bill then moves on to a conference committee, which is made up of members from each House. The committee's primary role is to work out any differences between the House and Senate versions of the bill. The revised bill is sent back to both houses for their final approval. Once approved, the bill is printed by the GPO in a process called enrolling. The clerk from the introducing house certifies the final version. The Speaker of the House and then the vice president sign the enrolled bill. Finally, the bill is sent to the president for his signature and enactment into law.

What options does the president of the United States have once both houses have passed a bill?

Once both houses of Congress have passed a bill, the president has three choices: First, he can sign the bill within ten days (Sundays excepted), whereupon it becomes a law.

Second, the president may veto the bill—that is, return it to Congress, stating his objections, without a signature of approval. In this case, Congress may override the veto with a two-thirds vote in each House. The bill would then become a law despite the president's veto. Third, the president may hold the bill without taking any action. Two different developments are possible in this situation, depending upon whether Congress is in session. If Congress is in session, the bill becomes law after ten days (excluding Sundays), even without the president's signature. If Congress has adjourned, the bill does not become law, and this procedure is called a pocket veto.

What is the difference between a veto and a pocket veto?

According the Constitution, a veto is the procedure by which the president of the United States refuses to approve a bill or

108TH CONGRESS
1ST SESSION

H. R. 1

To amend title XVIII of the Social Security Act to provide for a voluntary program for prescription drug coverage under the Medicare Program, to modernize the Medicare Program, and for other purposes.

IN THE HOUSE OF REPRESENTATIVES

JUNE 25, 2003

Mr. HASTERT (for himself, Mr. DELAY, Mr. BLUNT, Ms. PRYCE of Ohio, Mr. THOMAS, Mr. TAUZIN, Mrs. JOHNSON of Connecticut, Mr. BILIRAKIS, Mr. PETERSON of Minnesota, Mrs. CAPITO, Ms. GINNY BROWN-WAITE of Florida, Mr. BRADLEY of New Hampshire, Mr. BURNS, Ms. DUNN, Mr. FLETCHER, Mr. GOSS, Mr. GRAVES, Mr. McCRERY, Mr. NUNES, Mr. SIMMONS, and Mr. SULLIVAN) introduced the following bill; which was referred jointly to the Committees on Energy and Commerce, and Ways and Means, in each case for consideration of such provisions as fall within the jurisdiction of the committee concerned

A BILL

To amend title XVIII of the Social Security Act to provide for a voluntary program for prescription drug coverage under the Medicare Program, to modernize the Medicare Program, and for other purposes.

1   *Be it enacted by the Senate and House of Representa-*
2 *tives of the United States of America in Congress assembled,*

An example of a House bill—in this case, it is the 2003 bill called the Medicare Prescription Drug, Improvement, and Modernization Act, which overhauled Medicare for the first time in nearly four decades.

joint resolution and thus prevents its enactment into law. A regular veto occurs when the president returns the legislation to the house in which it originated. The president usually returns a vetoed bill with a message indicating his reasons for rejecting the measure. The veto can be overridden only by a two-thirds vote in both the Senate and the House. The Constitution grants the president ten days to review a measure passed by the Congress. If the president has not signed the bill after this time period, it becomes law without his signature. However, if Congress adjourns during the ten-day period, the bill does not become law, and this is known as a pocket veto.

What role does debate play in the legislative process?

The standing rules of the Senate and House promote deliberation by permitting senators and representatives to debate at length and by precluding a simple majority from ending a debate when they are prepared to vote to approve a bill. Although the right to debate is considered one of the most pivotal for shaping what occurs on the House and Senate floors, it has its limitations. In the House, no matter may be debated for more than one hour—usually equally divided between the majority and the minority—without unanimous consent. Moreover, the majority can call for the "previous question" and bring the pending matter to an immediate vote. In the Committee of the Whole, the period of time spent in general debate is determined in advance. Amendments are subject to the five-minute-per-side rule, but debate can be extended beyond ten minutes when unanimous consent is granted or when "pro forma" amendments are offered. A nondebatable motion to close debate is necessary to end debate on any specific amendment and bring it to a vote.

In the Senate, debate is normally without restriction unless time limits are agreed to by unanimous consent. The ability to extend debate at will—to filibuster—enables a senator to delay the final vote on a measure or even to prevent it altogether. Filibusters can be broken only by negotiation or through the use of a formal procedure known as cloture. A successful cloture motion requires at least a three-fifths vote, or sixty senators. If they vote for cloture, the filibuster comes to a gradual end. Thirty hours of further debate are permitted in the post-cloture period prior to the vote on final passage. However, senators do not usually extend debate after they have voted for cloture.

What is a filibuster?

The word "filibuster" is an informal term for any attempt to block or delay Senate action on a bill or other matter by debating it at length, by offering numerous procedural motions, or by any other delaying or obstructive actions. The lack of debate limitations in Senate rules creates the possibility of filibusters. Individual senators or minority groups of senators who adamantly oppose a bill or amendment may speak against it at great length in the hope of changing their colleagues' minds, winning support for amendments that meet their objectives, or convincing the Senate to withdraw the bill or amendment from further consideration on the floor. Opposing senators also can delay final floor action by offering numerous amendments and motions, insisting that amendments be read in full, demanding roll call votes on amendments and motions, and using a variety of other devices. The only formal procedure that can break a filibuster is cloture.

How are conference committees used to resolve differences in legislation?

From the days of the early republic, differences on legislation between the House and Senate have been assigned to conference committees to work out a settlement. The most usual case is that in which a bill passes one chamber with amendments unacceptable to the other. In such a case, the chamber that disagrees with the amendments generally asks for a conference, and the Speaker of the House and the presiding officer of the Senate appoint "managers," as the conferees are called. Generally, they are se-

What is cloture?

Cloture is the only procedure by which the Senate can vote to place a time limit on consideration of a bill or other matter and thereby overcome a filibuster. Under the cloture rule, the Senate may limit consideration of a pending matter to thirty additional hours but only by a vote of three-fifths of the full Senate, normally sixty votes.

lected from the committee or committees in charge of the bill. After attempting to resolve the points in disagreement, the conference committee issues a report to each chamber. If the report is accepted by both chambers, the bill is then enrolled and sent to the president of the United States for signature. If the report is rejected by either chamber, the matter in disagreement comes up again for debate as if there had been no conference. Unless all differences between the two houses are resolved, the bill fails.

How does a member of Congress decide how to vote?

Members of Congress are asked hundreds of times a year to cast their "yea" or "nay" votes on a variety of bills, motions, and amendments that cover every conceivable issue of the day from gun control and abortion rights to trade with China. The overall rate of participation—tallied at 95 percent of all votes held in the last few congresses—suggests that members take this responsibility seriously. Amid conflicting opinions regarding any piece of legislature, a member must make a decision, often in very little time. Because members are accountable to their constituents for the way they vote on a particular issue, they almost always do some form of research into any public policy issue. They review statistics, legal analyses, newspaper editorials, and arguments from special-interest groups. Members consider the cost to the taxpayer and spend time trying to gain an accurate idea of how their constituents feel about any given legislative proposal. In addition, party caucuses and senior members exert their own influence over members, supplying research and analysis to members in an effort to promote a specific argument or position. In addition to these influences, the president of the United States voices his opinion, and a member must assess whether the president's threatened veto might block passage of a measure.

When does a bill "die"?

A bill may be introduced at any point during a two-year Congress. It remains eligible for consideration throughout the duration of that Congress until the Congress ends or adjourns *sine die* ("without a specified day"). If it is not considered within that time frame, the bill fails, or "dies."

What happens to a bill after it becomes a law?

The provisions of a law take effect immediately unless the law itself specifies another date. The law may also indicate which executive departments, agencies, or officers are empowered to carry out or enforce the law. The written document is sent to the National Archives and Records Administration, where it is assigned a number. It is then published in individual form as a "slip law." At the end of each session of Congress, these new laws are consolidated in a bound volume called *U.S. Statutes at Large*. In addition, all permanent, general laws currently in force are included in the Code of Laws of the United States of America, commonly called the U.S. Code. The Office of Law Revision Counsel, part of the institutional structure of the House of Representatives, is responsible for preparing and issuing annual supplements to keep the U.S. Code current.

What is logrolling?

The term "logrolling" derives from the early American practice of neighbors gathering together to help clear land by rolling off and burning felled timber. In the political arena, it has to do with exchanging political favors, specifically the trading of votes among legislators to achieve passage of projects that are of interest to one another. Logrolling mainly occurs when members of Congress must vote on bills about which they are not experts, or in fact know very little, and turn to a more knowledgeable congressional colleague for advice. If the issue is of little interest to the uninformed member of Congress, he will often pledge his "yea" vote for that bill in exchange for a similar favor: the promise of a "yea" vote from his more knowledgeable colleague on a future piece of legislation. Logrolling often takes place on specialized legislation that targets money or projects for selected congressional districts.

When it comes to politics, log rolling is not a lumberjack sport performed on logs; rather, it is the exchange of favors and votes.

What is meant by the term "pork barrel" legislation?

The term "pork barrel" came into political parlance in the post–Civil War era, when plantation owners would hand out rations of salt pork to their former slaves, distributing them from wooden barrels. When the term is used in reference to a particular bill, it implies legislation loaded with benefits from members of Congress to their constituents back home, courtesy of the federal taxpayer. However, there is wide disagreement about what makes a bill "pork." Those critical of the practice feel it is unfair that a member with political skill can obtain federal funds for his district or state, when the same benefits are not received by other parts of the nation with similar needs. Proponents argue that the nature of America's diverse geographic and cultural regions warrants projects that may only benefit one area. For example, areas that regularly suffer from severe flooding or other destructive acts of nature consider federal funds to build dams essential to their recovery and would never call that project "pork." Furthermore, proponents argue that projects such as water reclamation, environmental cleanup, and highway improvements generate local jobs and bring political kudos to the member of Congress who worked to get the project funded, making it a part of the member's obligation to his constituency rather than simply an indiscriminate benefit to his or her region.

What role does Congress play in the federal budget-making process?

The federal budgeting process has three main components: formulation of the budget by the president and the Office of Management and Budget (OMB); congressional action on the budget; and, finally, implementation. Congress considers the president's budget proposals and approves, modifies, or disapproves them. Congress can—and often does—change funding levels, eliminate programs, or add programs that are not at the president's request. It can add or eliminate taxes and other sources of receipts or make other changes that affect the amount of receipts. Through the process of adopting a budget resolution, Congress agrees on levels for total spending and receipts, the size of the deficit or surplus, and the debt limit. The budget resolution then provides the framework within which congressional committees prepare appropriations bills and other spending and receipts legislation, such as changes in the tax code. After negotiating back and forth, the president and Congress reach a consensus on a budget they feel is

The origin of the term "pork barrel" comes from when there were still slaves in America. They were given rations of pork (stored in brine in a barrel), and sometimes, they would rush to grab as much as they could for themselves. The same idea applies to politicians grabbing money for their personal projects today.

in the best interests of the American people. During the execution of the budget, government agencies may not spend more than Congress has appropriated.

Does Congress ever allocate more money?

Yes. While the federal budget is being executed, the government often finds that it needs to spend more money than Congress has appropriated for the fiscal year because of circumstances that were not anticipated when the budget was created. For example, more money might be needed to provide assistance to a city struck by a natural or unforeseen disaster, and in these types of circumstances, Congress often grants additional funds. For example, Congress approved $40 billion in emergency funds to aid the city of New York immediately following the September 11, 2001, terrorist attacks and $51 billion in relief aid for the victims of Hurricane Katrina.

What is sequestration, and what does it have to do with Congress?

Established in 1985 by the Balanced Budget and Emergency Deficit Reduction Act, also known as the Gramm-Rudman-Hollings Act, sequestration is an across-the-board cut in federal spending by presidential order. A sequestration order can only be issued if Congress fails to meet a budgetary requirement, such as a deficit target or spending limit.

THE PRESIDENT

WHO CAN BECOME PRESIDENT?

Can anyone run for president?

No. According to Article II, Section 1 of the Constitution, any person seeking the presidency must be a natural-born citizen, at least thirty-five years old, and a resident of the United States for at least fourteen years. Constitutional scholars have debated whether a child born abroad of an American parent constitutes "a natural-born citizen." While most maintain that such a person should qualify as a natural-born citizen, no definitive consensus has been reached.

How many terms can a president serve?

Article II, Section 1 of the Constitution mandates that the president serve a four-year term. This time period was chosen because the framers agreed that four years was enough time for a president to have learned the ropes, demonstrated his leadership abilities, and established sound policies. The Constitution placed no limit on the number of terms that a president might serve until the 1951 adoption of the Twenty-second Amendment, which states that "no person shall be elected to the office of the President more than twice, and no person who has held the office of President, or acted as President, for more than two years of a term to which some other person was elected President shall be elected to the office of the President more than once." As a result, each president can serve a maximum of eight years in office; however, a president who succeeds to the office beyond the midpoint in a term to which another person was originally elected could potentially serve for more than eight years. In these exceptional cases, the president would finish out his predecessor's term and then seek two full terms on his own. Under these conditions, the maximum amount of time that he could serve would be ten years.

Has any president served more than two terms?

Yes. While early presidents, beginning with George Washington, declined to seek more than two terms of office and established the unwritten rule of not pursuing a third term, Franklin D. Roosevelt broke tradition by winning a third term in 1940 and a fourth term in 1944. He was the only president ever to serve more than two terms, since shortly thereafter the Twenty-second Amendment was passed, placing term limits on the executive office.

Have other term limits been suggested?

Since the Twenty-second Amendment was passed in 1951, several presidents—including Harry Truman, Dwight Eisenhower, and Ronald Reagan—have called for its repeal. Their main argument has centered on the fact that the amendment places an arbitrary time limit on the office and that the will of the people should be heeded in electing their chief officer, regardless of the amount of time that he has already served. Critics of the amendment concur, saying the time limit undercuts the authority of a two-term president, especially in the latter half of his second term. Still other presidents, most recently Jimmy Carter, have lobbied for a single, nonrenewable six-year term, arguing that this time period would allow the president to focus on implementing long-term policies that would benefit the nation and release him from the pressure of campaigning for a second term—a cumbersome task that automatically distracts him from the day-to-day responsibilities of the office.

When does the president actually begin his term?

When the Constitution was ratified, Congress was given power to determine the starting date of the new presidential administration, and it set the date of March 4, 1789. Although George Washington did not take the oath of office until April 30 of that year, his term officially began on March 4. Later, the Twentieth (or "lame duck") Amendment, which was ratified in 1933, established January 20 as the date on which presidents would be inaugurated. In 1937, Franklin D. Roosevelt became the first president to take the oath on January 20.

What is the presidential oath?

The oath of office for the president is found in Article II, Section 1 of the Constitution and reads as follows: "I do solemnly swear (or affirm) that I will faithfully execute the office of President of the United States, and will, to the best of my ability, preserve, protect, and defend the Constitution of the United States." Usually, the chief justice of

President Bill Clinton is seen here taking the oath of office in 1993. Chief Justice William Rehnquist administered the oath.

the Supreme Court administers the oath, although there is no provision made for this in the Constitution. In fact, throughout American history other judges have administered the oath at times of unexpected presidential succession.

What are the president's salary and benefits?

According to Title 3 of the U.S. Code, the president's salary is $400,000 per year. Congress sets the president's salary, which cannot be increased or decreased during a presidential term. In addition, the president is allocated a $50,000-a-year taxable expense allowance to be spent however the president chooses. During his term in office, the president also enjoys many perks, including living in the White House, managing office suites and a large staff, sailing on the presidential yacht, flying in his private jet (*Air Force One*), holding meetings at the Camp David resort, and enjoying abundant travel and entertainment funds, among other benefits. In addition, since 1959 each former president has received a lifetime pension.

Have any women ever run for president?

Beginning with Victoria Claflin Woodhull, the presidential nominee of the People's Party (Equal Rights Party) in 1872, women have consistently appeared on the presidential ballots of a variety of parties. The first woman presidential candidate selected at a major political party convention was Margaret Chase Smith of Maine. Smith was placed in nomination on July 15, 1964, at the Republican National Convention in San Francisco, California. Notable female presidential candidates include Shirley Chisholm (1972), Elizabeth Hanford Dole (1999), Michele Bachmann (2012), Jill Stein (2012 and 2016), and Hillary Clinton (2008 and 2016).

THE PRESIDENT'S ROLES AND RESPONSIBILITIES

What is the executive branch?

The executive branch of the federal government, headed by the president of the United States, consists of various entities and organizations of an administrative, regulatory, or policy-implementing character. The fourteen departments are the most visible of these entities, and their heads make up the cabinet. These departments include the Department of Defense, the Department of State, the Department of Energy, and the Department of the Interior. In addition, the executive branch includes a number of agencies, such as the Central Intelligence Agency (CIA) and the Environmental Protection Agency (EPA), as well as distinct smaller boards, committees, commissions, and offices created either by law or presidential directive. Immediately assisting the president are the agencies and entities of the Executive Office of the President, including, for example, the Council of Economic Advisors and the National Security Council.

What is the president's job description?

The president's chief duty is to protect the Constitution and enforce the laws made by Congress. However, he also has a host of other responsibilities tied to his job description: recommending legislation to Congress, calling special sessions of Congress, delivering messages to Congress, signing or vetoing legislation, appointing federal judges, appointing heads of federal departments and agencies and other principal federal officials, appointing representatives to foreign countries, carrying on official business with foreign nations, acting as commander in chief of the armed forces, and granting pardons for offenses against the United States.

What are the president's various roles?

Although the Constitution only clearly assigns to the president the roles of chief executive and commander of the country's armed forces, today the president of the United States assumes six basic roles: chief executive; chief of state/foreign relations; commander in chief; chief legislator; chief of party; and chief citizen, or popular leader.

What are the president's duties and roles as chief executive?

When wearing the hat of chief executive, sometimes called chief administrator, the president has four main duties: (1) enforcing federal laws and court rulings; (2) developing various federal policies; (3) appointing federal officials; and (4) preparing the national budget. Within the executive branch, the president has broad powers to manage national affairs and the workings of the federal government. The president can issue rules, regulations, and instructions called executive orders, which have the binding force of law for federal agencies but do not require congressional approval. With foreign countries, the president may negotiate executive agreements that are not subject to Senate confirmation. The president nominates, and the Senate confirms, the heads of all executive departments and agencies, together with hundreds of other high-ranking federal officials. In addition, the president alone appoints other important public officials, including aides, advisors, and hundreds of other positions. Presidential nominations of federal judges, including members of the Supreme Court, are subject to confirmation by the Senate. Another significant executive power involves granting a full or conditional pardon to anyone convicted of breaking a federal law—except in the case of impeachment. In addition, as the nation's chief executive, the president prepares the national budget.

What are the president's duties and roles as chief of state?

As the chief of state, the president is the ceremonial head of the United States. Under the Constitution, the president is the federal official primarily responsible for the relations of the United States with foreign nations. As chief of state, the president appoints ambassadors, ministers, and consuls, subject to confirmation by the Senate, and receives foreign ambassadors and other public officials. With the secretary of state, the president manages all official contacts with foreign governments. On occasion, the president may personally participate in summit conferences, where chiefs of state meet for direct consultation. For example, President Woodrow Wilson headed the American delegation to the Paris conference at the end of World War I; President Franklin D. Roosevelt met with Allied leaders during World War II; and every president since Roosevelt has come together with world leaders to discuss economic and political issues and to reach foreign policy agreements.

Through the Department of State, the president is responsible for the protection of Americans abroad and of foreign nationals in the United States. The president decides whether to recognize new nations and new governments and negotiate treaties with other nations, which become binding on the United States when approved by two-thirds of the Senate.

President Barack Obama is seen here meeting with Prime Minister Alexis Tsipras of Greece. One of the chief duties of a U.S. president is to meet with foreign heads of state and other dignitaries.

How is the president commander in chief?

Article II, Section 2 of the Constitution states that the president is the commander in chief of the U.S. Army, Navy, and, when it is called into federal service, state militias (now called the National Guard). Historically, presidents have used this authority to commit U.S. troops without a formal declaration of war. However, Article I, Section 8 of the Constitution reserves to Congress the power to raise and support the armed forces as well as the sole authority to declare war. These competing powers have been the source of controversy between the legislative and executive branches over warmaking, so much so that in 1973, Congress enacted the War Powers Resolution, which limits the president's authority to use the armed forces without specific congressional authorization in an attempt to increase and clarify Congress's control over the use of the military. In addition, the armed forces operate under the doctrine of civilian control, which means that only the president or statutory deputies—such as the secretary and deputy secretary of defense—can order the use of force. The chain of command is structured to ensure that the military cannot undertake actions without civilian approval or knowledge.

How is the president the chief legislator?

Despite the constitutional provision that "all legislative powers" shall be vested in the Congress, the president, as the chief formulator of public policy, plays a major legislative role. The president can veto any bill passed by Congress and, unless two-thirds of the members of each house vote to override the veto, the bill does not become law. Much of the legislation dealt with by Congress is drafted at the initiative of the executive branch. In his annual and special messages to Congress, the president may propose legislation he believes is necessary. If Congress should adjourn without acting on those proposals, the president has the power to call it into special session. But beyond this official role, the president, as head of a political party and as principal executive officer of the U.S. government, is in a position to influence public opinion and thereby the course of legislation in Congress.

To improve their working relationships with Congress, in recent years presidents have set up a Congressional Liaison Office in the White House. Presidential aides keep abreast of all important legislative activities and try to persuade senators and representatives of both parties to support administration policies.

How does the president exercise veto power?

There are two types of vetoes available to the president. The regular veto, called a qualified negative veto, is limited by the ability of Congress to gather the necessary two-thirds vote of each house for a constitutional override. The other type of veto is not explicitly outlined in the Constitution but is traditionally called a pocket veto. An absolute veto that cannot be overridden, it becomes effective when the president fails to sign a bill after Congress has adjourned and is unable to override the veto. The president's veto authority is one of his most significant tools in legislative dealings with Congress. It is not only effective in directly preventing the passage of legislation undesirable to the president but serves as a threat, thereby bringing about changes in the content of legislation long before a bill is ever presented to the president.

A president may veto legislation passed by Congress, but Congress, in turn, can override the veto if two-thirds of its members vote to approve it (President Barack Obama pictured).

How often does the president use his veto power?

Although the first presidents used their veto power sparingly (George Washington used it just twice during his two terms in office), use of both kinds of veto power has become more common over the course of American presidential history. Presidents Franklin D. Roosevelt, Grover Cleveland, and Harry Truman hold the record for the most legislation vetoed. Of recent presidents, Ronald Reagan exercised seventy-eight vetoes, George H. W. Bush forty-four vetoes, Bill Clinton thirty-seven vetoes, and George W. Bush and Barack Obama twelve each. Congress has overridden only a handful of regular vetoes from Washington to Clinton, overriding about 7.1 percent of the regular vetoes during this period. The presidents with the highest percentage of vetoes overridden are Franklin Pierce, Andrew Johnson, Gerald Ford, Richard Nixon, Woodrow Wilson, and George W. Bush.

Does the president have any control over the sessions of Congress?

Under the Constitution, the president may convene Congress or either house "on extraordinary occasions." It is usual for the president, when calling an extra session, to indicate the exact matter that needs the attention of Congress. However, once convened, Congress cannot be limited in the subject matter that it will consider. The president is also empowered by the Constitution to adjourn Congress "at such time as he may think proper" when the House and Senate disagree with respect to the time for adjournment; however, to date no president has exercised this power. Many constitutional experts believe the provision applies only in the case of extraordinary sessions.

How is the president the chief of party?

As chief of party, or party leader, the president is the acknowledged leader of the political party that controls the executive branch. He helps form the party's position on policy issues and strives to elect party members to Congress so that his party dominates in

What was the line-item veto?

The Line Item Veto Act of 1996 gave the president the authority to cancel certain new spending and entitlement projects as well as to cancel certain types of limited, targeted tax breaks. The president could make these cancellations within five days after the enactment of a money bill providing such funds. These line-item vetoes could then be overridden by a two-thirds vote of the House and Senate. President Bill Clinton used the line-item veto to make eighty-two cancellations, and Congress overrode thirty-eight of them, all within a single military construction bill. In 1998, the U.S. Supreme Court ruled the line-item veto unconstitutional, in violation of the Presentment Clause in Article I, Section 7 of the Constitution, which requires that every bill that passes the House and Senate be presented to the president for either approval or disapproval.

both the House and the Senate. While most presidencies are divided governments—that is, one party controlling the executive office and another party controlling the Congress—single-party control over both the executive and legislative branches makes it much easier for the president to propel his legislative agenda.

In what ways is the president the chief citizen?

President Franklin D. Roosevelt (1882–1945) probably best summed up the duties of this role when he said that the presidency "is preeminently a place of moral leadership." As a representative of the people, the president automatically assumes the role of chief citizen, or popular leader. The nature of this role mandates a certain trust between the president and the people, since it is the president's duty to work for the public interest amid competing private interests and to place the nation's best interests above the interests of any one group or citizen. In turn, the president relies on public support to help pass his legislative agenda through Congress, gaining the trust of the public with regard to these issues through exposure, straightforwardness, and strong leadership.

PRESIDENTIAL POWERS

What are the enumerated constitutional powers of the president?

Article II of the Constitution vests the "executive power" in the president. There is some dispute among scholars as to whether such executive power consists only of the powers enumerated for the president or whether it also includes those implied in Article II. These are the powers granted to the president in Article II, Sections 2 and 3 of the Constitution.

The president is commander in chief of the U.S. Army, Navy, Air Force, and, when it is called into action, the National Guard. The president may require the written opinion of military executive officers and is empowered to grant reprieves and pardons, except in the case of impeachment. The president receives ambassadors and other public ministers, ensures that the laws are faithfully executed, and commissions all officers of the United States. The president has the power—by and with the advice and consent of the Senate—to make treaties, provided that two-thirds of the senators present concur. The president also nominates and appoints ambassadors, other public ministers and consuls, justices of the Supreme Court, federal judges, and other federal officers, by and with the advice and consent of the Senate. The president has the power to temporarily fill all vacancies that occur during the recess of the Senate. In addition, the president may, under extraordinary circumstances, convene emergency sessions of Congress. Furthermore, if the two houses disagree as to the time of adjournment, the president may adjourn the bodies. In addition to these powers, the president also has enumerated powers that allow him to directly influence legislation. The Constitution directs the president to periodically inform Congress on the State of the Union and to recommend legislation that is considered necessary and expedient.

President Barack Obama gives a speech at the Commander in Chief's Ball in 2009. The president is the head of all branches of the U.S. military.

Also, Article I, Section 7 of the Constitution grants the president the authority to veto acts of Congress.

What are the implied constitutional powers of the president?

The president possesses certain powers that are not enumerated in the Constitution. The implied powers are the subject of continued debate among scholars for three primary reasons: the degree of the presidency's importance in the political strategy of the Constitution is not cut-and-dried; the president's authority in international relations is extensive and vaguely defined in the Constitution; and the president is often said to have inherent or residual powers of authority. For example, although the Constitution does not grant the president the express power to remove administrators from their offices, the president, as the chief executive, holds power over executive-branch officers unless such removal power is limited by public law. Note, however, that the president does not have such implied authority over officers in independent establishments: When Franklin D. Roosevelt removed a member of the Federal Trade Commission, an independent regulatory agency, the Supreme Court ruled the act invalid in 1935.

Another implied constitutional power is derived from the president's authority as commander in chief. Although Congress has the explicit power to declare war, the president is responsible for protecting the nation from sudden attack and has the ability to initiate military activities overseas without a formal declaration of war. Through the

125

War Powers Resolution of 1973, Congress sought to clarify the conditions under which presidents can unilaterally authorize military action abroad.

Because of these multiple powers and roles, has the presidency ever been criticized as being too powerful?

Yes. Because of the vast array of presidential roles and responsibilities, coupled with a prominent national and international presence, political analysts have tended to place great emphasis on the president's powers. Some have even spoken of the "imperial presidency," referring to Franklin D. Roosevelt's terms in office.

However, seldom does the public hear about the sobering realities a new president discovers when assuming office: an inherited bureaucratic structure that can be difficult to manage and slow to change direction, the power to appoint officials that extends only to some three thousand people out of a government workforce of about three million, and a "machinelike" system that often operates independently of presidential intervention. Rather than "all-powerful," analysts have often described the president as feeling "all-bureaucratic": new presidents are immediately confronted with a backlog of decisions from the outgoing administration; they inherit a budget formulated and enacted long before they entered office; and they must comply with treaties and informal agreements negotiated by their predecessors. After only a short time in office, a new president often discovers that Congress has become less cooperative with his agenda and the media more critical—even of his personal life. The president is forced to build at least temporary alliances among diverse, often conflicting interests and must strike compromises with Congress in order to get legislation passed.

How does the separation of powers keep the president from becoming too powerful?

The cornerstone of the U.S. government—a division of power among executive, legislative, and judicial branches—is called the separation of powers. Officials of each branch are selected differently, have different responsibilities, and serve different terms. By distributing the essential business of government among three separate but interdependent branches, the framers of the Constitution ensured that the government's powers were not concentrated in any one branch. The separation of power is not absolute, however, because of the system of checks and balances, which says that these branches must cooperate with one another, oversee one another, and enforce and support one another's decisions according to established rules. For example, Congress's authority to make laws can be "checked" by presidential veto; the president has the authority of commander in chief of the armed forces, but only Congress can declare war; and the Supreme Court has the authority to "check" on both the legislative and executive branches by declaring their acts unconstitutional.

Despite these constraints, every president achieves at least some of his legislative goals and vetoes other laws he believes not to be in the nation's best interests. Moreover, the president uses his unique position to articulate ideas and advocate policies on national issues, which then have a better chance of entering the public consciousness than those held by his political rivals—thus adding to his political power. The president's authority in the area of foreign relations and his careful execution of multilateral policy add to his clout as a world leader. So while a president's power and influence are limited in some areas, they are still greater than those of any other American, in or out of political office.

What is the difference between executive power and executive privilege?

These two similar terms have vastly different meanings. Executive powers are those powers granted to the president by Article II of the Constitution and include the power to execute, or enforce, federal law; the power to issue and implement executive orders, or directives, that have the effect of law; the power to nominate ambassadors, top-ranking government officials, officers, and judges of the Supreme Court; and the power to remove government officials from office. "Executive privilege," on the other hand, generally refers to the president's right to withhold information. Executive privilege is a claim that presidents generally make in asserting that, as the nation's chief executive, they have the discretion to decide that certain information be withheld from the public, Congress, or the courts for national security reasons. Although the Supreme Court has ruled that presidents are entitled to this privilege, it has maintained that the privilege is not unlimited and its scope is subject to judicial determination.

When have recent presidents tried to invoke executive privilege?

Generally maintaining that it is in "the public's best interest" not to disclose certain information, presidents have attempted to invoke executive privilege at various times—most notably Richard Nixon's refusal to turn over White House tapes during the Watergate investigation. Arguing that executive privilege may not be invoked to deny the courts access to evidence needed in a criminal proceeding, the prosecutor asked the U.S. Supreme Court to compel Nixon to release all of his taped conversations with his advisors. Bill Clinton tried to evoke executive privilege twice. First, claiming "client-lawyer confidentiality," he initially refused to turn over

Initially arguing that executive privilege allowed him to not turn over any White House tapes to investigators, President Richard Nixon relented in an April 29, 1974, speech to the public. Ultimately, the tapes showed his attempt to cover up the Watergate scandal, leading to his resignation.

notes taken during meetings with his lawyer to a Senate committee during the Whitewater investigation. Later, he tried to prevent the testimony of two of his advisors before the grand jury during independent counsel Kenneth Starr's investigation of his sexual relations with White House intern Monica Lewinsky. Ultimately, the grand jury denied his request.

What is an independent counsel?

In 1988 the Supreme Court upheld the constitutionality of the independent counsel law. These independent counsels investigate and prosecute alleged criminal conduct of high-ranking officials. They can only be removed by the attorney general of the United States, not the president, and then only for "good cause, physical disability, mental incapacity, or other impairing conditions."

What is impeachment?

Impeachment is the process by which the president, vice president, federal judges and justices, and all civil officials of the United States may be removed from office. Officials may be impeached for treason, bribery, and other high crimes and misdemeanors. The House of Representatives has sole authority to bring charges of impeachment by a simple majority vote, and the Senate has sole authority to try impeachment charges. An official may be removed from office only upon conviction, which requires a two-thirds vote of the Senate. The Constitution provides that the chief justice shall preside when the president is tried for impeachment.

How many presidents have been impeached?

In America's history, only two presidents have been impeached: Andrew Johnson and Bill Clinton. In 1868, impeachment proceedings were initiated against Johnson by the House of Representatives, who charged Johnson with usurpation of the law, corrupt use of veto power, interference at elections, and various misdemeanors. However, the fifty-four-member Senate proceedings acquitted Johnson by one vote. In December 1998, the House of Representatives brought two articles of impeachment against President Clinton: perjury—lying under oath before a federal grand jury about the precise nature of his sexual relations with White House intern Monica Lewinsky—and obstruction of jus-

President Bill Clinton was only the second American president to be impeached by Congress. He was impeached for lying under oath; however, in the end, he was not forced out of office.

tice by withholding evidence about, and influencing others to conceal, his affair with Lewinsky. Ultimately, the Senate rejected both charges, and Clinton remained in office.

Many also cite Richard Nixon in the list of impeached presidents, but that is a misconception. Amid the Watergate scandal, in July 1974 the House Committee on the Judiciary approved three articles of impeachment against Nixon, including the obstruction of justice and the abuse of presidential power. However, the charges never went to trial. On August 8, 1974, President Nixon publicly announced his resignation, making him the first president in American history to resign from office.

How many presidents have resigned from office?

Just one president has ever resigned from office: Richard Nixon. Under the threat of impeachment, Nixon resigned as the thirty-seventh president of the United States on August 9, 1974. Nixon, who had completed a little over a year and a half of his second term, was succeeded by Vice President Gerald Ford.

If the president is incapacitated, who is in charge?

The vice president serves concurrently with the president and holds the right of succession. The Twenty-fifth Amendment to the Constitution, adopted in 1967, details the process of presidential succession. It describes the specific conditions under which the vice president is empowered to take over the office of president if the president should become incapacitated. It also provides for resumption of the office by the president in the event of his recovery. In addition, the amendment enables the president to name a vice president, with congressional approval, when the second office is vacated.

If a president dies, resigns, or is removed from office, what happens?

According to the Twenty-fifth Amendment, adopted in 1967, the vice president succeeds to the office if the president dies, resigns, or is removed from office by impeachment.

Who would succeed to the presidency if the office becomes vacant and there is no vice president?

According to Article II, Section I of the Constitution, Congress determines the order of succession following the vice president. According to the effective law on succession, the Presidential Succession Act of 1947, should both the president and vice president vacate their offices, the Speaker of the House of Representatives would assume the presidency. Next in line is the president pro tempore of the Senate (a senator elected by that body to preside in the absence of the vice president), then cabinet officers in designated order: secretary of state, secretary of the treasury, secretary of defense, attorney general, secretary of the interior, secretary of agriculture, secretary of commerce, secretary of labor, secretary of health and human services, secretary of housing and urban development, secretary of transportation, secretary of energy, secretary of education, and secretary of veterans affairs.

THE EXECUTIVE ORGANIZATION

What is the federal government?

The federal government is the national government of the United States of America under the Constitution, including the executive, legislative, and judicial branches, as opposed to state or local governments. The executive branch is responsible for enforcing the laws of the United States. Its main components include the president, the vice president, the various government departments, and independent agencies. The president is leader of the country and commander in chief of the armed forces; the vice president is president of the Senate and first in line for the presidency should the president be unable to serve; the departments and their heads (called cabinet members) advise the president on policy issues and help execute those policies; and the independent agencies also assist in executing policy and provide special services. The legislative branch is the lawmaking branch of the federal government. It is made up of a bicameral (or two-chamber) Congress: the Senate and the House of Representatives. The judicial branch, made up of the Supreme Court and other federal courts, is responsible for interpreting the meaning of laws, how they are applied, and whether or not they violate the Constitution.

What is the Executive Office of the President?

The Executive Office is more like an umbrella agency than an individual office. As the president's right hand, the Executive Office includes the White House Office (which has more than four hundred staff members) as well as about a dozen separate agencies, or offices, staffed by the president's most trusted advisers and assistants.

Which offices are included in the Executive Office of the President?

The Executive Office includes various offices that directly assist the president. These include the Council of Economic Advisers, the Council on Environmental Quality, the Domestic Policy Council, the National Economic Council, the National Security Council, the Office of Administration, the Office of Faith-Based and Community Initiatives, the Office of Homeland Security, the Office of Management and Budget, the Office of National AIDS Policy, the Office of National Drug Control Policy, the President's Foreign Intelligence Advisory Board, the Office of the United States Trade Representative, and the White House Military Office.

What is the role of the White House staff?

The White House Office is the workplace of the White House staff—key personnel and political staff whose offices are located in the East and West wings of the White House. The White House staff exists to help the president carry out the role of chief executive officer. The president's staff of more than four hundred are directed by the chief of staff. The staff includes the president's most trusted aides, the counselor to the president, a number of senior advisors, and top officials who work with the president in the areas of foreign policy, the economy, national health care, the media, and defense. It also includes the president's press secretary, the president's physician, and the staff of the First Lady.

What is the role of the first lady?

Although this position is unpaid, unelected, and unappointed, the first lady—the wife of the president—is a dynamic force unto her own. Today, the role of the first lady is in itself a "powerful political institution, complete with office, staff, and budgetary resources rivaling those of key presidential advisors," according to political science professor Robert Watson, author of *The Presidents' Wives: Reassessing the Office of First Lady.* Although the Constitution is silent on the first lady's role, and by law, immediate members of the president's family cannot be appointed to a position in the federal government, many first ladies have assumed informal powers that exceed even those of cabinet secretaries. The first lady acts as the social host of the White House and performs at least a

Eleanor Roosevelt (shown here in 1932) was one of the most influential first ladies in U.S. history. She was a lifelong advocate of human rights and was a delegate to the United Nations General Assembly after her husband's death.

minimum level of campaigning, hosting, social activism, advocacy of pet projects, and public appearances. In addition, many recent first ladies—including Barbara Bush in her family literacy promotion; Hillary Clinton in her role as task force leader in President Bill Clinton's effort to reform health care; and Michelle Obama for her promotion of physical and mental health, especially in children—have embraced key responsibilities, necessitating large staffs and budgets.

Including roles the public generally expects of first ladies and responsibilities commonly undertaken by twentieth-century first ladies since Eleanor Roosevelt (who was first lady from 1933 to 1945), Watson has identified eleven fundamental duties of the modern office: wife and mother, public figure and celebrity, nation's social hostess, symbol of the American woman, White House manager and preservationist, campaigner, social advocate and champion of social causes, presidential spokesperson, presidential and political party booster, diplomat, and political and presidential partner.

Do the White House staff and the first lady ever work together?

Absolutely. Rosalyn Carter, first lady from 1977 to 1981, was one of the late twentieth century first ladies who followed the suit of early first ladies by utilizing the services of various executive agencies. In effect, Carter reorganized the modern office of the first lady so that today it includes roughly twenty to twenty-eight full-time, paid employees. In addition, today's first ladies use staff from the president's office, including speech-writers, schedulers, and policy experts. Nancy Reagan's office, for example, had eighteen to twenty-two employees, in addition to the use of clerical White House staffers. Hillary Clinton drew on fifteen staff positions to aid her in her role as first lady, including assistant to the president/chief of staff to the first lady, press secretary to the first lady, special assistant to the first lady, and deputy social secretary.

What is the president's cabinet?

The president's cabinet has been commonly regarded as an institution whose existence relies more on custom than law. Article II, Section 2 of the Constitution states that the president "may require the Opinion, in writing, of the principal Officer in each of the executive Departments, upon any subject relating to the Duties of their respective Offices." The historical origins of the cabinet can be traced to the first president, George Washington. After the First Congress created the State, Treasury, and War departments and established the Office of the Attorney General, Washington made appropriate appointments and subsequently found it useful to meet with the heads, also known as secretaries, of the executive departments. The cabinet could act as the president's primary advisory group; in practice, however, presidents have used it, along with other advisors and ad hoc arrangements, as they deemed necessary.

Who are the cabinet members?

Traditionally, the cabinet has consisted of the heads of the executive departments, such as the Department of Defense and the Department of Energy. All departments are headed by a secretary, except the Department of Justice, which is headed by the attorney general. From the earliest days, presidents have also included others in cabinet meetings. In recent years, the president's chief of staff, the director of the Central Intelligence Agency, and the director of the Office of Management and Budget, among others, have been accorded cabinet rank.

How are cabinet members chosen?

The president appoints each head of the fourteen executive departments. While each of these appointments is subject to confirmation by the Senate, rejections are rare. Many factors influence whom the president chooses: appointees are generally members of the president's party, those who played a role in the president's recent campaign, or those who have outstanding professional qualifications and personal experience related to the appointed position. In broad terms, the president also takes into account geographic location—thus, the secretary of the interior is often from the western United States, where most of the department's work is executed—as well as personal characteristics, such as gender and race.

How are executive departments and agencies created?

Executive departments, like the Department of Defense or the Department of Justice, must be created by statute. Today there are fifteen executive departments. Agencies in the executive branch, by contrast, may be created by a variety of means: statute, internal departmental reorganizations, or, in some cases, presidential directive. In his constitutional capacity as chief executive or commander in chief, or by delegation of authority from Congress, the president can create various agencies or units by executive order. All agencies, however, must ultimately be given statutory authority if they are to receive appropriations and their decisions are to have legal force.

What are the fifteen cabinet departments currently in place?

As of 2017, the following departments make up the president's cabinet: the Department of Agriculture, Department of Commerce, Department of Defense, Department of Education, Department of Energy, Department of Health and Human Services, Department of Housing and Urban Development, Department of the Interior, Department of Justice, Department of Labor, Department of State, Department of Transportation, Department of the Treasury, Department of Veterans Affairs, and the Department of Homeland Security.

What is the Department of Agriculture?

Created in 1862, the U.S. Department of Agriculture (USDA) is one of the country's oldest federal departments. The USDA supports agricultural production to ensure fair prices and stable markets for producers and consumers, works to improve and maintain farm income, and helps to develop and expand markets abroad for agricultural products. The department attempts to curb poverty, hunger, and malnutrition by issuing food stamps

The headquarters of the U.S. Department of Agriculture are located in the Jamie L. Whitten Building in Washington, D.C. The USDA was the first federal department to be organized.

to low-income individuals and families; by sponsoring educational programs on nutrition; and by administering other food assistance programs, primarily for children, expectant mothers, and the elderly. It maintains production capacity by helping landowners protect the soil, water, forests, and other natural resources. The USDA administers rural development, credit, and conservation programs that are designed to implement national growth policies, and it conducts scientific and technological research in all areas of agriculture. Through its inspection and grading services, the USDA ensures standards of quality in food for sale.

What is the Department of Commerce?

The Department of Commerce—originally part of the Department of Commerce and Labor, which was created in 1903 and split into two separate departments in 1913—serves to promote the nation's international trade, economic growth, and technological advancement. It offers assistance and information to increase U.S. competitiveness in the global marketplace; administers programs to create new jobs and to foster the growth of minority-owned businesses; and provides statistical, economic, and demographic information for business and government planners.

The department is made up of a variety of agencies. The National Institute of Standards and Technology, for example, promotes economic growth by working with industry to develop and apply technology, measurements, and standards. The National Oceanic and Atmospheric Administration, which includes the National Weather Service, works to improve understanding of the Earth's environment and to conserve the nation's coastal and marine resources. The Patent and Trademark Office promotes science and the useful arts by securing for authors and inventors the exclusive right to their creations and discoveries. The National Telecommunications and Information Administration advises the president on telecommunications policy and works to foster innovation, encourage competition, create jobs, and provide consumers with better-quality telecommunications at lower prices.

What does the Department of Defense do?

The Department of Defense was created in 1947 with the merger of the Department of War (established in 1789), the Department of the Navy (established in 1798), and the Department of the Air Force (established in 1947). Headquartered in the Pentagon, the Department of Defense is responsible for all matters relating to the nation's military security. It provides the military forces of the United States, which consist of more than one million men and women on active duty. They are backed, in case of emergency, by 1.5 million members of state reserve components, known as the National Guard. The National Security Agency, which coordinates, directs, and performs highly specialized intelligence activities in support of U.S. government activities, also comes under the direction of the Department of Defense.

The department directs the separately organized military departments of the U.S. Army, U.S. Navy, U.S. Marine Corps, and U.S. Air Force, as well as the four military service academies and the National War College, the Joint Chiefs of Staff, and several specialized combat commands. The Defense Department maintains forces overseas to meet treaty commitments, to protect the nation's outlying territories and commerce, and to provide air combat and support forces. Nonmilitary responsibilities include flood control, development of oceanographic resources, and management of oil reserves. Although the secretary of defense is a member of the cabinet, the secretaries of the Army, Navy, and Air Force are not.

Why is the Department of Education necessary?

While schools are primarily a state responsibility in the U.S. system of education, the Department of Education provides national leadership to address critical issues in American education and serves as a clearinghouse of information to help state and local decision makers improve their schools. Created in 1979, and formerly part of the Department of Health, Education, and Welfare, the department establishes policy for and administers federal aid-to-education programs, including student loan programs, programs for disadvantaged and disabled students, and vocational programs. Beginning in the 1990s and continuing to the present, the Department of Education has focused on raising standards of education for all students; improving teaching; involving parents and families in children's education; making schools safe, disciplined, and drug free; increasing access to financial aid so that students can attend college; expanding antibullying programs; and helping all students become technologically literate.

What does the Department of Energy do?

Created in 1977 as the result of growing concern over the nation's energy problems in the 1970s, the Department of Energy assumed the functions of several government agencies already engaged in the energy field. Staff offices within the Energy Department are responsible for research on, development, and demonstration of energy technology; energy conservation; civilian and military use of nuclear energy; regulation of energy production and use; pricing and allocation of oil; and a central energy data collection and analysis program. The Department of Energy protects the nation's environment by setting standards to minimize the harmful effects of energy production and by conducting environmental and health-related research, such as studies of energy-related pollutants and their effects on biological systems.

What is the role of the Department of Health and Human Services?

Established in 1979, when the Department of Health, Education, and Welfare (created in 1953) was split into separate entities, the Department of Health and Human Services (HHS) directly touches the lives of millions of Americans. The department oversees more than three hundred programs. Its largest component, the Health Care Financing Administration, administers the Medicare and Medicaid programs, which jointly provide health care coverage to more than sixty million elderly, disabled, and low-income individuals, including fifteen million children. HHS also administers the National In-

135

The intense political debate over how to handle health care in the United States has put the Department of Health and Human Services on center stage in the news (shown here is the department's headquarters near the National Mall in Washington, D.C.).

stitutes of Health (NIH), the world's premier medical research organization, supporting some forty thousand research projects on diseases like cancer, Alzheimer's, diabetes, arthritis, heart ailments, and AIDS. Other HHS agencies ensure the safety and effectiveness of the nation's food supply and drugs; work to prevent outbreaks of communicable diseases; provide health services to the nation's American Indian and Alaska Native populations; and help to improve the quality and availability of substance-abuse prevention, addiction treatment, and mental health services.

What does the Department of Housing and Urban Development do?

Created in 1965, the Department of Housing and Urban Development (HUD) manages programs that assist community development and help provide affordable housing for low-income families. Fair-housing laws, administered by HUD, are designed to ensure that individuals and families can buy a home without being subjected to discrimination. HUD directs mortgage insurance programs that help families become homeowners and a rent-subsidy program for low-income families that otherwise could not afford appropriate housing. In addition, it operates programs that aid neighborhood rehabilitation, preserve urban centers, and encourage the development of new communities. HUD also protects the homebuyer in the marketplace and fosters programs to stimulate the housing industry.

What is the Department of the Interior?

Created in 1849 as the nation's principal conservation agency, the Department of the Interior is responsible for most of the federally owned public lands and natural resources in the United States. The U.S. Fish and Wildlife Service administers five hundred wildlife refuges, dozens of wetland-management districts, dozens of national fish hatcheries, and a network of wildlife law enforcement agents. The National Park Service administers more than 370 national parks and monuments, scenic parkways, riverways, seashores, recreation areas, and historic sites, thus preserving America's natural and cultural heritage. Through the Bureau of Land Management, the department oversees millions of hectares of public land and resources located primarily in the West—from rangeland vegetation and recreation areas to timber and oil production. The Bureau of Reclamation manages scarce water resources in the semiarid western United States. The department regulates mining in the United States, assesses mineral resources, and has major responsibility for protecting and conserving the trust resources of American Indian and Alaska Native tribes.

What is the function of the Department of Justice?

Formed in 1870, the Department of Justice represents the U.S. government in legal matters and courts of law and renders legal advice and opinions upon request to the president and to the heads of the executive departments. The Justice Department is headed by the attorney general of the United States, the chief law enforcement officer of the federal government. Its Federal Bureau of Investigation (FBI) is the principle law enforcement body for federal crimes, and its Immigration and Naturalization Service (INS) administers immigration laws. A major agency within the department is the Drug Enforcement Administration (DEA), which enforces narcotics and controlled-substance laws and tracks down major drug-trafficking organizations.

In addition to aiding local police forces, the department directs U.S. district attorneys and marshals throughout the country, supervises federal prisons and other penal institutions, and investigates and reports to the president on petitions for paroles and pardons. The Justice Department is also linked to INTERPOL, the International Criminal Police Organization, charged with promoting mutual assistance between law enforcement agencies in almost two hundred member countries.

What is the job of the Department of Labor?

Established in 1913, the Department of Labor promotes the welfare of wage earners in the United States, helps improve working conditions, and fosters good relations between labor and management. It administers federal labor laws through such agencies as the Occupational Safety and Health Administration (OSHA), the Employment Standards Administration, and the Mine Safety and Health Administration. These laws guarantee workers' rights to safe and healthy working conditions, hourly wages and overtime pay, freedom from employment discrimination, unemployment insurance, and workers' compensation for on-the-job injuries. The department also protects workers' pension rights, sponsors job training programs, and helps workers find jobs. Its Bureau of Labor Statistics monitors and reports changes in employment, prices, and other national economic measurements.

The Department of State offices are housed in the Harry S. Truman Building in Washington, D.C. The Secretary of State advises the president on matters of foreign policy.

What are the functions of the State Department?

Created in 1789, the Department of State advises the president, who has overall responsibility for formulating and executing the foreign policy of the United States. The department assesses American overseas interests, makes recommendations on policy and future action, and takes the necessary steps to carry out established policy. It maintains contacts and relations between the United States and foreign countries, advises the president on recognition of new foreign countries and governments, negotiates treaties and agreements with foreign nations, and speaks for the United States in the United Nations and other major international organizations. The department maintains more than 250 diplomatic and consular posts around the world. In 1999, the Department of State integrated the U.S. Arms Control and Disarmament Agency and the U.S. Information Agency into its structure.

What is the Department of Transportation?

Formed in 1966, the Department of Transportation establishes the nation's overall transportation policy through almost a dozen operating units that manage highway planning, development, and construction; urban mass transit; railroads; civilian aviation; and the safety of waterways, ports, highways, and oil and gas pipelines. For example, the Federal Aviation Administration operates a network of airport towers, air traffic control centers, and flight service stations across the country. The Federal Highway Administration provides financial assistance to the states to improve the interstate highway system, urban and rural roads, and bridges. The National Highway Traffic Safety Administration establishes safety performance standards for motor vehicles and motor vehicle equipment. The Maritime Administration operates the U.S. merchant marine fleet. The U.S. Coast Guard, the nation's primary maritime law enforcement and licensing agency, conducts search-and-rescue missions at sea, combats drug smuggling, and works to prevent oil spills and ocean pollution.

What does the Department of the Treasury do?

Created in 1789, the Department of the Treasury is responsible for serving the fiscal and monetary needs of the nation. The department performs four basic functions: it formulates financial, tax, and fiscal policies; serves as financial agent for the U.S. government; provides specialized law enforcement services; and manufactures coins and currency. The Treasury Department reports to Congress and the president on the financial condition of the government and the national economy. It regulates the sale of alcohol, tobacco, and firearms in interstate and foreign commerce; supervises the printing of stamps for the U.S. Postal Service; operates the Secret Service, which protects the president, the vice president, their families, and visiting dignitaries and heads of state; suppresses counterfeiting of U.S. currency and securities; and administers the Customs Service, which regulates and taxes the flow of goods into the country. The department includes the Office of the Comptroller of the Currency, the treasury official who executes the laws governing the operation of approximately three thousand national banks. The Internal Revenue Service (IRS) is responsible for the determination, assessment, and collection of taxes—the source of most of the federal government's revenue.

Why is the Secret Service part of the Department of the Treasury?

Although it may seem strange today that the Secret Service falls under the jurisdiction of the Department of the Treasury, the hierarchy is based in historical logic. During the Civil War, approximately one third of all the currency in circulation was counterfeit, there were about 1,600 state banks designing and printing their own notes, and there were approximately four thousand varieties of counterfeit notes, making it difficult to tell a counterfeit from a genuine note. Officials believed that the adoption of a national currency in 1863 would solve the counterfeiting problem, but the national currency was soon being counterfeited. It became necessary for the government to take enforcement measures, and the Secret Service was thus formed as a bureau of the Treasury Department on July 5, 1865, with its major responsibility being the elimination of counterfeiting.

Soon after that, the Secret Service began to evolve into the entity we are familiar with today. Public sentiment after the assassination of President William McKinley in 1901 demanded better protection of the nation's chief executive. Because the Secret Service was the only law enforcement agency of the federal government at the time, it was logical to place the protection of the president under its jurisdiction. This unique mission officially became a permanent responsibility of the Secret Service in 1906. Today, the Secret Service also protects various other important government officials.

What does the Department of Veterans Affairs do?

Originally established as an independent agency in 1930 and elevated to cabinet level in 1989, the Department of Veterans Affairs dispenses benefits and services to eligible veterans of the U.S. military and their dependents. The Veterans Health Administration provides hospital and nursing home care and outpatient medical and dental services through a range of medical centers, retirement homes, clinics, nursing homes, and Vietnam Veteran Outreach Centers across the United States. The Department of Veteran Affairs also conducts medical research in such areas as aging, women's health issues, AIDS, and post-traumatic stress disorder. The Veterans Benefits Administration (VBA) oversees claims for disability payments, pensions, specially adapted housing, and other services, while the VA's National Cemetery System provides burial services, headstones, and markers for veterans and eligible family members at more than one hundred cemeteries throughout the United States.

What is the new cabinet-level department President Bush introduced during his presidency?

In an effort to defend the United States from terrorist attacks, eliminate security gaps, and unite Washington in its defense of the country, in June 2002, President George W. Bush created a cabinet-level department to oversee homeland defense. The Department of Homeland Security was charged with overseeing all aspects of homeland defense: protecting the nation's borders, ensuring airline security, responding to emergencies, and analyzing potential terrorist threats to the United States. The Department of Homeland Security encompassed agencies from eight existing cabinet departments at the time, including the Immigration and Naturalization Service, the Border Patrol, the Coast Guard, and the Transportation Security Administration. At a cost of $37 billion, the new department was the largest overhaul of the national government since 1947, when the Department of Defense was created. The Department of Homeland Security became the third-largest

The Department of Homeland Security is the newest cabinet-level department. It was established in 2002 after the 9/11 attacks; it is tasked with border and airport security and, in general, protecting the nation from terrorist attacks.

cabinet department and the first new one since 1989, when the Department of Veterans Affairs was formed.

Who are the current cabinet secretaries?

The cabinet includes the vice president of the United States and, by law, the heads, or secretaries, of fifteen executive departments as well as select others who have been afforded cabinet-level status. Under the Trump Administration, as of August 2017, the following people make up the president's cabinet: Secretary of State Rex W. Tillerson, Secretary of the Treasury Steven T. Mnuchin, Secretary of Defense James Mattis, Attorney General Jeff Sessions, Secretary of the Interior Ryan Zinke, Secretary of Agriculture Sonny Perdue, Secretary of Commerce Wilbur L. Ross, Jr., Secretary of Labor Alexander Acosta, Secretary of Health and Human Services Thomas Price, Secretary of Housing and Urban Development Benjamin S. Carson, Sr., Secretary of Transportation Elaine L. Chao, Secretary of Energy James Richard Perry, Secretary of Education Elisabeth Prince DeVos, Secretary of Veterans Affairs David J. Shulkin, Secretary of Homeland Security John F. Kelly, White House Chief of Staff John F. Kelly, U.S. Trade Representative Robert Lighthizer, Director of National Intelligence Daniel Coats, Representative of the United States to the United Nations Nikki R. Haley, Director of the Office of Management and Budget Mick Mulvaney, Director of the Central Intelligence Agency Mike Pompeo, Administrator of the Environmental Protection Agency Scott Pruitt, and Administrator of the Small Business Administration Linda E. McMahon.

What is the history of women in the executive branch?

Since the cabinet was established in 1789, there have been thirty-one female cabinet members. The first woman to serve in the cabinet was Frances Perkins, appointed by President Franklin D. Roosevelt as secretary of labor in 1933.

Former North Carolina Senator Elizabeth Dole is the first woman to have served in two different cabinet positions in two different administrations. She was appointed by President Ronald Reagan as secretary of transportation in 1983 and was the secretary of labor during the tenure of George H. W. Bush—Reagan's successor. Czechoslovakia-born Madeleine Albright became the first foreign-born woman to serve in the cabinet when she was appointed secretary of state in 1997; her appointment also made her the highest-ranking female cabinet member at that time. Condoleezza Rice was appointed secretary of state in 2005 and thus became the highest-ranking woman in the United States presidential line of succession. In 2006, Nancy Pelosi replaced Rice as the highest-ranking woman in line when she was elected Speaker of the House.

In 2009, President Barack Obama named four women to the cabinet: Arizona governor Janet Napolitano as secretary of homeland security, former First Lady and New York senator Hillary Clinton as secretary of state, California representative Hilda Solis as secretary of labor, and Kansas governor Kathleen Sebelius as secretary of health and human services. Clinton became the only first lady to serve in the cabinet and the third female secretary of state. Napolitano became the first female secretary of homeland security. Barack Obama appointed eight women to cabinet positions, more than any other president, surpassing George W. Bush's record of six. Donald Trump's cabinet is noticeably light on women, being composed mostly of white males.

What are independent agencies and regulatory commissions?

In general, independent agencies are all federal administrative agencies not included under the executive departments or under the direct, immediate authority of the president. These many and diverse organizations range from regulatory commissions to government corporations, such as the U.S. Postal Service, to a wide variety of boards and foundations. Some of these, such as the Smithsonian Institution, are longstanding, while others have been created over the years as the federal government's responsibilities have increased. Independent regulatory commissions have been established by Congress—beginning in the 1880s with the now-defunct Interstate Commerce Commission—to regulate some aspects of the U.S. economy. Among these are the Securities and Exchange Commission, the Federal Communications Commission, the Federal Trade Commission, and the Nuclear Regulatory Commission. Such agencies are not independent of the U.S. government and are subject to the laws that are approved by Congress and executed by the president.

What are the various independent agencies in operation today?

Called independent because they are not part of the executive departments, the more than one hundred independent agencies of the federal government vary widely in scope and purpose. While some are regulatory groups with powers to supervise certain sectors of the economy, others provide special services either to the government or to the people. In most cases, the agencies have been created by Congress to deal with matters that

Created by Benjamin Franklin, the U.S. Postal Service was a department of the government until 1971, when President Richard Nixon got rid of the postmaster general as a cabinet position and turned the mail-carrying service into a corporation that was still owned by the government. Many in Congress are calling for the complete privatization of the USPS.

have become too complex for the scope of ordinary legislation. Among the most important independent agencies are the Central Intelligence Agency (CIA), the Environmental Protection Agency (EPA), the Federal Communications Commission (FCC), the Federal Emergency Management Agency (FEMA), the Federal Reserve Board, the Federal Trade Commission (FTC), the General Services Administration (GSA), the Immigration and Naturalization Service (INS), the National Aeronautics and Space Administration (NASA), the National Archives and Records Administration (NARA), the National Labor Relations Board (NLRB), the National Science Foundation (NSF), the Office of Personnel Management (OPM), the Peace Corps, the Securities and Exchange Commission (SEC), the Small Business Administration (SBA), the Social Security Administration (SSA), the United States Agency for International Development (USAID), and the United States Postal Service (USPS).

How has the United States Postal Service changed from a federal department to a quasi-public corporation?

The U.S. Postal Service (USPS) is operated by an autonomous public corporation that replaced the Post Office Department in 1971. In May 1969, after years of financial neglect and fragmented control had impaired the Post Office Department's ability to function, Postmaster General Winton M. Blount proposed a basic reorganization of the Post Office, then one of the federal government's many departments. President Richard Nixon asked Congress to pass the Postal Service Act of 1969, calling for removal of the postmaster general from the cabinet and creation of a self-supporting postal corporation wholly owned by the federal government. As a result, the Post Office Department was transformed into the United States Postal Service, an independent establishment of the executive branch of the government of the United States.

The U.S. Postal Service is responsible for the collection, transportation, and delivery of the mail and for the operation of thousands of local post offices across the country. It delivers hundreds of millions of messages and billions of dollars in financial transactions each day to eight million businesses and 250 million Americans. It also provides international mail service through the Universal Postal Union and other agreements with foreign countries. An independent Postal Rate Commission, also created in 1971, sets the rates for different classes of mail.

What is the Presidential Transition Act?

One of the key responsibilities of a new administration is staffing the executive branch. A number of efforts were made during the Clinton Administration to ease the burden of presidential appointees and better prepare them for leading the federal government. The Presidential Transition Act of 2000, signed into law by President Bill Clinton on October 12, 2000, provides for an efficient transfer of authority from one administration to the next and outlines specific roles for a number of federal agencies, including the General Services Administration (GSA), the Office of Personnel Management, the Office

143

of Presidential Personnel, and the U.S. Archivist. As a result of the law, a transition-co-ordinating council was specifically created to provide the president-elect's team with an orderly transition to the new administration.

Why has the government been likened to a bureaucracy?

Describing the structure of the Federal Bureau of Investigation (FBI) before the Senate Judiciary Committee in June 2002, FBI agent Coleen Rowley called it an "ever-growing bureaucracy" of "endless, needless paperwork." The word "bureaucracy," in the sense that it is any large and complexly organized administrative body, has often been used to describe the federal government. In fact, many Americans simply use the word "bureaucracy" as a synonym for big government. The sense of the word, however, implies more than that. A bureaucracy is hierarchical in structure, meaning that the people at the top dictate work to the people at the bottom, and every person follows a chain of command. Each person in the bureaucracy has a specialized job to do, and there are definite rules and regulations that mandate how the organization is run. In these ways, the federal bureaucracy encompasses all of the agencies, people, and procedures through which the government operates—from the way that it makes and executes public policy to the way that it deals with the public and the media.

What is the discussion in recent years about downsizing government?

With nearly 3.5 million employees and a combined payroll of over $190 billion, it's easy to see why Americans have argued for downsizing the federal government—that is, decreasing the number of personnel and simplifying the machinery through which the executive branch operates in an effort to expedite decision-making and implement policy more effectively. However, when one considers the size and scope of the executive branch as well as the many duties it carries out for the American public, it's hard to imagine how this task might be accomplished. Many argue that it is the nearly 150 independent agencies within the executive branch that make Americans' lives manageable—by delivering the mail, collecting taxes, regulating business procedures, and administering Social Security programs. Although there has been a concerted effort in most recent administrations to cap big government, the daily workings of the federal government don't appear likely to be downsized anytime soon.

THE ROLE OF THE VICE PRESIDENCY

What role does the vice president serve?

The limited role of the vice president is introduced in Article II, Section 1 of the Constitution, which provides that the president "shall hold his Office during the Term of four Years … together with the Vice President…." In addition to his role as president of the Senate, the vice president is empowered to succeed to the presidency under Article II and the Twentieth and Twenty-fifth Amendments to the Constitution. His right of succession has often been mentioned as his most coveted privilege. The executive functions of the vice president include participation in cabinet meetings and, by statute, membership on the National Security Council and the Board of Regents of the Smithsonian Institution.

However, although the Constitution spends little time assigning any roles to the office of vice president, and traditionally the office has not been highly regarded, more recent presidents have given larger roles to their vice presidents. These include advising the president on domestic and foreign policy matters and carrying out a host of political and diplomatic duties in the name of the executive office. Unlike other members of the president's staff, the vice president is not subject to removal from office by the president. Under no circumstances may the president formally remove his vice president.

What are the qualifications for vice president?

The qualifications for vice president are the same as for president. According to Article II, Section 4 of the Constitution, the vice president must be a natural-born citizen, at least thirty-five years old, and have been a resident of the United States for at least fourteen years.

What happens if there is a vacancy in the office of the vice president?

According to the Twenty-fifth Amendment, ratified in 1967, whenever there is a vacancy in the office of the vice president, the president has the authority to nominate a vice president, who can then take office upon confirmation by a majority vote of both houses of Congress.

Has a vice president ever resigned?

Yes. Two vice presidents have resigned. John C. Calhoun (1782–1850) resigned on December 28, 1832, three months before his term expired, to become senator from South Carolina. Spiro T. Agnew (1918–1996) resigned on October 10, 1973, after pleading no contest to a charge of federal income tax evasion. Following Agnew's resignation, President Richard Nixon nominated Gerald Ford (1913–2006), the minority leader of the House, to fill the vice presidential vacancy. In accordance with the provisions of the Twenty-fifth

The office of vice president, assumed by Mike Pence in 2017, initially commanded almost no power or responsibilities at all. Today, the veep is president of the Senate, is the successor to the president, when needed, and participates in important cabinet meetings.

145

Amendment, under which Ford had been nominated, the Senate and House approved the nomination, and Ford was sworn into office on December 6, 1973. On August 9, 1974, less than a year later, Ford became president following Nixon's resignation. Shortly thereafter, Ford nominated Nelson A. Rockefeller (1908–1979) to be vice president, and Rockefeller was confirmed and sworn into office on December 19, 1974. In a span of just over one year, two situations arose for using the provisions of the Twenty-fifth Amendment to fill a vacancy in the vice presidency.

Which vice presidents succeeded to the presidency upon the death or resignation of the presidents under whom they served?

A total of nine vice presidents succeeded to the presidency in this way: John Tyler, Millard Fillmore, Andrew Johnson, Chester A. Arthur, Theodore Roosevelt, Calvin Coolidge, Harry Truman, Lyndon Johnson, and Gerald Ford. Four of these nine who succeeded to the presidency were elected for additional four-year terms: Theodore Roosevelt, Calvin Coolidge, Harry Truman, and Lyndon Johnson.

How many vice presidents have been elected to the presidency at the conclusion of their terms?

Only four vice presidents have been elected to the presidency at the conclusion of their vice presidential terms: John Adams, Thomas Jefferson, Martin Van Buren, and George H. W. Bush. Many people also incorrectly add Richard Nixon to this list; however, Nixon was the first vice president elected president several years after his vice presidential term. Nixon was vice president under President Dwight Eisenhower from January 1953 to January 1961 and, after losing to John F. Kennedy in the 1960 presidential election, did not return to government service again until January 1969, when he was inaugurated president of the United States.

When was the first and only time that a president/vice president team was not elected by the people?

The Gerald Ford/Nelson Rockefeller team ran the United States federal government without being elected to their posts as president and vice president. Both took office under the provisions of the Twenty-fifth Amendment.

Under the Richard Nixon presidency, Vice President Spiro Agnew resigned on October 10, 1973, leaving the position vacant. In accordance with the Twenty-fifth Amendment, President Nixon nominated Gerald Ford, House Republican leader from Michigan, as his vice president. Upon Senate confirmation, Ford assumed that role on December 6, 1973. When President Nixon resigned the presidency on August 9, 1974, Ford succeeded to the presidency, becoming the thirty-eighth president of the United States. He was then left to nominate a vice president, choosing former New York governor Nelson Rockefeller on August 20, 1974. After protracted hearings, Rockefeller was sworn in on December 19, 1974, as the new vice president of the United States.

THE COURTS

THE FEDERAL COURT SYSTEM

How and when was the federal court system established?

During the period of the Articles of Confederation, from 1781 to 1789, the laws of the United States were not subject to a national court system or judiciary. Rather, they were interpreted haphazardly by the individual states, which often ignored interstate disputes or settled them unfairly. When the Founding Fathers shaped the Constitution, they followed the words of Alexander Hamilton, who maintained that "laws are dead letters without courts to expound and define their true meaning and operation." The articles and clauses they wrote were developed to meet the need for an arbiter (reviewer) of law with a national jurisdiction. Thus, Article III provides for one Supreme Court and such inferior courts as Congress may "ordain and establish." Additionally, Article I, Section 8 states that Congress has the power "to constitute tribunals inferior to the Supreme Court." The Judiciary Act of 1789 formally established the Supreme Court and federal court system.

What role does Congress play with respect to the federal courts?

The Constitution gives Congress the power to create federal courts other than the Supreme Court and to determine their jurisdiction, or area of authority and control. In addition, Congress controls the types of cases that are addressed in the federal courts. As part of the system of checks and balances, Congress has three other basic responsibilities that determine how the courts operate. First, it decides how many judges there should be and where they will serve. Second, through the confirmation process, Congress determines which of the president's judicial nominees ultimately become federal judges. Third, Congress approves the federal courts' budget and grants money for the judiciary to operate—an amount that constitutes less than 1 percent of the federal budget.

How is the federal court system structured?

The Supreme Court is the highest court in the federal judiciary. Congress has established two levels of federal courts under the Supreme Court: trial courts (also known as district courts) and appellate courts (also known as circuit courts). Together, the courts make up a three-tiered system of justice.

There are ninety-four major trial courts, or district courts, in the United States. Each state has at least one, and no district court's jurisdiction includes more than one state. District court cases are usually heard by a single judge, who must be a resident of the district in which he or she presides. In addition to the district courts, Congress has created several special courts that have original jurisdiction over certain types of cases—for example, tax courts, customs courts, and military tribunals. Decisions of district courts, special courts, administrative agencies, and state supreme courts may be appealed to the thirteen U.S. courts of appeals. Often referred to as "circuit courts," these appellate courts also respect state boundaries, with several states making up one federal judicial circuit. There is a separate court of appeals for the District of Columbia and another called the Federal Circuit, both of which handle appeals generated by agencies of the federal government. Judges on circuit courts usually sit in panels of three; for especially controversial cases, all the judges on the circuit will hear the case *en banc* ("together"), although this rarely occurs. At the peak of the federal judicial system is the U.S. Supreme Court, which is the final arbiter of the law: the ultimate authority in deciding legal matters. It is the court of last resort for all legal cases in the United States, including matters of administrative law and constitutional questions.

What are district courts, and how are they organized?

The United States' ninety-four district courts are the trial courts in the federal judicial system. Over six hundred judges handle 80 percent of the federal caseload—more than 300,000 cases per year. The ninety-four districts include at least one district in each state, the District of Columbia, and Puerto Rico. Each district includes a United States bankruptcy court as a unit of the district court. In addition, three territories of the United States—the Virgin Islands, Guam, and the Northern Mariana Islands—have district courts that hear federal cases, including bankruptcy cases. Most federal cases are first tried and decided in district courts and are generally heard by a single judge. Within limits set by Congress and the Constitution, district courts have jurisdiction to hear nearly all categories of federal cases, including both civil and criminal matters. These cases include everything from personal injury to tax fraud.

There are two special trial courts that have nationwide jurisdiction over certain types of cases. The Court of International Trade addresses cases involving international trade and customs issues. The United States Court of Federal Claims has jurisdiction over most claims for money damages against the United States, disputes over federal contracts, unlawful "takings" of private property by the federal government, and a variety of other claims against the United States.

What are the courts of appeal, and how are they organized?

The ninety-four judicial districts are organized into twelve regional circuits, each of which has a U.S. court of appeals, often called circuit courts. Each court has from six to twenty-eight judges. A court of appeals hears appeals from the district courts within its circuit as well as appeals of decisions of federal administrative agencies. Cases are generally presented to the courts sitting in panels of three judges. There also is a Court of Appeals for the Federal Circuit with nationwide jurisdiction to hear appeals in specialized cases, such as those involving patent, trademark, and copyright laws and cases decided by the Court of International Trade and the Court of Federal Claims.

Appellate courts hear cases on appeal from district courts and from federal administrative agencies.

What are the special courts?

Within the federal court system, Congress created certain special courts to hear a narrow range of cases pertaining to specific matters. These include the Court of Appeals for the Armed Forces, which reviews court martial convictions in all of the armed services, and the Court of Veterans Appeals, which reviews decisions of the Board of Veterans' Appeals. Also grouped in this category are the United States Court of Federal Claims, which hears various claims against the United States, and the Tax Court, which hears controversies involving the payment of taxes. Various territorial courts and the courts of the District of Columbia are also special courts. In addition, there are a few other courts composed of regular U.S. district and appellate judges who provide their services in addition to their regular duties.

How is the power of the federal courts limited?

First and foremost, the power of the federal judiciary is limited by the system of checks and balances that exists in the federal government, which divides power among the executive, legislative, and judicial branches. The Constitution allows Congress to change the Supreme Court's jurisdiction; propose Constitutional amendments that, if ratified, can reverse judicial decisions; and impeach and remove federal judges. Only the president of the United States, with the advice and consent of the Senate, can appoint federal judges.

According to the Constitution, the federal courts can only exercise judicial powers and perform judicial work. They cannot make laws, which is the job of Congress, or enforce and execute laws, which is the job of the executive branch. Within their power to perform judicial work, the federal courts can only hear certain types of cases, those that fall within the scope defined by Article III, Section 2 of the Constitution and congressional statutes. Types of cases that may be heard in the federal courts include cases in which the U.S. government or one of its officers is either suing someone or being sued. In addition, the federal courts may decide cases for which state courts are inappropriate or might be suspected of partiality.

What kinds of cases do the federal courts hear?

In general, federal courts decide cases that involve the U.S. government, the U.S. Constitution or federal laws, or controversies between states or between the United States and foreign governments. A case that raises such a "federal question" may be filed in federal court—including, for example, a claim by an individual who may be entitled to money under a federal government program such as Social Security, a claim by the government that someone has violated federal laws, or a challenge to actions taken by a federal agency.

A case also may be filed in federal court based on the "diversity of citizenship" of the litigants (those involved in the case), such as between citizens of different states or between citizens of the United States and those of another country. To ensure fairness to an out-of-state litigant, the Constitution provides that such cases may be heard in a federal court but only if such cases involve more than $75,000 in potential damages. Claims below that amount may only be pursued in state court. Federal courts also have jurisdiction over all bankruptcy matters, which Congress has determined should be addressed in federal courts rather than the state courts. Through the bankruptcy process, individuals or businesses that can no longer pay their creditors may either seek a court-supervised liquidation (selling off for cash) of their assets, or they may reorganize their financial affairs and work out a plan to pay off their debts.

Can anyone observe a federal case in process?

Yes. With certain very limited exceptions, each step of the federal judicial process is open to the public. A person who wishes to observe a court in session may go to the federal courthouse, check the court calendar, and watch a proceeding. Anyone may review the pleadings and other papers in a case by going to the clerk of court's office and asking for the appropriate case file. By conducting their judicial work in public view, judges enhance public confidence in the courts, and they allow citizens to learn firsthand how America's judicial system works. In a few situations, the public may not have full access to court records and court proceedings, and these restrictions usually relate to high-profile trials. In these cases, there is often not enough space in the courtroom to accommodate all observers, and courtroom access may be restricted for security or privacy reasons. In addition, a judge may choose to place certain documents "under seal," meaning that they are not available to the public. Examples of sealed information include confidential business records, certain law enforcement reports, and juvenile records.

Unlike most of the state courts, the federal courts generally do not permit television or radio coverage of trial court proceedings.

THE SELECTION OF FEDERAL JUDGES

How are federal judges chosen?

According to the Constitution, Supreme Court justices, court of appeals judges, and district court judges are nominated by the president of the United States and confirmed by the Senate. The Senate Judiciary Committee typically conducts confirmation hearings for each nominee. Often, senators and members of the House who are of the president's political party recommend the names of potential nominees. However, the nomination process is often at odds with the confirmation process. The Senate is often leery of the nomination of judges whom they view as either too liberal or too conservative. For example, the Democratic-controlled Senate played a major role in shaping the federal judiciary during President George W. Bush's administration. Democrats objected to Bush's judicial nominees on many grounds, including their contention that Bush's candidates tend to be conservative. As of May 2002, of the one hundred candidates Bush had nominated to the federal bench, the Senate had confirmed half, and nine of Bush's thirty nominees to federal appeals courts had been confirmed. In addition, from June 2001 to January 2003, when the 107th Congress was controlled by Democrats, many conservative appellate nominees were stalled in the Senate Judiciary Committee and never granted hearings or committee votes.

How long are the terms of federal judges, and how are they compensated?

The Founding Fathers believed that an independent federal judiciary was essential to ensure fairness and equal justice for all citizens of the United States. Therefore, the Constitution makes specific allowances for federal judges' terms and salaries. According to Article III, federal judges—those of the Supreme Court, courts of appeals, and most federal district courts—have "good behavior" tenure as specified in the Constitution, which is generally considered to be a lifetime appointment. They can be removed from office only through impeachment and conviction by Congress. A few exceptions to the

Presidents such as George W. Bush have often struggled to get their federal judge nominees confirmed, especially when the Senate is controlled by an opposing party.

151

life term exist. Judges of the Court of Federal Claims, Tax Court, Court of Appeals for the Armed Forces, and Court of Veterans Appeals have fifteen-year terms, and judges of the territorial district courts in Guam, the Virgin Islands, and the Northern Mariana Islands have ten-year terms.

Congress sets the salaries and benefits that all federal judges receive. Judicial salaries are roughly equal to salaries of members of Congress. The Constitution states that the compensation of federal judges "shall not be diminished during their Continuance in Office," which means that neither the president nor Congress can reduce the salary of a federal judge. These two protections help an independent judiciary to decide cases free from popular opinion and political influence.

What are federal judges' qualifications?

The Constitution does not specify any requirements for federal judgeships. However, members of Congress, who typically recommend potential nominees, and the Department of Justice, which reviews nominees' qualifications, have developed their own informal criteria for selecting judges. In addition, the president, who appoints all federal judges, typically has a variety of individuals in mind for nomination, especially if he is considering appointments to the Supreme Court. Critics agree that the criteria for nomination include competency (including judicial or government experience), ideology or policy leanings (including justices with the president's party affiliation), religion, race, and gender. Historically, nominees have often been close friends of the president or those within his administration. However, presidents of late have looked beyond their immediate circle, typically nominating very accomplished private or government attorneys, judges in state courts, magistrate judges or bankruptcy judges, or law professors.

Has a federal judge ever been impeached?

Yes. In United States history, only thirteen federal judges have been impeached—that is, accused and tried of certain wrongdoings. Of these, seven were convicted and removed from their positions by the Senate. Three late-twentieth-century examples include Harry E. Claiborne (1917–2004) of the U.S. District Court in Nevada in 1986, on charges of income tax evasion and remaining on the bench following criminal conviction; Alcee Hastings (1936–) of the U.S. District Court in Florida in 1989, on charges of perjury and conspiring to solicit a bribe; and Walter Nixon (1928–) of the U.S. District Court in Mississippi in 1989, on charges of perjury before a federal grand jury.

THE SUPREME COURT AT WORK

What is the Supreme Court, and how is it organized?

As mandated by the Constitution, the Supreme Court of the United States is the highest court in America. The Supreme Court was created as outlined in the Constitution and by authority of the Judiciary Act of September 24, 1789. It was organized on February 2, 1790. The Court is composed of the chief justice of the United States and, since 1869, eight associate justices. Congress, which governs the Court's organization by legislation, varied the number of justices between five and ten in the period prior to 1869. Congress requires six justices for a quorum—that is, a minimum number present—to do Court business.

What is the jurisdiction of the Supreme Court?

The Constitution limits the Supreme Court to dealing with "cases" and "controversies." The first chief justice of America, John Jay, clarified this restriction early in the Court's history by declining to advise President George Washington on the constitutional implications of a proposed policy decision. The Court does not advise the government or heads of state; rather, its function is limited to deciding specific cases.

The Constitution states that the Supreme Court has original jurisdiction in all cases that affect ambassadors to the United States, other public ministers and consuls, and those in which a state is a party. The Constitution provides Congress with the authority to regulate the appellate jurisdiction of the Court; that is, Congress has authorized the Supreme Court to review judgments of lower federal courts and the highest courts of the states. The Supreme Court also has original jurisdiction in a select number of cases arising out of disputes between states or between a state and the federal government. In addition, the Supreme Court has the power of judicial review, granted in 1803 when it was invoked by Chief Justice John Marshall in *Marbury v. Madison*. In that decision, Chief Justice Marshall ruled that the Supreme Court had a responsibility to overturn unconstitutional legislation and that this power was a necessary consequence of its sworn duty to uphold the Constitution.

What is the importance of judicial review?

The Supreme Court's authority to overturn legislation or executive actions that, in the Court's judgment, conflict with the Constitution is based in America's democratic system of checks and balances. This power of judicial review—the authority to review acts of the other branches of government and the states and determine their constitutionality—has given the Court a crucial responsibility. Through the power of judicial review, the Court is charged with ensuring citizens' individual rights as guaranteed by the Constitution

The first U.S. Supreme Court justice was John Jay (1745–1829), who also served as governor of New York after leading the court from 1789 to 1795.

153

as well as with maintaining a "living Constitution" whose broad provisions are continually applied to complicated new situations.

While the function of judicial review is not explicitly described in the Constitution, it was considered before the Constitution's adoption. Before 1789, state courts had already overturned legislative acts that conflicted with state constitutions. Moreover, many of the Founding Fathers expected the Supreme Court to assume this role in regard to the Constitution. Alexander Hamilton and James Madison, for example, underlined the importance of judicial review in *The Federalist Papers*. Since the first time judicial review was exercised in *Marbury v. Madison* (1803), the Court has used this power sparingly: between 1803 and 1999, the Court found a federal law unconstitutional in only 143 cases. While most of these decisions affected outdated laws no longer supported by either the president or Congress, some of the Court's rulings in this area were extremely controversial, including *Dred Scott v. Sandford* (1857), which declared the Missouri Compromise unconstitutional; *Lochner v. New York* (1905), which ruled that New York State could not regulate bankers' working conditions; and *Schechter Poultry Corp. v. United States* (1935), which declared the National Industrial Recovery Act unconstitutional.

What is the significance of *Marbury v. Madison*?

Marbury v. Madison (1803) was the first Supreme Court case in which the Court exercised the power of judicial review. In that case, William Marbury (1762–1835), a last-minute judicial appointment by President John Adams (1735–1826) at the end of Adams' term, sued James Madison (1751–1836), the secretary of state under the new administration, for not upholding the appointment. The basis for Marbury's lawsuit was the Judiciary Act of 1789, which said that anyone not properly appointed could request a court order to obtain a due appointment and that the Supreme Court had original jurisdiction in this type of case. Chief Justice John Marshall (1755–1835) ruled that the Supreme Court was not the place to address Marbury's case because the Constitution did not grant the Supreme Court "original jurisdiction" in this area. Thus, the terms of the Judiciary Act of 1789 violated the Constitution, and therefore the act was void. Chief Justice Marshall's logic was that because the Constitution is the highest law in the land, established by the people, no entity expected to follow the laws of that document (i.e., Congress) should be able to make other laws that are in conflict with it.

Under the John Marshall Court, the important case of *Marbury v. Madison* was decided, reinforcing the principle of judicial review and invalidating an act of Congress for being unconstitutional.

With the *Marbury* decision, the Court took on the authority to declare acts of Congress unconstitutional if those acts exceeded the powers granted by the Constitution. Perhaps more importantly, however, the Court established itself as the arbiter of the Constitution, a role it has performed ever since. It is because of this role that the Court was able to greatly expand people's civil liberties throughout the twentieth century.

How do Supreme Court justices interpret the Constitution?

Rarely is interpreting the Constitution a straightforward task. Because Supreme Court cases are complex, the Supreme Court has adopted various perspectives of constitutional interpretation, or doctrines, in exercising judicial review. The first is the doctrine of original intent. Original intent involves determining the constitutionality of a law on the basis of the original intent of the Founding Fathers. Justices who follow the doctrine of original intent often review key documents in order to "get inside the founders' heads," including *The Federalist Papers,* James Madison's notes at the Constitutional Convention, and speeches made during the ratifying campaign. Those who criticize this theory claim that the issues before the Court today are more complex than two hundred years ago and were probably never considered by the Constitution's authors. Instead, they view the Constitution as a living document, adaptable in light of the changing times, and maintain that a law's constitutionality should be judged in the context of the entire history of the United States as a nation. In short, whether or not a given law is constitutional should reflect current societal conditions and values. Critics say this doctrine is highly subjective, since it reduces constitutional interpretation to an individual justice's perception of history.

From these two viewpoints emerged a third type of interpretation, often called the "plain meaning of text" doctrine. Under this doctrine, a law's constitutionality is measured against what the words of the Constitution obviously seem to say. Adherents to this perspective say that, unlike original intent, this measuring stick does not require debates about the intentions of a small group of men hundreds of years ago, and unlike the living Constitution theory, it does not invite a personal perspective on the country's history. However, reviewing the Constitution in terms of what it "seems to say" is not uncontroversial, since the framers purposely included ambiguous language in order to win ratification.

What is meant by the terms "judicial restraint" and "judicial activism"?

The various theories of constitutional interpretation govern how any given justice will vote on a particular case. "Judicial restraint" maintains that the Court should use restraint when deciding whether or not to overturn a prior Court decision. "Judicial activism," on the other hand, says that sometimes precedents need to be overturned in light of today's societal conditions.

What is the role of the solicitor general?

The solicitor general is a key officer in the Department of Justice. Often called the federal government's "chief lawyer," the solicitor general's job is to represent the United States in all Supreme Court cases in which the United States is a party. In addition, the solicitor general decides which cases the federal government should ask the Supreme Court to review and what position the United States should take in cases before the Supreme Court. When the government wants to present its point of view in a certain case, it is the solicitor general who files the *amicus curiae* brief (a brief filed by a person or group that is not directly involved in a case but who has a vested interest in how it is decided).

How does a case reach the Supreme Court?

Most cases that reach the Supreme Court come from either the highest state courts or the federal courts of appeal. Most reach the Court by writ of certiorari, which in Latin means "to be made more certain." In essence, this writ is an order that the Court issues to a lower court to send up the record in a given case for the Court's review. Either party in a legal case can petition the Supreme Court to issue a writ of certiorari, although the Court only considers a limited number of petitions. If the Court denies a certiorari, then the decision of the lower case stands. A handful of cases also reach the Supreme Court by certificate, whereby a lower court asks the Supreme Court to clarify the rule of law that should apply in a particular case.

In order to have access to the courts, cases must meet certain criteria: the case before a court must be an actual controversy, rather than just a hypothetical one, and there must be two opposing parties involved; the parties to the case must prove a substantial stake in the case's outcome; and the case must be heard while it is still relevant. Cases that reach the Supreme Court are also dependent upon the justice's priorities, and often the Court's criteria for hearing a case are subjective. Justices consider a blend of information, such as whether a lower-court decision conflicts with an existing Supreme Court ruling, whether the issue at hand was decided differently by two lower courts and needs the Court to resolve it, and whether the issue potentially has social significance beyond the interests of the parties directly involved.

How does the Supreme Court reach a decision, and who determines this procedure?

The Court's internal review process has largely developed over time by custom, while the procedures to be followed by petitioners to the Court are established in rules set forth by the Court. Each year the Court receives more than seven thousand petitions from state and lower federal courts. The Court reviews all of the cases submitted and agrees to hear oral arguments on about ninety each term. The justices also decide a limited number of other cases without hearing oral arguments—usually fewer than seventy-five. The rest of the petitions are denied.

After initially reviewing each case submitted, the justices hold a private conference to decide which cases to schedule for oral argument, which to decide without argument, and which to deny. If at least four justices agree, a case will be taken by the Court for a decision, with or without oral argument, and the other petitions for review will be denied. If oral argument is heard, the parties are generally allowed a total of one hour to argue the issues and respond to questions from the justices. Later, in conference, the justices reach their decision by a simple majority or plurality vote. A tie vote means that the decision of the lower court is allowed to stand. It is possible for such a vote to occur when one or three justices do not participate in a decision.

What are briefs and *amicus curiae* briefs?

Briefs are detailed documents filed with the Court before the oral argument is presented. Often running to hundreds of pages, these critical documents are carefully crafted statements that support a particular side of the case. *Amicus curiae* ("friend of the court" in Latin) briefs are filed by individuals or public interest groups that are not parties in the case but who have a vested interest in its outcome. They are often a part of highly charged cases that involve issues such as abortion, the death penalty, or the separation of church and state. However, no matter how much a third party wants to express its opinion to the Supreme Court, *amicus curiae* briefs can only be filed with the Court's permission and by its specific request.

What is opinion writing?

In short, opinion writing is the way Supreme Court decisions are explained. The Court's opinion outlines the Court's decision on a particular case and the Court's logic, or justification, for having reached the conclusion it did. The Court's opinion is often called the majority opinion. In addition, one or more of the justices who agree with the Court's decision will write a concurring opinion, which, in essence, makes or emphasizes a point that was not expressed in the majority opinion. Similarly, justices also write dissenting opinions, which voice a justice's reasons for disagreeing with the Court's majority opinion.

Who writes the opinions of the Supreme Court?

When the justices have decided a case, the chief justice, if voting with the majority, may write the opinion himself or assign an associate justice to write the opinion of the Court. If the chief justice is in the minority, the senior associate justice in the majority may write the opinion or assign another associate justice in the majority to write the opinion. The individual justices may write their own concurring or dissenting opinions on any decision, and these statements often become references for discussing the implications of the case.

What happens once a decision has been reached?

Once the Supreme Court rules on a particular case, it does not implement its decision. Rather, the case is sent back to the lower court from which it came, with instructions for that court to act in accordance with the Supreme Court's opinion. The lower court often has quite a bit of leeway in interpreting the Court's decision. In cases where the

Supreme Court's decision affects only one central-government agency, the decision usually becomes effective immediately. However, the majority of the Court's rulings, which affect many administrative and elected officials, often take years to put into place. For example, many school districts remained segregated years after the Court declared the unconstitutionality of public school segregation in *Brown v. Board of Education of Topeka* (1954). A decision on the ways that warrantless searches are conducted would affect more than just police officers and chiefs of police but also state attorneys general, local prosecutors, and trial court judges—all of whom must follow a new code of conduct in order for the Court's decision to be truly meaningful at an everyday level.

Why is so much importance placed on a Supreme Court decision?

The finality of the Court's decisions and the implications those decisions have for America's civil liberties is sobering. Article VI of the Constitution states that the Constitution and the laws of the United States made "in Pursuance thereof" shall be the supreme law of the land. When the Supreme Court rules on a constitutional issue, that judgment is virtually final; its decisions can only be altered by the procedure of constitutional amendment or by a new ruling of the Court. When the Supreme Court decides a case, particularly on constitutional grounds, it becomes the standard for lower courts and legislators when a similar question arises, thus setting a precedent for how future laws are made. By virtue of its power of judicial review, the Court can declare laws unconstitutional, thus making them null and void.

What is the role of the chief justice?

In addition to hearing cases and writing opinions, the chief justice, as presiding officer of the Court, is responsible for the Court's administration. Federal law outlines these administrative duties, which range from assigning associate justices and himself to the circuit courts to approving regulations for the protection of the Court building and grounds. In practice, the chief justice oversees all matters affecting the justices and procedures of the Court. The statutory duties of the chief justice reach beyond the Court itself and include the administrative leadership of the entire federal judicial system. The chief justice is chair of the Judicial Conference of the United States (a board of trustees for the federal court), chair of the Federal Judicial Center, and overseer of the Administrative Office of the United States Courts, unofficially dubbed the "housekeeper" and statistician for the federal court system. By statute, the chief justice sits on the boards of the National Gallery of Art, the Smithsonian Institution, and the Hirshhorn Museum.

Who were the Supreme Court chief justices over history?

Seventeen Supreme Court chief justices have served the United Sates since the Court's inception. They are: John Jay (1789–1795), John Rutledge (1795), Oliver Ellsworth (1796–1800), John Marshall (1801–1835), Roger B. Taney (1836–1864), Salmon P. Chase (1864–1873), Morrison R. Waite (1874–1888), Melville W. Fuller (1888–1910), Edward D. White (1910–1921), William Howard Taft (1921–1930), Charles Evans Hughes (1930–1941), Harlan Fiske Stone (1941–1946), Fred M. Vinson (1946–1953), Earl Warren (1953–1969), Warren E. Burger (1969–1986), William H. Rehnquist (1986–2005), and John G. Roberts Jr. (2005–present).

Who are the Supreme Court justices today?

Although Congress has periodically altered the size of the Court (the lowest number of justices serving being six and the most ten), since 1869 the number of justices has held steady at nine. Today, the Supreme Court is comprised of the chief justice of the United States, John G. Roberts Jr., and eight associate justices: Anthony M. Kennedy, Clarence

The U.S. Supreme Court of 2017 includes (back row, left to right) Elena Kagan, Samuel A. Alito, Sonia So-tomayor, and Neil Gorsuch, and (front row, left to right) Ruth Bader Ginsburg, Anthony Kennedy, Chief Justice John Roberts, Clarence Thomas, and Stephen Breyer.

Thomas, Ruth Bader Ginsburg, Stephen G. Breyer, Samuel Anthony Alito, Sonia Sotomayor, Elena Kagan, and Neil M. Gorsuch.

Which chief justices also served as associate justices?

Only five men in Supreme Court history have held both positions: John Rutledge, Edward D. White, Charles Evans Hughes, Harlan Fiske Stone, and William H. Rehnquist.

Which justice served the shortest term? Which justice served the longest?

The justice who served the least amount of time is John Rutledge, who served one year as associate justice and four months as chief justice, although he never received confirmation from the Senate. William O. Douglas served the longest, for more than thirty-six years. Other contenders were just two years off this record: Stephen J. Field, John Marshall, Joseph Story, Hugo Black, and William J. Brennan all served for thirty-four years or slightly more. Marshall's tenure of over thirty-four years was the longest for a chief justice.

Who became the first woman member of the Supreme Court?

Appointed by President Ronald Reagan in 1981, Justice Sandra Day O'Connor (1930–) became the first woman justice on the Supreme Court. Known for her moderate leanings, O'Connor was regarded as one of the Court's most influential members. Prior to her Court appointment, O'Connor held several posts in Arizona: assistant attorney general, state senator, and superior court judge. Governor Bruce Babbitt appointed her to

Thurgood Marshall (left) was chosen by President John F. Kennedy as the first African American to serve on the U.S. Supreme Court, which he did from 1967 to 1991; Sandra Day O'Connor was the first woman justice of the U.S. Supreme Court. She was nominated by President Ronald Reagan and served in that post from 1981 to 2006.

the Arizona Court of Appeals in 1979. Other female Supreme Court justices include Ruth Bader Ginsburg (appointed by Bill Clinton in 1993) and two who were nominated by Barack Obama: Sonia Sotomayor, who was appointed in 2009, and Elena Kaga, who took her seat in 2010.

Who was the first African American justice?

Thurgood Marshall (1908–1993)—Howard University Law School valedictorian, civil rights activist, and great-grandson of a slave—was nominated to the Supreme Court by President Lyndon Johnson in 1967. As chief counsel for the National Association for the Advancement of Colored People (NAACP) for two decades prior to his Supreme Court tenure, the liberal Marshall argued many precedent-setting cases. He is best known for his representation in *Brown v. Board of Education of Topeka* (1954), in which racial segregation of American public schools was declared unconstitutional. President John F. Kennedy appointed Marshall to the United States Court of Appeals for the Second Circuit in 1961, and from 1965 to 1967 Marshall served as solicitor general under President Lyndon Johnson. Marshall retired from the Court bench in 1991, after which the conservative African American justice Clarence Thomas took his seat.

What were some of the more interesting highlights of Ruth Bader Ginsburg's appointment?

Ruth Bader Ginsburg (1933–), the second woman in history to sit on the Court, was appointed in 1993 by President Bill Clinton. When Justice Byron White announced in March 1993 that he would retire from the Supreme Court, the Clinton Administration put together its list of potential nominees. However, Ginsburg's name was not on the list until her husband, Martin Ginsburg, began lobbying for his wife's seat on the Court through an intensive letter-writing campaign. Mr. Ginsburg called on legal scholars, academics, the presidents of Stanford and Columbia universities, and Texas governor Ann W. Richards, who called or wrote the White House rallying for Ginsburg's nomination. Clinton was commended by many for nominating Ginsburg, a woman of Jewish faith, to fill the traditionally "Jewish seat" on the Court, which had been vacant for over twenty years.

Which Supreme Court justice nomination came under Senate scrutiny, ending in a highly publicized Senate confirmation trial?

President George H. W. Bush's 1991 nomination of Clarence Thomas, the second African American to sit on the Court, was extremely controversial. Thomas, a past chair of the Equal Employment Opportunity Commission (EEOC), was opposed to affirmative action programs that he felt gave preferential treatment to minorities. As a conservative, Thomas stood in stark contrast to the man he was replacing, African American civil rights activist Thurgood Marshall, raising eyebrows among the Democratic-controlled Senate Judiciary Committee. Generally supported by the black population and civil rights groups, Thomas initially escaped a certain degree of media criticism. However,

Anita Hill, a former EEOC lawyer and past employee of Thomas, soon came forward with charges of sexual harassment, igniting fiery confirmation hearings before the Senate Judiciary Committee. After a sensational examination, the Senate finally confirmed Thomas by a narrow margin. However, many commentators note that Thomas' nomination was perhaps most costly to George H. W. Bush, who as a result of his choice lost the support of women voters in the 1992 presidential election.

Which president appointed the most justices?

President George Washington appointed the most justices—a total of eleven—but only ten actually served. In the twentieth century, President Franklin D. Roosevelt appointed a total of nine justices during his terms in office, including such notables as Hugo Black, Felix Frankfurter, and William O. Douglas.

What was Franklin D. Roosevelt's Court-packing plan?

After President Roosevelt's New Deal programs were put in place, the Supreme Court ruled several of those measures unconstitutional, including the National Recovery Act and the Guffey Coal Act of 1935. The Court invalidated FDR's Agricultural Adjustment Act, ruling that the processing tax that funded federal subsidies to farmers was unconstitutional and that the states, not the federal government, held the power to regulate agriculture. Fearful that the Court would apply its states'-rights reasoning to multiple New Deal measures and that his carefully crafted domestic policy would falter, in February 1937, Roosevelt sent Congress a bill to reorganize the federal judiciary. Dubbed the Court-packing plan by its critics, the bill cited the inability of the federal courts to handle their overwhelming caseload and proposed multiple judicial reforms, including the president's appointment of one justice to the Supreme Court for every justice who refused to retire by age seventy. It also called for a maximum of six new Supreme Court justices. Roosevelt's argument lost relevance when the Supreme Court began ruling in Roosevelt's favor, upholding both a Washington State minimum wage law and the Social Security Act. The bill died in July 1937, with an angry citizenry voicing its outrage over what it branded as Roosevelt's plan to rig the American judiciary. Despite this upheaval, due to deaths and retirements on the Court, Roosevelt was able to appoint seven new associate judges over the next four years.

Which full-term presidents did not appoint a Supreme Court justice?

In the twentieth century, only President Jimmy Carter failed to appoint any Supreme Court justices to the bench. In addition, three other presidents in U.S. history made no appointments: William Henry Harrison, Zachary Taylor, and Andrew Johnson.

POLICYMAKING AND THE COURTS

How has the Supreme Court's power gradually expanded?

In the early years of the nation's existence, the judiciary was the weakest of the three branches of government. Chief Justice John Marshall greatly strengthened the judiciary when he established the principle of judicial review by declaring an act of Congress unconstitutional in *Marbury v. Madison* (1803). Although the Supreme Court only exercised this power one more time prior to the Civil War (in *Dred Scott v. Sandford,* 1857), the establishment of judicial review made the judiciary more of an equal player with the executive and legislative branches. In fact, some scholars contend that the power of judicial review makes the Supreme Court in many ways a lawmaking body unto itself.

Since that time of equal footing, the Supreme Court has slowly expanded its power, particularly in the last sixty years. The Court has made substantive changes in policy areas, including school desegregation, legislative apportionment, obscenity, abortion, and voting rights. Without a doubt, the framers never imagined that the authority of the Supreme Court would encompass decisions on everything from gay rights to euthanasia, let alone that the federal judiciary would have a hand in educational policy, hiring decisions, and affirmative action. In addition, since the 1960s the Court has broadened the way it does business by allowing class-action suits and aligning itself with various constituencies, such as civil rights, consumer, and feminist groups.

Still a controversial ruling to this day, the *Roe v. Wade* case in which the Supreme Court allowed women to legally have abortions, continues to inspire public protests among more conservative and religious Americans.

163

What kinds of cases does the Supreme Court hear today?

Few people are unaware that the Supreme Court has issued dozens of landmark decisions throughout the twentieth century, including *Brown v. Board of Education of Topeka* (1954), *Baker v. Carr* (1962), *Engel v. Vitale* (1962), *Miranda v. Arizona* (1966), *Roe v. Wade* (1973), and *United States v. Nixon* (1974), to name a few. Both the cases themselves and the Supreme Court's rulings—as far-reaching as segregation in public schools and the president's executive privilege—reflected the climate of the Court and the conflicts facing America at critical points in the nation's history. The appointment of four justices in the 1990s—David H. Souter, Clarence Thomas, Ruth Bader Ginsburg, and Stephen G. Breyer—resulted in an overall conservative Court, as reflected in rulings that placed limits on affirmative action, voting rights, the separation of church and state, and the power of the federal government in relation to the states. However, the Court has expanded several rights, including free speech, women's rights, and gay rights.

Perhaps no time is more contentious than the early twenty-first century, when the Court has ruled on a variety of issues, including the 2000 presidential election, the Fifth Amendment, hospital drug testing, religious activities for schools, heat-sensing police surveillance, freelance copyright protection, Internet pornography, and granting homosexuals the right to marry throughout the United States. George W. Bush added a conservative chief justice, John G. Roberts Jr., and Associate Justice Samuel A. Alito to the court, and Donald Trump added another conservative justice, Neil M. Gorsuch, in 2017. This tipped the scale back to conservatism after the nominations of Sonia Sotomayor and Elena Kagan by Barack Obama.

How is the Court subject to public opinion?

Although the framers of the Constitution intended the Supreme Court to rule on cases solely on the basis of facts and law and to be above the pressures of the general public, today's Supreme Court is indeed pressured by the citizenry. Virtually every public interest group—from pro-lifers to environmentalists—seek out good test cases to present

What does the term "equal justice under law" mean?

"Equal justice under law" is the main principle of the judicial system in the United States. Engraved above the entrance of the Supreme Court building, it means that every person in the United States is entitled to receive equal and fair treatment from the law. These words express the ultimate responsibility of the Supreme Court, which, as the nation's highest tribunal, hears all cases and controversies arising under the Constitution and the laws of the United States. As the final reviewer and judge of the law, the Court is charged with ensuring the American people equal justice under law and thereby also functions as guardian and interpreter of the Constitution.

to the Court in hopes of advancing their policy positions. In fact, in most cases heard by the Supreme Court, either the government or a public interest group acts as the sponsoring party or an *amicus curiae* (third party). Groups as varied as the American Civil Liberties Union, the NAACP Legal Defense Fund, Concerned Women for America, and Americans United for Life Legal Defense Fund routinely act in this way, highlighting lower-court decisions and ideological conflict for the judges in their amicus briefs. In addition, because of its controversial decisions on everything from gun control and abortion to affirmative action and gay rights, the Supreme Court has routinely been the target of interest-group protests outside the courtroom.

STATE VERSUS FEDERAL COURTS

What is the supreme law of the land?

The term "supreme law of the land" refers to all laws of the United States made according to the Constitution as well as treaties made under the authority of the United States. All judges throughout the country, both state and federal, must uphold them, regardless of any statutes or acts that exist in individual state constitutions or laws.

What are the two types of court systems in the United States?

There are two types of court system, or judiciaries, in the United States: federal and state. The federal judiciary is made up of more than a hundred courts. Each state has its own number of courts, which can run into the thousands, and these state courts are responsible for trying the majority of cases in the country.

How is the U.S. court system organized?

The U.S. judicial system is not one single system but rather a collection of multiple, independently functioning courts. The federal court system is an integrated system divided into many geographic units and levels of hierarchy. In addition to this system, each state has a system of local courts. In this dual federal/state court structure, the U.S. Supreme Court is the final judge of federal law, while the highest court of each state (usually called state supreme courts) has the ultimate authority to interpret the law of its state. When federal constitutional or statutory matters are involved, the federal courts have the power to decide whether a state law violates federal law. The functioning of these systems is complicated by the fact that there are multiple sources of law, and courts in one system are often called upon to interpret and apply the laws of another jurisdiction. In addition, more than one court may have the authority to hear a particular case.

The federal judiciary and each state judicial system are constructed like pyramids. Entry-level courts at both the state and federal levels are called trial courts, in which witnesses are called, evidence is presented, and a jury or sometimes a judge reaches a conclusion based on the law. At the top of each pyramid is the court of last resort, which has the authority to interpret the law of that jurisdiction. At the federal level, this court is the U.S. Supreme Court; at the state level, it is the state supreme court. Most states and the federal system also have a midlevel court of appeals. The vast majority of courts at both the state and federal level are "courts of general jurisdiction," meaning that they have authority to decide many different types of cases. There are no special constitutional courts in the United States: any court has the power to declare a law or action of a government executive to be unconstitutional, subject to review by a higher-level court.

What is due process of law?

The Fifth Amendment's words that no person shall "be deprived of life, liberty, or property without due process of law" express one of the most important principles of the Constitution. The Founding Fathers shaped this constitutional guarantee because they believed that a person's life, liberty, and property should not be threatened or taken away because of the arbitrary or unreasonable action of the government but could only be limited if the government followed a proper course of legal action. The Fourth, Fifth, Sixth, and Eighth Amendments provide a number of procedural guarantees for those accused of crimes, and, taken together, those guarantees are often called due process rights. The due process clause appears in both the Fifth and Fourteenth Amendments, the latter of which holds the states to the same restrictions as the former.

The Sixth Amendment provides that Americans accused of a crime are guaranteed a speedy trial, legal defense, and to have their case presented in front of a jury of their peers.

> ## Do we as citizens have an obligation to the judicial process?
>
> Absolutely. A fundamental right of citizens is to have their judicial case heard and decided by a jury of their peers. Since "peers" means all U.S. citizens, each, in his or her role as a juror, performs a vital role in America's judicial system. As jurors, citizens support this fundamental right of their fellows and perform a basic civic function essential to the concept of democracy.

What are the two types of jury system in the United States?

There are two types of juries serving distinct functions in the federal trial courts: trial juries (also known as petit juries) and grand juries. A civil trial jury is typically made up of six to twelve members. In a civil case, the role of the jury is to listen to the evidence presented at a trial, to decide whether the defendant injured the plaintiff or otherwise failed to fulfill a legal duty to the plaintiff, and to determine what the compensation or penalty should be. A criminal trial jury is usually made up of twelve members. Criminal juries decide whether the defendant committed the crime as charged. A judge usually sets the sentence. Verdicts in both civil and criminal cases must be unanimous. A jury's deliberations are conducted in private, out of sight and hearing of the judge, litigants, witnesses, and others in the courtroom.

A grand jury, which normally consists of sixteen to twenty-three members, has a more specialized function. The prosecutor in federal criminal cases, the United States attorney, presents evidence so that the grand jury can determine whether there is probable cause to believe that an individual has committed a crime and should be put on trial. If the grand jury decides there is enough evidence, it will issue an indictment against the defendant. Grand jury proceedings are not open to the public.

How are jurors selected?

Before potential jurors are summoned for service, their names are randomly drawn from voter lists (or sometimes from the licensed-driver lists of the Department of Motor Vehicles). Random selection allows for a fair cross-section of the community and prohibits discrimination in the selection process. Because the Jury Act calls for a random selection of names, individuals cannot volunteer for service. The people whose names are selected are then mailed a questionnaire to determine whether they meet the legal qualifications for jury service. In order to be eligible, a potential juror must be at least eighteen years old, be a citizen of the United States, and have resided within the judicial district that the court serves for one year. In addition, a potential juror must be able to read, write, understand, and speak the English language; be mentally and physically sound; and not have been convicted of a felony or have felony charges pending. Individuals who receive questionnaires are legally required to complete and return them to the clerk's office, which then screens the completed questionnaires to determine who is eligible. In some courts, however, qualification questionnaires and summonses—documents that legally require a citizen to report for jury duty—are mailed together. Members of the armed forces on active duty, professional fire and police department personnel, and active public officers of federal, state, and local governments are exempt from serving on juries.

What is the role of state courts?

The primary function of the state courts is to hear disputes between private parties as well as between private parties and the government. Because almost every state court has the power to exercise judicial review, they act as "watchdogs" on the conduct of other state and local government agencies.

What kind of law applies to state courts?

Four basic forms of law are applied in state courts: constitutional law, statutory law, administrative law, and common law. Constitutional law deals with laws based on the articles of the Constitution. Laws affecting a citizen's civil liberties fall under constitutional law. Statutory law consists of those laws or statutes that are adopted by legislative bodies (such as the U.S. Congress and the state legislatures), the people (through the powers of initiative or referendum), and civil councils. (Initiative is the petition process by which voters put a proposed constitutional amendment or statute on the ballot; referendum is the process whereby a measure passed by a legislature is submitted to voters for their approval or rejection.) "Administrative law" is the term used to cover the rules and regulations of federal, state, or local executive officers. "Common law" refers to unwritten law that has formed over centuries and is based on the generally accepted ideas of the court. Common law applies to those situations where a violation has already occurred; equity, on the other hand, is a code of law that seeks to prevent wrongdoings before they occur and is often carried out in the form of an injunction.

What kinds of cases do the state courts hear?

Most cases are handled in the state court system. In fact, 99 percent of legal disputes in American courts are decided in the separate state court systems. State courts have jurisdiction over virtually all divorce and child custody matters, probate and inheritance issues, real estate questions, and juvenile matters. In addition, they handle most criminal cases, contract disputes, traffic violations, small claims, and personal injury cases.

How are state courts structured?

Because states are free to structure their judicial systems as they choose, state systems vary somewhat. However, most states have chosen a four-level model. At the lowest level are courts of limited jurisdiction, which hear minor civil and criminal cases—for example, traffic, juvenile, and small claims courts that settle disputes involving small sums of money. These are the "workhorses" of the state judicial system because they process the majority of the state's legal cases. The next level consists of state courts of general jurisdiction. These are the major trial courts of the state, empowered to hear more serious criminal cases and civil cases in which large sums of money are involved. Most states have a third tier, the intermediate court of appeals, where a party can appeal a case. Finally, there is the top level, called the state supreme court. Legal custom allows each losing litigant one appeal (with the notable exception of prosecution in a criminal case). In states without an intermediate appellate court, the state supreme court must hear these appeals.

What is the state supreme court's role, and how is it organized?

As the highest court in the state judicial system, the state supreme court primarily reviews decisions appealed to it by lower courts. The size of the state supreme court is determined by each state's constitution, although in most states, somewhere between five and seven justices sit on the bench. Like the U.S. Supreme Court in the federal system, the state supreme court is the court of last resort at the state level, having the final say in all state law. State supreme court cases that raise questions of federal law may be appealed to the U.S. Supreme Court, although few are. An appeal from a state supreme court will only be heard in the U.S. Supreme Court if a matter of federal law is involved in the case and the Supreme Court agrees to hear the appeal.

How are state judges selected?

Another detail left to the states' discretion is the method of selecting judges. While all federal judges are appointed for life terms by the president of the United States with the approval of the Senate, four primary methods are currently used to select state judges: partisan elections, nonpartisan elections, election by the state legislature, and appointment by the governor, the latter method including a merit system for selecting candidates. In the merit system, sometimes called the Missouri Plan after the first state to adopt it, judicial nomination boards screen applicants for judicial posts and send a list of the best-qualified candidates to the governor of the state, who makes the final selection. In twenty-three states, the governor appoints the justices; in four states, the legislature selects the judges; and in twenty-three states, voters choose.

DIFFERENCES BETWEEN CIVIL LIBERTIES AND CIVIL RIGHTS

What are civil liberties?

Civil liberties are those fundamental freedoms that together guarantee the rights of free people and protect the people from improper government actions against them. The specific rights that together make up the civil liberties of the people of the United States are written in the Bill of Rights, the first ten amendments to the Constitution. Examples of civil liberties include freedom of religion, freedom of speech, freedom of the press, and the guarantee of a fair, unbiased trial.

What are substantive liberties?

Some of the restraints put on the government are substantive liberties, which limit what the government shall and shall not have the power to do, including establish a religion, quarter troops in private homes without consent, or seize private property without just compensation.

How do civil liberties differ from civil rights?

Although these two terms are often used interchangeably, scholars generally agree that civil liberties are those liberties that protect people from the government—those that guarantee the safety of people, their opinions, and their property from the government as listed in the Constitution. The term "civil rights," on the other hand, is generally used to refer to acts of government that make constitutional guarantees real for all people, ensuring that they receive equal treatment under the law, as outlined by the Equal Protection Clause of the Fourteenth Amendment. Landmark civil rights legislation is found in the Civil Rights Act of 1964, which prohibits discrimination based on race or sex.

Does the Constitution grant Americans their civil rights and liberties?

No. It doesn't grant them, it only guarantees them. According to the Ninth Amendment, "The enumeration in the Constitution, of certain rights, shall not be construed to deny or disparage others retained by the people." The people of America had all their rights and liberties before they wrote the Constitution. The Constitution was formed, among other purposes, to secure the people's liberties—not only against foreign attack but also against oppression by their own government. The First Amendment to the Constitution, for example, does not *give* freedom of religion or speech to the people; rather, it prohibits Congress from passing any law interfering with freedom of religion, speech, and peaceful assembly.

What are some of the rights established in the original Constitution?

The Constitution strives to uphold several core democratic principles, one of which is the protection of individual rights and civil liberties. Thus, individual rights are at the heart of the Constitution, as expressed by the framers in the document's preamble with key phrases like "to establish Justice" and "to secure the Blessings of Liberty to ourselves and our Posterity." To establish justice, the Constitution makes no dis-

One inalienable right guaranteed by the Constitution is free speech, as well as freedom of expression, religion, and assembly. These rights are essential to the continuation of a democratic and free society.

tinction as to the wealth or status of any person; all are equal before the law, and all are equally subject to judgment and punishment when they violate the law. The same holds true for civil disputes involving property, legal agreements, and business arrangements. The emphasis on personal liberty is one of the main features of the Constitution, and the framers were careful to protect the rights of all people by limiting the powers of the national and state governments. As a result, Americans are free to move from place to place; make their own decisions about jobs, religion, and political beliefs; and go to court for justice and protection when they feel these rights have been violated.

What are inalienable rights?

Because the American Revolution was fought to preserve and expand the rights of the individual against the government, America's Founding Fathers boldly proclaimed these rights in the opening of the Declaration of Independence: "We hold these truths to be self-evident, that all men are created equal, that they are endowed by their Creator with certain unalienable Rights, that among these are Life, Liberty, and the pursuit of Happiness." In this document, the authors expressed their belief in certain inalienable, God-given rights that all people are inherently created with and entitled to enjoy simply because they are human beings, including the rights to life, liberty, and the pursuit of happiness. These rights are not destroyed when civil society is created, and neither society nor government can remove or "alienate" them. Most democratic societies agree that inalienable rights include freedom of speech and expression, freedom of religion and conscience, freedom of assembly, and the right to equal protection before the law. Since these rights exist independently of government, they cannot be taken away by legislation nor are they subject to the whim of an electoral majority.

THE BILL OF RIGHTS

What is the Bill of Rights?

The Bill of Rights—collectively, the first ten amendments to the U.S. Constitution—guarantees rights and liberties to the American people. These amendments were proposed by Congress on September 25, 1789, and ratified as a block by three-fourths (eleven) of the states on December 15, 1791, thereby officially becoming part of the Constitution. The first eight amendments outline substantive and procedural individual rights guaranteed to all people, while the Ninth and Tenth Amendments are general rules of interpretation of the relations among the people, the state governments, and the federal government. Although the Bill of Rights was originally written to restrict the national government, the Supreme Court has nationalized the Bill of Rights by upholding that most of the provisions also apply to the states, as outlined by the Fourteenth Amendment's Due Process Clause.

How does the Bill of Rights protect individual liberties?

The Bill of Rights limits the ability of government to intrude upon certain individual liberties, guaranteeing freedom of speech, press, assembly, and religion to all people. Nearly two-thirds of the Bill of Rights was written to safeguard the rights of those suspected or accused of crimes, providing for due process of law, fair trials, freedom from self-incrimination and from cruel and unusual punishment, and protection against double jeopardy: being tried more than once for the same crime. In short, the Bill of Rights places certain liberties beyond the reach of those in power on the premise that depriving citizens of fundamental rights diminishes their civil standing and ultimately their humanity. Since the adoption of the Bill of Rights, only seventeen additional amendments have been added to the Constitution. While a number of these amendments revised how the federal government is structured and operates, many followed precedent established by the Bill of Rights and expanded individual rights and freedoms.

How do the Ninth and Tenth Amendments relate to individual rights?

The Ninth and Tenth Amendments contain very broad statements of constitutional authority. The Ninth Amendment declares that the listing of individual rights is not meant to be comprehensive and that the people have other rights not specifically mentioned in the Constitution. The Tenth Amendment provides that powers not delegated by the Constitution to the federal government or withheld by it from the states are reserved to the states or the people.

Why was the Bill of Rights written?

Although the Constitution, as it was originally written, contained a number of important guarantees in Articles I and III, it did not include a general list of the people's rights. One explanation for this omission is that the framers assumed that the powers of the newly created national government were so carefully limited that individual rights really required no additional protections. Nevertheless, the states contested this omission so strongly that several refused to ratify the Constitution until the Continental Congress promised that a Bill of Rights would be added.

One of the loudest proponents of a bill of rights was George Mason (1725–1792), the author of the Declaration of Rights of Virginia. As a delegate to the Constitutional Convention, Mason refused to sign

The stubborn resolve of Virginia delegate to the Constitutional Convention, George Mason, is a big reason we have a Bill of Rights today. He refused to ratify the Constitution without it.

the Constitution, and his opposition almost blocked ratification by Virginia. Because of similar sentiment in Massachusetts, that state made its ratification conditional on specific guarantees of individual rights. By the time the first Congress convened, agreement to adopt such amendments was nearly unanimous, and the Congress began to draft the Bill of Rights.

How are a person's individual rights relative?

While the Constitution guarantees a number of rights, people can only exercise those rights as long as they do not infringe on the rights of others. For example, while everyone in the United States enjoys the right to free speech, no one has absolute freedom of speech. A person can be convicted under the law for using obscene language or for using words in a manner that cause another person to commit a crime, as seen in the example of rioting. Recently, the relativity of individual rights was exemplified in *Apollo Media Corporation v. United States* (1999), where the U.S. Supreme Court upheld a federal law that makes it illegal for anyone to send obscene email over the Internet.

Does the Bill of Rights apply to all people?

Most constitutional rights are extended to all the people of the United States. The Supreme Court has oftentimes determined that the word "persons," as it appears in the Constitution, includes both aliens, or foreign-born residents, and citizens. However, certain rights, such as the right to travel freely, as guaranteed by the two Privileges and Immunities Clauses (found in Article IV and the Fourteenth Amendment), are only guaranteed to citizens.

Does the Bill of Rights limit only the national government?

No. One of the most far-reaching amendments to the Constitution is the Fourteenth Amendment, ratified in 1868, which establishes a simple definition of citizenship and guarantees equal treatment to all persons under the law. With the words "No State shall … deprive any person of life, liberty, or property, without due process of law," in essence the Fourteenth Amendment requires the states to abide by the protections of the Bill of Rights, thereby applying those rights to more than just the national government. It wasn't until the 1960s, however, that most of the civil liberties outlined in the Bill of Rights were applied to the states.

How and when did the Supreme Court nationalize the Bill of Rights?

While the Supreme Court ruled in 1833 that the Bill of Rights limited only the national government, the Court slowly expanded Bill of Rights protections to the states. For example, in 1897, the Court used the Fourteenth Amendment to prohibit states from taking private property for public use without just compensation to the original owner. It wasn't until 1925, in *Gitlow v. New York,* that the Supreme Court applied the Bill of Rights to states in protecting individual liberties by ruling that freedom of speech is protected at the state level.

However, despite these milestones, as late as 1937 the Court held that only certain parts of the Bill of Rights applied to the states. Starting in 1961, most of the important provisions of the Bill of Rights were incorporated one by one into the Fourteenth Amendment and legally mandated for the states. During this decade, for example, the Supreme Court applied the Fourteenth Amendment to several important cases, including: *Robinson v. California* (1962), applying the Eighth Amendment's right against cruel and unusual punishment to the state of California; *Klopfer v. North Carolina* (1967), applying the Sixth Amendment's right to a speedy trial to the state of North Carolina; and *Duncan v. Louisiana* (1968), applying the Sixth Amendment's right to a trial by jury to the state of Louisiana. Today, the Fourteenth Amendment imposes all the Bill of Rights provisions on the states, except those of the Second, Third, Seventh, and Tenth Amendments and the grand jury requirements of the Fifth Amendment.

Could the Supreme Court reverse the nationalization of the Bill of Rights?

In theory, yes. Some scholars are quick to point out that, since none of the decisions made in the 1960s that nationalized most of the Bill of Rights clauses have actually been reversed, a reversal is unlikely. However, other scholars disagree, maintaining that, because in the 1980s and 1990s, the Supreme Court gave narrower and more restrictive interpretations of some of its earlier decisions, a reversal may be possible. Specifically, they cite the narrowing of abortion rights, noting *Webster v. Reproductive Health Services* (1989), in which the Court narrowly ruled that restrictions on the use of public medical facilities for abortion are constitutional, and *Planned Parenthood v. Casey* (1992), which narrowed the scope of the landmark *Roe v. Wade* (1973) decision, which upheld a woman's right to privacy through her right to have an abortion. In the 1990s, state power over capital punishment was extended when the Supreme Court severely limited repeated *habeas corpus* petitions from state prisoners, which would have required that they be brought before a judge to decide the legality of their detention.

The terms "substantive restraints" and "procedural restraints" are both used in the Bill of Rights. What's the difference?

Substantive restraints limit what the government has the power to do, such as restricting freedom of speech, religion, or the press. Procedural restraints limit how the government can act and are usually grouped under the general category of due process of law. For example, citizens are guaranteed due process of law when they are charged with a crime, and the government may not infringe upon this basic civil liberty.

Have Americans' basic civil liberties changed over the years?

No. Since the addition of the Bill of Rights, no amendments have been added to the Constitution to alter the civil liberties guaranteed by these first ten. After the Supreme Court ruled in *Texas v. Johnson* (1989) that flag burning was an expression of free speech and overturned the conviction of Gregory Johnson (1956–), who was arrested for torching the American flag in 1984, many citizens rallied to add a constitutional amendment that would ban flag burning. This proposal resurfaced in the 1990s, although reluctance to alter the

The 1989 *Texas v. Johnson* case involved free speech rights. Gregory Johnson (at right with his lawyer) burned an American flag in violation of a Texas flag desecration law. The U.S. Supreme Court ruled 5–4 in favor of Johnson's rights.

First Amendment eventually won out, and no amendment has been added to date. The Christian Coalition's 1995 Contract with the American Family set out to alter many civil liberties, including by passing legislation that would place limits on second-trimester abortions and adopting the Religious Equality Amendment to allow prayer in public schools. Although no amendment has been passed, state legislation to restore school prayer has been initiated in Pennsylvania, South Carolina, and Florida, and certain legislators support an amendment that would permit students to pray aloud in schools, marking a growing trend toward increasing religious expression in school.

THE FIRST AMENDMENT: FREEDOM OF RELIGION, SPEECH, PRESS, ASSEMBLY, AND PETITION

What is freedom of religion?

Guaranteed by the First Amendment, freedom of religion—or, more broadly, freedom of conscience—means that no person should be required to profess any religion or other belief against his or her desires. Additionally, because a person's religious faith is a profoundly personal matter, no one should be penalized in any way because he or she chooses one religion over another or chooses no religion at all. With nine out of ten Americans expressing some religious preference and approximately 70 percent belonging to religious congregations, America has long been a country made up of a variety of religious faiths and one that upholds religious tolerance. The First Amendment forbids Congress to set up or in any way provide for an established church. In addition, Congress may not pass laws limiting worship, speech, or the press or preventing people from meeting peacefully.

What is the Establishment Clause?

The First Amendment phrase "Congress shall make no law respecting an establishment of religion" is referred to as the Establishment Clause. Simply put, it prohibits the national government from establishing a national religion. However, the Establishment Clause does not prevent government from meeting the needs of religious groups, although the Supreme Court has often interpreted the clause to forbid government endorsement of or aid for religious doctrines.

What is the Free Exercise Clause?

The second clause of the First Amendment, "or prohibiting the free exercise thereof," known as the Free Exercise Clause, prohibits the national government from interfering with an American's rights to practice his or her religion.

What does the phrase "separation of church and state" mean?

Prescribed by the First Amendment, separation of church and state provides in part that "Congress shall make no law respecting an establishment of religion, or prohibiting the free exercise thereof...." Thomas Jefferson declared that this clause in essence creates

Among other things, the separation of church and state principle means that a nativity creche such as this one cannot be displayed on the grounds of a public building, such as a city hall or public school.

a "wall of separation" between church and state or between the government and any religious activity. Although there are situations where this wall has been lowered—for example, each session of Congress opens with prayer—the doctrine of the separation of church and state has been applied stringently by the Supreme Court to most types of state-supported religious activity. As a result of the separation of church and state, students in public schools may not pray aloud publicly as part of the school day, they may not study the Bible as a sacred text, and they may not celebrate religious holidays. Furthermore, cities may not display a Christmas crèche on certain public property, such as a courthouse, and students may not receive federal grants or loans specifically to attend religious elementary or secondary schools.

What is the Lemon test?

Although the Supreme Court has historically debated how to interpret the Establishment Clause and measure the constitutionality of state laws that appear to further religion, the Supreme Court decision *Lemon v. Kurtzman* (1971) established a test by which to measure the constitutionality of these types of laws. Thus, in what is commonly referred to as the Lemon test, a law or practice dealing with church/state issues must: (1) have a secular legislative purpose; (2) have a primary effect that neither advances nor inhibits religion; and (3) not involve an excessive government entanglement with religion. In *Lemon v. Kurtzman,* state funding of parochial schoolteachers' salaries failed this test and is therefore prohibited by the Constitution. A decade later, the Lemon test was applied to a Kentucky law that required the posting of the Ten Commandments in public school classrooms and invalidated that law because the Court ruled the posting had no "secular legislative purpose." Since this time, the Supreme Court has ruled more flexibly where issues of church and state are concerned as long as the hot button—school prayer—has not been pushed. Consistently, the Court has ruled for a strict separation of church and state with regard to school prayer.

Why is there so much controversy over school prayer?

Perhaps no aspect of the church/state controversy generates more discussion than the subject of prayer in public schools, primarily because this topic cuts right to the core of what Americans think religious freedom is. The First Amendment protects both advocates and critics of school prayer by mandating government neutrality between religious belief and nonbelief. At the heart of the school prayer debate is the intense conflict between the Establishment Clause and the Free Exercise Clause. The Supreme Court has ruled that it is unconstitutional for the government—through the educators who run public schools—to lead children in prayer or force them to pray a certain way. However, all children have the right to pray voluntarily before, during, or after school, and students have the right to discuss their religious views with their peers so long as this is not disruptive. Because the Establishment Clause does not apply to purely private speech, students have the right to read their Bibles or other scriptures, say grace before meals, and pray before tests.

Despite these rights, some proponents of school prayer call for increased religious freedom in the school and advocate amending the Constitution so that the government would legally sponsor the activity of prayer. A majority of the American public say they support such an amendment, and Republican presidential candidates have generally favored adopting such an amendment. In its 1990 decision *Board of Education v. Mergens,* the Supreme Court moderated the ban on prayer in school by saying that students may form Bible reading and school prayer clubs as long as they are not exclusive, since banning religious groups while allowing secular ones to meet impedes students' right to free exercise of religion as guaranteed by the First Amendment. However, despite these and other examples of leniency, the Supreme Court ruled in *Lee v. Weisman* (1992) that even nonsectarian prayer at public school graduation ceremonies violated the Establishment Clause of the Constitution, both because of its inevitably coercive effect on students and because it conveyed a message of government endorsement of religion. Because of varying Supreme Court decisions, abundant arguments on both sides, and the time-consuming and often difficult process of signing an amendment into law, it's likely the school prayer controversy will remain alive for some time to come.

What role do school vouchers play in the freedom of religion debate?

School voucher programs, which are used in several states and give parents of school-aged children yearly stipends to pay for their children's tuition at the school of their choosing, including private religious schools, have not been deemed either constitutional or unconstitutional by the Supreme Court. Although proponents of school voucher programs maintain that the main purpose of vouchers is educational, not religious, and that vouchers are in accordance with the Free Exercise of Religion Clause because they allow families to choose the religious environment in which their children will be raised, others feel differently. The critics of school vouchers argue that they violate the Establishment Clause because they allow parents to use state-provided stipends to pay for religious education, in essence mandating government financial support of religious institutions, thus breaching the wall of separation between church and state.

How are issues of religion and politics related?

The most controversial aspect of religion in the United States today is probably its role in politics. In recent decades, some Americans have come to believe that separation of church and state has been interpreted in ways hostile to religion. Religious conservatives and fundamentalists have joined forces to become a powerful political movement known as the Christian Right. Their goals include overturning, by law or constitutional amendment, Supreme Court decisions allowing abortion and banning prayer in public schools. Ralph Reed, former executive director of the Christian Coalition, estimates that one-third of the delegates to the 1996 Republican Convention were members of this or similar conservative Christian groups, an indication of the increased involvement of religion in politics.

What does "freedom of speech" mean?

"Congress shall make no law ... abridging the freedom of speech, or of the press." Freedom of speech and expression is the lifeblood of any democracy. Actions such as debating and voting, assembling and protesting, and worshipping rely on the unrestricted flow of speech and information. In contrast to authoritarian states, democratic governments do not control, dictate, or judge the content of written and verbal speech, and the First Amendment thus guarantees this basic civil liberty. A democratic nation depends upon a literate, knowledgeable citizenry whose access to the broadest possible range of information enables it to participate as fully as possible in the public life of society, and democracy can only thrive when it is supported by citizens who enjoy a free flow of ideas and opinions.

What are the limits on free speech?

Although free speech is guaranteed by the First Amendment, not all speech is free from government control. Specifically, three types of speech—commercial speech, libel and slander, and obscenity—are not protected under the First Amendment and may be regulated. Commercial speech includes advertising or other speech for business purposes, including print, radio, and television advertising. Libel is a false statement made about someone in print, while slander involves the spoken use of malicious words; both have the intent of injuring a person's character or reputation. Obscenity includes publicly offensive language or images of no social value. Whether pornography is considered "obscene" depends on whether it is deemed to have some artistic or literary value. According to the Supreme Court's 1942 decision *Chaplinsky v. New Hampshire,* obscenity, lewdness, libel, and "fighting words" are not protected because "such expressions are no essential part of any exposition of ideas."

What is meant by "prior restraint"?

Freedom of speech has its origins in the early colonial period of American history, when speech and press were governed by the doctrine of prior restraint, which maintained that the government could not censor written materials before they were published. This doctrine still holds today, and legally, people have the right to publish material of their choosing without being required to submit the material beforehand to a government censor. Furthermore, the government cannot block publication of materials, as upheld by the Supreme Court in the famous *Pentagon Papers* case. This 1971 ruling maintained that the U.S. government could not block

Free speech does not include malicious speech or written words deliberately intended to hurt someone. That is why, for example, online bullying can lead to criminal prosecution.

the publication of Defense Department documents illegally given to the *New York Times* by anti-Vietnam War activists.

What is strict judicial scrutiny?

The Supreme Court has adhered to the Constitution's underlying premise that certain rights are essential to individual liberty in American society by deeming them worthy of strict judicial scrutiny. These include the liberties found in the Bill of Rights, specifically the First Amendment. Thus, when a case comes before the Supreme Court that deals with civil liberties issues, the Court assesses that case in terms of its "real and appreciable impact on, or a significant interference with the exercise of the fundamental right" and applies the strict scrutiny doctrine, meaning it gives a close or rigid reading and interpretation of the law.

How does the phrase "clear and present danger" relate to freedom of speech?

The phrase arose out of the Supreme Court case *Schenck v. United States* (1919), in which the Court was asked to review a World War I soldier's conviction for espionage after he printed and mailed antiwar leaflets to draft-aged men. In that decision the Court upheld the clear and present danger doctrine, which states that people should have complete freedom of speech unless their language presents a "clear and present danger" to the nation or brings about "evils that Congress has a right to prevent." Although the Court upheld Schenck's conviction, it marked the first time the Court had limited the regulation of speech with a definite standard.

How does the popular phrase "them's fightin' words" relate to freedom of speech?

In *Chaplinsky v. New Hampshire* (1942), the Supreme Court utilized the fighting words doctrine to maintain that some words constitute violent acts. In that case, they upheld the conviction of a Jehovah's Witness because he had used words against a police officer that were considered threatening and "by their very utterance inflict injury or intend

Is a symbol "speech"?

In addition to the protection guaranteed to pure, spoken speech, the Supreme Court has generally extended the First Amendment to cover other means of expression called symbolic speech, including symbols, logos, and signs, as well as to activities such as picketing, sit-ins, and demonstrations. Although the Court has historically been sympathetic to symbolic speech—as in instances of flag desecration and the wearing of symbols such as armbands to protest the Vietnam War, as seen in the historic *Tinker v. Des Moines* ruling of 1969—it has not given blanket First Amendment coverage to symbolic speech. Thus, what some have maintained is symbolic speech, such as burning draft cards, hasn't held up under Supreme Court scrutiny.

to incite an immediate breach of the peace." Prior to this decision, the Court had protected most speech under the clear and present danger doctrine.

What is meant by the term "speech plus"?

The communication of political, social, and other views is not limited to one-on-one, direct speech, web pages, and newspaper editorials but often extends into the area of "speech plus," which includes picketing and marching, distributing leaflets and pamphlets, addressing public audiences, soliciting door to door, and conducting many forms of sit-ins. However, because all of these means of expression involve action rather than mere speech, they are much more subject to regulation and restriction by the government than straightforward speech. While the First Amendment protects some forms of speech plus, the Supreme Court does not extend that coverage to all.

What is confidentiality?

Many federal courts have rejected the news media's assertion of their right to confidentiality, that is, their right to refuse to testify in court to reveal their sources and other confidential information. In fact, the Supreme Court ruled in *Branzenburg v. Hayes* (1972) that reporters, like other citizens, must "respond to relevant questions put to them in the course of a valid grand jury investigation or criminal trial." Despite this ruling, approximately thirty states have passed "shield laws," giving news journalists some protection against disclosing their sources in those states.

What are speech codes?

Meant to promote what is sometimes called "politically correct" speech, speech codes are those speech impositions adopted by universities and colleges that have attempted to ban what they consider to be offensive speech—usually racial epithets and comments regarding sexual orientation. Since 1989, more than two hundred colleges and universities across the United States have adopted speech codes that prohibit racial comments directed at minorities. In recent years the American Civil Liberties Union (ACLU), which maintains that speech codes violate the First Amendment's guarantee of free speech, has been active in defending students accused of violating university speech codes and continually and aggressively seeks the dismantling of such codes.

How is saluting the flag related to freedom of speech?

In the twentieth century, the relationship between church and state evolved into a conflict between civic duty and individual conscience, as seen in a number of Supreme Court rulings. In *West Virginia State Board of Education v. Barnette* (1943), certain members of the Jehovah's Witness religion refused to salute the American flag during the school day, as commanded by state law. Because their religion forbade such pledges of loyalty, the Jehovah's Witnesses argued they were being forced to violate their consciences. The justices determined that saluting the flag was a symbol of speech, which the state could not force its residents to perform. In 1985 it upheld its decision that burning the American flag is a form of symbolic protected speech in *Texas v. Johnson* by overturning the conviction of Gregory Johnson, who had been found guilty of setting fire to an American flag during the 1984 Republican National Convention.

How is the banning of books in schools related to freedom of speech?

Because banning books involves the restriction and/or censorship of materials by an individual or group that feels the books' opinions are unorthodox or unpopular, it cuts to the heart of freedom of expression as guaranteed by the First Amendment. Challenges to books in schools or libraries are often motivated by a desire to protect children from "inappropriate" sexual content or "offensive" language; however, censorship of constitutionally protected

Because saluting the American flag is legally considered a form of free speech, the Supreme Court ruled that a person could not be forced to do so.

speech by librarians or school officials, even if for a child's protection, violates the First Amendment. According to Herbert N. Foerstel's *Banned in the U.S.A.* and other sources, frequently challenged books of the 2000s included *Of Mice and Men* by John Steinbeck, *The Catcher in the Rye* by J. D. Salinger, *I Know Why the Caged Bird Sings* by Maya Angelou, *Lord of the Flies* by William Golding, *Slaughterhouse-Five* by Kurt Vonnegut, and *The Color Purple* by Alice Walker.

How do freedom of speech and freedom of the press relate?

Of all the liberties listed in the Bill of Rights, scholars and civil libertarians maintain that there is a "trio of rights" that are so closely related they are often discussed together as one: freedom of speech, freedom of the press, and freedom of assembly. In a democratic society, if free speech is to have an effect, it must be disseminated through a free media. An audience must also have the freedom to gather to listen to a speaker who is communicating his or her ideas in order for a free exchange of thought and information to be possible. Because democracy involves public debate and open decision making, the communication of ideas, opinions, and information is essential, both through the spoken and printed word. Newspapers, magazines, radio, and television serve as both forums for debate and sources of information on which decisions can be based.

What are the limits on a free press?

Under the First Amendment, the press—which is also referred to as mass media and includes all print and electronic media—is protected, although different constitutional rules apply to each kind of media. Besides issues of copyright infringement and libel, the print media are for the most part unregulated. The electronic media—radio, television, and the Internet—are subject to limited regulation based on the Federal Communications Act of 1934, administered by the Federal Communications Commission (FCC). Because radio and television use public airwaves to broadcast their programs, they must do so with the public's permission and thus have a license to broadcast that is subject to FCC renewal. While the FCC cannot censor program content, it can prohibit the use of indecent language. In general, the Supreme Court has given cable programming broader First Amendment freedom than it has traditional television.

Can obscene films be banned under the First Amendment?

Yes. Although the Supreme Court has determined that liberty of expression through motion pictures is guaranteed by the First and Fourteenth Amendments, state or local governments are within their constitutional rights to ban an obscene film (as states like Massachusetts and Maryland have in times past) but only under a law that mandates a judicial hearing where the government must prove obscenity. Today, local review boards are rare, having been replaced with a rating system created by the movie industry that most viewers respect.

How does the Internet factor into the discussion of free speech?

Internet regulation—including communications that contain indecent words or pictures that can easily be accessed by minors and child pornography sites—first became a major concern during the Clinton Administration, leading to the passage of the 1996 Communications Decency Act. In a landmark 1997 decision, the Supreme Court ruled that the Communications Decency Act violated the First Amendment's guarantee of freedom of speech, deeming the Internet a unique medium entitled to the highest protection under the Constitution's free speech protections. The ruling in effect gave the Internet the same free speech protection as print, making it the first electronic medium to enjoy this privilege, primarily because of its unique construction, including low barriers to access, abundance of sites, and the variety of perspectives and opinions disseminated.

Is rap music protected under freedom of speech?

Yes. Although rap groups and other performers of popular music came under increased scrutiny in the 1990s and 2000s by

Even if some may find the lyrics offensive, rap music (and other forms of such entertainment) is protected under the law as a form of free speech.

concerned parent groups and child advocates such as Tipper Gore, wife of former vice president Al Gore and author of *Raising PG Kids in an X-Rated Society,* rap artists have cited First Amendment protection when called on to defend their controversial lyrics, considered by some to be degrading and violent. Women's groups and even police departments have objected to what is known as "gangsta rap" for its sexually explicit and anarchistic lyrics; their arguments, however, consistently lose out to these expressive artists and their music labels, who maintain that their viewpoint is unique and protected by the free speech provisions of the Constitution.

What is freedom of assembly?

The corollary to freedom of speech is the right of the people to assemble and peacefully demand that the government hear their grievances. Without this right to gather and be heard, freedom of speech would be devalued. For this reason, freedom of speech is considered closely linked to, if not inseparable from, the right to gather, protest, and demand change. Democratic governments can legitimately regulate the time and place of political rallies and marches to maintain the peace, but they cannot use that authority to suppress protest or to prevent groups from making their voices heard.

What are time, place, and manner regulations?

According to several Supreme Court rulings, the government can make and enforce reasonable, precisely defined, and fairly administered laws regarding the time, place, and manner of public assemblies, including, for example, city ordinances that prohibit making noise or causing disturbances near schools or state laws that forbid parades near courthouses when they are intended to influence court proceedings. Because these laws must also be neutral in content, meaning they cannot regulate assemblies based on what might be said in that location, the Supreme Court has been careful in its review of ordinances that are vague or attempt to pinpoint a particular group of people.

What are people's rights in relation to demonstrations on public property?

Although it is within a person's constitutional rights to freely assemble and petition in public, the Supreme Court has often upheld laws that, in order to avoid unnecessary violence and conflict, require advance notice and permits for demonstrations in public places. Public forums include streets, sidewalks, parks, and other public places where people naturally assemble. Other kinds of public property, such as rooms in a city hall or classrooms in public schools used for after-hours activities, are known as limited public forums and thus are available only for limited assembly and speech. In the 1990s, the most controversial demonstrations were those held by anti-abortion groups such as Operation Rescue. Although these groups have the right to assemble outside of abortion clinics, in 1994 the Supreme Court ruled that it was well within the domain of a Florida judge—whose order drew a thirty-six-foot neutral zone around the clinic—to direct protesters not to block access to abortion clinics in that state. Congress responded by passing the Freedom of Access to Clinic Entrances Act later that year, which makes it a federal offense to threaten or interfere with anyone providing or receiving abortions and allows abortion clinic employees or patients to sue for damages and seek federal injunctions against violators.

Can public schools ban political protests?

Yes. The Supreme Court determined that, although public facilities like libraries, schools, and government offices are open to the public, they are not public forums. Schools, for example, have the right to exclude those who engage in activities other than those for which the school was created. Students, parents, and visitors have no right to interfere with educational programs or occupy facilities in order to further a political goal or stage a political protest. Even if the actions are peaceful, they occur on what the Court has called nonpublic property and are thus not constitutionally protected.

What is freedom of association?

The constitutional guarantee of freedom of association is found in the right to assemble and petition, meaning that a person has the right to freely associate with others to promote political or social issues. Although it is not explicitly referred to in the Constitution, the Supreme Court deemed freedom of association one of the guarantees of free expression in its 1958 ruling *National Association for the Advancement of Colored People v. Alabama* by saying, "Freedom to engage in association for the advancement of beliefs and ideas is an inseparable aspect of 'liberty' assured by the Due Process Clause of the Fourteenth Amendment, which embraces freedom of speech." Freedom of association applies to state and congressional regulation of the amount of money candidates and political parties can raise and spend for their interests. Although the Court ruled that there are limits on the amount of money people may contribute to candidates, it struck down limits on the amounts people may contribute to associations created to support or oppose ballot measures. Furthermore, the government cannot set limits on the amounts that people, including candidates, spend on politics—as seen with presidential candidates Ross Perot in 1992, Steve Forbes in 1996, and Donald Trump in 2016 as well as New York City mayor Michael Bloomberg in 2001, all of whom used their personal fortunes to finance their candidacies.

THE SECOND, FOURTH, FIFTH, SIXTH, AND EIGHTH AMENDMENTS: FROM THE RIGHT TO BEAR ARMS TO THE RIGHTS OF THE CRIMINALLY ACCUSED

What is the right to bear arms?

The Second Amendment was originally adopted so that Congress could not disarm a state militia and thus prohibits only the national government from limiting the right to carry weapons. At its heart was the idea of preserving the "citizen-soldier"; however, it does not guarantee a citizen's right to keep and bear arms free from government restriction. Because the Supreme Court has never found the Second Amendment to be within the meaning of the Fourteenth Amendment's Due Process Clause, each state has the authority to limit its citizens' rights to keep and bear arms.

Is the right to bear arms restricted in any way?

Yes. Each state imposes its own limits on its citizens' rights to keep and bear arms. While the Brady Law imposes a seventy-two-hour waiting period before gun purchases, many states have adopted longer waiting periods, and some states have banned so-called Saturday night specials, inexpensive guns that can be easily concealed. States have also implemented laws that bar the possession of handguns by those under eighteen years of age; require adults to use a gun-locking device or store guns in a place that is not accessible to minors; and require permits to purchase and carry firearms, firearm registration, and licensing by owners. Permit, registration, and licensing laws specify the types of guns these laws apply to—for example, rifles and shotguns versus handguns. California, a gun control-conscious state, enacted a one-handgun-per-month law and a stricter assault weapons ban. Maryland, which limits the carrying of concealed weapons, has a one-handgun-per-month law and a strong juvenile possession law and enforces its child access prevention law. In 1999, Connecticut adopted a groundbreaking law that gives law enforcement and the courts the authority, under limited conditions, to re-

While all Americans still have a right to bear arms, the Constitution allows states to impose some restrictions. For example, California bans some types of assault rifles.

move guns from the homes of those who are found to pose a significant threat to the community. States with more permissive gun control laws include Kentucky, Louisiana, Maine, Montana, and Wyoming.

Why is the issue of gun control so controversial?

As violence and murder rates escalated in America throughout the 1980s and 1990s, the issue of gun control provoked much heated debate. After the attempted assassination of President Ronald Reagan in 1981, gun control legislation was at the forefront of Congress's agenda, but it wouldn't be until 1994—with the passage of the Brady Handgun Violence Prevention Act, or Brady Law, which mandates a seventy-two-hour waiting period for the purchase of handguns, and the Violent Crime Control and Law Enforcement Act, which bans the manufacture, sale, and possession of nineteen kinds of semiautomatic assault weapons—that any substantial gun control laws would take effect. In opposition to these laws, the National Rifle Association (NRA) and other groups maintain that the Second Amendment forbids the federal government to obstruct the right to bear arms and that laws that attempt to do so are therefore unconstitutional.

A central question in the gun control debate is whether or not there is an individual right to keep and bear arms under the Second Amendment or whether the amendment guarantees only the right of individual states to have their own militias, making it a community right. Groups like the NRA view the Second Amendment as recognizing a right to be armed for individual as well as community protection and the right of the states to have militias. These groups also maintain that regulation should stay where it belongs, in the hands of the states. Because the Supreme Court has ruled on only a handful of cases regarding the Second Amendment, and because the wording of the Second Amendment is vague and subject to interpretation, it is unlikely that the gun control debate will be settled anytime soon.

What does the Fifth Amendment allow for?

The Fifth Amendment covers a lot of ground. According to this amendment, a capital crime is punishable by death, while an infamous (serious) crime is punishable by death or imprisonment. This amendment guarantees that no one has to stand trial for such a federal crime unless indicted by a grand jury. Furthermore, a person cannot be put in double jeopardy, or tried twice, for the same offense by the same government. The amendment also guarantees that a person cannot be forced to testify against him- or herself and forbids the government to take a person's property for public use without fair payment. Finally, this amendment deals with the due process of law, for which it is probably best known.

What does "due process of law" mean?

The statement that no person shall "be deprived of life, liberty, or property without due process of law" expresses one of the most important tenets of the Constitution. These words of the Fifth Amendment uphold the idea that a person's life, liberty, and property are not subject to the uncontrolled power of the government but rather can be limited only through a due course of legal action. This concept has its roots in the Magna Carta, a thirteenth-century British charter that provided that the king could not imprison or harm a person "except by the lawful judgment of his peers or by the law of the land." The Fourth, Fifth, Sixth, and Eighth Amendments provide a number of procedural guarantees for those accused of crimes, and those guarantees are often called due process rights. Language found in the Fifth Amendment is repeated in the Fourteenth Amendment as restrictions on the power of the states.

However, due process is a vague clause, and the Supreme Court has applied it to widely different cases. Until the mid-1900s, the court used the Due Process Clause to strike down laws that prevented people from using their property as they wished; for instance, in *Dred Scott v. Sandford* (1857), the Court overturned the Missouri Compromise, which regulated the extension of slavery in the U.S. territories. The Court upheld that the compromise unjustly prevented slave owners from taking slaves—their property—into the territories. Today, the courts use the due process rule to strike down laws that interfere with a person's civil liberties.

How do the Fourth, Fifth, Sixth, and Eighth Amendments provide for due process of law?

Taken together, these amendments provide for due process of law by protecting those accused of a crime. The Fourth Amendment says that federal law enforcement officials may not search people or their homes without a search warrant that describes the location to be searched and/or the items to be removed. The Fifth Amendment safeguards the rights of people accused of crimes that may result in the death penalty. The Sixth Amendment guarantees those who are arrested a speedy, public trial by jury. And the Eighth Amendment prohibits courts from setting excessive bail and fines and forbids cruel and unusual punishment.

What is a writ of *habeas corpus*?

From the Latin *habeas corpus,* meaning "you should have the body," a writ of *habeas corpus*, also referred to as a writ of liberty, was written into Article I, Section 9 of the Constitution to prevent unjust arrests and imprisonments. As a court order that is directed to an officer holding a prisoner, it mandates that the prisoner be brought before the court and that the officer show cause why the prisoner should not be released. The writ challenges only whether a prisoner has been accorded due process of law, not whether he or she is guilty or innocent. Today, the most common usage of the writ is to appeal state criminal convictions to the federal courts in cases where the petitioner believes his or her constitutional rights were violated by state judicial procedure.

Because the colonists regarded this writ as fundamental to their rights, and the wrongful refusal to issue it was one of their grievances leading up to the American Revolution, the framers of the Constitution provided that "the privilege of the Writ of Habeas Corpus shall not be suspended, unless when, in cases of rebellion or invasion,

Habeus corpus is a Latin term that, when it comes to the law, means that any accused criminal has to be brought before a court so that they may receive due process.

the public safety may require it." Although President Lincoln suspended *habeas corpus* at the beginning of the Civil War, since that time the writ has only been suspended once (in Hawaii during World War II), and the Supreme Court ruled that action illegal, based on its decision in 1866 that neither Congress nor the president can legally suspend the writ where there is no actual fighting. While the Supreme Court's liberal decisions regarding prisoners' rights in the 1950s and 1960s encouraged many inmates to file writs challenging their convictions, the late twentieth century witnessed the Court refusing to allow multiple *habeas corpus* filings, primarily from death row.

What is the Takings Clause, and how does it relate to eminent domain?

The Takings Clause of the Fifth Amendment states that private property cannot be taken by the government for public use without just compensation to the property owner. The drafters of the Bill of Rights included a Takings Clause to address outright physical appropriations of private property, such as government expropriation of private land for the construction of roads, since colonial governments often confiscated private property for public projects without paying (or justly paying) its owners. Today, the government uses its right of eminent domain to acquire land for highways, schools, and other public facilities, but constitutionally it must always pay a fair price for its acquisition.

What are the rights of an accused criminal from the time of arrest until the time of trial?

Until suspects are proved guilty of crimes, their individual rights are fully respected under the Constitution. The Fourth Amendment safeguards against illegal search and seizure, and illegally collected evidence cannot be introduced in court. In most cases, law enforcement officers must obtain a court-ordered search warrant based on probable cause before searching property, and arrests cannot be made without probable cause. The Fifth Amendment provides that no person in a criminal case may be compelled to be a witness against him- or herself. As a result, police are required to advise a suspect of his or her right to remain silent and the right to have an attorney present during any questioning. Furthermore, no one may be tried twice for the same crime. The Sixth Amendment allows for the right to a speedy and public trial by an impartial jury of one's peers and the right to counsel. The Eighth Amendment puts a limit on the amount of bail imposed and guards against cruel and unusual punishment. In their totality, the rights outlined in the Bill of Rights are meant to place the burden of proof on the government, rather than on the accused, who is presumed innocent until proven guilty.

What is the right to remain silent?

Because certain seventeenth-century English courts forced confessions of heresy from religious dissenters, the framers of the Bill of Rights were careful to include in the Fifth Amendment the provision that a person has the right to remain silent and shall not be compelled to testify against him- or herself in a criminal prosecution. Although the provision against self-incrimination applies to criminal prosecutions, it has also been interpreted to protect anyone questioned by a government agency, including a congressional committee.

What does it mean to Mirandize someone?

In *Miranda v. Arizona* (1966), the Supreme Court declared that no federal or state conviction could stand in court based on evidence obtained by the police during interrogation unless the suspects have been (1) notified that they are free to remain silent; (2) told that what they say may be used against them in court; (3) told that they have the right to have attorneys present at the time of questioning; (4) told that attorneys will be provided for them in the event that they cannot afford to hire their own; and (5) allowed to terminate any stage of a police interrogation. Known as the Miranda warning, this announcement is read to a suspect by a police officer before questioning. If a police officer fails to read a suspect his or her Miranda rights, charges against the suspect can be dropped

Because of the 1966 *Miranda v. Arizona* decision, people who are arrested by the police must be informed of their rights, including the right to an attorney and to remain silent.

and convictions reversed, even if there is enough evidence to establish the suspect's guilt. If a suspect answers questions without an attorney present, then the burden of proof is on the prosecution to demonstrate that the suspect knowingly and willingly gave up his or her right to remain silent and have an attorney present.

Where did the phrase "I take the Fifth" come from?

The phrase comes from the Fifth Amendment's provision that a person cannot be forced to testify against him- or herself. Made familiar to the public through motion-picture screenplays and Court TV, "I take the Fifth" has often been used as a catchall phrase by defendants on trial to avoid answering questions that might incriminate them.

What does the term "double jeopardy" mean?

According to the Fifth Amendment, double jeopardy means that a person cannot be tried twice for the same crime by the same government. However, he or she may be tried a second time if a jury cannot agree on a verdict, if a mistrial is declared for some other reason, or if he or she requests a new trial.

What is a speedy and public trial?

According to the Sixth Amendment, a person accused of a crime must have a prompt, public trial by an open-minded jury. The requirement for a speedy and public trial grew out of the fact that some political trials in England had been delayed for years and then were held in secret. Accused individuals must be informed of the charges against them and must be allowed to meet the witnesses against them face-to-face. Otherwise, innocent persons may be punished if a court allows the testimony of unknown witnesses to be used as evidence. Furthermore, the Sixth Amendment guarantees that individuals on trial can face and cross-examine those who have accused them. Finally, accused persons must have a lawyer to defend them if they want one. If a criminal defendant is unable to afford a lawyer, the Supreme Court has held that one must be appointed by the government to represent the accused individual.

What is the right to counsel?

The Supreme Court decision *Gideon v. Wainwright* (1963) established that all persons accused of serious crimes are constitutionally entitled to legal representation under the Sixth Amendment and that if the accused cannot afford to hire an attorney, the court must assign one. This is known as a person's right to counsel. Most states have established an office of the public defender, an attorney who is responsible for the defense of impoverished criminal suspects.

What is an indictment?

An indictment is a formal complaint that is presented before a grand jury by the prosecutor charging an accused person with one or more crimes.

What is the role of a grand jury?

A grand jury determines whether a person can be tried for a crime. Guaranteed by the Fifth Amendment, the right to a grand jury is meant to protect the accused from unjust prosecutors. In federal cases, a grand jury consists of between sixteen and twenty-three people drawn from the area of the federal district court that it serves. When a case comes before a grand jury, at least twelve jurors must agree that there is enough evidence to return an indictment and allow the case to be heard in court. If the grand jury determines that there is enough evidence to warrant a trial, the accused is then held for prosecution. If there is not enough evidence to warrant a trial, the charges are dropped. Because a grand jury's proceedings are not a trial, the sessions are not publicized, and only the prosecution is present.

What is trial by jury?

The framers of the Constitution considered the right to jury trial so important that in the Sixth Amendment they provided for jury trials in criminal cases. In the Seventh Amendment, they provided for such trials in civil suits where the amount contested exceeds twenty dollars. The amendment applies only to federal courts, but most state constitutions also call for jury trials in civil cases. Not all criminal prosecutions require a jury trial, and the Supreme Court has consistently excluded petty offenses—so called because of their punishment or the nature of the offense—from the right to a trial by jury. In both state and federal courts, an accused person may waive the right to a trial by jury in exchange for a bench trial before a judge.

What are bills of attainder?

A bill of attainder is a legislative act that targets an individual or group for punishment without a trial. According to Article I, Sections 9 and 10 of the Constitution, neither Congress nor the states can pass such laws. While they can pass laws that define a crime and set appropriate penalties, it is unconstitutional for them to decide whether or not a person is guilty of that crime and then impose punishment.

What are *ex post facto* laws?

From the Latin phrase *ex post facto,* meaning "after the fact," these are laws that define a crime or provide for its punishment and are applied to an act committed before the law was passed. According to the Constitution, these laws, which clearly work to the disadvantage of those accused, may not be enacted by either Congress or the states. For example, a law making it a crime to sell narcotics cannot be applied to a person who sold narcotics before the law was passed. However, *ex post facto* laws only apply to criminal law; retroactive civil laws, on the other hand, are not unconstitutional.

What factors have led to increased public cynicism about jury trials?

Although it's hard to cite all the factors that have led to increased public cynicism about jury trials, many commentators have noted that the sensational newspaper and television coverage of trials of the 1990s, coupled with questionable convictions or acquittals for what appear to be obvious crimes, has led the public to be cynical about the jury process overall. Trials criticized for what some perceive as blatant injustice include the 1992 acquittal of Los Angeles police officers after the extended beating, captured on videotape, of Rodney King; the 1990s trials of Lyle and Eric Menendez, who confessed to killing their parents but whose first trials resulted in hung juries that could not come to a consensus about the exact nature of their crime; and the highly debated 1995 acquittal of O. J. Simpson in his criminal trial for the murder of his ex-wife, Nicole Brown Simpson, and Ronald Goldman. Although questions of racial equality and justice were paramount in the Simpson debate, many also criticized jury trial procedures and called for their overhaul.

O. J. Simpson's attorney, the late Johnnie Cochran, was able to get murder charges dismissed. Many Americans thought the trial was a farce, that Simpson was clearly guilty, and that his acquittal was a slap in the face to the justice system.

What is a plea bargain, and how does it relate to the three-strikes law?

In an effort to speed up the criminal justice process, defenders and prosecutors have established the plea bargain, which is an agreement between the prosecution and defense that the accused person will plead guilty to a crime, provided that other charges are dropped and a reduced sentence is recommended to the judge. While the Supreme Court has approved of plea bargaining in general, extensive use of this tactic has been an issue with many politicians who believe that those convicted should serve longer sentences. In response, they proposed the three-strikes law (adapted from the baseball phrase "three strikes and you're out"), which says that, after having been convicted of three felonies, a convict must receive a mandatory life sentence, whether or not a plea bargain has been struck.

The three-strikes concept came to the forefront of national attention in 1994 when California voters approved the law, which also doubles the minimum terms for second-time offenders, and Congress passed its federal version. Currently, twenty-eight states have heavier sentences for repeat offenders: Arizona, Arkansas, California, Colorado, Connecticut, Florida, Georgia, Indiana, Kansas, Louisiana, Maryland, Massachusetts, Montana, Nevada, New Hampshire, New Jersey, New Mexico, North Carolina, North Dakota, Pennsylvania, South Carolina, Tennessee, Texas, Utah, Vermont, Virginia, Washington, and Wisconsin. Massachusetts became the latest state to introduce heavier sentences for repeat offenders when it passed its own version of the law in 2012.

How does the Eighth Amendment relate to capital punishment?

The Eighth Amendment states, "Excessive bail shall not be required, nor excessive fines imposed, nor cruel and unusual punishments inflicted." Simply put, bail, fines, and punishments must be fair and humane. In the case of *Furman v. Georgia* (1972), the Supreme Court ruled that capital punishment, as it was then imposed, violated this amendment. Because it was deemed "arbitrary and capricious" and not applied fairly and uniformly across the states, the Court held that the death penalty was "cruel and unusual punishment" in violation of the Eighth Amendment and the due process guarantees of the Fourteenth Amendment. After that decision, many states adopted new capital punishment laws designed to meet the Supreme Court's objections. The Court has since ruled that the death penalty may be imposed if certain standards are applied to guard against arbitrary results in capital cases.

How many states have the death penalty?

While more than a hundred countries have abolished the death penalty, over the twentieth century the United States increased its rate of executions and the number of crimes punishable by death. Currently, thirty-two states exercise the death penalty. Eighteen states and the District of Columbia have abolished the death penalty.

For which crimes has capital punishment been used?

Under the federal system of the United States, most serious crimes, such as murder, are tried by individual states, not by the federal government. However, the U.S. government and the U.S. military have also employed capital punishment for certain federal offenses, primarily murder or crimes resulting in murder. Since the federal death penalty was first used on June 25, 1790, convictions for piracy, rape, rioting, kidnapping, and spying and espionage have resulted in federal executions. The states reserve the penalty for the most brutal crimes, which are not subject to review by the president, although they can be appealed to the U.S. Supreme Court. Although the states can seek the death penalty for several different serious crimes, such as terrorism, in practice it is only used in cases of first-degree murder.

Do Americans support the death penalty?

A 2016 Gallup Poll found that 60 percent of Americans support the death penalty—down one percentage point from the previous year—while opposition remained at 37 percent, its highest level since the U.S. Supreme Court struck down the death penalty in 1972. However, while most Americans favor the death penalty, many have expressed reservations about whether all prisoners on death row have received fair trials. In 2000 the governor of Illinois, George Ryan, declared a moratorium on further executions in that state in an effort to study why there had been a high number of errors found in recent death penalty cases and to ensure that no innocent person would face the death penalty. In 2002, the Supreme Court ruled that the execution of mentally retarded criminals was unconstitutional, thus limiting the scope of capital punishment.

CIVIL LIBERTIES VS. SECURITY ISSUES

How have civil liberties been threatened throughout U.S. history?

Since the late 1700s, the United States has witnessed actions by Congress or the president that have either restricted civil liberties or led to controversies about those rights. For example, in 1861 President Abraham Lincoln suspended the writ of *habeas corpus* in several states before extending the suspension to all states in 1863, thus denying those accused of crimes the right to be brought before a judge to consider whether the charges were valid; and in 1942 President Franklin D. Roosevelt signed an executive order that resulted in the internment of more than 120,000 Japanese Americans at "war relocation" camps in America during World War II. Although in 1944 the Supreme Court upheld the forced evacuation as a necessary wartime act, the action has been strongly criticized. The twentieth century saw additional threats as well. The Cold War era passage of the 1950 Internal Security Act made it illegal for a member of a "communist-action" organization in the United States to hold any nonelective office, be employed in a defense organization, or apply for or use a passport. The 1978 Foreign Intelligence Surveillance Act allows for electronic eavesdropping and wiretapping when collecting foreign intelligence. And the 1996 Antiterrorism and Effective Death Penalty Act established membership in a terrorist organization as grounds for denying noncitizens entry into the United States and allows federal officers to use wiretapping when investigating immigration offenses.

What are some examples of how civil liberties have been threatened since the September 11, 2001, terrorist attacks on the World Trade Center and the Pentagon?

Historians agree that many threats to civil liberties arise in times of war or threats of terrorism. Most recently, many criticize the USA Patriot Act, which eases search warrant requirements to allow the Federal Bureau of Investigation (FBI) to monitor certain Internet activity and allows the agency to monitor and search any phone line a suspect uses, despite the Fourth Amendment's requirement that a search warrant specifically describe a physical place being searched. Critics say the increased protection from terrorists comes at the cost of privacy, a basic civil

Although known as the Great Emancipator, President Abraham Lincoln did some pretty frightening things during the Civil War that affected civil rights, including suspending the writ of *habeas corpus*.

liberty. The Justice Department's new policy of monitoring communications between terrorist suspects and their lawyers has been sharply criticized primarily because of its limitation on the constitutional right to legal representation. Critics say the policy violates both the Sixth Amendment, which grants a criminal defendant the right "to have the assistance of counsel for his defense," and the Fourth Amendment, which relieves citizens of "unreasonable searches and seizures." In addition, the USA Patriot Act has been criticized by the American Civil Liberties Union (ACLU) because it significantly increases the government's law-enforcement powers while continuing a trend of decreasing the checks and balances that Americans have traditionally relied on to protect individual liberty. Specifically, the act expands the government's ability to conduct secret searches, grants the FBI broad access to sensitive business records about individuals without having to show evidence of a crime, and provides for large-scale investigations of American citizens for "intelligence" purposes.

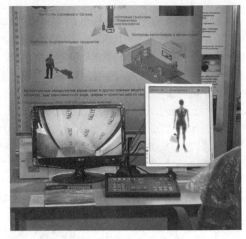

Many Americans have increasing concerns about personal privacy after the passage of the Patriot Act, one of which has been the use of body scanners at airports, which some feel is going too far when it comes to searching people not even accused of a crime.

In fact, in the wake of the October 2001 passage of antiterrorism legislation, many criticized the Bush Administration's detention of hundreds of unnamed suspects associated with the September 11 terrorist attacks without charging them with specific crimes as well as its plans to try suspected terrorists before military tribunals, thus eliminating judicial review and replacing public criminal trials guaranteed by the Sixth Amendment. Furthermore, many constitutional safeguards provided to U.S. criminals would not apply to those being tried: suspects would not be advised that they can remain silent, and evidence would most likely not be challenged because of the circumstances under which it was gathered. Although the Constitution makes provision for certain tribunals, the United States has generally opposed them in other nations because they fail to provide adequate due process.

Finally, the USA Patriot Act and new immigration legislation authorizes U.S. authorities to jail and deport any noncitizen whom the attorney general considers a threat under the new definitions of terrorist groups, allows the deportation of suspicious legal U.S. residents, and broadens the grounds on which foreigners may be denied entry to the United States. Because the tightening immigration policies expand the government's power to detain and expel residents, civil libertarians are concerned that these newfound powers might be used against minorities and other disenfranchised people to compromise their civil liberties.

What has the relationship been between individual liberties and national security since September 11, 2001?

The issue of balancing civil liberties and national security came to the forefront of American discussion when the Bush Administration proposed its antiterrorist legislation. After its passage, many civil libertarians expressed fear that the hasty adoption of sweeping limitations on personal freedom came at a cost that would ultimately reach beyond the Bush Administration. While acknowledging that terrorist activities must be countered in order to maintain national security, they argued that the Antiterrorism Act is ultimately too threatening to civil liberties because it greatly expands the investigative authority of government agencies and the conduct of surveillance and intelligence-gathering organizations. Civil libertarians argued that the administration and Congress could have struck a better balance between national security and civil liberties—for example, modifying statutes perceived as restricting law-enforcement officials to make exceptions only for terrorist investigations and better determining how to share a narrow class of information relating to terrorist activities with the intelligence community.

THE RIGHT TO PRIVACY

What is the right to privacy?

The right to privacy is a person's right to be free of government interference in those areas of personal life that do not affect other citizens. The Supreme Court justice Louis Brandeis defined it as "the right to be let alone." Although the word "privacy" doesn't appear in either the Constitution or the Bill of Rights, nor is it directly addressed in *The Federalist Papers,* the Ninth Amendment allows for this right by stating, "The enumeration in the Constitution, of certain rights, shall not be construed to deny or disparage others retained by the people." In other words, there are some rights that people may retain even though they are not spelled out in the Constitution, and the Supreme Court has held that the right to privacy is one such right.

How is the right to privacy contained in the First, Third, Fourth, Fifth, and Ninth Amendments?

Although not explicitly mentioned in the Bill of Rights, the Supreme Court has found support for a right to privacy in the First, Third, Fourth, Fifth, and Ninth Amendments. Since the late 1950s, the Supreme Court has upheld a series of privacy interests under the First Amendment and Due Process Clause—for example, "associational privacy," "political privacy," and the "right to anonymity in public expression." However, many constitutional scholars acknowledge that it wasn't until the Supreme Court case *Griswold v. Connecticut* (1965), when a statute prohibiting the use of contraceptives was struck down as an infringement of the right to marital privacy, that privacy was defined by the Court. In this landmark case, the Court found a "zone of privacy" to be embedded in the Constitution. The Court maintained that the First Amendment's right of association, the Third Amendment's prohibition against quartering soldiers in citizens' homes, the Fourth Amendment's protection against illegal searches and seizures, the Fifth Amendment's protection against self-incrimination, and the Ninth Amendment's guarantee that individuals are entitled to rights not specifically defined in the Constitution, in combination, create the "penumbra" of a right to privacy.

How are the right to privacy and the right to an abortion linked?

Although the Supreme Court has not been specific with regard to the range of sexual acts covered under one's right to privacy, in *Roe v. Wade* (1973), it ruled that the right to privacy includes a woman's right to have a safe and legal abortion. The Court argued that the right to privacy was "founded in the Fourteenth Amendment's concept of personal liberty and restrictions on State action." This landmark decision spurred the right-to-life, or pro-life, movement, which holds that human life begins at conception and that abortion is thus comparable to infanticide, and its pro-choice counterpart, which maintains that a woman's right to choose how to use her own body is intrinsically connected to her constitutional right to privacy. Although the Supreme Court has reacted to these two groups and various political pressures by declaring certain restrictions on abortion constitutional and severely limiting *Roe*'s scope since the early 1970s, it has yet to overturn the decision completely. As late as 2001, the Supreme Court upheld its position on privacy and abortion, ruling that states could not ban what is commonly referred to as partial-birth abortion. Access to a safe and legal abortion is still fundamentally a privacy issue and constitutionally guaranteed, although many scholars agree that the Court no longer gives abortion the same measure of constitutional scrutiny it once did. Over the years, the composition of the Supreme Court, the partisan composition of Congress, and the views of the president (in terms of legislation he will support or justices he will nominate) have all played a role in the evolving abortion issue.

How are sexual orientation rights and the right to privacy related?

Sexual relations between members of the same sex have been deemed constitutional under the banner of the right to privacy since the Supreme Court overturned Georgia's sodomy law in 1998. A little more than a decade earlier, however, the Court had ruled in *Bowers v. Hardwick* (1986) that Georgia's anti-sodomy law was constitutional in that privacy rights did not extend to homosexual couples. Since that time, state courts—including those in Louisiana and Maryland—have overturned anti-sodomy laws because they interfere with the right to privacy. Today, thirteen states have anti-sodomy laws. For that same reason, the Vermont legislature ruled to legalize civil unions between same-sex couples (colloquially referred to as "gay marriage") in April 2000 and voted to provide comprehensive legal status to lesbian and gay couples, allowing them to share all the protections and benefits of marriage under state law. However, partly because of the 1996 Defense of Marriage Act and overwhelming public opinion—a January 2000 Gallup

While controversial for many years, the U.S. Supreme Court finally recognized in 2015 that same-sex marriage is covered under right-to-privacy laws.

poll found that 62 percent of Americans believe marriages between homosexuals should not be recognized by the law—other states have been slow to legalize civil unions between same-sex couples. Proponents of gay marriage include the American Civil Liberties Union, which argues that keeping gay marriage illegal violates the Due Process Clause of the Fifth Amendment in that it discriminates on the basis of sex, making one's ability to marry dependent on one's gender. Furthermore, numerous activist groups maintain that gay marriage involves civil liberties issues in that a legal union allows for basic marriage rights afforded to same-sex couples, including tax exemptions, Social Security benefits, inheritance rights, and property rights.

Do random drug tests violate students' right to privacy?

The move toward drug testing comes in an era of school safety crackdown that many say has restricted students' freedom and infringed upon their civil liberties. In its 1995 ruling *Vernonia School District v. Acton,* the Supreme Court upheld random drug testing of student athletes and ruled that it does not violate their right to privacy, primarily because athletes are subject to more regulations than other students and thus cannot be guaranteed the same level of privacy. Hundreds of school districts responded by adopting drug testing policies, but several state courts struck down broader programs that test nonathletes as an invasion of the students' privacy. In March 2001, for example, a federal judge rejected mandatory drug testing for all seventh- through twelfth-grade students in Lockney, Texas, and state courts in Indiana, New Jersey, Oregon, and Pennsylvania expressed similar objections to like policies. However, in June 2002, the Supreme Court extended its opinion to cover nonathletes, voting to uphold drug testing of students involved in extracurricular activities—even those not suspected of drug use. The Court reasoned that the importance of detecting and preventing drug use by "reasonable means" outweighed an individual's right to privacy.

Does wiretapping violate the right to privacy?

Citing the right to privacy as a basic right of citizens, state laws prohibit the interception or recording of a private conversation unless all those involved in the conversation first give their permission, and federal statutes prohibit these and similar activities. In *Olmstead v. United States* (1928), the Supreme Court ruled, "Whenever a telephone line is tapped, the privacy of the persons at both ends of the line is invaded, and all conversations between them upon any subject, and although proper, confidential, and privileged, may be overheard." However, special powers to monitor communications between citizens are granted to the federal government, and the FBI engaged in increased wiretapping and other forms of electronic surveillance during the Clinton Administration. In an effort to aid the Federal Bureau of Investigation (FBI) in doing its job, Congress passed the controversial 1994 Communications Assistance for Law Enforcement Act (CALEA), which requires the telecommunications industry to design its systems in compliance with FBI technical requirements to facilitate electronic surveillance. In addition, increased wiretapping privileges were granted to the federal government under President George W. Bush's antiterrorism legislation. However, many civil libertarians are concerned with the far-reaching surveillance rights the FBI has been granted and have asked Congress to remedy this situation by adopting legislation that would uphold the Fourth Amendment's protection against unwarranted searches and maintain a citizen's right to privacy.

How has the right to privacy been compromised in the information age?

Many civil libertarians assert that an individual's right to privacy has been compromised in this age of information, when technology makes it easier to access a person's private information—from websites that allow customers to uncover information about people's financial profiles to the government-sponsored global communications system Echelon, which many say monitors worldwide satellite, microwave, cellular, and fiber-optic communications for suspicious or "antigovernment" language. While the benefits of an electronic age provide for higher productivity and sheer convenience, advances in technology make it possible to collect, store, analyze, and retrieve information in ways that were previously impossible—and that are clear infringements of the right to privacy. Both Intel and Microsoft have been criticized for creating software that transmits unique identification numbers whenever a personal computer user logs on to the Internet. One company, Acxiom Corporation in Conway, Arkansas, has a database combining public and consumer information on more than 95 percent of American households.

Does the implantation of ID chips infringe on the right to privacy?

Developers of an identification chip implanted under the skin of Alzheimer's patients claim their chip will make health professionals' and patients' lives easier. However, this groundbreaking act—implanting a microchip that emits an identification number inside the human body, much like a human barcode—has civil libertarians and other concerned citizens objecting on grounds of privacy. By scanning a radio-frequency identification (RFID) chip, medical personnel can access a wealth of information: a person's name, address, and medical profile. The maker of the VeriChip is only just beginning to develop more sophisticated chips, among them one that is able to receive satellite signals that transmit a person's location. Although the

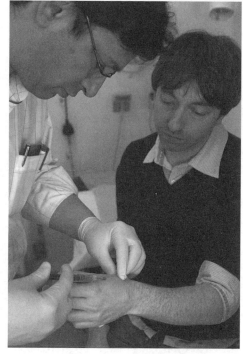

A doctor implants an RFID chip into a patient's hand in this 2009 photo. Currently, such implants are voluntary (except for some corporate employees), though many Americans worry they will become mandatory.

process is voluntary, critics say it creates a precedent for having others implanted, possibly involuntarily, including entire groups of people, such as prisoners, teenagers, or aging parents. Along with national identification cards and citizen-tracking databases, ID chips represent one of the most substantial threats that technology poses to individual liberties.

EXPERIENCES OF ETHNIC GROUPS, WOMEN, GAYS AND LESBIANS, AND JUVENILES

What is the history of African Americans and civil rights?

The history of African Americans in government and politics is multifaceted, with issues of equality, suffrage, civil rights, and full political participation at its heart. During the years that followed Reconstruction and in the first decade of the twentieth century (particularly in the late 1890s and early 1900s), African Americans were systematically stripped of their political and civil rights throughout the southern United States. While the Fifteenth Amendment was intended to secure the vote for African American men, it took Congress almost ninety years to pass the laws necessary to make the amendment applicable. The Civil Rights Act of 1960 strengthened voting rights by providing federal supervision of voter registration, but it was the Voting Rights Act of 1965 that truly made the amendment effective.

Because of the struggle involved in realizing their full political and civil rights, few African Americans have held office over the nation's history. While the number of black representatives in local and state governments totaled more than 1,500 in 1870, it would be close to a hundred years before African Americans were again represented in significant numbers in local, state, and national governments.

How did the post-World War II era bring about greater civil rights for African Americans?

The postwar era marked a period of unprecedented energy against discrimination among African Americans in many parts of the United States. Resistance to racial segregation and discrimination came through strategies such as civil disobedience, nonviolent resistance, marches, protests, and boycotts—all of which received national attention as the media documented the struggle to end racial inequality—and court cases in which African Americans legally challenged segregation. Supreme Court decisions and legislation—specifically the *Brown v. Board of Education of Topeka* decision in 1954, the Civil Rights Act of 1964, and the Voting Rights Act of 1965—all helped bring about greater civil rights for African Americans. While civil libertarians agree there is more to achieve in ending discrimination, milestones in civil rights laws have been passed to ensure African Americans' basic civil liberties, including regulating equal access to public accommodations, establishing equal justice before the law, and mandating equal employment, education, and housing opportunities. The black struggle for civil rights also inspired rights movements for other disenfranchised groups who recognized that their interests were not being upheld by the law, including those of Native Americans, Latinos, and women.

How did civil rights legislation affect voting turnout?

As a result of the Voting Rights Act of 1965 and its amendments, large-scale voter registration drives took place in the South, and the number of African Americans registered to vote rose dramatically. Prior to 1965, black turnout in Mississippi was less than 5 percent. By 1980, 65 percent of African Americans of voting age in the South were registered. In recent national elections, turnout by African American voters has come close to white voter turnout.

What is affirmative action?

Although the Civil Rights Act of 1964 is probably the most important piece of legislation outlawing discrimination in Americans' lives by establishing that discriminatory practices based on race, color, national origin, or sex are illegal, discriminatory practices still occur. In response to this, in 1965 the federal government adopted a policy of affirmative action, which requires that employers take positive steps to remedy the effects of past discrimination by having a multiethnic workforce. Affirmative action programs vary in scope, ranging from targeted advertising and recruitment techniques to factoring a person's race or sex into hiring or admissions decisions. The most aggressive form of affirmative action involves establishing a quota, or specified number of positions, for members of minority groups. Affirmative action applies to all federal government agencies, the states, and all private employers who sell goods or services to the federal government.

Affirmative action reverses discriminatory practices regarding race, sex, and national origin in school admissions and business hiring. One result has been a dramatic increase in the college enrollment of black students.

How does affirmative action relate to the politics of civil rights, and why has it come under scrutiny?

Because affirmative action programs involve race- and sex-based criteria, critics of the policy hold that these programs are unconstitutional—in effect, a kind of reverse discrimination against the majority because of preferences for females and nonwhites. The landmark *Regents of the University of California v. Bakke* (1978) set the standard for reverse discrimination by maintaining that the decision to deny a white applicant admission to the university's medical school because the school had set aside a number of spots for nonwhite students was unconstitutional and violated the Fourteenth Amendment's Equal Protection Clause. In the 1980s and 1990s, however, the Supreme Court made it more difficult for those charging discrimination to win their cases.

One recent affirmative action case, *Adarand Constructors v. Pena* (1995), marks a major departure from the Court's previous rulings. In that case, the Court held that preferential treatment by the government based on race or sex is in almost all cases unconstitutional, even when the result is intended to have a beneficial effect, such as righting past wrongs for minority groups. That same year, the University of California Board of Regents voted to end its affirmative action policies, a decision that was followed by the passage of Proposition 209, in which the state of California added an amendment to its constitution that bans affirmative action. Voters in Washington State passed a similar measure, and in 1997 a federal court ordered Texas to drop its affirmative action policy from its state university admissions requirements. Both 2000 presidential candidates

George W. Bush and Al Gore expressed their opposition to affirmative action, reflecting a trend of national ambivalence toward this policy.

How have Latinos, Asian Americans, and Native Americans fought for civil rights?

Many efforts by disenfranchised and minority groups to achieve civil rights parallel African American efforts. Neither the 1964 nor 1965 civil rights legislation identified any ethnic groups other than African Americans as deserving affirmative action; however, because the civil rights movement raised the issue of equal protection under the Constitution, other ethnic groups have made similar civil rights claims, and Congress has given them the recognition they lobbied for through voting rights legislation. Since the 1960s, Latinos, Asian Americans, and Native Americans have all had various successes in winning recognition under the law, depending on how effectively each group has been able to mobilize its members in elections. Latinos have been very active in this area; for example, George P. Bush, whose mother is of Mexican descent, campaigned for his uncle George W. Bush during the 2000 presidential primaries in order to help secure the Latino vote for Bush.

Latinos have become increasingly active in securing their civil rights, primarily through groups such as the Mexican American Legal Defense and Education Fund (MALDEF), which has focused on voting and immigration issues. MALDEF argued that English-language ballots and voter registration materials discriminated against Latinos, to which Congress responded in 1982 by requiring that these materials be printed in the language of any minority group that constitutes more than 5 percent of a county's population, in effect protecting not only Latinos from discrimination but Asian Americans and Native Americans as well. In 1994 the Latino community rallied to oppose California's Proposition 187, which if passed would have denied illegal aliens state and local public services. Although Asian Americans are only beginning to rally in national electoral politics, their biggest victory came in the area of civil rights, where they demanded that compensation be paid to Japanese Americans who were relocated by the U.S. government to internment camps during World War II.

Although the U.S. Constitution and U.S. antidiscrimination laws provide Native Americans protection against many different kinds of civil rights abuses, they were created without Native American representation and did not apply to tribal governments. In 1968, Congress created the Indian Civil Rights Act, which listed several rights that tribal goverments must respect, including rights to speech, assembly, press, and religion. Since this time, Native American tribes have been granted special rights, such as the right of Pacific Northwest tribes to fish for salmon. Recent tribal rights recognized in the late twentieth century include commercial gambling on tribal property and tribal religious freedom, provided for by the 1978 American Indian Religious Freedom Act.

How is the Voting Rights Act relevant for Latinos today?

Latinos, like African Americans, are once again seeing challenges to the franchise of voting. President Johnson's home state of Texas has become ground zero for implementing time-tested measures to restrict voting rights. Prior to 1965, in Texas and the rest of the South, political participation was suppressed by a variety of tactics, foremost among them the poll tax. In 2011, the Texas legislature passed a bill mandating that voters present a current state-issued voter identification card. On the face of it, the bill did not seem like a challenge to civil rights; however, indirect fees, coupled with the logistical difficulty of attaining an ID, placed an undue burden on poorer communities.

The Department of Justice blocked the Texas voter ID law under Section 4 of the Voting Rights Act, which allowed the federal government to block discriminatory legislation in jurisdictions with a history of voter suppression. However, in 2013 the Supreme Court struck down that portion of the act, freeing states like Texas to place new restrictions on voting. As the largest and most economically disadvantaged group in Texas, Latinos are the most likely to be affected by new voter ID laws.

How are civil rights and Arizona SB 1070 linked?

Certain political scientists maintain that anti-immigrant laws diminish the value of American civil rights and respect for liberties. In 2010, Arizona passed the Support Our Law Enforcement and Safe Neighborhoods Act (introduced as Arizona Senate Bill 1070 and thus often referred to as Arizona SB 1070), the broadest and strictest anti-illegal immigration measure in decades. U.S. federal law requires all aliens over the age of fourteen who remain in the United States for longer than thirty days to register with the U.S. government and to have registration documents with them at all times; violation of this requirement is a federal misdemeanor crime. The Arizona act additionally made it a state misdemeanor crime for an alien to be in Arizona without the required documents and required that state law enforcement officers attempt to determine an individual's im-

migration status during a "lawful stop, detention or arrest" when there is reasonable suspicion that the individual is an illegal immigrant. The law barred state and local officials and agencies from restricting enforcement of federal immigration laws and imposed penalties on those sheltering, hiring, and transporting unregistered aliens.

Although the stated purpose of the law was to combat illegal immigration, political scientists maintain that the effect has been to infringe on the rights of Latinos. The "show me your papers" provision, obligating local law enforcement to check the immigration status of anyone they suspect of being in the country illegally, is a shortcut to racial profiling, they maintain. The day before the law was to take effect, a federal judge issued a preliminary injunc-

Immigrants have been battling a plethora of anti-immigrant state legislation in recent years. Courts have often found such bills discriminatory or unconstitutional.

tion that blocked the law's most controversial provisions. In June 2012, the U.S. Supreme Court ruled on the case *Arizona v. United States,* upholding the provision requiring immigration status checks during law enforcement stops but striking down three other provisions as violations of the Supremacy Clause of the U.S. Constitution.

What is the history of women and civil rights?

"We hold these truths to be self-evident, that all men and women are created equal...." These words, written in 1848 at the first Women's Rights Convention, held at Seneca Falls, New York, announced a new American revolution in which the goal was to overthrow masculine "tyranny" and to establish political, social, and economic equality between the sexes. Although the campaign for the vote created the greatest public outcry, it was one facet of the larger struggle of women to enter the professions, to own property, and to enjoy the same legal rights as men. After the Seneca Falls convention, it would be seventy-two years before the Nineteenth Amendment to the Constitution universally gave women the right to vote, which they first exercised in the 1920 presidential election. Other rights of equality would come in the following years but more slowly.

What role did the Equal Rights Amendment play in women's political history?

The introduction and failure of the Equal Rights Amendment (ERA), which stated that legal rights could not be denied or changed based on a person's gender, had perhaps the most profound political effect on women's lives of any event. While it was several states short of the three-fourths majority it needed to become law, the campaign to pass the ERA placed women's issues on the political agenda. It tripled membership in the National Organization for Women, making it a powerful advocacy group for women's rights. It prompted some states to pass their own ERAs or to interpret statutes in a manner more favorable to women. Finally, it encouraged women on both sides of the issue to participate more in politics and to run for local, state, and national offices. The so-termed "year of the woman" elections in 1992 brought an increase in the number

An early champion of nondiscrimination regarding women was Congresswoman Martha Griffiths (D-MI; 1912–2003), who served in the House from 1955 to 1974 and later became the first woman lieutenant governor of Michigan.

of women elected to the Senate and House of Representatives, and in 1998 women's representation in the House increased again.

What other women's issues have come to the forefront in recent years?

Although NOW concentrated on the ERA, a large number of other women's groups addressed a spectrum of issues. One was the issue of domestic violence, and during the 1970s and 1980s women's rights advocates began opening shelters for battered women across the United States to house victims of abuse. The majority of the organized women's movement united behind the freedom of choice" at the cost of alienating potential women's rights supporters who favored the right-to-life position. Abortion became a national issue led by national organizations such as NARAL Pro-Choice America (formerly the National Abortion and Reproductive Rights Action League) and Planned Parenthood of America. The issue of pornography came to the forefront at this time and has continued to divide the women's movement into the twenty-first century. A majority of women found pornography demeaning, while many were strong supporters of pornography as a form of free speech. Others, including activists Andrea Dworkin and Catharine MacKinnon, felt that pornography was so central to the subjugation of women that First Amendment protections should not apply.

What milestones have been achieved for women in the military?

One of the most controversial issues involving women's rights has been the role of women in the armed forces. Although women have continuously served in the armed forces in various roles, since the early twenty-first century, women have gained ground as they have lobbied to serve in military combat units. In January 2013, the Department of Defense lifted the Combat Exclusive Policy, thus allowing women to compete for assignment to combat units, participation in which is usually a requirement for promotion to top military positions. In 2016, the Department of Defense announced that women can serve in frontline combat posts.

What are the issues surrounding gay men and women in the military?

Until the late twentieth century, the armed forces viewed homosexuality as incompatible with military service. Although President Bill Clinton had made a campaign pledge to repeal the longstanding ban on gay and lesbian military service, in 1993 he announced Don't Ask, Don't Tell, a new policy in which enlistees would not be asked about their sexual orientation, and gays and lesbians would be allowed to serve in the military as long as they did not declare that they were gay men or lesbians or commit homosexual acts. Despite this milestone, large numbers of gay men and women were expelled from the military in subsequent years. During his 2008 presidential campaign, Barack Obama promised to repeal Don't Ask, Don't Tell and allow gay men and lesbians to serve openly, but until 2010, Congress failed to act on legislation that would repeal the policy, even though 77 percent of the public supported the right of gays and lesbians to serve openly. In 2010, a U.S. district court judge ruled that the policy was unconstitutional and issued an injunction to prohibit its enforcement. After a federal court suspended the injunction, Congress passed gradual repeal legislation in 2010, and Don't Ask, Don't Tell was phased out in 2011.

How has the Defense of Marriage Act affected gay couples?

Controversy over the issue of same-sex marriage first arose in 1993 when the Hawaii Supreme Court ruled that denying marriage licenses to gay couples might violate the equal protection clause of the Hawaii state constitution. In response, Congress passed the Defense of Marriage Act of 1996, which prohibits federal recognition of lesbian and gay couples and allows state governments to ignore same-sex marriages performed in other states. In 1999, the Vermont Supreme Court ruled that gay couples are entitled to the same marriage benefits as opposite-sex couples. In April 2000, the Vermont legislature passed a law permitting gay and lesbian couples to form "civil unions." The law entitled partners who formed civil unions to receive state benefits available to married couples, including the rights to inherit a partner's property and to decide on medical treatment for an incapacitated partner. In subsequent years, a number of states permitted civil unions, and, in time, most of these states legalized same-sex marriage. As of 2015, thirty-seven states and the District of Columbia had legalized gay marriage. In a 2015 ruling, *Obergefell v. Hodges,* the U.S. Supreme Court held that the fundamental right to marry is guaranteed to same-sex couples by both the Due Process Clause and the Equal Protection Clause of the Fourteenth Amendment to the U.S. Constitution and required all states to issue marriage licenses to same-sex couples and to recognize same-sex marriages performed in other jurisdictions.

What methods did these groups use to gain access to the political process?

There are a number of ways that groups have realized their right to participate in the political process, including holding demonstrations and marches, lobbying, testifying at congressional hearings, and commenting on policy. Leaders such as Dr. Martin Luther King Jr. paved the way for unique methods of participation. King shaped thirteen years of civil rights activities with his philosophy of nonviolent social action and peace marches. Activists like Cesar Chavez and Dolores Huerta followed suit on behalf of farmworkers, women, and Hispanic Americans. Feminists Betty Friedan and Gloria Steinem launched a nationwide grassroots campaign in the 1970s to pass an Equal Rights Amendment (ERA) to the Constitution. Many people form public interest groups in an effort to unite for a common cause and influence public policy. In fact, many argue that the real impact of equal rights and greater political participation for these groups was felt—and continues to be felt—at the local level through grassroots movements and their own groups (labor, volunteer, pressure, women's, minority, LGBTI) that have won broader and greater rights for themselves and future generations.

POLITICAL OPINION

WHAT IS POLITICAL OPINION, AND HOW IS IT MEASURED?

How do Americans form political opinions?

People form political opinions—that is, attitudes or perspectives about political events, circumstances, or people—in a variety of ways and from a variety of sources. Inherent factors, such as race, gender, age, and religion, help shape people's belief systems and political opinions, as do the external factors of economic and social position, education, family origin, social groups, political leaders, peer pressure, and the mass media. The government itself also strives to manage public opinion, although the results of this have been mixed throughout history. In an openly democratic country like the United States, private groups and the government compete to shape opinion, often showcasing their positions through the media. A person's political opinions on issues, events, and leaders are formed as he or she evaluates the details according to his or her belief system and/or political ideology.

How is public opinion measured?

There are a number of ways in which public opinion is measured. While consumer behavior and group demographics play a role in measuring public opinion, researchers and politicians rely on public opinion polls—sampling techniques used to understand voters' attitudes and opinions on significant political issues—to help them with a myriad of decisions. Polls are used to obtain information about voters' attitudes toward issues and candidates, to profile candidates with winning potential, to plan campaigns, and to forecast voting patterns.

The process of polling in general has met with some skepticism from the public, who fail to see how polling a limited number of people could represent the views of the majority. Furthermore, many Americans have been soured by a technique called push polling (asking a participant a loaded question in order to elicit a certain response) and thus have become ambivalent about participating in polls and surveys. Experts say that, when analyzing poll data, politicians should bear in mind that public opinion on a given topic cannot be understood simply through the polling process and that alternative methods of measuring public opinion—such as monitoring citizen behavior and garnering public opinion directly from the people—should also be considered. In addition, the misinterpretation of specific trends in public opinion and biases about the public adds to the challenge of measuring public opinion.

What is a representative sample?

Assessments of citizen attitudes about political candidates are based on polling a representative sample, or select portion, of the total population. Therefore, if 1,000 persons are polled, and 750 of them select candidate A as their presidential choice, then, according to pollsters, that statistic should linearly scale up to the entire population: if there are one million votes to be cast, then 750 X 1,000, or 750,000—give or take a 5 percent or less margin of error—should select the same candidate. However, because some segments of the voting population may not be included in the "representative" sample, critics maintain that there is a larger margin of error than pollsters are willing to account for.

How is polling done on election night to forecast the winner?

As a routine part of election campaigns, polls are used to forecast the results of an election. On election night, communications companies conduct exit polls, which, unlike electoral surveys, are not concerned with the intended vote but are based on the answers given by voters selected at random after they have voted. Although these are not results that have been counted and verified after the closing of the polls, they do reflect how a person says he or she has actually voted, and they are relatively reliable.

Is measuring public opinion a new phenomenon in politics?

Relatively speaking, yes. Although early politicians often tried to gauge public opinion by the turnout at an event or the roar of a crowd, the systematic measurement of mass public attitudes began in the twentieth century. Although opinion polls were occasionally conducted before the 1930s, they were neither systematic nor scientific. Public opinion polling improved in the 1930s, when business and educational organizations began to develop methods that allowed the relatively unbiased selection of respondents and the systematic gathering of data from a wide cross-section of the public. Among the pioneers was statistician George H. Gallup, who in 1935 created the Gallup Poll, which is still widely used to assess public opinion today. The Harris Survey, which began in 1956, and the Gallup Poll are probably the two best-known polling organizations. Nonprofit polling organizations include the Princeton Office of Public Opinion Research (1940), the National Opinion Research Center (1941), and the National Council of Public Polls (1968).

What landmark event "forced" polling techniques to improve?

A well-publicized 1948 political event encouraged polling agencies to further refine their methods. In that year's presidential election, most polls mistakenly predicted a victory for the Republican candidate, Thomas E. Dewey, over President Harry Truman, primarily because voters with a lower income level were underrepresented and also because the polling agencies missed last-minute attitude changes among the voting public. Since 1948, techniques of public opinion research and

Political pollsters got it very wrong when they predicted that Thomas E. Dewey had defeated Harry Truman for president in 1948.

polling have improved considerably, but there is still no foolproof method for gauging public opinion. Politicians use public opinion polls to assess voting trends, determine values among the voting population, decide how to target their campaigns, and help determine how to vote on certain legislation. And the media still publish polls reflecting candidate popularity to predict which candidates will win certain elections.

Is the government responsive to public opinion?

In a democracy, where the government operates with the consent of the people, it is the leaders' obligation to attend to public opinion, and recent survey results suggest that they do. Major shifts in policy tend to occur when there are major shifts in public opinion, and generally both the president and Congress respond to public preferences, such as those for more or less government regulation, more or less government spending, foreign policy issues, welfare reform, and issues affecting the environment. Because often public opinion is not specific, and ways of measuring public opinion are not always accurate, the government has some leeway in the way that it responds to public opinion. The prominence of public interest groups that represent the voice of select population groups has evolved in order to meet this challenge.

POLITICAL PREFERENCES AND VOTING BEHAVIOR

Who is eligible to vote?

Any citizen of the United States over the age of eighteen who meets certain state requirements may vote in federal elections. The most common state requirement is registration, although registration requirements and deadlines vary from state to state.

North Dakota is the only state that does not require voters to register. In addition, thirty states and the District of Columbia require that voters be residents for a period of between one and five days prior to election day, and most states bar registration and voting by convicted felons and those deemed mentally incompetent.

How many people in the United States are registered to vote?

According to Federal Elections Commission statistics, there were 200 million registered voters at the time of the 2016 presidential elections. This means that more than fifty million new people have registered to vote in the past eight years. Only 146.3 million were registered as recently as 2008, when Barack Obama first won the U.S. presidency—a remarkable surge of over 34 percent in the electorate during a single presidency.

How has the right to vote been extended since the Civil War?

Before the Civil War, only white males aged twenty-one years or older and some black males in certain nonslave states were eligible to vote. Since this time, through a series of constitutional amendments and legislative enactments, Congress and the states have progressively extended the right to vote to other groups. The Fifteenth Amendment (ratified in 1870) guarantees the right to vote regardless of "race, color, or previous condition of servitude"; the Seventeenth Amendment (1913) provides for direct popular election to the Senate; the Nineteenth Amendment (1920) extended the vote to women; the Twenty-third Amendment (1961) gave residents of the District of Columbia the right to vote in presidential elections; the Twenty-fourth Amendment (1964) prohibits the payment of any tax as a prerequisite for voting in federal elections; and the Twenty-sixth Amendment (1971) extended the vote to citizens aged eighteen years or older.

How have race, ethnicity, gender, and class affected the right to vote?

By not allowing a certain race, ethnicity, or gender to vote, the law restricts such groups' participation in politics. The Declaration of Independence states that "all men are created equal"; however, when Thomas Jefferson penned that phrase in 1776, blacks were enslaved and women were not recognized as full citizens. Political equality applied to white, male property owners, who were the only segment of the population granted suffrage. The Thirteenth, Fourteenth, and Fifteenth Amendments to the Constitution, passed during Reconstruction (1865–1878), made some gains in granting African Americans the right to vote, but it would not be until the Voting Rights Act of 1965 that legal protection of voting rights would be extended to African Americans and other minority groups. Women were given the right to vote by the Nineteenth Amendment (1920).

When did women get the right to vote?

Although women received the right to vote with the ratification of the Nineteenth Amendment in 1920, it took many years of organized struggle for women to gain the right to vote. The women's rights convention held at Seneca Falls, New York, on July 19 and 20, 1848, was considered a historical step in gaining women the right to vote, and between that time

Suffragists protesting at the White House in 1917 are shown here getting arrested by police. The struggle for women's voting rights took years and was hard-won.

and the ratification of the Nineteenth Amendment, certain states granted women the right to vote. After years of vigorous lobbying by suffragettes such as Elizabeth Cady Stanton, Susan B. Anthony, Lucretia Mott, and Lucy Stone, in 1893 women got the vote in Colorado, followed by Utah (1896), Idaho (1896), Washington (1910), California (1911), Arizona (1912), Kansas (1912), Oregon (1912), Illinois (1913), Nevada (1914), and Montana (1914).

When did African Americans get the right to vote?

Technically, African Americans received the right to vote with the Fifteenth Amendment. However, it wasn't until the 1960s—with the passage of the Civil Rights Acts of 1957, 1960, and 1964 and the Voting Rights of Act 1965, which suspended all literacy tests and similar devices that had been used to discriminate against minority groups, particularly blacks—that African Americans began to experience less discrimination at the polls and truly gained the opportunity to exercise their voting rights. In 1975 Congress again extended the Voting Rights Act, enacting a permanent nationwide ban on the use of literacy tests and devices, expanding the act to cover minority groups not literate in English, and requiring affected states and jurisdictions to offer certain types of bilingual assistance to voters. Although voter rights for blacks and other minorities have come a long way, as recently as the 2000 presidential election, the National Association for the Advancement of Colored People (NAACP) maintained that voting irregularities plagued African American voters in Florida, charging that voters were unlawfully turned away from polls by sheriff's deputies and improperly stricken from voter rolls.

215

What is turnout?

Voter turnout is the number of people who actually show up and vote at the polls. This is different from the number actually registered as not all registered voters show up at the polls on election day. Since 1996, the number of citizens eligible to vote has increased in every presidential election, as has the number who report voting, according to the U.S. Census Bureau. Overall, 133 million people reported voting in 2012, a turnout increase of about two million people since the election of 2008. Between 1996 and 2008, turnout increases varied but were always larger than in 2012, reaching a high of about fifteen million additional voters in 2004.

What are the major characteristics of voting behavior?

One way to understand an election's outcome is by understanding how and why voters made up their minds. Based on recent polls and voting-trend statistics, political scientists have determined that a number of attitudinal and social factors are related to individual voting behavior. Among attitudinal factors, assessments of the personal characteristics of candidates, evaluations of government performance, orientations on specific policy issues, party identification, and ideology are the primary determinants of candidate choice among voters. Among social factors, race, religion, region, and social class appear to be the characteristics that have most closely related to voting over the past several decades. Examining how these factors are related to the vote in particular elections helps political scientists explain election outcomes.

What is the difference between partisan voters and nonpartisan voters?

Voters who consistently identify themselves with one political party and vote for its candidates from one election to the next are called partisan voters. Sometimes certain identifiable groups in society, such as various socioeconomic classes, religious groups, or ethnic groups, have a general tendency to support a favorite party over long periods of time. This phenomenon is called stable partisan alignment: the same social groups vote for the same party time after time. But when large numbers of voters disengage their established loyalties to their favorite party and become less partisan and more independent, partisan dealignment is said to occur. Partisan dealignment means that once-solid supporters of a particular party no longer vote for that party's candidates automatically. They may vote for certain of its candidates depending on the stance those candidates take on various issues, or they may gravitate to another party, or they may switch back and forth between parties from one election to the next. Voters who move back and forth in this way are called swing voters.

What is split-ticket voting?

Sometimes called ticket splitting, "split-ticket" voting refers to voting for candidates of different political parties in the same election—for example, when a citizen votes for a Republican president and a Democratic senator. Because ticket splitters do not vote for all of one party's candidates in any given election, they are said to split their votes between parties.

Who votes?

Statistics reveal that only about half of U.S. citizens vote. In the 2016 presidential primaries, voter turnout fell to 55 percent, nearly its lowest point in two decades; voter turnout scores were well below the 50 percent mark in congressional elections. Beyond this general statistic, studies on voter demographics reveal the following specifics: whites are more likely to vote than minorities, although there is not much difference in voter turnout between whites and African Americans; college graduates are much more likely to vote than people with fewer than eight years of education; senior citizens are much more likely to vote than people in the eighteen to twenty-four age category; and higher-income groups are more likely to vote. Although America is generally regarded by scholars and citizens alike as one of the most treasured democracies compared to other societies, its citizens are not as likely to vote.

What does "majority rule with minority rights" mean?

In a democracy, decision making is done by majority rule, with each person having one vote equal to that of his or her neighbor. It is the will of the people and not the dictate of a select ruling leadership that determines public policy. Majority rule is not a matter of coming up with the "right" answers but instead of finding satisfactory solutions to

What is straight-ticket voting?

"Straight-ticket" voting refers to casting a blanket vote for all candidates of a particular party—for example, when a Republican votes only for Republican candidates in any given election. In certain states, a voter can vote for all candidates of a certain party by checking one box on the ballot.

217

When it comes to presidential elections, only about half of the Americans eligible to vote actually do so. State and local election turnouts are even lower.

public issues and problems, so although the majority's decisions are not always right, majority rule means that all people have an equal say in decisions that affect them. Because majority rule, if unchecked, has the potential to destroy its opposition (and, hence, the democratic process), democracy upholds majority rule restrained by minority rights. This means that the majority must always recognize the rights of the minority and be willing to hear their voice.

How has immigration affected the American political community?

The United States is a nation made of immigrants, and the belief systems and values of their diverse cultures have greatly affected American political culture. According to the U.S. Census Bureau's Center for Immigration Studies, as of the year 2015, 43.3 million immigrants lived in the United States, the largest number ever recorded in the nation's history. As a percentage of the population, immigrants account for more than one in ten residents, the highest percentage in seventy years. Half of today's immigrants to the United States come from ten countries: Mexico, China, the Philippines, the Dominican Republic, Vietnam, India, Poland, Ukraine, El Salvador, and Ireland. This influx of diverse peoples makes for a rich political community with a wide array of interests, needs, and concerns. Today, the politics of immigration centers on both cultural and economic conflicts: policymakers are divided over whether to preserve language and cultural differences, and economists debate the economic impact of immigration. Furthermore, the immigration policies adopted during President Trump's first year in office—including limited and carefully scrutinized immigration—fuel the immigration discussion.

How has social class played a role in political participation?

Early voting requirements kept the vote in the hands of wealthier citizens and away from various ethnic groups. Early in this nation's history, property ownership was a common suffrage requirement. The poll tax was a tax payment required by some states before a person could vote, and it remained in effect in certain southern states until the Twenty-fourth Amendment outlawed the tax in 1964. Certain states required literacy in order to vote and used that to discourage poorer groups, and African Americans in the South, from voting. Even in southern states where the poll tax was no longer used, closed registration lists and straightforward intimidation were used to prevent blacks and the poor from voting.

What does the 2010 Census have to do with the political community?

The accuracy of the U.S. Census is of great concern to many public interest groups and their multicultural members. The national census, conducted every ten years, is the constitutionally required count of all people in the United States. Data from the census are used to determine the number of U.S. representatives from each state, draw the boundaries of congressional districts, and allocate hundreds of billions of dollars in federal grant money. Historically, the census has tended to undercount minorities, meaning that the regions in which they live tend to receive less representation in government and less federal funding.

What is particularly significant about Hispanics and the vote?

Census data show that the Hispanic population (Mexican Americans, Puerto Ricans, Cubans, and other people of Spanish-speaking descent) has grown faster than the over-

The U.S. Hispanic population is having a growing influence on the country's politics. While many lean toward the left, more conservative Hispanics also have a substantial contingent.

all U.S. population since 1990 and is projected to become the largest U.S. minority group by 2020. Between 2012 and 2016, about 3.2 million young, U.S.-citizen Latinos advanced to adulthood and became eligible to vote. Nearly all of them are U.S.-born; on an annual basis, some 803,000 U.S.-born Latinos reached adulthood in recent years. This is by far the largest source of growth for the Hispanic electorate, but it is not the only one. The second-largest source is adult Hispanic immigrants who are in the United States legally and decide to become U.S. citizens. It was estimated that some 1.2 million would do so between 2012 and 2016. Another source is the exodus from Puerto Rico. Since 2012, some 130,000 more Puerto Ricans have left the island than moved there. Florida has been the biggest recipient of these Puerto Rican adult migrants, all of whom are U.S. citizens and eligible to vote in U.S. elections.

What is significant about Asian Americans and voter turnout?

The 10.2 million Asian Americans living in the United States have established a growing presence in the country. Advocacy groups who represent this population are working toward advancing their civil rights, supporting immigration policies that benefit Asian Americans living in the United States and encouraging bilingual education programs for Asian Americans.

The November 1996 elections were viewed as historically significant for Asian Americans because of the election of a number of Asian Americans throughout the country. The most notable was the election of Gary Locke as the governor of the state of Washington, the first Chinese American to capture a state's top post as well as the first Asian American to become governor outside of Hawaii. In California, the election of Mike Honda of San Jose to the California Assembly was hailed as a major political achievement because he became only the second Asian American in the 120-member California legislature. According to UCLA's Asian American Studies Center, in 1998–1999 there were nearly two thousand elected and appointed Asian American and Pacific Islander officials across the nation. One of the lowest rates of voter turnout, however, is found among the Asian American population in general. Various studies of California voter demographics in the mid-2000s, for example, found that Asian American citizens turned out for elections at rates that were 10 to 15 percent lower than that of whites and African Americans. Advocacy and public interest groups are working to increase voter participation for upcoming national elections.

How are the youth represented in the political community?

According to experts and young adults themselves, there is widespread cynicism about the political community among many eighteen- to twenty-nine-year-olds and much uncertainty as to how many will bother to vote in upcoming elections. A recent poll conducted for the Pew Research Center for the People and the Press revealed that 55 percent of eighteen- to twenty-nine-year-olds are registered to vote. In the 1996 presidential election, voters under thirty years of age made up about 28 percent of total participants; in the 1998 midterm elections, those aged eighteen to twenty-four made up just 12 percent of the voter population, while only 8 percent of those aged eighteen to twenty-one voted.

Furthermore, the 2000 U.S. Census reported that, among eighteen- to twenty-four-year-old African Americans, 62.4 percent were not registered to vote in November 1998. The percentage of nonregistered citizens of voting age for other races is high as well, with the eighteen- to twenty-four-year-old age group topping the charts in terms of eligible voters who are not registered. Experts cite busy schedules, disillusionment with the government, apathy, a highly individualistic nature, and lack of trust in the political process as the reasons fewer and fewer young people are turning out at the polls.

POLITICAL OPINION AND THE POLITICAL PROCESS

What are Americans' core political values?

Although Americans have a vast array of political opinions, at the heart of these are the fundamental ideals of democracy, liberty, equality, and individualism upon which the U.S. government was established.

Where do these core political values come from?

The political values and beliefs that Americans hold dear are rooted in a philosophical tradition known as classical liberalism, an ideology that influenced the founders of the early republic and continues to play a part in democratic movements around the world today. Classical liberalism emphasizes the importance of the individual and individual freedom, equality, private property, limited government, and popular consent.

Are politics and political values ever in conflict?

Many of the political debates and events that have occurred over history involve conflict over the nation's values and what words like *liberty, equality,* and *justice* mean. Events such as the Civil War, the civil rights and suffrage movements, and the assassination of presidents reflect this conflict. Additionally, there is conflict within the system of government itself. Because of the separation of powers between the three branches of government and the system of checks and balances that keeps each branch's actions accountable to the others, political values are often in conflict, and such conflicts cannot be worked out in cases where one major party holds the presidency and another controls Congress. With power divided between the legislative and executive branches, it can take months to arrive at an agreement, and branches of the government are often pursuing different policies.

Is patriotism a political value?

Patriotism, or love for one's country, is considered a citizen trait more than an inherent political value. The last time patriotism came to the forefront as a major national

221

theme was in September 2001, when terrorist attacks triggered an outpouring of nationalist sentiment on a scale not seen since World War II. Symbols of patriotism—including images of the national flag, lyrics from "The Star-Spangled Banner," the recitation of the Pledge of Allegiance, and phrases such as "United We Stand"—flooded the national consciousness in the months following the attacks. Whether patriotism will resurface and affect such things as citizens' involvement in government or voter turnout in future elections is yet to be seen.

What do Americans think about their government?

While opinion about the government of the United States is as varied as its citizens, overall there are two major trends that indicate how Americans perceive the federal government: in recent years, the public's trust in government has declined, and the

Patriotism might not be a strong indicator of voter behavior, but it certainly comes into play when a nation is in crisis, such as after the 9/11 terror attacks, when Americans all over the country pulled together to support one another.

average person feels that there is little he or she can do to influence the government. For example, 66 percent of Americans said that government officials don't really care what people think, according to a recent poll.

According to a 2005 joint survey by Democratic and Republican pollsters, three out of four Americans indicated they distrust government. The bipartisan poll stated that 76 percent of the people questioned said they rarely or never trust "government to do what is right." This surpasses polls dating back to the late 1950s that showed dramatic discontent in times of political crisis: 61 percent were distrustful in 1974 after the Watergate scandal, 69 percent in 1980 after the Iran hostage crisis, and 62 percent in 1990 following the Iran-Contra affair.

Why has trust in the government declined?

Americans' trust in their government is closely tied to their perception of the government and its performance. According to public opinion polls and expert opinion, Americans may not trust the government for the following reasons: they believe that the government does not always tell the truth; they feel that the government has become too big and nonresponsive to citizens' needs; there are few benefits that can be obtained from the government; and the government is too intrusive in matters of privacy. According to various reports, there is also a public sense that the government has spent large sums of money on problems that have not improved, thus fueling the public's distrust of the government in general.

How is distrust in government linked to voter turnout?

Experts say declining trust in the government (specifically cynicism concerning the political process), coupled with a sense that a person's vote does not really matter, is one of the primary reasons that fewer and fewer voters are showing up at the polls. The inconvenience of polling locations and times is another reason cited by some. Furthermore, the fact that voting rights are taken for granted by many Americans and the feeling among some citizens that they are uninformed about the issues and thus unqualified to vote also contribute to decreased voter turnout. In addition, because the 2016 presidential election was won with a majority of electoral rather than popular votes, citizens may have lost faith in the voting process.

Why should I vote?

If half the people in the United States vote, can it be said that the government truly represents the people? And are the people of the United States active citizens if they don't vote? What are the policy consequences if America's people don't vote? Democratic governments such as the United States cannot disregard the interests of a voting population, but if citizens do not vote, then politicians do not necessarily need to heed their interests. It is necessary for the people of a democratic country to constitutionally voice their opinions as to which political party best supports the overall interests of the nation and ultimately their own interests. One of the most effective ways to represent oneself is to vote; choosing not to vote can be equated with not voicing one's opinion. Not voting also adds to the increasing sense of political alienation already prevalent in America, and when members of a particular demographic group (such as those in a low-income bracket or a certain age group) don't vote, they become more powerless because they don't have the voice to influence social policy. In order for citizens to have a say in the nation's future, voting is imperative.

How does a citizen register to vote?

A citizen registers to vote by filling out a registration application, which can be obtained either from a local election official in the citizen's county or city or through registration outreach programs sponsored by such groups as the League of Women Voters. In addition, citizens can also register to vote at state Department of Motor Vehicles offices, state offices providing public assistance, state offices administering state-funded programs for the disabled, and armed forces recruitment offices. Many states also offer registration opportunities at public libraries, post offices, unemployment offices, and public high schools and universities.

How can citizens change their party affiliation?

Each state's board of elections has specific requirements and deadlines for changing party affiliations. In most states, if you want to change your party affiliation, you must reregister to vote. Citizens can change their party affiliation on their state's voter registration form.

PUBLIC INTEREST GROUPS

THE ROLE OF PUBLIC INTEREST GROUPS

What is a public interest group?

Although public interest groups are referred to by a variety of names—special interest groups, organized interest groups, pressure groups, and lobby groups—their common denominator is that such a group is a formally or informally organized association of people with common interests and demands that attempts to influence public policy.

What does the concept of pluralism have to do with interest groups?

Pluralism, or the theory that all interests are and should be free to compete for influence in the government, is the underlying philosophy of public interest groups. The fact that numerous groups compete for their agendas at the national, state, and local levels ensures balance and compromise in public policy.

What are the benefits of joining a public interest group?

Interest groups allow like-minded individuals to come together and take their claims directly to the government and thus fill the void left by traditional political parties. Interest groups provide a vehicle for the unrepresented or underrepresented to have their voices and positions heard, thereby making the policy-making process more representative of diverse populations and varying perspectives. As an organized effort, public interest groups provide a support mechanism for the individual, often making headway in political policy in ways no individual could.

How are public interest groups organized?

Interest groups vary in the way they are organized, depending primarily on their size and scope. Most of the established groups have state affiliates and numerous local chapters.

All groups have a leader who mobilizes members and acts to a certain extent as their public voice, such as Marian Wright Edelman of the Children's Defense Fund, Pat Robertson (and more recently Roberta Combs) of the Christian Coalition of America, and Nadine Strossen of the American Civil Liberties Union. Membership can range from anywhere in the low hundreds to many tens of thousands. Funding comes primarily from membership contributions, dues, and fundraising activities.

TYPES OF INTEREST GROUPS

What different kinds of interests are represented by public interest groups?

Interest groups are defined by the causes and issues they represent; thus, as many groups as interests exist: property rights groups, states' rights groups, civil rights and civil liberties groups, environmental groups, animal rights groups, children's advocacy groups, peace groups, right-to-carry-arms groups, right-to-life groups, and church groups, to name a few. They include good-government groups like Common Cause and Public Citizen, Inc., civil liberties groups like the American Civil Liberties Union, environmental groups like Greenpeace USA and the Sierra Club, and religious groups, such as the Christian Coalition. Some, such as the American Federation of Labor and Congress of Industrial Organizations (AFL-CIO)—the umbrella organization for seventy-eight labor unions in the United States—represent more than one issue. Public interest groups that have received widespread attention for their lobbying efforts include the American Association of Retired Persons (AARP), Amnesty International, the National Rifle Association (NRA), and the National Right to Life Committee. Others that are dedicated to representing the needs of certain ethnic groups include the National Association for the Advancement of Colored People (NAACP), the Mexican American Legal Defense and Education Fund, and the Native American Rights Fund. Although most interest groups focus on domestic issues, some are concerned with foreign policy. The American Israel Public Affairs Committee (AIPAC), for example, focuses on the Middle East and the relationship between the United States and Israel.

The American Federation of Labor and Congress of Industrial Organizations (AFL-CIO) is the largest federation of labor unions in the United States and, as such, represents a powerful public interest group that can influence politics on the local and national levels.

What are some examples of conservative interest groups?

Conservative interest groups dominated the political landscape during the Bush and Clinton administrations and have grown ever since, fueled by factors such as the growth of conservative talk radio and the desire of some Americans to return to the moral foundations of the mid-twentieth century. Examples include the two-million-member Christian Coalition, a dominant force in the pro-life debate; the National Taxpayers Union; the Home School Legal Defense Association; and the National Federation of Independent Business, to name a few. Conservative groups have been able to pressure the national government into considering their agenda and have become a substantial presence at the state and local levels, introducing property rights and gun owner rights legislation in a large number of states.

Are there government interest groups?

Yes. Given the structure of the American federal system, it is not surprising that there are organizations to bring the issues of local and state government before Congress and the administration. Government interest groups include the National League of Cities, the National Conference of Mayors, and the National Governors Association. One critical task performed by these groups is to help state and local governments get federal grants. These funds are important because they are a central means by which states get back money taken away through federal taxes. As the budget has tightened and as more Republicans have won governorships, these groups have become more likely to seek greater local control over policies instead of more cash.

What are some examples of civil rights interest groups?

The National Association for the Advancement of Colored People (NAACP), the Mexican American Legal Defense and Education Fund (MALDEF), the National Organization for Women (NOW), and the National Gay and Lesbian Task Force represent groups that historically have faced legal discrimination and in many respects continue to lack equal opportunity. Their concerns involve more than civil rights and encompass social welfare, immigration policy, affirmative action, a variety of gender issues, and political action.

How are ideological interest groups classified?

Ideological interest groups view all issues—federal spending, taxes, foreign affairs, court appointments—through the lens of their political ideology, typically liberal or conservative. Their support for legislation or policy depends exclusively on whether they find it ideologically sound. Americans for Democratic Action (ADA), a liberal group, and the American Conservative Union (ACU) rate elected officials by the same standard. A Republican challenger might point to an incumbent's high ADA rating to show that he or she is too liberal to represent the district.

What are some well-known single-issue interest groups?

Some interest groups are formed to advocate for or against a single issue. Although other interest groups may have a position for or against gun control, it is the only issue in the political arena for the National Rifle Association (NRA) and the National Coalition to Ban Handguns (NCBH). The same is true of abortion, which pits the National Right to Life Committee (NRLC) against the National Abortion Rights Action League (NARAL). However, single-issue interest groups don't always generate their opposite. Mothers Against Drunk Driving (MADD), which campaigns for stiffer sentences for driving while intoxicated and mandatory penalties for the first offense, is one group that doesn't.

What are some examples of economic interest groups?

Economic interest groups include organizations that represent big business, such as the U.S. Chamber of Commerce and the National Association of Manufacturers (NAM), as well as big labor: the American Federation of Labor and Congress of Industrial Organizations (AFL-CIO) and the International Brotherhood of Teamsters, for example. Large corporations and individual unions also have offices in the capital. Trade associations represent entire industries. The members of the American Public Power Association (APPA), for example, are municipally owned electric utilities, rural electric cooperatives, and state power authorities.

What is the New Politics movement?

Formed during the 1960s in opposition to the Vietnam War, the New Politics movement is a coalition of citizens that has rallied for such issues as environmental protection, the rights of women and children, and nuclear disarmament. The movement has been called the number-one contributor to the expansion of interest group activity in the late twentieth century because many of its constituents created the public interest groups that are so prominent today, such as Common Cause, the Sierra Club, the National Organization for Women, and the Environmental Defense Fund as well as several of consumer activist Ralph Nader's organizations. They called themselves public interest groups in order to be distinguished from other business groups and to suggest that their issues were public, rather than self-serving. Because in the 1960s and 1970s these groups were particularly effective in laying the groundwork for influencing Congress and the courts and securing various consumer and safety legislation, they spawned the interest group activity that is so prevalent today.

STRATEGIES THAT MAKE
INTEREST GROUPS SUCCESSFUL

What do public interest groups do to gain influence?

Interest groups represent the interests of their members to policymakers at all levels of state and national government. Thus, the elderly play a lead role in pushing the government to adopt affordable health care legislation and Social Security programs, people with disabilities fight for improved access to public buildings, and right-to-life groups press for increased protection for the unborn. While increasing public awareness about their issues and helping to set the public agenda, most public interest groups lobby the government directly to put pressure on the lawmaking process, including shaping the government's agenda by raising new issues or calling attention to previously ignored problems. Besides lobbying Congress, regulatory agencies, and the courts, many engage in protest activities, such as marches and demonstrations. Many also become more directly involved in the electoral process by endorsing candidates, evaluating candidates or officeholders, and even creating political parties.

What does it mean to lobby?

Public interest groups use the process of lobbying to assert their influence over the policy process. A lobbyist is any person who attempts to influence policy through

A former chair of the American Conservative Union, Cuban-born attorney Al Cardenas is one of the most influential lobbyists working in Washington, D.C., today. Lobbyists try to influence politicians on behalf of special interest groups for whom they work.

what are known as lobbying techniques, such as testifying at court hearings, contacting government officials directly to present a certain point of view, presenting research results to back a certain position, entering into coalitions with other organizations to shape the implementation of policies, soliciting the media to advance a particular cause, consulting with government officials to plan legislative strategy, even helping to draft legislation. Lobbyists initiate letter-writing campaigns, undertake grassroots lobbying efforts, and engage in fundraising projects. While some public interest groups, such as Common Cause, Mothers Against Drunk Driving, and the National Coalition for the Homeless, maintain permanent lobbies in Washington and in state capitals, others, such as colleges and trade associations, hire lobbying firms that are adept at navigating Congress and the bureaucratic maze.

Who is a lobbyist?

Most estimates place the number of lobbyists in Washington, D.C., at close to twenty thousand. According to the 1995 Lobbying Disclosure Act, a lobbyist must spend at least 20 percent of his or her time lobbying Congressional members or executive branch officials or their staffs. Because lobbying plays such an important role in passing Congressional legislation, many lobbyists are those who know the system inside out: former members of Congress, former staff aides, former White House officials, and former cabinet officers.

What is grassroots lobbying?

Grassroots lobbying is a form of political lobbying that strives to involve ordinary citizens in a special interest group's campaign. It involves door-to-door information drives, mass mailings, and print ads in an effort to persuade voters to act as advocates for a special interest group's agenda—urging them to write or call their representatives or senators to express their support. Beyond knocking on doors, interest groups have grown savvy in their use of the Internet and computerized fax machines to recruit thousands of Americans at the grassroots level.

How do public interest groups use the media to their advantage?

Solicitation of the media is one of the most powerful tools that can be used in grassroots lobbying. Because the media have a large and powerful influence on the government and its agenda, the more media attention that a cause receives, the more likely Congress is to act upon it. Public interest groups gain media attention by courting reporters and keeping them up to date on the nuances of their issues, writing stories themselves for newspapers and magazines, discussing their issues on television talk shows, and buying ad space in newspapers, in special interest magazines, and on billboards.

In what ways is litigation used by interest groups to advance their causes?

Interest groups use litigation to fight for their causes in court. A number of interest groups, or their specially created divisions, are specifically dedicated to working within the judicial system. Examples include the Pacific Legal Foundation, which was created to fight environmental protection groups in court; the Christian Legal Society, which concentrates on issues of church and state; and the U.S. Chamber of Commerce, which developed its National Chamber Litigation Center to support business interests in courts. Activities include litigating cases, demonstrating in front of courthouses, sending letters to judges, and filing *amicus curiae* (Latin for "friend of the court") legal briefs in cases in which they are not directly involved.

What is reverse lobbying?

Rampant in Washington during the 1990s, reverse lobbying is a form of lobbying where government officials work with interest groups to pressure other government officials. For example, the Clinton Administration formed relationships with dozens of health care reform groups in 1993 and 1994, asking them to lobby Congress on behalf of the president's ambitious health care reform package. Along those same lines, Republican House leaders in 1995 organized Project Relief, an ambitious coalition of over a hundred trade associations formed to push regulatory reform legislation through the House and Senate by means of grassroots efforts.

What is a PAC?

PAC—which stands for political action committee—is a political committee organized for the purpose of raising and spending money to elect and defeat political candidates. The term refers to those political committees that are not the official committees of any candidate or political party but rather are affiliated with corporations, labor unions, and

Ellen Malcolm (shown at far right) is a political activist who in 1985 founded EMILY's List, a pro-choice Democratic PAC.

public interest groups. Most PACs have specific legislative agendas and play a significant role in congressional elections, contributing large amounts of money to candidates, and engaging in other election-related activities.

How do PACs and public interest groups differ?

Public interest groups promote their causes primarily by attempting to influence government policy rather than by means of fundraising or elections. However, like a political party, an interest group will often form a PAC, which then becomes the group's federally registered fundraising arm, making campaign contributions to candidates that the interest group supports. A well-known and powerful PAC is EMILY's List, which helps elect pro-choice Democratic women candidates to office. In 2000, EMILY's List contributed a record $9.3 million to candidates for the two-year election cycle. It is associated with many women's special interest groups, including the National Organization for Women (NOW) and the National Partnership of Women and Children.

How much can PACs contribute to candidates' campaigns for federal office?

PACs may contribute up to $5,000 per candidate per election. However, a PAC must meet the legal requirements for a multicandidate committee: it must be a political committee that has been registered with the Federal Elections Commission for at least six months, have received contributions from more than fifty people, and have at least five federal candidates. PACs can also give up to $15,000 annually to any national party committee and $5,000 annually to any other PAC. PACs may also receive up to $5,000 from any one individual, PAC, or party committee per calendar year.

231

What are some examples of influential PACs?

PACs have increased significantly in number and influence since the late twentieth century. In 1976, there were 608 PACs, but by 1998 the number had increased to more than four thousand. Through their PACs, the following industries and companies are the largest contributors to federal candidates: law firms, the retired, securities and investment groups, the real estate industry, pharmaceutical companies, insurance companies, computer companies, the entertainment industry, and the oil and gas industry. One of the most influential industries is the tobacco industry; since 1995, tobacco industry PACs have contributed $7.4 million to congressional candidates. In the 2000 election cycle, these PACs gave $2.4 million to candidates for federal office. The pharmaceutical industry also ranks high as an influential industry; since 1991, companies belonging to the Pharmaceutical Research and Manufacturers of America (PHRMA), the trade group for brand-name drug makers, have given more than $18.6 million in political contributions, primarily through their PACs. The gun rights lobby gave more than $6.1 million to federal parties and candidates in PAC and individual donation money.

What are the most generous PACs, and how much did each contribute to the 2000 presidential election campaign?

According to the Federal Elections Commission, during the 1999–2000 election campaign cycle, PACs contributed about $245 million to federal candidates (up 19 percent from $206.8 million in the 1997–1998 cycle) and just under $30 million to the political parties. PACs in the top twenty list of contributors to federal candidates include the National Association of Realtors (which gave $3.4 million), the International Brotherhood of Electrical Workers ($2.6 million), the Association of Trial Lawyers of America ($2.6 million), the Teamsters Union ($2.5 million), the United Auto Workers ($2.1 million), the American Medical Association ($2 million), and the American Federation of Teachers ($1.5 million). The International Brotherhood of Electrical Workers gave the most to Democratic federal candidates ($2.5 million), and the National Association of Realtors gave the most to Republican federal candidates ($2 million). Other generous PACs include the American Federation of State, County, and Municipal Employees; Democrat, Republican, Independent Voter Education; the National Association of Home Builders; and the National Automobile Dealers Association.

How are PAC donations and political decisions linked?

Advocates of campaign finance reform have long held that PAC donations can be directly linked to the way elected officials vote on issues that are dear to those PACs. The League of Women Voters, for example, cites these specific examples: In the 1997–1998 midterm election cycle, tobacco industry PACs gave $1.4 million to federal candi-

The National Association of Realtors, which is headquartered in this Washington, D.C., building, spent $3.4 million supporting candidates in the 2000 election, making it one of the most financially influential PACs in the country.

dates; in 1998, the Senate voted against teen antismoking programs by failing to increase the Food and Drug Administration's budget. Similarly, managed health care PACs gave more than $742,000 to federal candidates; in 1998, the House of Representatives defeated regulations to guarantee greater access to necessary care. PACs associated with the gun lobby and opposed to criminal background checks distributed $889,000 to federal candidates; in 1998, the Senate passed an amendment to bar taxes levied on gun dealers to fund a database of criminal records. Finally, timber industry PACs gave $818,000 to federal candidates; in 1997, the Senate voted to continue subsidies to timber companies for the construction of logging roads. In addition, corporations seeking to restrict the ability of the Occupational Safety and Health Administration (OSHA) to enforce worker health and safety regulations increased their political contributions when the issue came before Congress in 1995; since the early 1990s, the food industry has given more than $41 million to the campaigns of Washington lawmakers and managed to influence every bill that has promised meaningful improvement to that industry.

REGULATING LOBBYISTS

What does the First Amendment have to do with lobbyists?

The perception that lobbyists and the interest groups they represent have adversely affected the political process has led to state and federal legislation that regulates lobby-   233 ists. Nevertheless, a fundamental conflict remains over the extent to which government may regulate lobbyists and lobbying activities. Those opposed to restrictions on lobbying argue that the First Amendment guarantees the right of citizens to petition the government for redress of grievances. Placing restrictions on lobbyists impairs this right. On the other hand, critics of lobbyists assert that regulations are needed to preserve the democratic process and to ensure the legitimacy of government.

Lobbyists believe the First Amendment protects their activities. Although the U.S. Supreme Court has never stated that there is a constitutional right to petition the government, supporters of lobbying note that several state supreme courts have acknowledged a fundamental right to do so. Therefore, any regulation of lobbying must be the least restrictive means to further a compelling state interest.

How does regulation of lobbying impair the democratic process?

Lobbyists and their supporters maintain that intrusive regulation of lobbying can impair the democratic process. Laws that seek to identify contributors to lobbying groups may have a negative effect on the exercise of citizens' rights. If made public, a contribution to an unpopular lobby can discourage similar contributions by others. Because many unpopular lobbies are small and poorly funded, discouraging even a few donors may significantly affect the support for a wide variety of viewpoints.

Supporters of strict regulation of lobbyists dispute these arguments. They contend that regulation is needed to prevent special interests from controlling the political process, to ensure ethical behavior on the part of lawmakers and government officials, and to enhance the public's confidence in the government. Numerous scandals have been linked to lobbying at the federal and state levels, providing ample justification for such regulation. Lobbyists have a place in the legislative process, concede many critics, but they must be prevented from using money and favors improperly to influence legislators and their staffs.

Why do critics of lobbying support regulation?

Critics of lobbying note that the courts have generally supported reasonable regulation of lobbying activity. This type of regulation does not prevent lobbyists from openly and appropriately communicating with government in regard to legislation. The regulation does restrict traditional practices, such as giving legislators and their staffs tickets to sporting events, paying for meals and entertainment, and underwriting golf and skiing trips. These practices have contributed to the public perception that gifts and favors buy access to legislators and sometimes even votes. Critics of lobbying also support regulation requiring the public disclosure of the clients that lobbyists represent. Registration of lobbyists is a minimally restrictive means of serving the public interest, yet it gives the public information on which interest groups are involved in pending legislative matters. Critics argue that lobbyists should not be permitted to exert influence in anonymity, primarily because the public has a right to know what interest groups have shaped legislation.

How are interest groups regulated by the government?

The Federal Regulation of Lobbying Act of 1946 was a statute enacted by the U.S. Congress to reduce the influence of lobbyists. Section 308 of the bill forced lobbyists to register with the Clerk of the House of Representatives and the Secretary of the Senate, to provide information including the names and addresses of their employers, and to identify those in whose interests they work. The 1946 act expanded the definition of who could be considered a lobbyist. It included in this category any person who directly or indirectly solicits, collects, or receives money or any other thing of value to be used principally to aid the passage or defeat of any legislation.

Why do critics of lobbying argue that additional reform is needed?

Despite the reforms legislated in the federal Lobbying Disclosure Act of 1995—legislation aimed at bringing a level of accountability to federal lobbying practices in the United States—critics of lobbying argue that additional reform is needed. The act addresses disclosure, registration, and a ban on gifts and meals, but it leaves large loopholes, such as the ability of lobbyists to make large contributions to the campaign committees of members of Congress. The critics point out the irony of banning small gifts, yet permitting senators and representatives to accept $5,000 donations for their campaign committees from PACs controlled by lobbyists. Even more distressing, note critics, is the change this situation has produced in the dynamics between lobbyist and legislator: it is now the legislator who calls the lobbyist to ask for a political contribution. Critics charge that the unceasing quest for campaign cash has distorted the political system. The only way to prevent lobbyists and the special interests they represent from dominating the legislative process is to institute public financing of congressional campaigns. Once campaign contributions are no longer an issue, critics conclude, lobbyists will lose their last effective means of improperly influencing legislation.

POLITICAL PARTIES

FUNCTIONS OF POLITICAL PARTIES IN THE U.S.

What is a political party?

A political party is a group of political officeholders, candidates, activists, and voters who identify with a group name and platform and seek to elect to office those who share their identity. Although party members are diverse and not always of one mind, a party shares the common goal of coming together to get its candidates elected to office.

What are the major responsibilities of political parties?

While political parties perform a variety of functions, they are mainly involved in nominations and elections. Their major responsibilities include recruiting candidates for local, state, and national office; nominating candidates through caucuses, conventions, and primary elections; "getting out the vote" for their candidates and providing voters with information about candidates and their parties; and facilitating mass electoral choice—that is, helping voters recognize their options and encouraging electoral competition. In addition, they influence the institutions of national government and the policy-making process. For example, Congress is organized around the two-party system, and the Speaker of the House is a party office. Parties determine the makeup of congressional committees, including who will chair committees, where positions are no longer based solely on seniority.

How are political parties organized?

Political parties are organized on national, state, and local levels. At the national level, the national committee is directly in charge of the national party; for example, the Democratic National Committee and the Republican National Committee are the committees that run the Democratic and Republican parties, respectively. The national party chair is the committee's top official, formally elected by the national committee but selected by the presidential candidate. Chairs play a major role in running the national campaign and planning the presidential nominating convention and after the election serve as a liaison between the party and the White House. As the primary spokesperson for the committee, the chair tries to manage party factionalism, negotiate disputes between candidates, raise money, and prepare for the next presidential election. The national committee usually elects a new chair after every electoral defeat. While winning the White House is the major goal of the national party committee, winning congressional elections is the goal of the congressional and senatorial campaign committees, which are composed of senators and representatives chosen for two-year terms by their fellow party members in the Senate and House. The party leadership appoints the chairs of these committees.

How are political parties at the state and local levels organized?

Parties at the state and local levels are organized much as they are at the national level, although state law determines how their committees are structured and run. Each state committee is headed by a chair who is normally elected by the committee, although approximately 25 percent of state chairs are chosen at state conventions. Members of the state committees are usually elected from local areas and are usually dominated by governors, senators, or a coalition of local business leaders. Today's trend is toward stronger state organizations, most of which operate independently of the national party. Republicans are typically better funded than other parties at the state level. Below state committees are county committees, which vary widely in scope. Their key job is to recruit candidates for offices such as county commissioner, sheriff, and treasurer, but they perform a variety of other functions as well: distributing campaign literature, organizing telephone campaigns, distributing posters and lawn signs for their candidates, and soliciting door to door. Party committees also appear at the city, town, and village level.

What is the concept of divided government?

A divided government is a government in which the president is a member of one political party, and at least one chamber of Congress, either the Senate or the House of Representatives, is controlled by the opposite party. While this term is generally applied to the federal government, it can also be applied at the state level, when one party controls the governor's office and another controls the state legislature. Divided government is a frequent historical occurrence, working to discourage radical changes in policy and to motivate politicians of both parties to compromise on proposed legislation. In the post-World War II era, the majority of national elections produced divided governments, and rarely has the United States seen administrations where the White House and Congress were aligned with the same party. Divided government has also increased at the state level in the postwar era.

When the government is divided between the two major parties—Democrats and Republicans—the result can be a series of stalemates that prevent progress in legislation.

How do the differences between liberals and conservatives affect Congress and policymaking?

Divided government influences which issues are on the congressional agenda as well as the outcome of proposed legislation. To the extent that the president and members of the majority party in Congress support some issues instead of others, more issues arise when control of government is divided rather than unified, often leading to a high level of partisan conflict and the stunting of proposed legislation. For example, throughout most of the 1990s, divided party control of the government caused incessant conflict between President Bill Clinton, a Democrat, and the Republican-controlled Congress. The congressional Republicans and Democrats exhibited sharp policy differences and an unusually high level of unity within their respective parties. This atmosphere contrasts with that of a unified government: when the president's party controls both houses of Congress, it is likely to introduce, consider, and pass bills that are on the president's agenda.

What are political machines?

Throughout history, political parties have sometimes failed to maintain transparency and integrity in their pursuit of elected office. In American politics some regional and local political party organizations have been called "political machines," the "machine" being that part of the political party that operates like a well-oiled mechanism, headed by a boss or small group of autocratic leaders whose orders are carried out by a small group of loyal members. In some cases, the machines are simply extensions of the politician himself. In the nineteenth and early twentieth centuries, these machines were known for their unethical methods of maintaining their positions in elected office, including bribery, patronage, control over nominations, and election rigging. The power of these political machines was greatly reduced by the introduction of primaries to select a party's candidate as well as by citizen activism that pressed to restore government accountability.

Infamous political machines include Tammany Hall, led by William "Boss" Tweed in New York City in the 1860s, which was accused of defrauding New York City of between $75 million and $200 million in an effort to control city politics. Huey "Kingfish" Long's Louisiana machine helped him obtain the governorship in 1928, after which he controlled every level of Louisiana state politics until his election to the Senate in 1930. James Michael Curley, intermittent mayor of Boston between 1914 and 1950 and governor of Massachusetts in the mid-1930s, was known for his leadership of Boston's Democratic political machine. Tom Pendergast and his Kansas City machine suggested that Harry Truman run for Senate and provided his machine's backing in Truman's successful 1934 primary and general election races. Mayor Richard J. Daley's Chicago political machine singlehandedly ruled the city for three decades of the mid-twentieth century.

What is partisanship?

"Partisanship" refers to a person's or candidate's loyalty to a particular political party.

THE TWO–PARTY SYSTEM

What is the two-party system in American politics?

Political parties were not envisioned by America's Founding Fathers, but they gradually took hold as the electorate expanded. By the late 1820s, two political parties, the Democrats and the Whigs, dominated the U.S. political system. During the 1850s, a third political party, the Republicans, gained widespread popularity because of its opposition to slavery, and since 1852 every U.S. president has been either a Republican or a Democrat. These two parties remain at the forefront of the U.S. political system, known as a two-party system, in contrast to most of the world's other democracies, which have multiple parties.

Approximately two-thirds of Americans today consider themselves to be Republicans or Democrats. Even those citizens who maintain they are independents (not subscribing to any party) generally have partisan leanings and show high levels of partisan loyalty. On average, 75 percent of those independents who leaned either toward the Republicans or the Democrats voted for their preferred party's presidential candidate in the presidential elections held between 1980 and 2016.

What is the Democratic Party?

The Democratic Party of the United States is one of the nation's two major political parties. It is represented by the Democratic National Committee (DNC), which serves as the national party organization for the Democrats. The DNC plans the party's quadrennial presidential nominating convention; provides technical and financial support for the election of party candidates; and works with national, state, and local party organizations, elected officials, candidates, and constituencies to respond to the needs and views of the Democratic electorate and the nation. Often referred to as "the party of the people," the Democra-

The Republican Party was founded in Jackson, Michigan, in 1854 at a place called Under the Oaks. The founders of the party were anti-slavery, and, of course, the first Republican president, Abraham Lincoln, freed the slaves.

tic Party has traditionally been associated with its commitment to support immigrants, blue-collar workers, women, and minorities—a reputation due in part to President Franklin D. Roosevelt and his New Deal social programs. Democrats tend to take a more liberal stand on society's issues and believe that the federal government should take a more active role in people's lives, particularly the disenfranchised.

What is the Republican Party?

The Republican Party is the other major political party in the United States. It is represented by the Republican National Committee (RNC), which is the national party organization for the Republicans. The RNC functions as the DNC's counterpart and performs many of the same functions. The Republican Party is also referred to as the GOP, although the acronym's meaning has changed over time. In 1875, GOP stood for the "Gallant Old Party," 1876 references called it the "Grand Old Party," and during the 1964 presidential campaign, "Go Party" was briefly used as the meaning behind the acronym. The Republican Party tends to take a more conservative stand on issues, maintaining that the federal government should not play a major role in individuals' lives. Most Republicans favor lower taxes and less government spending on social programs as well as less government intervention in business and the economy.

A HISTORY OF
POLITICAL PARTIES IN THE U.S.

What are the historical origins of the Democratic Party?

The Democratic Party was founded by Thomas Jefferson (1743–1826) in 1792 as a congressional caucus to fight for the Bill of Rights and against the elitist Federalist Party. Known at the time as the Jeffersonian Republicans, in 1798 the "party of the common man" was officially named the Democratic-Republican Party and in 1800 elected Jefferson as the first Democratic president of the United States. In 1830, the name was shortened to the Democratic Party. In 1848, the party's national convention established the Democratic National Committee, now the longest-running political organization in the world, and charged it with "promoting the Democratic cause."

What are the historical origins of the Republican Party?

The Republican Party was formed in the early 1850s by antislavery activists and individuals who believed that government should grant western lands to settlers free of charge. The first official Republican meeting took place on July 6, 1854, in Jackson, Michigan, during which the name "Republican" was chosen because it alluded to equality and reminded people of Thomas Jefferson's Democratic-Republican Party. At the Jackson convention, the new party adopted a platform and nominated candidates for office in Michigan. In 1856, the Republicans became a national party when John C. Frémont was nominated for president. Even though they were considered a third party because the Democrats and Whigs constituted the two-party system at the time, it wasn't long before they supplanted the Whigs. In 1865, Abraham Lincoln became the first Republican to assume the White House.

What is the link between the Civil War and an era of one-party domination?

The Civil War era is closely tied to the Republicans and their strength as a party. In 1861 the fledgling Republican Party was a coalition of men who had belonged to groups as di-

Where do the party symbols of the donkey and the elephant come from?

The symbol of the Democratic Party is the donkey, while the symbol of the Republican Party is the elephant. During the midterm elections of 1874, Democrats tried to convince voters that Republican president Ulysses S. Grant would seek an unprecedented third term. Thomas Nast, a cartoonist for *Harper's Weekly,* depicted a Democratic jackass trying to scare a Republican elephant, and both symbols have stuck to this day.

verse as Whigs, Anti-Slavery Democrats, Free-Soilers, Know-Nothings, and Abolitionists. By the outbreak of the Civil War, these parties had melded into three basic factions—conservatives, moderates, and radicals—and it was President Abraham Lincoln's job to shape these factions into a government that could win the war without politically and economically destroying the South. The most aggressive and eventually most influential of the three was the Radical Republican faction, which vehemently opposed slavery. Although they weren't a majority within the Republican Party, the Radicals dominated the other factions because of their commitment to their cause and the determination of their members—some of whom chaired key committees in Congress—to foreground such issues and legislation as the Confiscation Acts, emancipation, the enlistment of blacks in the war, the Thirteenth Amendment, and Reconstruction policies. The Union victory and the destruction of slavery did not end the Radical agenda, and with Lincoln's assassination and Andrew Johnson's succession, the Radicals' domination of the Republican Party and Congress increased. These committed politicians would shape the reconstruction of the nation and continue to play an active role in politics through Johnson's presidency.

Which administrations were Republican, and which were Democrat?

Presidents during most of the late nineteenth century and the early part of the twentieth century were Republicans. While the Democrats and Franklin D. Roosevelt tended to dominate American politics in the 1930s and 1940s, for twenty-eight of the forty years from 1952 through 1992, the White House was in Republican hands. The following presidents were Republican: Abraham Lincoln (1861–1865), Ulysses Grant (1869–1877), Rutherford Hayes (1877–1881), James Garfield (1881), Chester Arthur (1881–1885), Benjamin Harrison (1889–1893), William McKinley (1897–1901), Theodore Roosevelt (1901–1909), William Howard Taft (1909–1913), Warren Harding (1921–1923), Calvin Coolidge (1923–1929), Herbert Hoover (1929–1933), Dwight Eisenhower (1953–1961), Richard Nixon (1969–1974), Gerald Ford (1974–1977), Ronald Reagan (1981–1989), George H. W. Bush (1989–1993), George W. Bush (2001–2009), and Donald Trump (2017–).

The following presidents were Democrats: Andrew Jackson (1829–1837), Martin Van Buren (1837–1841), James Polk (1845–1849), Franklin Pierce (1853–1857), James Buchanan (1857–1861), Andrew Johnson (1865–1869), Grover Cleveland (1885–1889, 1893–1897), Woodrow Wilson (1913–1921), Franklin D. Roosevelt (1933–1945), Harry Truman (1945–1953), John F. Kennedy (1961–1963), Lyndon Johnson (1963–1969), Jimmy Carter (1977–1981), Bill Clinton (1993–2001), and Barack Obama (2009–2017).

Who are the New Democrats?

The New Democrats were first most closely associated with the Clinton Administration and its policies. The New Democratic, or Third Way, philosophy has three fundamental principles: the idea that government should promote equal opportunity for all, while granting special privilege to none; an ethic of mutual responsibility that equally rejects the politics of entitlement and the politics of social abandonment; and a new approach to governing that empowers citizens to act for themselves. Some New Democrat ideas that have become law include national service, work-based welfare reform, charter schools, community policing, an expanded earned-income tax credit, and market incentives for environmental protection. According to the Democratic Leadership Council, which leads the movement, "The Third Way approach to economic opportunity and security stresses technological innovation, competitive enterprise, and education rather than top-down redistribution or laissez-faire. On questions of values, it embraces 'tolerant traditionalism,' honoring traditional moral and family values while resisting attempts to impose them on others. It favors an enabling rather than a bureaucratic government, expanding choices for citizens, using market means to achieve public ends and encouraging civic and community institutions to play a larger role in public life."

President Bill Clinton (right) with his vice president, Al Gore. The Clinton Administration ushered in a group of New Democrats whose philosophy was to pass legislation to give Americans more opportunities but also more responsibility.

How did the New Democrats change after the Clinton Administration?

During the two terms of George W. Bush (1946–), the evolving New Democrat movement was dominated by socially liberal economic conservatives on Wall Street and in Silicon Valley. These centrist Democrats jettisoned the white, working-class southerners and westerners who had been wooed by the original New Democrats and focused instead on winning over former moderate Republicans in the Northeast and on the West Coast who combined liberal attitudes on abortion, gay rights, and environmentalism with opposition to big government and concern about federal deficits.

In 2008, many Wall Street Democratic donors began supporting a relatively unknown first-term senator from Illinois named Barack Obama (1961–). Although Obama called himself a New Democrat in 2009, many have said that Obama in his first term governed as an "Eisenhower Democrat." He combined a foreign policy realism reminiscent of Republican realists like Eisenhower, Brent Scowcroft, and Colin Powell (who voted for him in 2008 and endorsed him in 2012). In domestic policy, his major success was the Affordable Care Act, or Obamacare, which was based on the individual mandate system promoted in the 1990s by the moderate Republican senator Lincoln Chafee (1953–) of Rhode Island and adopted by RomneyCare in Massachusetts. To the dismay of progressive and populist Democrats, Obama refused to support radical reform of the financial sector, which had largely funded his campaign in 2008, and surrounded himself with Wall Street insiders like Timothy Geithner and William Daley. As president, Barack

Obama reflected the priorities of the second New Democrat coalition, uniting donors from Wall Street, Hollywood, and Silicon Valley with a "new majority" coalition of racial minorities, immigrants, liberal women, and young voters.

When did the first presidential election with two dominant parties take place?

The first election featuring two dominant parties was in 1796. Federalist John Adams was elected president, and Republican Thomas Jefferson was elected vice president, prompting Congress in 1804 to pass the Twelfth Amendment, which prevented the election of a president and vice president from two different parties.

Are there other political parties?

Yes. Any political party that is not Republican or Democratic, has a base of support, and plays a role in influencing the outcome of an election is referred to as a minor party or third party. Today's third parties include the American Independent Party, the Reform Party, the Libertarian Party, the Socialist Labor Party, the Communist Party USA, the Peace and Freedom Party, and the USA Green Party. Third parties are often formed to voice a protest against one or both of the major parties—for example, Theodore Roosevelt's Bull Moose Party in 1912 and George Wallace's American Independent Party in 1968.

Who were the National Republicans?

The National Republicans made up the administration party during John Quincy Adams' presidency (1825–1829). Adams' supporters adopted the name National Republicans because they favored strong economic nationalism, much like the former Federalist Party. The National Republicans stood in opposition to Andrew Jackson's Democratic-Republican Party, which favored a limited national government and opposed economic aristocracy. As the National Republicans dissolved in the mid-1830s, the Whigs emerged.

Who were the Anti-Masonics?

Formed in New York in 1828, the Anti-Masonic Party was the first third party to appear in American national politics. It was formed primarily in response to America's suspicion of secret societies like the Masons and to what some perceived as a Masonic threat to public institutions at that time. The Anti-Masonic Party was the first party to hold a nominating convention and the first to announce a platform, nominating William Wirt (1772–1834) of Maryland for president and Amos Ellmaker (1787–1851) of Pennsylvania as his running mate in September 1831. However, the political effect of the first-time entrance of a third party into a United States presidential election was to siphon support from presidential contender Henry Clay and help then-president Andrew Jackson, who was a Mason, win reelection by a wide margin. Although the Anti-Masonics enjoyed some success (Vermont elected an Anti-Masonic governor, William A. Palmer), after the elections of 1836, the Anti-Masonic party declined and was eventually absorbed into the Whig Party.

245

Who were the Whigs?

The Whig Party was formed during the second quarter of the nineteenth century to oppose President Andrew Jackson and the Democratic Party. The term "Whig" came into popular parlance in 1834 and persisted until the party disbanded after the presidential election of 1856. The anti-Jackson group drew on the political history of two revolutions for its name: the American Revolution and the seventeenth-century English Glorious Revolution. During the latter, the opposition to the king had called themselves Whigs. The party's leading figures, Henry Clay (1777–1852) of Kentucky and Daniel Webster (1782–1852) of Massachusetts, supported a nationalistic economic policy called the "American System," which involved a program of tariff protection, federally sponsored communication projects (internal improvements), continuation of the na-

Four U.S. presidents were members of the Whig Party: William Henry Harrison (1941; died in office), John Tyler (1941–1945), Zachary Taylor (1849–1850; died in office), and Millard Fillmore (1850–1853; pictured here).

tional bank, and a conservative public land sales policy, harkening back to Alexander Hamilton's Federalist economic policy of 1791. Although they enjoyed some successes, ultimately they were hindered by the rising power of the Jacksonians, who were thereafter called Democrats.

Who were the Know-Nothings?

The Know-Nothing Party, more formally known as the American Party, was founded in New York City in 1849. It was organized to oppose the large influx of immigrants who entered the United States after 1846. Because Know-Nothings believed that these primarily Irish and Roman Catholic immigrants threatened to destroy America, the party strove to use government power to uphold their vision of an Anglo-Saxon Protestant society. Their platform outlined a limited immigration policy, proposed that only native-born Americans could hold public office, and advocated a twenty-one-year mandatory waiting period before immigrants would be granted citizenship and voting rights. They also sought to limit the sale of liquor, restrict public school teaching to Protestants, and allow only the Protestant version of the Bible to be read daily in classrooms. Despite their strength and appeal, the Know-Nothings declined as a national party when many members defected to the Republican Party. Although their numbers remained strong in several northern states in the late 1850s, the party had eroded as a national presence before the election of 1860.

What was the Populist Party?

Also known as the People's Party, the Populist Party was formed by a group of small farmers and sharecroppers to oppose large-scale commercial agriculture that they feared would put them out of work. The national party was officially founded in 1892 through a merger of the Farmers' Alliance and the Knights of Labor. That year the Populist presidential candidate, James B. Weaver (1833–1912), won over one million votes. Between 1892 and 1896, however, the party failed to make further gains, in part because of fraud and intimidation by southern Democrats.

Populists advocated federally regulated communication, transportation, and banking systems to offset the economic depression and prevent poverty among working-class families. Progressive Republican Theodore Roosevelt resurrected many Populist ideas and recast them in new forms as he expanded the federal regulation of business corporations and addressed many People's Party concerns in his Progressive Party. Other Populist planks—particularly those calling for aid to farmers and employment on public works projects in times of economic depression—became reality during the 1930s under the New Deal administrations of President Franklin D. Roosevelt, a Democrat.

What was the Progressive Party?

Also known as the Bull Moose Party, the Progressive Party was formed in 1912 by former Republican president Theodore Roosevelt (1858–1919). Progressives supported women's suffrage, environmental conservation, tariff reform, stricter regulation of industrial combinations, and prohibition of child labor. Many liberal Republicans went to the new party, which nominated Roosevelt for president and Hiram W. Johnson for vice president. Although the Progressives greatly outpolled Republicans in the election, the net result was a victory for the Democratic candidate, Woodrow Wilson. Progressive candidates for state and local offices did poorly, and the party disappeared in 1916 when Roosevelt returned to the Republican Party. Presidential candidates Robert La Follette

Who were the Dixiecrats?

Also known as the States' Rights Party, the Dixiecrats were a small group of southern Democrats in the elections of 1948 who opposed President Harry Truman's civil rights program and revolted against the civil rights plank adopted at the Democratic National Convention. A group of States' Rights leaders then met in Birmingham, Alabama, and proposed Governor Strom Thurmond of South Carolina for president, hoping to force the election into the House of Representatives by preventing either Truman or his Republican opponent, Thomas E. Dewey, from obtaining a majority of the electoral votes. However, their plan failed (Thurmond garnered only thirty-nine electoral votes and 1.1 million popular votes), and many Dixiecrats became Republicans.

and Henry Wallace briefly resurrected their own versions of the Progressive Party, and the party officially disbanded after the 1952 presidential election.

Which third-party presidential bids have been noteworthy in the post-World War II era?

No third-party candidate has ever come close to winning the presidency, and only eight minor parties have managed to win a single state's electoral votes. However, historians agree that there have been four noteworthy third-party presidential bids since World War II, where third-party or independent candidates have garnered more than 7 percent of the popular vote: In 1948, two independent candidates for president challenged the Republican candidate, Thomas E. Dewey, and the Democratic contender, then-president Harry Truman. On the right, Strom Thurmond (1902–2003)—then a Republican senator from South Carolina—ran as the nominee of the Dixiecrats, or States' Rights Party, a group of dissident Democrats in favor of racial segregation. On the left, Henry Wallace (1888–1965), a former vice president under Franklin D. Roosevelt, ran as the nominee of the Progressive Party. Thurmond won 22 percent of the vote in the South, the only area of the country in which he campaigned; Wallace garnered slightly more than 2 percent of the vote.

In 1968, George Wallace (1919–1998), the pro-segregation governor of Alabama, ran as the presidential nominee of the American Independent Party. Wallace, who won 13.8 percent of the vote, was thought to have taken votes away from both major-party candidates, Democrat Hubert Humphrey and Republican Richard Nixon. In 1980, Illinois congressman John Anderson (1922–) ran as the presidential nominee of the National Unity Movement. It was assumed that Anderson, a moderate, would take votes away from both the Democratic nominee, President Jimmy Carter, and the Republican nominee, Ronald Reagan. In the end, Anderson won 7 percent of the vote, which hardly dampened Reagan's landslide victory. The most recent example involves Ross Perot (1930–), who in 1992 ran as the presidential nominee of United We Stand America, the precursor of the Reform Party. Political commentators argue that Perot's strong garnering of 19 percent of the vote probably hurt the Republican candidate, President George H. W. Bush, thus helping to elect Democratic nominee

A former U.S. congressman from Illinois, John Anderson ran for president as an Independent in 1980. Some felt that his candidacy as a moderate would pull votes from incumbent Jimmy Carter, but Ronald Reagan won by such a landslide that Anderson's winning of 7 percent of the votes made no difference.

Bill Clinton, and some could argue that Ralph Nader's (1934–) presence in the 2000 presidential race siphoned votes from Democratic candidate Al Gore, who, despite gaining the majority of popular votes, lost the electoral vote to George W. Bush.

What were some third-party issues that changed America?

Many of American politicians' ideas about social issues and reform had their roots in the fledgling campaigns of third-party politicians. Although they were eventually adopted by a major political party and quickly became part of the public political debate, movements advocating Prohibition (introduced by the Prohibition Party in the late 1800s), women's suffrage (advocated by the Prohibition and Socialist parties before being supported by both major parties in 1916), prohibition of child labor (a mainstay of the Socialist Party), unemployment insurance (another social issue advocated by the Socialist Party), and a tough stance on crime (advocated by the American Independent Party in 1968 and adopted by the Republican Party) had humble beginnings on third-party platforms.

What is the Reform Party?

The most successful third party in recent years has been the Reform Party, founded by billionaire Texan Ross Perot, who enjoyed a fair measure of success in the presidential election of 1992 as an independent and again in 1996 under his newly formed party. In the 1992 elections, Perot garnered 19 percent of the popular vote (the largest percentage of the popular vote won by a third-party candidate since Theodore Roosevelt's Progressive ticket) and 9 percent in 1996. In fact, no other third-party presidential candidate in history has ever received more than 5 percent of the popular vote in two consecutive elections. After Perot's presidential campaigns, grassroots efforts continued to mount in the fifty states in which the party had established itself; however, typical of many third-party experiences, attempts to reach voters were quickly blocked. For example, in 1997, when Perot attempted to buy airtime for an infomercial on campaign finance reform, the networks rejected him. During the 1996 presidential campaign, Perot was kept out of the presidential debates. Still active today, Reformists seek to limit the power of special interest groups and return political power to the people. They have advocated term limits for members of Congress, campaign reform, and the creation of a new federal tax system. Jesse Ventura became the first Reform Party candidate to win statewide office when he was elected governor of Minnesota in 1998.

Why have third parties been unsuccessful in America's political system?

The elections of Reform Party candidate-turned-Minnesota governor Jesse Ventura (1951–) and Green Party candidate-turned-state legislator Audie Bock of California have brought the role of third-party and independent candidates to the forefront of American consciousness. Although a number of political parties exist, and some have been somewhat effective at certain times over the course of American political history, Stephen Rockwood, author of *American Third Parties Since the Civil War,* cites several reasons why third parties have not been successful in the United States. First, the U.S. election system is based on winner-takes-all voting rather than proportional representation (granting legislative seats in proportion to the number of votes received). Second, the historic tradition in which the two parties act as umbrella groups for a variety of interests inhibits the voice of third parties; in essence, third parties have a hard time succeeding because one or both of the major parties often adopt their most popular issues and thus their voters. Finally, the media tend to concentrate on the Republicans and Democrats rather than giving airtime to smaller parties.

In addition, most states have laws that require third parties to secure their place on the ballot by submitting large numbers of voter signatures, in contrast to the Democrats and Republicans, who are given automatic ballot access. Furthermore, in the state legislatures, both the Democrats and Republicans strive to keep the political agenda limited to two parties, fearing increased conflict and stress with the addition of a third party. Finally, the public funding of campaigns favors the two main parties, and at the national level, third-party presidential candidates receive funds after the general election (as opposed to the major-party candidates, who receive funds after their summer nominations) and only if they have received more than 5 percent of the vote. Many third-party and independent candidates and their supporters complain about these aspects of the campaign system, holding that the process is so biased against them that they are automatically pushed to the fringe of elections. Nevertheless, even when they don't win, these candidates can play an important part in raising issues, mobilizing new voters, introducing campaign innovations, and tipping elections from one major-party candidate to another.

What is an independent candidate, and has one ever won a presidential election?

An independent candidate is one who has no party affiliation, choosing to run for office independently of the Democratic and Republican parties, or any third party, for that matter. An independent candidate gets on the ballot by petition. Key independent candidates include Ross Perot in his 1992 presidential campaign and John B. Anderson in his 1980 campaign. Independent candidates continue to appear on the ballot, although none have received any significant attention or share of the popular vote. In fact, no independent candidate has ever won a presidential election, and less than a handful have received 5 percent or more of the popular vote. Rarely does an independent candidate garner any electoral votes.

Why do some people think Ralph Nader cost Al Gore the 2000 election?

Because of the presence of third-party candidates, 40 percent of the presidents elected since 1840 have lacked a popular-vote majority, greatly affecting their terms in office. In the 2000 presidential elections, consumer advocate and Green Party nominee Ralph Nader (1934–) appeared to be a significant factor in garnering votes in states that had close races between Democratic candidate Al Gore (1948–) and Republican candidate George W. Bush (1946–), ultimately keeping Gore from winning the popular vote in those states. According to the Associated Press, exit polls in states including Colorado,

Florida, Nevada, New Hampshire, Oregon, Washington, and Wisconsin suggested that at least half the Nader voters would have voted for Gore if it had been a two-way race. In many of those states, it was enough to throw the state to Bush. While obviously not all of Nader's supporters would have voted for Gore, according to ABC's *This Week*, prior to the election, 56 percent of Nader's supporters said that if Nader wasn't running they'd pick Gore, 23 percent would pick Bush, and the rest wouldn't vote. Despite Democratic Party accusations that "a vote for Nader is a vote for Bush," Nader maintained that he was a viable third-party candidate and "did not run for president to help elect one or the other of the two major candidates." Even though he may not have had a real chance at winning the White House, if Nader had received over 5 percent of the vote, it would have entitled the Green Party to millions of dollars in federal matching funds in the 2004 elections.

Why is Bernie Sanders notable?

Several grassroots campaigns to elect Bernie Sanders president as a write-in candidate were established on social media in the run-up to the 2016 U.S. presidential election. Though Sanders continued to campaign for Democrat nominee Hillary Clinton (1947–), supporters pointed to alleged DNC bias in the Democratic Party's presidential primaries against Sanders and to Clinton's email scandal and continued to support him. Both Clin-

ton and Donald Trump would have had to win fewer than the required 270 electoral college votes for Sanders to have denied either candidate the presidency and for the election to be passed to the House of Representatives; thus, the initial write-in campaign in Vermont, offering only three electoral college votes, was unsuccessful. The campaign expanded to include all twelve eligible states and relied on states such as California, with a high electoral college vote count and large support for Sanders, to be successful in denying both Trump and Clinton. He received over 100,000 popular votes and one electoral vote. Two other electoral votes were disallowed. Sanders came in third in Vermont, ahead of both Gary Johnson and Jill Stein, and took 5.67 percent of the vote, a first in U.S. presidential history.

Although he ran as a Democrat, in many ways, U.S. Senator Bernie Sanders (I-VT) ran a campaign like a third-party candidate, giving Secretary of State Hillary Clinton a run for her money in the 2016 presidential race.

MECHANISMS OF POLITICAL PARTY CHANGE: REALIGNMENT, DEALIGNMENT, TIPPING

What is electoral realignment?

In the United States, party politics have taken an interesting course generally referred to by political scientists as "electoral realignment." Typically, one party has dominated the national electoral arena for a period of approximately thirty years, after which a new party supplants the dominant party. This electoral realignment is usually followed by a long period in which the new party is the dominant political force, not necessarily winning every election but maintaining control of the Congress and the White House. At least five such realignments have taken place since the founding of the American Republic: (1) in 1800, when the Jeffersonian Republicans defeated the Federalists, thus becoming the dominant force in American politics; (2) in 1828, when the Jacksonian Democrats gained control of both the White House and Congress; (3) in 1860, when Abraham Lincoln's newly founded Republican Party displaced the Whig Party, which had formerly been one of the country's major parties; (4) in 1896, when the Republicans gained control of the national government; and (5) between 1932 and 1936, when Franklin D. Roosevelt's Democratic Party took control of the White House and Congress, where the party remained dominant through the 1960s. Since the 1960s, party politics in the United States have been primarily characterized by the term "divided government."

Has electoral realignment happened recently?

Yes. A recent example of realignment came at the end of George W. Bush's presidency. In the 2008 elections, the Democrats expanded their majorities in the Congress and won the presidency decisively. This was due to momentum from the Democrats' 2006 successes as well as the continued unpopularity of President George W. Bush, whose administration was now faced with a financial crisis and economic recession. Some people believe that 2008 may have been a realigning election with a long-lasting impact, as were the election of Franklin D. Roosevelt in 1932 and the election of Ronald Reagan in 1980.

How does dealignment affect political parties?

Under conditions of partisan dealignment—when large numbers of voters disengage their established loyalties to their favorite party and become less partisan and more independent—it becomes more difficult for parties to produce long-term programs that will attract a long-term following. Having to make frequent shifts and revisions in their programs to attract increasingly fickle and unpredictable voters, parties find it harder to represent their constituents' views in a stable fashion and support policy initiatives that may take many years to translate into effective governmental action. In short, party dealignments further complicate the task of establishing responsible party government.

Many scholars argue that the trends in elections in the United States over the last several decades are best characterized as dealignment.

What is electoral tipping?

"Tipping" refers to the end of one era and the crystallization of another. More specifically, an electoral tipping point is a point in time when a group—or a large number of group members—rapidly and dramatically changes its behavior by widely adopting a previously rare practice. The phrase was first used in sociology by Morton Grodzins, who borrowed the phrase from physics, where it referred to adding small amounts of weight to a balanced object until the additional weight caused the object to suddenly topple, or tip. Grodzins studied integrating American neighborhoods in the early 1960s. He discovered that most of the white families remained in the neighborhood as long as the number of black families remained relatively small, but, at a certain point, when "one too many" black families arrived, the remaining white families would move out en masse in a process known as white flight. He called that moment the "tipping point."

CAMPAIGNS AND ELECTIONS

HOW ARE ELECTIONS CONDUCTED?

What is the difference between elections in the United States and those in authoritarian and totalitarian states?

In a democracy like the United States, elections are considered free and fair. For an election to be free and fair, certain civil liberties such as freedom of speech, association, and assembly are required. Democratic elections are characterized by political parties and civic groups who mobilize and organize supporters and share alternative platforms with the public. Elections are competitive and their results considered to reflect the will of an informed citizenry. Democratic elections are periodic, inclusive of all citizens, and definitive. Quite the opposite is true of totalitarian states. Elections staged by right-wing dictatorships, Marxist regimes, and single-party governments may lend an aura of legitimacy but in fact lack opposition parties and fair and free voting methods. Suffrage in totalitarian and authoritarian states is an expression of the power of the state rather than of the free choice of citizens. Because abstaining from the vote might be interpreted as an expression of hostility toward the government in power, election results are generally heavily skewed in favor of the government. These scenarios are typical of authoritarian/totalitarian regimes today, including those in Iran, North Korea, and Cuba.

In recent years, elections have been a prime vehicle for democratization as authoritarian governments have increasingly conceded to democratic principles. By the close of the twentieth century, electoral democracies clearly predominated in the world, including much of the post-Communist world, Latin America, and parts of Asia and Africa. According to Freedom House, a nonpartisan organization that monitors political rights and civil liberties around the world, electoral democracies—political systems whose leaders are elected in competitive multiparty and multicandidate

255

processes in which opposition parties have a legitimate chance of attaining power—now make up 120 of the 192 existing countries and represent 62.5 percent of the world's population.

What are the types of elections in the United States?

In the United States, there are generally three types of elections: presidential elections, congressional elections, and regional or local government elections. Within these three general types, there are primary elections, which are either open or closed and whose main function is to decide which candidates will represent their parties in the general election, and general elections, during which voters decide which candidates will actually fill public offices. Primaries are contests between candidates within each party, whereas general elections are contests between candidates of opposing parties. In addition, there are three other types of elections: the initiative, which gives citizens an opportunity to propose legislation and present it to the state electorate for popular vote; the referendum, which allows a state legislature to submit proposed legislation to the state's voters for their approval; and the recall, which is an election to remove a politician from office by popular vote.

What is the process of electing the president of the United States?

The process of electing the president is usually divided into four main stages: (1) the prenomination stage, during which candidates compete in state primary elections and caucuses for delegates to the national party conventions; (2) the national conventions themselves, held in the summer of the election year, in which the two major parties nominate candidates for president and vice president and ratify platforms of policy positions and goals; (3) the general election campaign, during which the major party nominees and independent candidates compete for votes from the entire electorate, culminating in the popular vote on election day in November; and (4) the electoral college phase, in which the president and the vice president are officially elected.

How does the presidential election process of the twenty-first century differ from the election process of a century ago?

Today's presidential elections differ in many ways from those held earlier in America's history. First, voter participation today is a major factor in determining who the party nominees will be. In recent years the political parties have given a much greater role to party voters in the states (versus party leaders) when determining nominees. Secondly, in the twenty-first century's technically advanced society, the media (and more recently the Internet) play a large role in conveying information to voters and shaping the course of the campaign. Finally, the financing of presidential campaigns is substantially governed in the various election phases by a system of public funding enacted in the 1970s as a result of increasing campaign costs and fundraising pressures on the candidates.

Part of the process of electing a U.S. president is the national party convention, during which parties also ratify their official platforms.

How often are presidential elections held?

The president and vice president of the United States are elected every four years in even-numbered years divisible by the number four by a majority vote of presidential electors who are elected by popular vote in each state.

How often are Senate and House elections held?

Both Senate and House elections are held during the midterm election season in the second year into a president's four-year term. They occur on the first Tuesday after the first Monday in November of even-numbered years.

What are midterm elections?

Midterm elections are those elections for seats in the Senate and House of Representatives that take place two years into a four-year presidential term. Midterm elections determine some members of the Senate and all members of the House of Representatives as well as many state and local officials, but the results are sometimes interpreted as a popular referendum on the president's performance during the first two years of his term.

What is a nonpartisan election?

A nonpartisan election is a contest in which candidates campaign and run for office without being formally identified or associated with a particular political party.

What is a primary?

A primary is an electoral contest held to determine each political party's candidate for a particular office. In primary elections, voters decide which political candidates within a party will represent that party in the general election. Primaries are held at all levels of government, including local contests for mayor, district races for the House of Representatives, statewide elections for governor or U.S. senator, and presidential elections.

257

The most publicized primary is the presidential primary, which is the state-run election held for the purpose of nominating presidential party candidates. Presidential primaries perform this function indirectly, primarily because voters do not directly select presidential nominees but rather choose delegates from their respective states who will attend a national party convention to nominate a presidential candidate for their party. Most states restrict voting in a primary to party members, and these are called closed primary states. In contrast, open primary states allow voters to choose either party's ballot in the voting booth on primary day. None of the open-primary states require voter registration by party. Some states, such as Massachusetts, hold semiclosed primaries, which means that independents can participate; one state, Louisiana, holds completely nonpartisan elections. In 2000, thirty-nine Democratic and forty-two Republican primaries took place in the states and the District of Columbia.

What is the main advantage and disadvantage of open primaries and closed primaries?

Advocates of open primaries argue that voters should be able to choose which primary they will vote in at each election and that this ultimately increases voter participation and is the most democratic form of election. Party organizations prefer closed primaries because they promote party unity and keep those with no allegiance to a party from influencing its choice, as happens in crossover voting, when members of rival parties vote for the weakest candidate in the opposition's primary.

When is the official primary season?

Although the increasingly early dates that mark the beginning of the primary season make it harder to set an official time period for the season, based on the 2000 primaries, the season usually begins in February and ends in June. In 2000, New Hampshire kicked off the primary season—as it traditionally does—on February 1, with the largest group of states (California, Connecticut, Georgia, Maine, Maryland, Massachusetts, Missouri, New York, Ohio, Rhode Island, and Vermont) holding their primaries on March 7. The last date of the primary season was June 6, when a handful of states held their primaries. However, both the Republican and Democratic parties decided to allow states to hold their presidential primaries more than a month earlier in 2004 than in 2000.

Super Tuesday refers to the primary date in presidential elections when a large block of states hold votes at the same time. Since the first Super Tuesday in 1988, the term has lost some meaning as such multistate votes tend to happen several times in the election season.

What is Super Tuesday, and why did both major parties support its development?

Widespread use of the term "Super Tuesday" dates from 1988, when on March 9 of that year, a group of southern states came together to hold the first large and effective regional group of primaries in order to increase the importance of southern states in the presidential nomination process and lessen the impact of early votes in the New Hampshire primary and Iowa caucuses. Super Tuesday does not fall on a particular date, however, and the term has since become muddied, largely because during the presidential primary season there may be several groups of state primaries in various regions of the United States falling on one or more Tuesdays. For the 2000 election, a large number of states (including California and New York) held their primary elections on March 7, one week before the dates usually associated with Super Tuesday. However, major parties support these regional or multiregional elections because, as so many convention delegates are selected at once, the weight of such a large, simultaneous vote tends to make or break would-be presidential nominees.

What is a political caucus?

In the most general sense, a caucus is a meeting of people who gather to effect political or organizational change. In American presidential politics, the term "political caucus" has come to mean a meeting of each party's local political activists, party members, and leaders to select nominees for public office and conduct other business. In the presidential nominating process, the caucus is often used in combination with a state convention to elect delegates to the national nominating convention. In what is referred to as a layered caucus system, local party activists work at the precinct level to select delegates to county meetings, who in turn select delegates to state meetings. The state-level conventions select delegates to their party's national nominating convention, thus indicating which presidential candidate is preferred by each state party's members. The overall effect of the political caucus is to democratize presidential nominations by determining candidate preferences at the precinct level and then moving them forward. In the 2000 presidential election, both state parties in nine states selected delegates using the caucus process; Democrats scheduled caucuses in three additional states.

What is frontloading?

"Frontloading" refers to the process of pushing up the date of a state's presidential primary in hopes of gaining influence over the nomination process. In 2000, approximately three-quarters of the parties' national delegates were chosen in the six weeks between February 1 and March 14. This trend toward an early, condensed primary season has been criticized by politicians and observers who say it discourages candidates who are not able to raise sufficient campaign funds early enough in the campaign process.

Do people ever argue that a primary is a more democratic type of election than a caucus?

Yes. The main argument for the primary as a presidential selection vehicle is that it is open to everyone who wants to vote, not just party activists. Representatives of a wide variety of groups are in theory eligible to win the presidency, and primaries are the most representative means of nominating presidential candidates because they both measure a candidate's popularity and challenge the candidate to display his or her leadership and communication skills under pressure. Advocates of caucuses argue that, although primaries attract more participants than caucuses, caucus participation allows for more time with the candidates: attendees spend several hours learning about the political process and the goals of the party, listening to candidate speeches, and sizing up party leaders and elected officials in ways that aren't possible in the fast-paced primary atmosphere. Because primaries tend to get extensive media coverage, voters can easily be swayed. Critics of primaries also argue that the way they are scheduled unfairly affects their outcome; New Hampshire, simply by virtue of being the first state to hold its primary, receives much more media attention than the other states. Although arguments for regional primaries—where the nation is divided into five or six distinct geographical regions that all hold their primary elections on the same day—occasionally surface, at present the primary is the preconvention contest preferred by a majority of the states.

What is a platform?

A platform is a political party's formal written statement of its principles and goals, which is put together and issued during the presidential nomination process.

How does the party nominate political candidates?

Party conventions are the ratifying bodies that confer the nomination upon the candidate who won it in state contests during the primary season. The primary season gradually reduces the playing field of major-party candidates as the accelerated pace of the primary winnows out candidates who fall short of expectations and thus find it difficult to raise the money they need to sustain their runs. The reforms of the past thirty years have changed the dynamics of the nominating process by closely tying the allocation of delegates to electoral performance. In years past, a candidate could compete in a select number of primaries to demonstrate his or her popular appeal; today, however, the nomination goes to the candidate who holds a majority of delegates in the primaries and caucuses.

Has the vice presidential candidate always been the choice of the presidential candidate?

No. While in current practice the choice of a vice presidential nominee is the prerogative of the presidential candidate, this was not always the case. Franklin D. Roosevelt is generally regarded as the first president who was able to impose his personal vice presidential choice. Prior to this precedent, party leaders usually chose the vice presidential nominee, often an unsuccessful presidential candidate who had wide support or was perceived as adding geographical balance to the ticket.

What is the concept of ticket balance?

An active ingredient in contemporary vice presidential nominations, "ticket balance" refers to matching the presidential candidate with a vice presidential nominee whose geographical support, age, and political ideology are different from those of the presidential candidate, thus maximizing the diversity of the ticket. For example, a presidential nominee perceived as liberal will often choose a more conservative running mate. In the interest of continuity, incumbent presidents seeking reelection usually select their current vice presidents as running mates, although there have been exceptions. In 1956, for example, Republican leaders unsuccessfully urged President Dwight Eisenhower to replace Vice President Richard Nixon, and in 1976 Vice President Nelson Rockefeller announced that he would not seek the nomination, widely interpreted by po-

When Al Gore ran for president in 2000, he balanced his ticket with Senator Joe Lieberman from Connecticut, the first time a Jewish man had ever been a running mate. Strategies like this are chosen by presidential candidates in the hope of gaining more votes.

litical analysts as an effort to allow a more conservative candidate to take his place in order to bolster President Gerald Ford's candidacy. In the November 2000 presidential elections, Al Gore broke new ground by nominating Connecticut senator Joseph Lieberman as his vice presidential running mate, marking the first time a person of Jewish descent had run on a major-party ticket.

How are the candidates on the ballot determined?

Candidates for the presidency and vice presidency representing the major political parties automatically have their names placed on the general election ballot in all of the states, while minor-party candidates must satisfy various state requirements, such as gaining a requisite degree of public support in the form of petition signatures, establishing a state-mandated organizational structure, or having polled a required number of votes in the most recent statewide election. All states also provide for independent candidates to be included on the general election ballot; in almost all cases, independent candidates must submit a requisite number of petitions signed by registered voters in order to gain ballot access. Some states also provide for write-in votes for candidates not included on the ballot. Major-party congressional candidates are given automatic ballot access in all states, while minor-party and independent candidates must meet various state requirements, such as the submission of petition signatures of registered voters, in order to be placed on the general election ballot.

What is the plurality system?

Used for legislative elections in the United States, the plurality electoral system is the oldest and the most frequently used voting system in the world. Known also as the winner-takes-all system, the plurality system is straightforward: voters simply place a mark next to their preferred candidate, and the candidate who receives the highest number of votes wins. Its more technical name, the "single-member district plurality system," captures the two basic attributes of the plurality system: first, votes are cast in single-member districts—districts in which only one member of the legislature is elected; second, the winner is the candidate who receives the most votes (or the plurality of the vote). Proponents of plurality electoral systems cite three main advantages: simplicity, stability, and constituency representation.

What is proportional representation?

The main rival of the single-member plurality system and the system most used by European democracies is called proportional representation. Although there are many different forms of proportional representation, all proportional representation systems have two things in common: First, proportional representation voting systems elect people in multimember districts. Instead of one member of the legislature being elected in a small district, proportional representation involves much larger districts, where five, ten, or more members are elected, resulting in multiple winners of office in each district. Second, the multiple seats are distributed according to the proportion of the vote won by particular parties or political groups. For example, if there was a ten-member proportional representation district in which the Republican candidates won 60 percent of the vote, they would receive six of those ten seats; with 30 percent of the vote, the Democrats would win three seats, and any third party that won 10 percent of the vote would receive the remaining seat.

THE NATIONAL CONVENTION

What happens at the national convention?

The spring of an election year is characterized by vigorous campaigning for primaries and caucuses nationwide, climaxing at the national conventions of the political parties. The national conventions are said to jump-start the general election campaign for the presidential candidates. Once at the national party conventions, delegates from the states cast votes for the person who will represent the political party in the November general election. In order to secure a party's nomination, a candidate must receive a majority of the delegates' votes. It is not unusual for delegates to vote several times before one candidate secures the majority of the votes and officially becomes that party's candidate for the presidential election. If a president is running for reelection, this nomination process must still be completed. Even if the president does not face any opposition from within his own political party, the national convention still takes place.

How are delegates to the national convention chosen?

There are significant differences from state to state in the way national convention delegates are chosen. Many states even have different rules for choosing Democratic and Republican delegates. Some states award delegates to candidates on a winner-takes-all basis, meaning that the candidate with the most votes in a state is awarded all of that state's delegates. Other states award delegates in proportion to each candidate's share of the primary vote. Some delegates are officeholders in state party organizations, but many others are chosen in primary elections held in most states to select delegates. In addition, delegates can be "pledged" or "unpledged" to vote for the same candidate the voters in his or her state or district supported in the primary, and these rules vary widely by state. The number of delegates has risen over the years. In 2000, the Democratic Na-

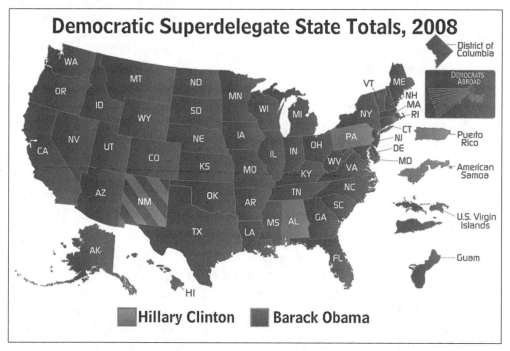

This map shows how Democrat superdelegates voted in the 2008 presidential election. Superdelegates decide which candidate they will vote for regardless of the popular vote in their state. This fact has made the practice of superdelegate votes controversial for many who feel it is not democratic.

tional Convention had 4,337 delegates and 610 alternates, while the Republican Convention had 2,066 delegates and an equal number of alternates.

What are superdelegates?

"Superdelegate" is a term used for an unpledged delegate to the national convention who is seated automatically and chooses for himself for whom he votes. Primarily associated with the Democratic National Convention, superdelegates consist of party leaders and elected Democrats that are typically more moderate and more politically seasoned than pledged Democrats. In 2016, 712 delegates made up approximately 15 percent of the total Democratic delegation.

When was the first national nominating convention?

The Anti-Masonic Party was the first to hold a national convention, meeting in Baltimore, Maryland, in September 1831 to choose William Wirt as its candidate; the Democrats and National Republicans each held national conventions the following year. By 1840 the Democrats and Whigs had adopted the national convention as the standing nominating device, which the major parties have used without exception ever since.

Are there convention rules?

Yes. At the national convention, each party establishes rules for the party as well as the convention. This is also when the party's platform—an outline of its philosophy and priorities—is adopted.

What is the two-thirds rule?

In the days when national conventions were often unruly and strongly contested gatherings, various party rules and political practices were in effect. One such rule was the so-called two-thirds rule, a Democratic Party requirement adopted at the 1832 convention (and not abandoned until 1936) mandating that the party's nominee receive a two-thirds majority of delegate votes. The record for the number of ballots cast is held

What was so special about the Election of 1832?

The election of 1824 brought an end to the use of a congressional caucus as a nominating device, but a brief transitional period followed in which state legislative caucuses and conventions and various other methods were used to nominate presidential candidates. In 1831 and 1832, the three parties contesting the election—Anti-Masonic, Democratic, and National Republican—used their respective national conventions as vehicles for nominating their presidential tickets for the first time. The use of nominating conventions reflected the growing trend toward greater democratic participation that characterized the Jackson era.

What was the "smoke-filled room"?

Convention deadlock was not unknown among Republicans, despite the fact that they required only a simple majority to nominate their candidates. At their 1920 convention, Ohio senator Warren Harding emerged as a compromise nominee. According to various stories, Harding's nomination was arranged at a secret, late-night meeting of party leaders held in a hotel suite, establishing the image of presidential nominees being selected in a smoke-filled room. The term came to imply choice of a nominee by a small group of party leaders meeting out of the public view.

by the Democrats, who required 103 ballots to nominate John W. Davis at the 1924 national convention.

What was a "dark horse" candidate?

Fear of deadlock among the most widely known candidates led to the occasional emergence of a "dark horse" candidate, a minor candidate or party figure who had not originally been considered as a candidate, as a compromise choice. Historians often cite James K. Polk of Tennessee, nominated by the Democrats in 1844, as the first dark horse candidate to win nomination. In 1936 the Democrats enacted rule changes that required only a simple majority for nomination, which largely ended the lengthy ballots that had once resulted in the selection of dark horse candidates.

Who are "favorite sons"?

The "favorite son" candidacy is another historical device that is less frequently seen now in national conventions. Favorite sons were political figures such as governors or senators who ran for the presidency, usually campaigning only in their home states, for the purpose of retaining control of state delegations. Once at the national convention, the favorite son typically used his delegates as bargaining chips to influence the party platform, help secure the nomination for a preferred candidate, seek future political favors, or enhance his own prospects as a vice presidential nominee. A 1972 rule change required that candidates garner pledges of support from at least fifty delegates, not more than twenty of whom can be from one state. This rule, which essentially required candidates to obtain a modest level of support from a geographically diverse base, helped reduce the number of names placed in nomination at subsequent conventions. Current Republican Party rules require that candidates obtain the support of a majority of delegates from five or more states in order to have their names placed in nomination.

Which national convention was a symbol of national disunity?

The 1968 Democratic National Convention, held in Chicago, was less notable for its politics than for its televised account of social unrest and national disunity. Recent events, including the assassinations of Martin Luther King Jr. and Robert Kennedy and the loss of young lives in the Vietnam War, triggered war protestors to barrage the convention and voice their concerns to the Democratic Party and its presidential candidate, Hubert Humphrey. Chicago mayor Richard Daley met the protestors with twelve thousand police officers and the Illinois National Guard, resulting in a bloody riot that led to hundreds of arrests and injuries. Captured by television cameras and broadcast across the nation, the convention doomed Humphrey's candidacy and intensified the revolutionary protests against the Vietnam War.

Five miles north of the 1968 Democratic National Convention in Chicago, the Youth International Party (Yippies) organized a war protest event. The convention probably had more protestors surrounding it than any political convention before or after it.

Which was the longest national convention?

The 1924 Democratic National Convention in New York, which lasted seventeen days and required 103 ballots to select conservative lawyer John W. Davis as the presidential nominee, was the longest in American history. Catholic New Yorker Al Smith and Protestant prohibitionist William McAdoo of California were the two candidates with the most support, but they were also the two candidates who were most disliked among the convention crowd. It took seventeen days of compromise before candidate John W. Davis was nominated for the Democratic ticket.

When was the last major convention at which the nomination was still in doubt and had to be decided at the convention?

The 1976 Republican National Convention was the most recent convention in America's history at which the identity of a major party's nominee was in question before the nominating ballots were cast. That year, President Gerald Ford fended off a strong challenge from former California governor Ronald Reagan to secure the nomination.

THE ELECTION CAMPAIGN

What are the factors in a successful election campaign?

Political scientists and scholars agree that campaigning for an office such as the presidency, a governorship, or a Senate seat is an art, involving many layers of activity that must come together successfully in order for a candidate to win office. First, there is a very personal aspect to campaigning, as the candidate and his supporters make appearances, meet voters, conduct press conferences, and give speeches around the nation; here, the candidate's diplomatic skill is tested, and a balance must be struck between campaign issues to appeal to everyday voters and leaders of various groups and voting blocs, such as business, labor, and key ethnic populations. There is also an organizational aspect, which involves planning sophisticated mass mailings, coordinating electronic telephone banks to reach voters, reaching special interest groups for money and endorsements, and raising money to support the campaign. The media aspect involves both running paid advertisements and soliciting the press in an effort to gain the maximum campaign coverage possible as well as managing the art of damage control, that is, responding to and turning around any form of controversial or negative press.

Who are the key players in a candidate's election campaign?

Depending on the candidate's level of office, an organizational staff consisting of anywhere from a dozen volunteers to hundreds of paid specialists carries out the day-to-day work of the campaign. In presidential campaigns, literally tens of thousands of volunteers are at work, directed by a paid staff of hundreds, including lawyers, accountants, and a variety of consultants. The campaign manager and a few political consultants run the campaign, providing both the strategy and the hands-on plan for carrying the strategy out. Key consultants include the media consultant, who is the chief liaison with the press; the pollster, who manages the public opinion surveys critical to the direction of the campaign; and the direct mailer, who oversees direct-mail fundraising efforts. Most argue that the most valuable player is the finance chair—directly responsible for soliciting and garnering the large contributions that pay the staff and keep the campaign running—because without adequate financing a campaign comes to a grinding halt.

How are presidential campaigns generally managed?

Recent presidential campaigns have been managed by separate candidate-centered organizations, ad hoc groups assembled for the specific purpose of winning the election. After the conventions, these committees are usually expanded to include key staff from the campaigns of rival contenders for the nomination. The campaign organization prepares the campaign plan, schedules appearances for the campaigners, conducts opposition and survey research, manages the national media campaign, and conducts both voter-registration and get-out-the-vote drives. Campaigns are organized on the national, state, and local levels, overlapping existing party structures, especially at the local level. One of the campaign organization's main goals is to broaden the candidate's appeal, bringing his or her message to the largest possible number of independent voters and to disgruntled members of the other party in order to win votes.

What is a campaign plan?

A campaign plan outlines the strategy and tactics that campaign organizations and candidates hope will bring a winning combination of electoral and popular votes in the gen-

While the official campaign season is still about a year long in America, candidates may start much earlier than that to raise interest in their cause. Donald Trump, for example, announced his candidacy in June 2015, seventeen months before the actual election.

eral election. The plan details the issues the nominees will emphasize and aspects of the candidates' personal images they hope to convey to voters. Specific points include a "plan of attack" on the platform, issues, and candidates of the opposition; methods for targeting socioeconomic, ethnic, and religious groups that the campaign organization feels will most likely accept the campaign message; an assessment of the ticket's strengths and weaknesses in various states; and geographic areas the candidates should target in order to secure an electoral college majority.

How long is a presidential election campaign?

Presidential candidates begin organizing their campaigns and raising money a year or more before the primary season. While the length of the nominating season has remained unchanged, pre-election maneuvering by candidates usually begins shortly after the previous presidential election, and exploratory committees are often in operation one or two years before an election.

Why are political campaigns sometimes called horse races?

The term "horse race" is sometimes used as a metaphor for an election campaign because it conveys the feeling of excitement that people experience when they watch a horse race or other sporting event. The term has also been applied to media coverage of

What is the coattail effect?

The term "coattail effect" refers to the ability of a popular officeholder or candidate, on the strength of his or her own popularity, to increase the chances for victory of other candidates of the same political party. The candidate carries others to victory "on his coattails."

campaigns, which frequently emphasizes the candidates' standings in public opinion polls as if they were horses in a race, rather than their positions on the issues.

When was the first public presidential debate held? What about the first televised debate?

The year 1948 saw the first public debate between presidential candidates Thomas E. Dewey and Harold Stassen, which was held as a radio broadcast in connection with the Oregon Republican presidential primary. The first televised debate took place in 1956 between contestants for the Democratic presidential nomination Adlai Stevenson and Estes Kefauver.

Have the number of debates increased, and what does this phenomenon have to do with the straw poll?

Yes. Campaign debates have become an increasingly important aspect of the nominating process, and an unprecedented number occurred during the 1988 primary season: approximately sixty debates, virtually all televised, were held among presidential candidates of one or both parties. In general, the increase in debates through the 2016 presidential campaigns has coincided with a decrease in the number of straw poll elections before and during the nominating season. Straw polls measure candidate popularity among party activists at state conventions but have no influence on the selection of delegates. To some extent, candidate debates offset one of the most frequently criticized aspects of the election process: the idea that the combined influence of the media and back-to-back primaries emphasizes candidate image over substantive issues.

What is the League of Women Voters, and what does it have to do with the debate system currently used in national campaigns?

The League of Women Voters (LWV) is a nonpartisan political organization that, according to its mission statement, "encourages the informed and active participation of citizens in government, works to increase understanding of major public policy issues, and influences public policy through education and advocacy." The organization's involvement in the debating process dates to 1952, when several presidential candidates and/or their representatives discussed the issues in a joint televised appearance before the LWV

269

national convention, the precursor of the modern televised debate. Because candidate debates are a key component of a political campaign, the LWV often sponsors or cosponsors presidential debates, as it did in 1976 (when it sponsored a series of three presidential debates between nominees Jimmy Carter and Gerald Ford) and in 1992 with cosponsor CNN.

What is the dirtiest presidential campaign on record?

In his book *Presidential Campaigns,* author Paul F. Boller, Jr., remarks, "Presidential campaigns are a lot nicer today than they used to be. What respectable person today would think of calling one of the candidates for the highest office in the land a carbuncled-faced old drunkard? Or a howling atheist? Or a pickpocket, thief, traitor, lecher, syphilitic, gorilla, crook, anarchist, murderer? Yet such charges were regular features of American presidential contests in the 19th century." Although many early campaigns had their share of derogatory remarks, historians agree that the 1828 presidential campaign between Andrew Jackson (1765–1845) and incumbent president John Quincy Adams (1767–1848) was probably history's dirtiest. The conflict had its roots in the 1824 election between the same two candidates, in which Jackson won the popular and electoral votes, but the House gave Adams the presidency. In 1828 the mudslinging ranged from accusations of adultery against Andrew and Rachel Jackson to suggestions that President Adams had spent thousands of federal dollars to stock the White House with gambling equipment. Attacks against Jackson included criticism of his leadership abilities, name calling involving his mother and wife, and allegations that he was involved in dueling and brawling. Words used to describe him included "slave trader," "gambler," and "promoter of cock fights and

horse races." Despite this unprecedented attack on the candidates' personalities, the campaign resulted in Jackson's landslide victory, the revival of a two-party system, and the creation of a new national party, the Democratic Party of the United States.

Who is repeatedly cited as one of the most colorful campaigners in America's political history?

The 1928 Democratic presidential candidate, Alfred E. Smith (1873–1944), is often noted for his commanding personality, razor-sharp wit, and ability to launch into impromptu speeches laden with humor. A New York Catholic and longtime member of the Tammany Hall machine, Smith's history and upbringing made it difficult for him to appeal to a wide electorate. He is most remembered for his trademarks: a

A governor of New York, Alfred E. Smith campaigned for president in 1928 as one of the more colorful figures that year. Although he was connected to the corrupt Tammany Hall political machine, his wit and humorous speeches were memorable. He was also the first Catholic to run for the White House.

brown derby hat, an upbeat campaign song ("The Sidewalks of New York"), and his habit of pronouncing "radio" as "raddio."

Which vice presidential and presidential candidates successfully hid illnesses during their campaigns?

Franklin D. Roosevelt kept his deteriorating heart condition quiet during his 1944 re-election campaign (Roosevelt's own personal physician asserting that there was "nothing wrong organically with him at all…. He's perfectly okay"). During the 1960 presidential campaign, John F. Kennedy successfully hid his long-rumored and publicly denied struggle with Addison's disease, a failure of the adrenal glands for which the Massachusetts senator received injections of cortisone and other medications. Edmund Muskie, an early 1972 Democratic hopeful who was being treated for depression, was considered unfit to hold office after he allegedly cried in public. George McGovern's 1972 running mate, Missouri senator Tom Eagleton, was forced to quit the ticket within a month of the Democratic National Convention after the media revealed allegations of electroshock therapy as treatment for his clinical depression. While in times past the media often went along with not publicizing candidates' or incumbents' health conditions, today the media make much of presidential hopefuls' health status, as witnessed by its coverage of Bill Bradley's irregular heartbeat and John McCain's recurring skin cancer during the 2000 campaign.

Which presidential candidates sought a place on the national ballot at least three times in their political career but never won office?

It is not unusual for a candidate to make several unsuccessful runs for political office, including the presidency. Consider these unlucky candidates: Henry Clay, who was nominated as a Democratic Republican in 1824, as a National Republican in 1832, and as a Whig in 1844 (he also ran two other times without a nomination as a Whig in 1840 and 1848); William Jennings Bryan, who ran as a Democrat in 1896, 1900, and 1908; Eugene Debs, who ran on the Socialist ticket five times: in 1900, 1904, 1908, 1912, and 1920; and Gus Hall, who ran on the Communist Party ticket in 1972, 1976, 1980, and 1984. However, the candidate who probably holds the record for the most unsuccessful runs for his party's top nomination is Republican Harold Stassen, who sought the nomination nine times between the years 1944 and 1992.

CAMPAIGN FINANCE

Who pays for the campaigns of candidates?

Most of the funding for federal candidates comes from voluntary contributions by individuals, groups, and political parties. Since 1976, presidential candidates have also had the option of public funding for their campaigns, which is supported by taxpayer

271

designations of three dollars. Public funding is not available to candidates running for Congress.

In the 1980s and 1990s, the money given to presidential campaigns usually came in the form of "soft money"—unlimited financial contributions made to the political parties by corporations, labor unions, and wealthy individuals. During the 1998 election, for example, the parties raised $172.5 million in soft-money contributions, Philip Morris being the largest single contributor of soft money to the political parties with donations totaling $1.7 million. Businesses and labor groups also make large "independent expenditures," such as media campaigns to endorse or oppose specific candidates, and the political parties themselves can also make campaign expenditures as long as these are independent of their own candidates. In addition, candidates may spend unlimited amounts of their own personal funds on their campaigns. Presidential and vice presidential candidates who accept public funds cannot spend more than $50,000 of their own and their immediate family's funds.

The Shays–Meehan/McCain–Feingold campaign finance reform bill, passed by Congress in March 2002 and signed into law by President George W. Bush as the Bipartisan Campaign Finance Reform Act, changed the terms of soft-money contributions. The bill prohibits national political parties from raising or spending soft money and also bars state and local parties from spending soft money on federal elections, with one exception: the bill allows parties to collect up to $10,000 per donor annually in those states that allow soft money, but the money can only be utilized for voter registration and turnout efforts.

What do the terms "hard money" and "soft money" mean?

These two terms are used to differentiate between campaign funding that is and is not regulated by campaign finance law. "Hard money" refers to money that is regulated by the Federal Elections Commission and that can be used to influence the outcome of federal elections because it supports the election of a specific candidate. In contrast, "soft money" is the term used for those funds raised and spent by political parties, corporations, labor unions, and other groups that are not regulated by law and can only be spent on activities that do not affect the election of candidates for national offices. These activities include voter registration drives, party-building events, and administrative costs for state and local candidates. In the 1990s, the term "soft money" came to be synonymous with unlimited financial contributions from influential labor and business groups. The most significant component of the Bipartisan Campaign Finance Reform Act is its clampdown on soft-money contributions: the act makes it illegal for national political parties to raise or spend soft money and bars states and local parties from spending soft money on federal elections, with the exception of voter registration and turnout efforts.

Was there an increase in the amount of soft money raised in the 1990s?

Yes. Republicans raised $138.2 million in soft money in the 1996 presidential election cycle, a 178 percent increase over 1992. During that same time, Democrats raised $123.9

million, a 242 percent increase over 1992. In the 1998 midterm election cycle, Republicans raised $93.7 million, a 144 percent increase over the funds they raised in 1994; Democrats raised $78.8 million, an 84 percent increase over their 1994 fundraising. This skyrocketing of soft money contributions led, in part, to the passage of the Bipartisan Campaign Finance Reform Act. Effective November 6, 2002, the act prohibits national political parties from raising or spending soft money.

How did incumbents have the advantage during the first decade of the twenty-first century?

An overwhelming proportion of special interest contributions went to candidates already in office, especially those whose seniority and influence were highly regarded by special interest groups. In the last several general election contests, Republican incumbents in the House of Representatives outspent their challengers by nearly an eight-to-one margin; for Democrats, the margin was four to one. Critics of the system were very vocal in maintaining that this process limited competition and intimidated those potential challengers who couldn't afford the television time they needed to become known among voters. The incumbent advantage had a particularly detrimental effect on the candidacies of minorities and women seeking to break through the political barriers that traditionally have stood in the way of their political involvement.

Soft money donations to political campaigns in Washington have been skyrocketing since the 1990s. The more the public knows about such dealings, the more it undermines Americans' confidence in their leaders.

How much can individuals donate to a particular candidate?

As a result of the Bipartisan Campaign Finance Reform Act, individuals can contribute up to $2,000 per candidate per election, with primary and general elections counted separately. Individuals can give $5,000 per year to a political action committee (PAC), $25,000 per national party committee per year, and $10,000 per state or local party committee per year. In addition, the act increases the aggregate limit on individual contributions from $25,000 per year to $95,000 per two-year election cycle, of which only $37,500 may be contributed to candidates over the two years. The two-year election cycle starts on January 1 of odd-numbered years and extends to December 31 of even-numbered years.

273

What does the Bipartisan Campaign Finance Reform Act of 2002 do?

The Shays-Meehan/McCain-Feingold campaign finance reform bill, the brainchild of Congressmen Christopher Shays (R-CT) and Marty Meehan (D-MA) and Senators John McCain (R-AZ) and Russ Feingold (D-WI), is the first bill since the Watergate era to seriously rein in the large donations of soft money that characterized national party fundraising efforts in the 1980s and 1990s. Signed into law by President George W. Bush as the Bipartisan Campaign Finance Reform Act of 2002, the law prohibits the national political parties from raising or spending the unlimited financial donations from labor unions, corporations, and wealthy individuals known as soft money. It also bars state and local parties from spending soft money on federal elections, with one exception: it allows parties to collect up to $10,000 per donor annually in those states that allow soft money. However, the money can only be used for voter registration and turnout. To balance this cut in soft money at federal and state levels, the act increases individual hard money contribution limits. It doubles individual contributions to candidates running for president and Congress so that individuals can donate $2,000 to candidates per election, for a total of $95,000 to parties and candidates every two years. The bill eases contribution limits even further for federal candidates who run against wealthy, self-financed opponents.

In addition, the bill prohibits special interest groups from using their general funds to finance radio or television ads that target a federal candidate within one month before a primary election and two months before a general election. Contribution limits for political action committees (PACs) remain unchanged. Most of the bill took effect on November 6, 2002; the hard money limitations took effect January 1, 2003. Analysts say that the act's most predictable impact on campaign finance in future elections will involve an increase in the influence of corporations, trade associations, and other organizations with large, hard-money PACs, while decreasing the influence of those that have relied primarily on large, soft-money contributions. If this is the case, the pressure many corporations and wealthy individuals feel to make large donations to the political parties in response to requests from members of Congress and White House officials. In contrast, pressure for smaller donations of hard dollars from individuals will increase.

What are some of the issues surrounding campaign finance reform?

Advocates of campaign finance reform maintain that campaign spending is a self-serving system spun out of control. In 1996, for example, congressional candidates spent more than $765 million on their races, a 5 percent increase over the record-breaking 1994 elections. According to reform advocates, unlimited campaign spending contributed to a number of problems in the 1990s, including an increasing reliance by candidates on special interest dollars to cover skyrocketing campaign costs; a tendency among incumbents to spend large amounts of their time raising funds rather than serving the people; and frustration among potential candidates who were dismayed at having to raise exorbitant amounts of money in order for their candidacies to have a chance at succeeding. In addition, campaign donations from political action committees (PACs) can be directly linked to the way elected officials vote on issues once they reach public office.

Advocates of campaign finance reform argued that the methods of financing political campaigns should enable candidates to compete more equitably for public office, allow maximum citizen participation in the political process, and combat corruption and undue influence. Specific suggestions for campaign finance reform included placing additional limits on contributions, which led mavericks like Congressman Christopher Shays (R-CT) and Senator John McCain (R-AZ) to sponsor the Shays-Meehan/McCain-Feingold campaign finance reform bill. Other suggestions continue to be discussed, including encouraging citizens to put voluntary limits on spending; introducing measures to close loopholes in the current law; encouraging the public financing of campaigns; and introducing new disclosure and reporting requirements.

Can the government regulate campaign spending?

Yes. By putting caps on donations and the amount of money that candidates can spend, the government regulates campaign spending. Money used to communicate with voters independently of a candidate's campaign is subject to federal regulation only if the message contains express advocacy (i.e., wording like "vote for Jones"). If an ad campaign or other media communication contains express advocacy and has not been coordinated with the candidate, it is considered an independent expenditure under the Federal Election Campaign Act, and there are no limits on the amounts that may be spent on these types of communications. If a media communication does not contain express advocacy but rather discusses a candidate's actions, voting record, or position on an issue, courts have generally held that funding for these messages is not subject to federal contribution limits, primarily because such speech is protected under the First Amendment. The Bipartisan Campaign Finance Reform Act of 2002 prohibits special interest groups from using their general funds to pay for radio or television ads that target a federal candidate within one month before a primary election and two months before a general election.

What did the Federal Election Campaign Act do?

Known colloquially as the FECA, this 1971 law, which was amended in 1974, 1976, and 1979, governs the financing of federal elections. The law requires candidates and political committees to disclose the sources of their funding and how they spend their money; regulates the contributions received and expenditures made during federal election campaigns; and governs the public funding of presidential elections. The provisions of the Bipartisan Campaign Finance Reform Act of 2002 amend the Federal Election Campaign Act.

The Federal Election Commission building in Washington, D.C., is where attorneys and administrators work to enforce campaign finance law, such as limits to contributions and management of public funding of elections.

What is the role of the Federal Election Commission?

The Federal Election Commission (FEC) is an independent regulatory agency charged with administering and enforcing federal campaign finance law. Established by Congress in 1975, the duties of the FEC are to disclose campaign finance information, to enforce provisions of the law such as the limits and prohibitions on contributions, and to oversee the public funding of presidential elections. The commission is made up of six members, each of whom is appointed by the president and confirmed by the Senate. Each member serves a six-year term, and two seats are subject to appointment every two years. By law, no more than three commissioners can be members of the same political party, and at least four votes are required for any official commission action.

THE POPULAR VOTE AND THE ROLE OF THE ELECTORAL COLLEGE

Is the presidential candidate who gets the highest number of popular votes the winner?

No. The president and vice president of the United States are not elected directly by popular vote but rather by electors, individuals who are chosen in the November general election in presidential election years. Known collectively as the electoral college, it is this entity that votes directly for the president and vice president.

Were presidents ever elected popularly?

No. The electoral college was established by the Founding Fathers as a compromise between election of the president by Congress and election by popular vote. They were attempting to create a blueprint that would allow for the election of the president without disturbing the carefully designed balance between the presidency and Congress and between the states and the federal government. Mandated by the Constitution and modified by the Twelfth and Twenty-third Amendments, the College of Electors (as the Founders called it) has served as the nation's method for selecting its highest official for over two hundred years.

What is the electoral college, and how does it elect the United States president and vice president?

Each state is allocated a number of electors equal to the number of its U.S. senators plus the number of its U.S. representatives. When Americans vote for a president and vice president, they are actually voting for presidential electors, known collectively as the electoral college. It is these electors, chosen by the people, who elect the chief executive. The Constitution assigns each state a number of electors equal to the combined total of the state's senators (always two) and House delegation (which may change each decade according to the size of each state's population as determined in the U.S. Census).

In each presidential election year, a group (ticket or slate) of candidates is nominated by political parties and other groupings in each state, usually at a state party convention or by the party state committee. It is these elector-candidates, rather than the presidential and vice presidential nominees, for whom the people vote in the November election, which is held on the Tuesday after the first Monday in November. In most states, voters cast a single vote for the slate of electors pledged to the party presidential and vice presidential candidates of their choice. The slate winning the most popular votes is elected; this is known as the winner-takes-all, or general ticket, system. Maine and Nebraska use the district system, in which two electors are chosen on a statewide, at-large basis, and one is elected in each congressional district. Electors assemble in their respective states on the Monday after the second Wednesday in December. They are pledged and expected, but not required, to vote for the candidates they represent. Separate ballots are cast for president and vice president, after which the electoral college ceases to exist for another four years.

How are electoral votes tabulated?

The electoral vote results are counted and certified by a joint session of Congress held on January 6 of the year following the election. A majority of electoral votes (currently 270 of 538) is required to win. If no candidate receives a majority, the president is elected by the House of Representatives and the vice president is elected by the Senate, a process known as a contingent election.

Who can serve as an elector?

Aside from members of Congress and employees of the federal government, who are prohibited from serving as electors in order to maintain the balance between the legislative and executive branches of the federal government, anyone may serve as an elector. Since electors are often selected in recognition of their service and dedication to their political party, they are often state-elected officials, party leaders, or persons who have a personal or political affiliation with the presidential candidate. The process for selecting electors varies throughout the United States. Generally, the political parties nominate electors at their state party conventions or by a vote of the party's central committee in each state.

Given the electoral college procedure, is the individual vote really meaningful?

Yes. Within his or her state, a person's vote has a great deal of significance. In the electoral college system, the people do not elect the president and vice president through a direct nationwide vote, but a person's vote helps decide which candidate receives that state's electoral votes. It is possible that an elector could ignore the results of the popular vote, but that occurs very rarely.

How can the electoral college defeat the will of a majority of the people in selecting a president?

The Founding Fathers devised the electoral college system as part of their plan to divide power between the states and the national government. Under the federal system adopted in the Constitution, the nationwide popular vote has no legal significance. As a result, it is possible for the electoral votes awarded on the basis of state elections to pro-

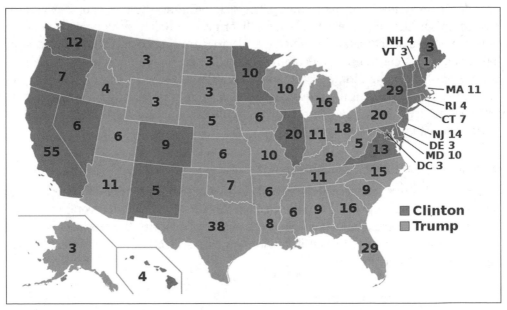

In the 2016 presidential election, Donald Trump had fewer popular votes than rival Hillary Clinton, but he ended up with more electoral votes and won. Previous presidents who entered the White House with a minority of popular votes include John Quincy Adams (1824), Rutherford B. Hayes (1876), Benjamin Harrison (1888), and George W. Bush (2000).

duce a result different from the nationwide popular vote. The electoral vote totals determine the winner, not the statistical plurality or majority a candidate may have in the nationwide vote totals. Forty-eight of the fifty states award electoral votes on a winner-takes-all basis (as does the District of Columbia). For example, all fifty-four of California's electoral votes go to the winner of that state election, even if the vote is split 50.1 percent to 49.9 percent.

Since the nation's first presidential election in 1792 there have only been a few times when the winner of the popular vote has not won the election or when the decision was thrown to the House of Representatives, as required by the Constitution. The first viciously contested election occurred in 1876, when Democrat Samuel Tilden won the popular vote and won the electoral college by one ballot, but the ballots in three southern states were contested (Louisiana, South Carolina, and Florida), eventually throwing the election to Republican Rutherford B. Hayes. One of the most contested elections in recent history was the 2000 presidential race, in which George W. Bush received less of the popular vote (48.4 percent) than opponent Al Gore (who garnered 48.6 percent) but picked up the key state of Florida, thus winning 271 electoral votes to Gore's 267.

Do electors ever switch votes?

Theoretically, yes, electors can switch votes but in reality never do and likely never will. There is no constitutional provision or federal law that requires electors to vote according to the results of the popular vote in their states. Some states, however, require electors to cast their votes according to the popular vote. These pledges fall into two categories: electors bound by state law and those bound by pledges to political parties. In the twenty-first century, it is rare for electors to disregard the popular vote by casting their electoral vote for someone other than their party's candidate. Electors generally hold a leadership position in their party or were chosen in recognition of years of loyal service to the party. Throughout United States history, more than 99 percent of electors have voted as pledged.

Has the electoral college ever voted unanimously for any president?

Yes. The electoral college voted unanimously on two occasions, both times for George Washington, for his terms beginning in 1789 and 1793. James Monroe just missed sharing this claim to fame, since in the presidential election of 1820 all of the electors except one voted to reelect Monroe.

Why does the United States still have the electoral college?

The electoral college process is part of the original design of the Constitution, and a constitutional amendment would need to be passed in order to change this system. While many different proposals to alter the presidential election process, such as direct nationwide election by the people, have been suggested over the years, none has been passed by Congress and sent to the states for ratification. However, the Twelfth Amendment, which deals with the expansion of voting rights and the use of the popular vote in the states as the vehicle for selecting electors, has substantially changed the electoral college process.

What is a referendum, and how does it differ from an initiative?

In many states, voters play a direct role in the lawmaking process, exercising the power of both referendum and initiative in local elections, where voting on issues such as those involving businesses, schools, neighborhoods, transportation, safety, and health can transform a community. If a law has been passed in the state legislature, it may be sent back to the voters to accept or reject, letting the voters decide directly whether a new law should be put into effect. This is known as the power of referendum. In the process of initiative, a group of voters signs a petition asking for a specific law. If enough people sign the petition, qualified voters must be given a chance to vote for or against the proposed law, which will go into effect if more than half (a majority) of the votes are in favor of the law.

During a presidential election, who is responsible in a given locality for voting procedures and counting the votes?

Each state's Secretary of State office is responsible for facilitating statewide voter registration in accordance with state laws; testing and certifying all voting systems used in state elections; preparing ballots and election forms and materials; tabulating, processing, and certifying election results; and responding to requests for advice, information, and interpretation on election laws and procedures.

What is a vote recount, and when is a recount necessary?

A vote recount involves just that—recounting votes cast in an election. Each state has specific procedures a candidate must follow when filing a protest that results in a recount as well as specific procedures for conducting recounts of paper ballots, voting machines, and electronic equipment. In general, a political candidate may choose to conduct a recount if there are reasonable grounds for alleging that the count of votes at any voting station was inaccurate or the number of invalid or rejected ballots was sufficient to affect the election results.

In the 2000 presidential election, how many votes were eventually not counted for either candidate in Florida, and what was the percentage of uncounted votes nationwide?

Although a definitive number was never reached, according to media sources, approximately 180,000 Florida ballots were cast but not counted. On a nationwide level, a July 2001 joint study conducted by the Massachusetts Institute of Technology and California Institute of Technology revealed that four million to six million of the one hundred million votes cast in November 2000 were not counted, citing faulty voting equipment, confusing ballots, voter error, and problems at polling places—including long lines, short hours, and inconvenient locations—as the main reasons. The estimate of lost votes is at least twice as high as one released earlier in July 2001 by House Democrats, who said that about two million votes, or nearly 2 percent of the total, had not been counted. The study also confirmed that Florida was just one of many states with ballot problems, citing Illinois, New York, South Carolina, Idaho, Wyoming, and Georgia as having high rates of spoiled, unmarked, or uncounted ballots.

What did the Supreme Court rule in its final decision affecting the 2000 vote?

In the Florida vote count certified on November 26, 2000, a total of 537 votes out of the more than 5.8 million cast separated Al Gore and George W. Bush. Whether additional votes from manual recounts would be counted was in litigation between the two candidates and their representatives until the evening of December 12, when the Supreme Court ruled that manual recounts could not continue on constitutional grounds because Florida's lack of uniform standards for the recount-

One of the controversies of the vote count in Florida concerned "hanging chads." Punch-card ballots were used, and, apparently, if the voter did not thoroughly punch a hole in the card, the card-reading machine would not count the vote correctly. Election staff had to examine cards manually, but many still felt the final count was not precise.

ing process violated the Fourteenth Amendment's equal protection guarantees. The Court's five-to-four ruling thus awarded the White House to George W. Bush, based on the original certified vote.

Have the results of any other national election ever been seriously opposed in U.S. history?

Yes. Historians generally agree on four close and disputed elections in the nineteenth century and two in the twentieth. In the election of 1800, presidential candidates Aaron Burr and Thomas Jefferson, both nominees of the Republican Party, tied in the electoral college vote with seventy-three votes each, throwing the election into the House of Representatives and triggering the passage of the Twelfth Amendment, which maintains that electoral delegates must vote separately for president and vice president. During the election of 1824, four candidates ran for the presidency, but none received either a majority of the popular vote or a majority of the electoral college; Andrew Jackson led runner-up John Quincy Adams in both popular and electoral votes but ultimately lost the presidency when the House of Representatives chose Adams. In the presidential race of 1876, Democrat Samuel Tilden won the popular vote and the electoral college by one vote against Republican Rutherford B. Hayes, but ballots contested in several southern states ultimately threw the White House to Hayes. During the election of 1888, Democratic incumbent Grover Cleveland won the popular vote but lost in the electoral college by sixty-five votes to Republican Benjamin Harrison, marking the first time in history that the electoral college had denied the presidency to the clear winner of the country's popular vote.

In the 1960 presidential election, a little over 100,000 votes ended up separating incumbent Republican vice president Richard Nixon and Democrat John F. Kennedy, making it one of the closest elections of the twentieth century. When it became clear that Kennedy had won the state of Illinois by approximately eight thousand popular votes, thus picking up that state's electoral votes, Nixon conceded the election. Despite these close races, no election in history has come down to such a margin as the 537-vote difference that ultimately decided the 2000 presidential contest.

How did the results of the 2000 presidential election play a role in election reform?

The 2000 presidential election exposed unprecedented weaknesses in America's voting systems, prompting many to push for reform. Critics cited problems such as antiquated voting machines, ballot systems that confused voters, an insufficient number of polling places, limited accessibility for people with disabilities, chaotic absentee ballot procedures, and a general lack of standardization and consistency. Under particular scrutiny was the punch-card voting system that became the focus of the Florida recount. In addition, civil rights concerns arose from the unfair application of voter identification requirements and from the fact that many of the oldest, faultiest voting machines found their way into low-income, minority neighborhoods.

Since the 2000 election fiasco, several states have implemented election overhaul measures, and several others have discussed revising their election laws. In April 2002 the Senate approved a landmark $3.5-billion bill that required states to upgrade their voting systems over a five-year period, including replacing outdated ballot-counting machines, improving access to polling places for the disabled, and increasing voter participation. The House passed its own voting reform bill in December 2001, authorizing $2.65 billion in federal aid to the states over three years. During this period, lawmakers agreed on certain areas of reform, most of which have come to pass to varying degrees of effectiveness: (1) states should maintain a statewide voter registration list that is linked to local precincts; (2) voters whose names do not appear on the registration list should have the right to cast a provisional ballot that would be counted if their registration is verified; and (3) in an effort to reduce the number of mistakes that occur at the polls, more time and money should be used in recruiting and training poll workers and educating voters about their rights and responsibilities. In an effort to provide fair elections for all eligible voters, states have taken a closer look at their voter registration procedures, provisional ballots, absentee and early voting procedures, and other key election reform issues, and procedures for counting overseas ballots and military votes have improved.

What types of voting methods and machines are currently used?

Counties across America vary in the voting methods and machines used, typically relying on antiquated equipment that may not count votes accurately. The oldest and simplest form of voting is the paper ballot, on which a voter simply places a check next to the name of his or her preferred candidate, and the votes are then counted by hand. Mechanical lever systems, which were developed in the 1890s, involve large displays of the entire ballot and small levers next to each choice; the voter flips a lever to choose a candidate and, once finished voting, pulls a large lever, which counts each vote. Developed in the 1960s, punch-card systems require that voters use a stylus to punch a hole in a pre-scored card next to their preferred candidate's name. According to an October 2001 study by the University of California at Berkeley, the trend in voting equipment is away from paper, punch-card, and lever systems and toward more modern systems, including those

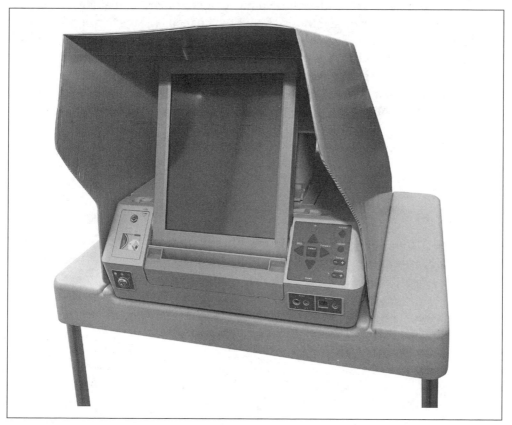

This modern touch screen voting machine is designed to assist the blind, deaf, and people with other disabilities with their voting.

utilizing optical scanning (in which an infrared or other scanner records the markings on a paper ballot) and computer touch screens (where voters push a button or touch the screen of an ATM-type machine to choose a candidate). Many jurisdictions are replacing older voting equipment with more modern technology, and some are considering the use of vote-by-mail and Internet voting to ensure greater degrees of accuracy.

Optical scanning and electronic systems perform better than other systems, especially in large counties, and the newer versions of both systems give voters feedback so that they can check their selections before submitting their ballots. Touch screen electronic voting systems allow individuals to select a ballot translated into a foreign language, and some of these systems allow disabled persons to vote by listening to recordings.

Can voters expect to eventually cast their votes online?

Although the Internet has allowed large numbers of Americans to get involved in politics in unprecedented ways, only thirty states offered online voting in the November 2016 presidential election, primarily for voters living overseas or serving in the military. However, fears of hackers tampering with or shutting down voting sites have led most states to proceed cautiously with online voting. Critics also argue that a gap exists between connected Americans and those without the financial means to own a computer or pay for Internet service, making at-home Internet voting a viable option only for a select demographic. Optimists, however, point to the potential of the Internet to create a more democratic America by implementing a foolproof cyberspace system that soon would be available to all. Few disagree that this medium holds vast possibilities for involving the United States citizenry in the political process in the twenty-first century.

THE MEDIA MACHINE

THE MEDIA AND PUBLIC OPINION

What is public opinion?

Public opinion is the complex collection of the opinions of many different groups of people and represents the sum total of all their views relating to matters of public affairs, namely politics and public policy. Rather than being the single, unified viewpoint of a robotic mindset, public opinion represents a variety of groups, each with a differing point of view on a particular subject.

What is the definition of "mass media"?

Mass media are the types of media that reach mass audiences—for example, television, radio, film, books, magazines, newspapers, the Internet, and social media.

How is public opinion measured through the media?

The general content of public opinion can be found within a variety of media sources, including books, journals, magazine and newspaper articles and editorials, comments made on radio and television, newsletters published by special interest groups, paid advertisements (print, billboards, and commercials), letters to the editor, and emails to politicians. While politicians often use these means of expression to familiarize themselves with certain issues, the views expressed aren't necessarily indicative of the size of the group that holds them or how strongly an opinion is held, so politicians often turn to other measuring sticks, such as public opinion polls, to supplement them. Polling is also a large part of major media outlet measurements, with entities like the *New York Times* and the Cable News Network (CNN) polling the public on political issues and politician approval on a regular basis.

Where do Americans get their news?

Americans get their news from the top four mass media: television, newspapers, radio, and magazines. With at least one television set in 98 percent of the nation's homes turned on for multiple hours each day, television is the primary vehicle for delivering the news. While television replaced newspapers as the primary source of people's political information in the 1960s, the more than eleven thousand newspapers published in the United States are still a major contender for people's opinions. And because many of today's major newspapers, including the *New York Times,* the *Los Angeles Times,* the *Chicago Tribune,* and the *Washington Post,* have credible reputations for delivering in-depth coverage of national and local news, they are still a favorite among their combined 150 million readers per issue. Radio has long been a choice of those wanting to pick up quick snippets of news and political information on their way to and from work, with at least one station in every major city broadcasting nothing but news. In addition, the popularity of talk radio and the many stations that cater to ethnic-specific audiences has helped this medium reach and influence an increasingly diverse public. Last but not least are the many news magazines that dominate the newsstands, including *Time* and *Newsweek,* which enjoy a combined circulation of nearly twelve million copies each week.

What is the most powerful form of mass media?

For disseminating ideas, influencing public opinion, and reaching voters, television wins hands-down as the most powerful form of mass media. With the typical American watching a minimum of three hours of television per day and the typical household running its television seven hours per day, television attracts a large and wide-reaching audience that no other form of communication can reach. With the 1980s deregulation of the U.S. telecommunications industry and the advent of cable television, the average community in the United States receives thirty television channels that cover every imaginable component of society. Americans can even watch the House and Senate at work on C-SPAN, something unimaginable to the country's Founding Fathers.

How has the nature of mass media changed in the twenty-first century?

Because media companies continue to consolidate at an ever-increasing pace, hard-and-fast rules as to who owns what and when have disappeared, and companies are now able to offer the American public an incomparable portfolio of media and content from the Internet and broadcast and cable television to film, music, magazines, and books. With the stamp of approval of the Federal Communications Commission, the following mergers represent the evolving culture of media today: the November 1998 $4.2 billion merger of Internet giants America Online (AOL) and Netscape; AT&T's 1999 acquisition of MediaOne, creating the nation's largest cable company; Viacom and CBS's 1999 $35 billion merger, at the time the biggest in media industry history; the creation of the world's largest media business with the 2000 AOL–Time Warner deal; the 2000 merger of Time Warner and EMI Group PLC, creating the world's second-largest music company just two weeks after Time Warner agreed to merge with America Online; and the March

2000 Tribune Company–Times Mirror Company $8 billion merger, the largest newspaper acquisition in U.S. history.

How has the Internet gained prominence as a major news outlet?

Besides revolutionizing public access to government documents and databases, public and private libraries, and archives of information, the Internet has changed public discussion of politics by allowing candidates to host websites and solicit feedback from the public. In 1996 all major presidential candidates developed websites to support their campaigns, and by the 2000 presidential election campaign, candidates were collecting cam-

Modern media outlets, ranging from twenty-four-hour news channels to the Internet and phone apps, have drastically altered how voter opinion is influenced.

paign contributions via the web. In addition, all major newspapers and cable and television networks have Internet sites, many of them with politics-specific components, such as CNN's allpolitics.com and the *Washington Post*'s "Politics" section on washingtonpost.com. Online magazines such as the *Drudge Report, Slate,* and *Salon* have made both news and gossip available to browsers at a lightning-fast pace, and a 2016 report by the Pew Research Center for the People and the Press found that Americans increasingly rely on the Internet (its major news sites and other less reliable sites alike) for news, and they trust what they read. Interest groups, too, have reached new audiences and expanded their membership via the web, creating the potential for even greater influence in Washington. As an interactive medium, the Internet provides the ability to disseminate information quickly and readily and at the same time solicit information from its audience, giving the American public a viable outlet for voicing its opinion and talking back on important political matters.

Is the Internet usurping the daily news functions of more traditional print media?

Although Microsoft's Bill Gates predicted that the Internet would abolish print media, this hasn't happened yet, partly due to Americans' propensity to read the morning paper over a cup of coffee and the increasing exposure newspapers have gained by creating news-dedicated websites on the Internet. However, when it comes to political news, more and more citizens are turning to the Internet for information about presidential elections and campaigns, especially as television coverage becomes more superficial. A study by the Annenberg Public Policy Center and the Alliance for Better Campaigns found that the three major networks' newscasts averaged less than a minute of candidate discourse per night during the 2016 presidential primaries, forcing interested Americans to seek out other media sources, print and online alike, for their news. However, because many online political "front pages" provide little original reporting and not all cover a story in depth, Internet users may just look at the day's headlines and then return to magazines and newspapers for more complete coverage.

How do the media shape public opinion?

Because the media are a primary vehicle for providing Americans with political information, their reporting inevitably shapes the way people think. Not only do the media set the agenda for what people will watch or read, they control the way that content is delivered. Whether people watch the hard facts of a live CNN report or read a political scientist's editorial about a candidate in a major newspaper, they are gathering information and forming an opinion about what they see or hear. To the extent that the media report accurately and truthfully, without bias or sensationalism, the public can form opinions more objectively. Conversely, to the extent that information is skewed, public opinion can be similarly affected. Thanks to cable television, the amount of public discourse on air has increased, allowing politicians to present their case on public issues as varied as national health care, terrorism, and the size of the federal budget. So, too, has this medium allowed people to take part in public debates more knowledgably and have a more immediate impact on Congress's policymaking.

How are media coverage and public perception of current events and politics related?

How the media report current and political events is directly linked to the public's perception of those events—whether they are evaluating a candidate's credibility and integrity, summing up the government's position on a legislative policy, or trying to make sense of a phenomenon as complex as the war on terrorism. Central to this discussion is the amount of time journalists spend editorializing during news segments by injecting their own viewpoints and how that commentary translates to the audience. The increasing coverage the press gives to a political candidate's character, its dissemination of unsubstantiated rumors, and what it chooses to emphasize, criticize, or applaud during a presidential or congressional campaign affect not only public perception of a candidate or issue but also the way the public acts at the polls, making or breaking legislation or a candidate's political campaign and career.

How do the media impact the public agenda?

Media coverage has had the ability to rally support for or create opposition to a host of national policies. The last half of the twentieth century provides dozens of examples of how the press has changed not only public opinion but public policy as well. Many cite the press coverage of the 1950s civil rights movement as the catalyst for mounting pressure on Congress to bring an end to segregation. Similarly, the media virtually single-handedly changed public opinion about the Vietnam War, portraying it as ill-fated and unwinnable, and brought pressure on the Nixon Administration to negotiate an end to the bloodshed. Also, few forget that the media were central to the Watergate scandal of the early 1970s, launching a series of investigations into then-president Richard Nixon's actions, which eventually led to his resignation. More recently, the press's coverage of the September 11, 2001, terrorist attacks ignited a newfound patriotism across America and may have played a role in Americans' acceptance of the national government's more stringent terrorist policies at the expense of hard-won civil liberties.

THE POWER OF THE PRESS: THE MEDIA AND POLITICAL CAMPAIGNS

What role do the media play in the coverage of political campaigns?

In presidential campaigns, news coverage—particularly television news coverage—is the main source of political information for voters. A January 2016 poll conducted for the Pew Research Center for the People and the Press reported that 75 percent of respondents stated that television was their main source of election campaign news. Reporting on campaigns tends to focus on the results of opinion polls, which are freely available and have a high entertainment value because they emphasize the competitive aspect of campaigns. There is also a focus on nominating conventions, which, aired in

Television news influences 75 percent of Americans when it comes to election campaigns, according to a Pew Research Center survey.

a three-hour evening segment, provide compelling visuals and quotable material akin to the Emmys, and on candidate advertisements, which are short "sound bites" that can stand alone or easily be fed into a two-minute news segment. These tools give reporters a jumping-off point for portraying both candidates and the election race. Carefully worded claims that a candidate has "momentum," is a "favorite," or has "suffered a political blow" can alter the course of an election. Because politicians understand how the press works, they adapt their campaigns accordingly, sending the results of their own opinion polls and copies of their advertisements to newspapers and television stations across the country in hopes of gaining coverage. Candidates are also well known for leaking their opponents' compromising histories and scandalous behavior to the press.

What role does political advertising play in the media and elections?

Televised political advertising today is the largest single expense in any presidential media campaign. In 1996, for example, more than 60 percent of the money spent by the Bill Clinton and Bob Dole general election campaigns was devoted to electronic media advertising, most of it for television. The use of paid media in U.S. elections consists mainly of thirty-second advertisements that run on national networks (such as ABC, CBS, or NBC) and individual television stations in specific cities. However, because most candidates must woo voters at the state level, most political advertising, even in presidential campaigns, is purchased from local television outlets. Candidates focus their advertising on states where votes are split evenly between parties and their advertising dollars can be used most effectively. In hotly contested states, voters typically view six presidential advertisements for every one ad that voters in other states see. While public financing (and thus spending limits) puts the presidential candidates who accept it on an equal footing, Congressional campaigns are financed entirely through private donations. Incumbent members of the House and Senate raise and spend three dollars for every dollar raised by their challengers, thereby giving sitting members of Congress an edge in advertising their candidacies and platforms through the broadcast media.

How do Americans feel about media coverage of elections and political campaigns?

Given the importance of election campaigns for the political process and policymaking, it is not surprising that the media's coverage of campaigns is controversial. Overall, Americans criticize the press for being poll- and candidate-centered—providing extensive coverage of poll results as well as campaign strategy analysis—but devoting little or no attention to the discussion of public policies. According to a November 2000 Brown University study, a majority of the public felt that the media's overall coverage of the 2000 election was either "excellent" or "good," but 28 percent felt that media coverage was biased against an individual candidate. Critics cite the media's overemphasis on candidates' personalities and personal scandals as the reasons for this turnoff. This dissatisfaction with press coverage translates to the candidates as well: A 1999 poll by the Institute for Global Ethics indicated that Americans were bored with candidates' antics at campaign time, with more than eight in ten voters saying that attack-oriented campaigning is unethical, lowers voter turnout, and produces less ethical elected officials, and 60 percent were "very concerned" that candidates attack each other instead of discussing the issues at campaign time.

How has the television coverage of presidential campaigns changed in recent years?

Political analysts cite the presidential campaign of 1992 as the event that marked a change in the power of the Big Three networks—CBS, NBC, and ABC—to dominate election coverage and campaign messages. That year the candidates turned frequently to cable TV, especially CNN, as an important alternative media outlet, with independent candidate Ross Perot announcing his availability on CNN's *Larry King Live* and Democratic candidate Bill Clinton choosing MTV to showcase his talent as a saxophone player. As the ability of cable TV to cover a campaign twenty-four hours a day has become more apparent, the major networks have shifted their emphasis to interpreting and analyzing campaigns rather than trying to cover them exhaustively. Although the Big Three networks were still clearly in control in 1992 with 55 percent of the audience for evening news programs, or twenty-two million U.S. households, cable TV encroached on these figures throughout the 1990s and 2000s and has clearly provided a viable alternative for viewers in the twenty-first century.

President Donald Trump has had an adversarial relationship with the media, which he claims are sensationalistic to the point of becoming "fake news."

Why do some consider the press to be too adversarial in its coverage of political issues?

Because the American news media constitute a highly competitive industry run by the private sector with very little government intervention, profits and programming choices drive the business, and the stories that make it into daily news broadcasts or special segments are often sensational stories. Reporters pride themselves on reporting thoroughly, objectively, and fairly; in their self-proclaimed role as advocates for the people, they often act as investigators of the government, so to speak—breaking controversial stories, revealing corrupt practices, and covering scandalous behavior in an effort to gain an audience and the respect of their peers. Consider, for example, the extraordinary amount of time that was given to the Bill Clinton–Monica Lewinsky sex scandal. While this coverage gained the station a favorable rating, it also fed the press's reputation of being too adversarial, triggering a backlash by candidates and disproportionately shaping a public opinion characterized by a lack of faith in government and public officials. Nevertheless, the public's right to know remains at the heart of America's free-press philosophy and governs the way the media conduct themselves, particularly in relation to the government. While some call this relationship adversarial, others think of it as objective monitoring.

Does the media's coverage of current events and politics ever backfire?

Interestingly, how and what the media report shape what the public thinks about the media as an entity, especially in times of conflict or war. During the Vietnam era, the press was criticized for its depiction of the U.S. government's role in the war. Seven weeks into the United States' war in Afghanistan, many Americans said the nation's news media were behaving irresponsibly (some said treasonously) by providing extensive raw coverage that they felt fueled the terrorists and unnecessarily alarmed U.S. citizens. According to a November 2001 *Los Angeles Times* poll, 48 percent of Americans claimed that the media had been irresponsible in their coverage by not balancing national security with the American people's right to know the details of the conflict in Afghanistan and the larger war on terrorism. While news editors maintain that the media's duty is to inform, including reporting unpleasant or unsettling news that may bring a barrage of criticism, critics maintain that controversial breaking stories only leave Americans skeptical about what they hear or read. While many news organizations insisted that they took special care to avoid overrepresenting or being manipulated by the Taliban and their propagandists, many people objected to the repeated gruesome portrayal of the casualties, citing overstimulation and the dispersal of "too much information"—a concept inconceivable to almost any journalist—as the cause for media turnoff.

Criticism of the media in times of war is nothing new. Polls immediately following the U.S. dispatch of troops to the Caribbean island nation of Grenada in 1984 and participation in the Persian Gulf War of 1991 indicated that the American public overwhelmingly supported the U.S. military's restrictions on media coverage of the two conflicts.

POLITICAL CAMPAIGNS
AND THE INTERNET

How do modern political campaigns reach voters?

Increasingly, the modern political campaign is committed to reaching voters via digital means. Whether advertising on search engines and social media, reaching out to email lists with millions of subscribers, analyzing data for trends and voter intentions, or asking for political donations, statistics support the claim that the Internet is often where modern political campaigning makes its most powerful impact. Analysts cite several reasons for the success of the Internet in campaigns, including its speed. Both radio and television allow for the live transmission of a political message or political event, but both of these technologies depend on the audience being present at the right time to receive the message. An event streamed via the Internet is just as live as radio or television broadcasts, yet is also easily accessed at any time after the event via any one of dozens of free video streaming services. The Internet is an interactive medium, allowing citizens to send and receive in real time. In addition, the versatility of the Internet and the options it offers to those seeking to communicate a political message to a pool of potential voters is unprecedented—Instagram feeds, Facebook photo albums, podcasts, and YouTube video playlists among them. The voter who would like to receive information tailored to his or her personal political preferences can click a couple of boxes on a list to ensure personalized receipt of newsletters. Via laptop, tablet, game console, or smartphone, the Internet is a technology that follows the user and is available on demand, 24/7. This ease of use is what makes the Internet particularly appealing to candidates. In addition, the Internet has brought more transparency to politics, since once information becomes available online, it is virtually impossible to hide it or keep it from being shared.

How many people learn about political campaigns via the Internet?

According to a 2008 report conducted by the Power Research Center, nearly one-quarter of Americans (24%) said they regularly learn something about presidential campaigns from the Internet, almost double the percentage at a comparable point in the 2004 presidential campaign (13%). Moreover, the Center said the Internet had become a leading source of campaign news for young adults, and social networking sites such as Facebook are a notable part of the story. Forty-two percent of those aged eighteen to twenty-nine said they regularly learn about presidential campaigns from the Internet, the highest percentage for any news source. In January 2004, just 20 percent of young people said they routinely received campaign news from the Internet. Compared with the 2000 campaign, far fewer Americans in 2008 said they regularly learned about presidential campaigns from local TV news, nightly network news, and daily newspapers. Cable news networks were up modestly as compared with 2000 but had shown no growth since the 2004 campaign.

The White House has its own Facebook page as one of several social media outlets for connecting to the American public.

Why has the Internet been called "news you can choose"?

With the Internet, YouTube, TiVo, and cable TV, the American people have become selective viewers. "They approach their news consumption the way they approach their iPod," Dan Pfeiffer, the White House communications director for President Obama, once famously said. "You download the songs you like and listen to them when you want to listen to them." That affects the way reporters spend their days formulating messages, the way campaigns craft their messages, and the way constituents select their messages.

How has sharing become a way of distributing the news?

Tweets and retweets have become the new, virtual form of word of mouth. Last-minute details for tea parties, town hall meetings, and other events get posted on Facebook and tweeted to supporters. During the Obama presidency, the White House's Facebook page had more than one million fans; its Twitter feed had 1.7 million followers. Many commentators have said that is not surprising, given that President Obama was the first candidate to announce his White House run via Web video and his vice presidential running mate by text message.

FREEDOM OF THE PRESS

What is the difference between an independent press and an official press?

An independent press is one that functions free from government control or interference and without prior restraints, such as licensing requirements or content approval, and without subsequent penalties for what is published or broadcast. An independent or free press differs from an official or government-sponsored press, which is owned, run, and/or censored by a country's government. Although well over half of the world's nations are self-proclaimed democracies, in an effort to preserve "public stability," most of them have instituted press laws that prohibit reporting on a wide array of subjects, ranging from the internal operations of government to the private lives of government leaders. In addition, many of these countries' journalists practice self-censorship in reaction to government pressure and fear of retribution.

Why has the press been called the fourth branch of the government?

The American press has assumed the role of the watchdog of government, constantly measuring the government's ethics and practices and reporting on them. The power that comes from this role has earned the press the title "the fourth branch" of the government, after the three official branches (legislative, judicial, and executive). A variety of court opinions have found that the press has an important function as a guardian of democracy and as a check upon government abuse, as echoed by U.S. Supreme Court Justice Hugo Black in his final concurring opinion in the 1971 *Pentagon Papers* case, which mandated that the *New York Times* could continue to publish the then-classified documents on a Department of Defense study of American activities during the Vietnam War. Here, the government's power to censor the press was abolished so that the press would remain free to question government activities and inform the people. It is this role as watchdog that prompted Founding Father Thomas Jefferson to say some two hundred years ago that, if he had to choose between government without newspapers or newspapers without government, he "should not hesitate a moment to prefer the latter."

What does the term "freedom of the press" really mean?

The Bill of Rights guarantees that Congress cannot enact a law infringing upon free speech or a free press, and this has provided the basis for America's tradition of a free press for more than two hundred years. In drafting the First Amendment, America's Founding Fathers affirmed the fundamental right of citizens to be informed about political issues without government interference. Belief in the importance of a press free of government control is the reason why the United States has remained "hands-off" when it comes to dealing with the press: unlike other countries, there is no ministry of information that regulates the activities of journalists, no requirement that journalists be registered, and no requirement that they be members of a union.

Because of this broad constitutional protection of press freedom and similar provisions in state constitutions, few press laws exist in the United States. Those that do exist tend to provide additional protections and legal rights for journalists; for example, the Privacy Act of 1974 regulates the collection and dissemination of personal information contained in any federal agency's files, and the Privacy Protection Act of 1980 established protection from police searches of newsrooms. There are also federal and state freedom of information and "sunshine" laws, such as the 1966 federal Freedom of Information Act, which allows executive-branch records to be reviewed by the public and press. As a result of this protection, the news media are somewhat buffered against potential backlashes by the government. For example, it is almost impossible for a public official to win a libel suit against the media because the courts have ruled that such officials must be open to special kinds of scrutiny and accountability in a democratic system. American journalists have also won a number of court cases to protect the anonymity of news sources from government inquiry.

Can the government restrict the press? Is there a difference in how the print and broadcast media are regulated?

While there is very little government interference to restrict media, regulation does exist. The print media enjoy the most freedom; there is no licensing requirement for newspapers and no enforceable definition exists of what constitutes a legitimate news publication. The press does not set minimum standards for membership, does not issue or revoke licenses, and does not regulate professional standards, although most outlets take pains to adhere to impartial reporting and thorough news coverage. In addition, there are unofficial checks and balances against journalistic excess, including external checks such as libel laws and self-appointed press monitors and internal checks such as the appointment by some newspapers of an ombudsman to investigate public complaints and publish self-criticism. The broadcast media, on the other hand, need a federal government license to operate because the limited airwaves it uses are deemed public property. There are, however, safeguards against political discrimination in the licensing process, and examples of political bias in issuing or revoking licenses are rare. For the most part, government decisions on broadcast licensing are aimed at ensuring competition and diversity in a free-market economy.

Under what circumstances, if any, is the government justified in limiting access to information? Are journalists within their rights in publishing such restricted information?

Political scientists and democratic governments agree that at times, especially times of war and national strife, governments are justified in limiting access to information considered potentially harmful or too sensitive for general distribution. However, journalists are fully justified in pursuing such information and publishing or broadcasting it as they deem fit. This is

Former White House press secretary Sean Spicer had the unenviable job of often telling the media that the president was refusing to release information to them. The tension between the Trump Administration and the press has raised concerns about what facts the government can and cannot keep from the public.

How does the press regulate itself?

In response to polls showing increased public distrust of the press, in the late 1970s, many editors showed a renewed interest in codes of ethics and other forms of self-regulation. Journalistic codes of ethics outlining how the press should behave have been in use in the United States since 1923, when the American Society of Newspaper Editors approved the first one, revised most recently in 1975. The Society of Professional Journalists and the Associated Press Managing Editors have adopted similar codes that encourage journalists to perform with objectivity, accuracy, and fairness, and many news organizations try to uphold these. In addition, some newspapers have experimented with the Scandinavian concept of an ombudsman, an individual appointed by a newspaper to investigate complaints concerning the paper's coverage and practices and to publish the results of the investigation. In 1967, the *Louisville Courier Journal* of Louisville, Kentucky, became the first U.S. newspaper to adopt the system, with only one of the powerful dailies—the *Washington Post*—following suit. The United Kingdom's news council concept has also been adopted in the United States, beginning with the formation in 1973 of the National News Council, which acted as an alternative to libel actions and other kinds of litigation by investigating complaints against media organizations where the plaintiff agreed not to bring civil actions against the accused. Since the National News Council's funding ended in 1984, only a few news councils at the state level—most notably the Minnesota News Council—have operated successfully.

often called the historical struggle between two rights: the government's right—some say obligation—to protect national security and the people's right to know, based on the journalist's right and ability to capture and disseminate the news. Certain scholars maintain that, from the journalist's perspective, if the publication of a story runs the risk of jeopardizing lives, the journalist must weigh whether the decision to publish or broadcast is for the ultimate good of the people. Although this involves very complex journalistic ethics, in the United States, the fact remains that it is the journalist's decision alone, not the government's.

What is the role of the Federal Communications Commission?

Established by the Communications Act of 1934, the Federal Communications Commission (FCC) is an independent U.S. government agency directly accountable to the U.S. Congress. The FCC is charged with regulating interstate and international communications by radio, television, wire, satellite, and cable in the nation's fifty states, the District of Columbia, and U.S. possessions. The FCC's responsibilities include processing applications for licenses and other filings, analyzing complaints, conducting investigations, developing and implementing regulatory programs, and contributing in court hearings.

What is the equal time rule?

The Communications Act of 1934 also established an equal opportunity, or equal time, rule which states that, if a political candidate obtains time on a broadcast station, other candidates for the same office (or their appointed representatives) must be allowed an "equal opportunity" on that station. An equal opportunity usually includes equal time, but the term means more than that. For example, it means the right to obtain time in a period likely to attract approximately the same size audience as the period in which the opposing candidate appeared. News shows are exempt from the equal time rule.

Why is the Telecommunications Act of 1996 important?

In an effort to address rapid technological advances in an era of fiber optics and microwave transmissions, Congress overwhelmingly passed the Telecommunications Act of 1996, which broke the monopolies in the telecommunications field and allowed companies to compete in areas they formerly could not by regulation or law. The bill created a nationwide marketplace for telecommunication services, replacing the segmented marketplace of local and long-distance telephone service and cable television. The legislation also replaced a decades-old system based on federal and state laws and a court order that broke up AT&T, a monopoly telephone company, into a long-distance carrier and regional ("Baby Bell") telephone companies. The act removed previous barriers between sectors of the industry, and American consumers can now receive local telephone service from their cable television company or a long-distance carrier, and local phone companies can provide television programming. Potentially, all of these services can be provided by a single company, such as a local public utility company.

How has regulation changed since the 1980s?

Deregulation of the media began in earnest in the 1980s. As media choices increased during this decade, the Federal Communications Commission began to relax regulations on U.S. broadcast media, expanding the number of outlets one owner could possess and announcing it would no longer enforce the fairness doctrine. To further

What is the fairness doctrine?

From 1949 to 1987, the FCC also enforced a fairness doctrine that required broadcast stations to devote a reasonable percentage of time to the coverage of controversial issues and provide a reasonable opportunity for the presentation of contrasting viewpoints on such issues. It eventually extended the right of rebuttal to public figures who were attacked.

increase competition, in January 1994, the Clinton Administration proposed eliminating restrictions that prevented cable TV and telephone companies from entering each other's markets, which eventually led to the Telecommunications Act of 1996. Despite this general trend toward deregulation, there has been an increase in the number of proposals that attempt to regulate the Internet, specifically limiting its content so that children cannot access pornographic or objectionable websites. The privacy protections granted to users of online computer services and the Internet have generally been upheld but were debated continually since the 1996 federal district court panel decision to strike down the new Communications Decency Act. In this decision the court held that Internet communications are entitled to the same degree of protection as printed communications.

Why have some people argued against cameras in courtrooms?

The argument against having cameras in courtrooms was raised by the televised O. J. Simpson case, which many maintained left viewers with a distorted impression of the American legal system, thanks largely to selected media footage shown on the eleven o'clock news and the occasional play to the camera by trial participants. Although almost all the states allow camera coverage of courtroom proceedings and have for decades, the federal courts do not. Many arguments have surfaced against such coverage, namely that it encourages sensationalism, subjects participants to undue publicity and pressure, infringes upon a person's right to privacy, and feeds into the entertainment and ratings games of television stations. However, proponents of the courtroom camera hold that responsible camera coverage is simply an extension of Americans' right to an open trial and promotes, rather than undermines, the judicial process by allowing an informed citizenry to see how the justice system works.

THE MEDIA UNDER VARIOUS ADMINISTRATIONS

Which early president was the first to have poor relations with the press?

The administration of John Adams (1797–1801), the second president of the United States, marks the beginning of adversarial president–press relations. Although the press did not begin attacking his predecessor, George Washington, until the end of Washington's administration, the press attacked Adams from the time of his address to Congress in May 1797 until he left the White House in March 1801. During his presidency, Federalist newspapers printed essays written by Adams' critics, most notably Federalist leader Alexander Hamilton, which accused Adams of conspiring with Republicans for peace with France. Republican newspapers called Adams a monarchist who sought to establish a dynasty with Great Britain. Although Adams' legacy included uniting moderate Federalists and Republicans, he blamed the Federalist and Republican newspapers for his downfall, saying, "Regret nothing that you see in the papers concerning me. It is impossible that newspapers can say the truth. They would be out of their element."

When did the press start using the term "whitewash"?

The term "whitewash," meaning to gloss over or cover up faults, was used by the press as early as 1762 by a writer for the *Boston Evening Post*. In a political sense, the term dates to 1800, when a *Philadelphia Aurora* editorial said, "If you do not whitewash President [John] Adams speedily, the Democrats, like swarms of flies, will bespatter him all over, and make you both as speckled as a dirty wall, and as black as the devil." Since that use, the term "whitewashing" has taken on the meaning of a

Conflict between the president and the media is nothing new; it goes back to America's second leader, John Adams.

predetermined exoneration of a public official accused of wrongdoing after he has been subject to an "investigation" by a committee with a friendly majority.

How and when did the term "off the record" originate?

Long used in the courtroom, the terms "off the record" and "on the record" entered the political vocabulary sometime in the late 1800s. Since 1893, when the official proceedings of Congress were first published in the Congressional Record, members called informal statements "off the record" and formal statements "on the record." At the 1919 Democratic National Convention, President Woodrow Wilson is recorded as saying, "Personally, and just within the limits of this room, I can say very frankly that I think we ought to …," thus ushering in an era when politicians believed they were justified in denying off-the-record statements if they were published without their consent, an ethical practice still adhered to by many today. The phrase "Let us take a look at the record" is attributed to 1928 Democratic presidential candidate Alfred E. Smith, who often used the expression to review issues.

How did a newspaper editor's remark actually help 1840 Whig presidential candidate William Henry Harrison of Ohio?

Even during the early nineteenth century, the press held the power to affect what the public believed. That year, a Democratic newspaper editor called Harrison a poor old farmer who would be content with three things: a pension, a log cabin, and a barrel of hard cider. However, instead of having the intended effect of hurting Harrison's candidacy, the editor's comments rallied large numbers of westerners who found it easy to identify with a candidate who shared their lifestyle. What they didn't know was that this image—which soon caught on with the public and became the hallmark of Whig rallies and parades—was only that: Harrison was very wealthy, lived in a sixteen-room mansion, and never drank hard cider. Although he was the exact antithesis of the editor's remarks, that image helped him build his campaign and gain voters, eventually winning him the White House.

Which nineteenth-century president was associated with a number of scandals during his presidency?

While Ulysses S. Grant's administrations (1869–1877) were known for their contributions to Reconstruction policy and Indian policy, frequent mention is made of the many scandals that plagued Grant's presidency. Black Friday (1869) on the New York gold exchange involved Wall Street conspirators who attempted to corner the available gold supply and prevent the government from selling gold by enlisting Grant's brother-in-law as co-conspirator. In the Crédit Mobilier scandal of 1872, the *New York Sun* accused Vice President Schuyler Colfax, vice presidential nominee Henry Wilson, and other prominent politicians of being involved in the operations of Crédit Mobilier, a corporation established by promoters of the Union Pacific to siphon off the profits of railroad construction. In 1875 a group of corrupt officials and businessmen known as the Whiskey Ring was exposed by the *St. Louis Democrat,* ultimately compromising important Grant appointees and General Orville E. Babcock, Grant's private secretary. Finally, Secretary of War William W. Belknap was impeached in 1876 on charges of accepting bribes from Indian agents, making Belknap the first cabinet official ever impeached in the United States.

Who was Lemonade Lucy?

"Lemonade Lucy" was the nickname the press teasingly gave First Lady Lucy Hayes (1831–1889) for her habit of excluding alcoholic beverages from White House functions, choosing instead to serve lemonade and fruit juices. Although the custom at the time was to serve alcohol at state functions, the First Lady's practice was supported by her husband, President Rutherford B. Hayes (1822–1893), an ex-poker-playing, cigar-smoking drinker who had given up his vices to join the Sons of Temperance and traveled to make speeches on their behalf.

President Rutherford B. Hayes' wife, Lucy, was called "Lemonade Lucy" by the press for refusing to serve alcohol at the White House.

Which president introduced the phrase "throwing the hat in the ring"?

Theodore Roosevelt (1858–1919) popularized the phrase in response to a reporter's question on his way to the Ohio Constitutional Convention in Columbus in 1912. Asked whether he intended to run for president again later that year, the former president drew on western sporting slang and replied, "My hat is in the ring; the fight is on and I'm stripped to the buff. You will have my answer on Monday." Since that time, the phrase "throwing the hat in the ring" has been associated with entering a political campaign or announcing one's candidacy for office.

Who coined the expression "pitiless publicity" in reference to drawing on the press to help solve political problems?

Although it was first used by poet Ralph Waldo Emerson (1803–1882), Woodrow Wilson (1856–1924) publicly coined this expression while running for governor of New Jersey in 1910. During his campaign Wilson was asked a series of questions about how he planned to rid the state of the "boss and spoils system" in politics, to which he replied, "I would propose to abolish it by the reform suggested in the Democratic platform, by the election to office of men who will refuse to submit to it … and by pitiless publicity." Because the public was taken with the phrase, Wilson continued to use it, and the phrase has ever since been associated with him.

Who was the first president to make regular use of press conferences?

Although he disliked the media, Woodrow Wilson made many attempts to interact with them. He was the first president to hold a presidential news conference and pioneered the concept as a way of molding public opinion and rallying support for the administration. Wilson's personal appeal to the media also translated to Congress: in 1913 he broke with Thomas Jefferson's precedent of submitting the annual message to Congress in writing by personally delivering the address to Congress orally, thus setting a precedent for today's State of the Union Address.

Which three presidents required the press to submit their questions in writing in advance?

Never wanting to be taken by surprise, three presidents in succession—Warren Harding, Calvin Coolidge, and Herbert Hoover—required the press to submit questions in writing to them or their secretaries in advance, ensuring ample time to prepare a politically advantageous response.

Which president holds the record for the most press conferences?

The media-savvy Franklin D. Roosevelt held 998 news conferences during his twelve-year presidency. He began the trend on March 8, 1933, as soon as he was sworn into office and continued holding press conferences steadily throughout his three terms. Unlike his predecessor, Herbert Hoover, who asked the press to prepare questions and submit them to him prior to any dealings with the press, Roosevelt's off-the-cuff, frank nature established a fresh relationship with the press.

Roosevelt also became the first president to appear on television when he spoke at the opening ceremonies of the New York World's Fair on April 30, 1939. NBC telecast the event from the Federal Building on the exposition grounds. Several years later, Roosevelt took another "first" as the first president to broadcast in a foreign language. On November 7, 1942, Roosevelt addressed the French in their own language from Washington, D.C., in coordination with the U.S. Army's invasion of German-occupied French possessions in Africa.

What important precedent did Warren G. Harding set for his successor, Calvin Coolidge?

Warren G. Harding (1865–1923) introduced the practice of holding biweekly press conferences throughout his term in office, and this was continued by Calvin Coolidge (1872–1933). Because of Coolidge's openness and availability to the press (having held some five hundred such meetings during his six years in the White House), he enjoyed great popularity among the Washington press corps.

What first-time service did reporter Judson Welliver provide to a U.S. president?

Judson Welliver (1870–1943) was the first person to be hired officially as a speechwriter—for President Calvin Coolidge. While even the earliest presidents had help preparing their speeches (George Washington often consulted Alexander Hamilton), Welliver was the first person employed for that sole purpose in the White House. During the last several presidencies, drafts have been prepared by full-time wordsmiths in the official Office of Speechwriting.

Beginning with the radio, how have the media been used to communicate the president's annual State of the Union address?

Calvin Coolidge was the first president to deliver what was then named the annual message to Congress via radio in 1923. With the advent of radio and television, the presi-

---

Who was the first president to address the nation by radio?

Warren G. Harding was the first president to deliver a speech broadcast by radio. On June 14, 1922, his speech at the dedication of the Francis Scott Key Memorial at Fort McHenry in Baltimore, Maryland, was broadcast by local Baltimore station WEAR (now WFBR). Harding is frequently confused with Calvin Coolidge, who was the first president to broadcast on radio to a joint session of Congress on December 6, 1923, and also the first president to broadcast from the White House, with his tribute to President Harding on February 22, 1924, which was broadcast by forty-two stations from coast to coast.

dent's annual message expanded from a conversation between the president and Congress to an address to the American people. Franklin D. Roosevelt began using the phrase "State of the Union" in 1935, which was the common name of the president's annual message from that time forward. Roosevelt's successor, Harry Truman, set a precedent in 1947, when his State of the Union speech became the first to be broadcast on television. Lyndon Johnson was the first president to have his State of the Union address broadcast on all three commercial television networks. George W. Bush broke the mold once again: his January 29, 2002, address marked the first time in history that the president's State of the Union message was available via a live webcast originating from the White House website.

How did Franklin D. Roosevelt use the media to his political advantage?

Probably one of America's most successful communicators was Franklin D. Roosevelt, who used the popular medium of the radio, by that time in over half of America's households, to his political advantage. From the room now known as the Diplomatic Reception Room of the White House, Roosevelt addressed the nation in more than thirty "fireside chats"—heart-to-heart conversations he held directly with Americans about the problems they were facing during the Great Depression of the 1930s and World War II in the 1940s. These chats—for which families and friends gathered around their living room fireplaces to listen to the president by radio—were immensely popular primarily because Roosevelt's calming voice and everyday language assured Americans that despite the country's crises, the United States had the resiliency to survive as a nation. The effect was ultimately to instill faith in Roosevelt as president, convincing Americans

Why was FDR's paralysis kept quiet by the media?

When Franklin D. Roosevelt died on April 12, 1945, few Americans knew the extent of his disability and the pains he took to conceal the fact that he had polio. During his early political career, Roosevelt denied his disability in order to present himself to the public as a viable candidate, and he continued to hide his polio throughout his presidency, fearing political ramifications. Sitting mostly at his desk or behind a lectern, the public did not see him in the wheelchair he used daily for two decades. Reporters and photographers followed a tacit rule to keep the disability secret, and media appearances were orchestrated with the president seated or able to reach a podium with minimal movement. Of the more than 35,000 pictures taken of Roosevelt, only two show him in a wheelchair, while political cartoonists did much to dispel the rumors of illness by drawing him running, jumping, or leaping. As was the trend in those times, the media emphasized the public performance and personality of the president and avoided examining his private life.

that he was working hard to correct their problems. Radio was also a means for the president to bypass the partisan newspapers that were generally critical of New Deal reforms, instead giving his administration direct access to citizens, which ultimately boosted his popularity as a leader and allowed him to move forward with his presidential agenda. Roosevelt's chats were so successful that presidents Jimmy Carter and Bill Clinton tried to replicate the technique, but they had little success.

Even though radio was eventually supplanted by television, how did it continue to have a role in communicating the politics of the day?

While television displaced radio in the 1950s as America's most popular electronic medium, radio still remained important in communicating politics. The U.S. government used radio as a Cold War weapon internationally by broadcasting anticommunist propaganda across the Soviet bloc with its Voice of America campaign and on the domestic front by broadcasting Senator Joseph McCarthy's (1908–1957) infamous anticommunist hearings. It wasn't too long before Americans were enjoying all-news radio, which remained a popular way of getting national headlines throughout the rest of the twentieth century as more and more commuters tuned in on their way to work. The 1990s witnessed a rebirth of political radio programming as a series of successful talk radio programs hosted by such conservatives as Rush Limbaugh, G. Gordon Liddy, and Oliver North informed listeners on the affairs of state.

Who was the first president to appear on television from the White House?

Harry Truman (1884–1972) became the first president to appear on television from the White House when he spoke about the world food crisis on October 5, 1947. Although

that speech was only seen in New York and Philadelphia, about ten million viewers watched Truman's inauguration on TV only two years later, and more than a hundred million heard it on the radio.

Why did Harry Truman frequently get in trouble with the press?

Critical of journalists and shy of the press, Harry Truman frequently got himself in trouble by coming unprepared to press conferences and offering impromptu answers. Truman frequently relied on his press secretary Charles Ross to brief him with trial questions and issue clarifications of his off-the-cuff answers, such as when he implied at a 1950 conference that he might use nuclear weapons in Korea.

In 1947, Harry Truman was the first U.S. president to appear on television from the White House.

305

John F. Kennedy's presidency took place in an era when the media were more apt to be "hands-off" when covering a president's personal life, especially in the areas of health and sexual relations. Although the media was vaguely aware of JFK's sexual exploits, they chose not to publicize them. This is almost unimaginable to a twenty-first-century citizenry, whose public officials are under the media spotlight and exposed to the press's tell-all philosophy. Prompted by the publication of a 1975 Senate committee report, journalists began linking Kennedy to various women, portraying him as a less-than-perfect husband with a penchant for extramarital affairs. Reports about Kennedy's well-disguised Addison's disease also began to surface at that time, forcing reporters to examine their responsibility to scrutinize the physical condition and private lives of public officials.

What prominent media stories did John F. Kennedy have to overcome when he campaigned in the 1960 presidential election?

The press paid particular attention to Democratic candidate John F. Kennedy's (1917–1963) Catholic religion. Many voters had ultimately rejected Democratic candidate Alfred E. Smith in 1928 because he too was Catholic, and Kennedy fought hard to overcome this prejudice. The media also focused on his age (at forty-two, many considered Kennedy too young to assume the White House), his extreme wealth (and the charge that he and his father, who funded his campaign, were trying to buy the White House), and his mediocre congressional record as a Massachusetts senator.

Why was JFK known for courting the press?

Kennedy always answered reporters in a respectful tone, engaging them with flattery and charm and consistently thanking them for the facts they chose not to publish. The elite of print and television journalism considered themselves Kennedy's friends and often mentioned their shared burden of helping Kennedy shape the country and its future. Kennedy was known for playing reporters against one another and for his unique way of managing to get only the most favorable stories about himself on the front page.

How did television help bring about the end of the Vietnam War?

In 1975 Marshall McLuhan said, "Television brought the brutality of war into the comfort of the living room. Vietnam was lost in the living rooms of America—not on the battlefields of Vietnam." Few disagree with the words of this well-known social commentator, which stress that television helped bring about Americans' disillusionment with the Vietnam War as night after night, viewers watched the country's young men carried off in body bags. After the media openly denounced America's involvement, Walter Cronkite, the most respected television newscaster of the era, spoke openly for a peace settlement.

President Lyndon Johnson realized television's effect on the public when he responded, "If I've lost Walter, I've lost the war." Although serious negotiations to end the war did not begin until Johnson chose not to seek reelection in 1968, the media attention given to the length of the war, the high number of U.S. casualties, and U.S. involvement in war crimes provided the public pressure necessary to initiate its conclusion.

Which president signed the act that created the Corporation for Public Broadcasting?

Lyndon Johnson signed the Public Broadcasting Act on November 7, 1967. The act authorized $38 million for educational television and radio for the next three years, created the Corporation for Public Broadcasting, and established the Commission of Instructional Technology to study instructional television and radio in the United States.

Which president has appeared the most on the cover of *Time?*

By 1994, men who served as president of the United States had appeared more than two hundred times on the cover of *Time* magazine. Herbert Hoover was the only occupant of the White House since *Time* began in 1923 who did not appear on its cover as president, although he was pictured there before and after his presidency. Franklin D. Roosevelt appeared on the cover nine times, and Ronald Reagan was pictured on forty-four covers. However, Richard Nixon appeared there fifty-six times, more than any other man or woman to date.

How do historians characterize Richard Nixon's relationship with the press?

"Adversarial" is the one word that defines Nixon's relationship with the press. His mannerisms, which lacked the grace of his recent predecessor John F. Kennedy, made him always appear uncomfortable before the press and the public. He had such an unpopular public image that most of the press and public didn't trust him even before the Watergate scandal broke. Nixon himself perpetuated this image by revealing to the press as little as possible and believing that secrecy was his prerogative as the nation's chief executive.

How did the press's coverage of the Watergate scandal usher in a new era in the power of the press?

The investigative efforts of *Washington Post* journalists Bob Woodward (1943–) and Carl Bernstein (1944–) exposed the tangled web of Watergate and influenced President Nixon's (1913–1994) 1974 resignation. While both of these were groundbreaking events, the team's coverage marked a new era of investigative journalism and forever changed the way the press would view, report on, expose, and critique presidents. Investigative reporters now viewed it as their duty to democracy to subject the presidency to intense scrutiny. The press, which had often been "hands-off" on the personal details of the president's life, was now given permission to continue to expose the government's most corrupt practices and by doing so altered America's consciousness with regard to the amount of privacy afforded to government officials.

Bob Woodward (left) and Carl Bernstein (shown in 2004 and 2007 photos, respectively) were investigative journalists with the *Washington Post* when they famously broke the Watergate scandal story.

In June 2002, thirty years after they broke the Watergate story, Woodward and Bernstein spoke of journalist lessons learned from the scandal. "The lessons have to do with being careful, with using multiple sources, to putting information into context, to not being swayed by gossip, by sensationalism, by manufactured controversy," said Bernstein, who won the *Washington Post* a Pulitzer Prize for his efforts. "All of which I think have come to dominate our journalistic agenda much more in the past 30 years."

How did the backlash from Watergate affect the office of president?

After the Watergate scandal and President Nixon's resignation, many people simply didn't trust the presidency. Every component of the executive office was turned inside out from the abuse of national security and executive privilege to the misuse of large campaign donations. The willingness of a president and his aides to use respected government agencies—namely, the Federal Bureau of Investigation, the Internal Revenue Service, and the Central Intelligence Agency—in unlawful and unethical ways against their enemies was a breach of trust between the citizenry and its leaders. As a result, Americans expressed great disillusionment with the national government in general and the presidential office in particular. In addition, Americans now welcomed viewing the life of the president and other public officials under the press's microscope—as seen with the 1988 withdrawal of Democrat Gary Hart from the presidential race after the press uncovered his relationship with Donna Rice as well as the many allegations, extramarital and otherwise, that dogged Bill Clinton's presidency.

What was Jimmy Carter's weakness when it came to dealing with the press?

Political commentators often cite Jimmy Carter's (1924–) inability to communicate with the press and public as his greatest weakness. Often viewed as the harbinger of bad news, Carter's nontelevision-friendly persona and elevated speaking style contributed to his image as an ineffectual leader who was overwhelmed by his administration's crises, including uncontrollable inflation rates at home, the hostage crisis in Iran, and the Soviet Union's invasion of Afghanistan. Carter was also apathetic toward the press, which fostered a new aggressiveness toward the executive office. Carter's crumbling relationship with the press mirrored his low approval ratings, which had dropped to 31 percent—lower than Richard Nixon's before his resignation—by the election of 1980.

How did the media use Ronald Reagan's previous career as an actor to undermine his presidency?

While some analysts claim that Ronald Reagan's (1911–2004) celebrity image as a Hollywood "good guy" probably helped him at the polls, the press frequently used his prior acting career to discredit his presidency, linking his weakness as a leader with a lack of qualifications. Many asserted that, as president, Reagan was simply playing a role or participating in a public performance. His detractors emphasized the fact that certain administration priorities were drawn from the scripts of his most popular movies, calling attention, for example, to his proposed 1983 Strategic Defense Initiative as a reworking of the Hollywood-devised "Inertia Projector" technology in his 1940 film *Murder in the Air*. Reagan himself did much to perpetuate his image as an actor, frequently drawing analogies to Hollywood when discussing his presidential responsibilities. When addressing students in Moscow during his 1988 summit meeting with Soviet leader Mikhail Gorbachev, Reagan presented his view of the presidency and role as president by comparing himself to the director of a film. He asserted that a good director makes sure that the star actors and all the bit players know their parts and comprehend the director's vision of what the film is all about.

Why were Ronald Reagan's old films rarely shown on television during the 1980s?

In 1976 the Federal Communications Commission ruled that rerunning old Ronald Reagan movies, even those in which he played a minor role, could be challenged by political opponents demanding equal time on television. Fans were thus hard-pressed to find a Reagan movie on air during most of his presidency.

Which first lady captured the media's attention when she ordered over $200,000 worth of china for the White House?

Nancy Reagan's attempt to make the White House elegant with the purchase of $209,000 worth of new china was not well received by the public once it made headline news. Her penchant for $20,000 designer dresses and other flamboyancies were often the subject of press reports, and reporters made no bones about listing the "gifts" the Reagans acquired during their tenure in the White House, including more than $1 million worth of dresses, jewelry, shoes, and accessories.

How did the media's sensationalizing of the Clinton/Lewinsky affair affect the public's perception of Washington?

The media's full-blown, graphic examination of President Bill Clinton's (1946–) relationship with Washington intern Monica Lewinsky (1973–) and Clinton's 1998 impeachment by the House of Representatives on charges of lying under oath and obstructing justice in an attempt to cover up the affair set new parameters of just how far the media are willing to go in exposing a president's sexual exploits. Entire transcripts of Clinton's testimony—including all the dirty details—were widely available to the American public. Because

Now a fashion designer and political activist, Monica Lewinsky was a White House intern when she had a physical relationship with President Bill Clinton that led to an unsuccessful attempt by Congress to remove him from office.

of the sensationalism surrounding this event, many Americans felt that Bill Clinton's actions irreparably undermined the office of the president with his impeachment, extramarital affairs, and way of playing "fast and loose" with the truth having eroded the chief executive's image as the moral authority of the nation. Despite his actions, however, Clinton's approval ratings continued to be strong overall, although his moral character was frequently the target of Republican Party criticism. In addition, the public's perception of Clinton's exploits became an issue for Vice President Al Gore during the 2000 presidential campaign.

How did the Clinton Administration's atmosphere of scandal reach beyond the office of the president?

The public's general lack of respect for the presidency and its fascination with scandal affected more than Bill Clinton's beleaguered public persona. Many of Clinton's aides were implicated by the media and questioned before the grand jury in Clinton's Whitewater investigation, and many members of Clinton's cabinet, including Agriculture Secretary Mike Espy, Interior Secretary Bruce Babbitt, and Energy Secretary Hazel O'Leary, were the subjects of their own investigations. In addition, although Clinton and his staff were found guiltless, an investigation into the Democratic Party's 1996 fundraising methods resulted in jail terms for some Democratic Party donors. Some of Clinton's rivals also felt the heat of media scrutiny. Republican Congressman Robert Livingston was slated to become Speaker of the House until his extramarital affair became the subject of news headlines. In fact, one of the most talked-about effects of Clinton's follies was the abrupt resignation of disillusioned Republican Speaker of the House Newt Gingrich.

What was Whitewater?

Whitewater is the name of an early scandal that broke during the Clinton Administration. Members of the Republican Party accused Bill Clinton and Hillary Clinton of covering up financial misdealings with regard to his Arkansas investments prior to becoming president. The accusation centered on a failed savings and loan company operated by Clinton business associates James and Susan McDougal, who had questionable business dealings in real estate on the Whitewater River in Arkansas. McDougal was accused of wrongly using money from his failing savings and loan in the 1980s to benefit the Whitewater venture he had created with the Clintons. The scandal soon centered on the mysterious resurfacing of previously "lost" billing records from Hillary Clinton's Rose Law Firm, which could have defined Hillary Clinton's legal work for McDougal and implicated her in the business transactions.

Once the charges of a possible cover-up were made, a special prosecutor was assigned. The position ultimately went to Kenneth Starr, a conservative attorney and former federal judge who headed the Whitewater investigation as well as the ensuing Paula Jones and Monica Lewinsky sex scandal investigations. By the end of 1999, no indictment or specific charges of criminal activity against the president or Hillary Clinton had resulted from the Whitewater or other Starr investigations; however, Starr did successfully urge for Clinton's impeachment in connection with his affair with Lewinsky. Fourteen of the Clintons' Arkansas associates were ultimately convicted and imprisoned for their Whitewater associations, including the McDougals and Jim Guy Tucker, Clinton's replacement as governor of Arkansas.

In March 2002 the saga came to an end when the third prosecutor, independent counsel Robert Ray, issued his final report, concluding that investigators lacked sufficient evidence to prove that either Bill or Hillary Clinton "knowingly participated in the criminal financial transactions used by McDougal to benefit Whitewater." According to the Associated Press, "The Clintons' lawyer called the five-volume report—the product of a $70 million, six-year investigation—the most expensive exoneration in history." Many political analysts understand that, while the Clintons may have ultimately been vindicated, the Whitewater investigation caused irreparable damage to the Clinton legacy, including prompting a presidential impeachment and creating bitter divisions between Republicans and Democrats.

What personality quirks did the media play up in George W. Bush's campaign and early presidency?

During his campaign and early presidency, the media frequently made light of George W. Bush's inarticulate nature, inability to accurately answer questions about history and foreign policy, and vague ideas about his presidential agenda. Often called a "bumbler"

311

who couldn't defend his proposals coherently, Bush's personal quirks, including his down-home Texas attitude, joke-cracking persona, and penchant for personally nick-naming members of his staff, were repeatedly highlighted in the press, often at the expense of his credibility.

How was President George W. Bush perceived by the media after his involvement in the war on terrorism?

In the aftermath of the September 11, 2001, tragedy, George W. Bush was perceived by both the American people and the media in a new light. After previously questioning his credibility and leadership at every turn, the news media exhibited a newfound respect for the president with such notable publications as *Time* reporting that "the president is growing before our eyes" and *Newsweek* portraying him as a confident, capable leader in full command of the war against terrorism. His job approval rating averaged 89 percent in the months following the attack, and many leaders and Democratic politicians complimented him as a leader. Although the news media at times criticized Bush for waging the war on terrorism at the expense of certain U.S. civil liberties and the domestic agenda, three-quarters of Americans felt the government was doing enough to protect the rights of average Americans, according to an *ABC News/Washington Post* poll of December 2001. At the time of public consensus, however, Bush was less than halfway into his first term.

What has been the role of Voice of America historically, and how has it changed post-September 11?

In observance of its sixtieth anniversary, on February 25, 2002, President George W. Bush said of Voice of America (VOM), "For decades, the Voice of America has told the world the truth about America and our policies. Through a Cold War—in crisis and in calm—VOA has added to the momentum of freedom." VOM is an international multimedia broadcasting service funded by the U.S. government. VOA broadcasts over nine hundred hours of news, informational, educational, and cultural programs every week to an audience of some 91 million worldwide. VOA programs are produced and broadcast in English and fifty-two other languages via radio, satellite television, and the Internet.

VOA began in response to the need of peoples in closed and war-torn societies for "a consistently reliable and authoritative source of news." While the Smith–Mundt Act of 1948 prohibits VOA from broadcasting to the United States, listeners from Albania to Thailand tune in to understand the United States' military actions across the globe. For example, the first VOA broadcast originated from New York City on February 24, 1942, just seventy-nine days after the United States entered World War II. Speaking in German, announcer William Harlan Hale told his listeners, "Here speaks a voice from America. Every day at this time we will bring you the news of the war. The news may be good. The news may be bad. We shall tell you the truth." On July 12, 1976, President Gerald Ford signed the VOA Charter into law, mandating that VOA broadcasts be "accurate, objective, and comprehensive."

Many people in the Arab world have a distorted view of America in general and its role in the war on terrorism specifically. Anti-American broadcasts are the norm, especially on Al Jazeera, the Qatar-based satellite network that aired Osama bin Laden's verbal attacks against the United States. Therefore, in an effort to reach this audience, Voice of America has increased its content and targeted lively dialogue at younger audiences. In addition, VOA broadcasts in Afghan languages were expanded to give opponents of the Taliban more airtime. Various VOA tactics assist in moving the Middle East away from overwhelming government-sponsored censorship toward a more independent media.

What was Barack Obama's relationship with the press?

"Controversial" and "adversarial" are two words that are often used to describe President Obama's relationship with the press. Obama's early use of Twitter and Facebook to make news was seen as controversial, as was the White House's use of its own videographer to record the president in settings to which the press had no access. Obama's use of nontraditional venues for major interviews, including *The Tonight Show*, *The Daily Show*, and ESPN, often frustrated reporters. A 2015 study conducted by the *Columbia Journal Review* concluded, "Evidence suggests that the relationship between the president and the press is more distant than it has been in a half century." However, the study also puts responsibility on the press for being "held prisoner by the demands of social media, chasing clickable quotes rather than substantive information." The pervasiveness of social media led White House press secretary Josh Earnest to put an end to off-camera morning meetings in his office because he said journalists would use the opportunity to tweet every word he said.

Which presidents have made notable public speeches?

In carrying out his roles as popular leader, chief executive, and addresser of the press, the president of the United States often makes compelling speeches in order to rally the

---

How did Donald Trump's use of social media early in his tenure set the tone for his relationship with the press?

Donald Trump's early use of social media established his style of communication with the press and relationship with the media. During his campaign, Trump gained notoriety for his use of social media, and particularly Twitter, to express his views and communicate directly with his supporters. Then and after taking office, President Trump routinely insisted that he was treated unfairly in the press (in one tweet calling the press "the enemy of the American people"), while many in the news industry openly expressed how difficult it was to report on him in today's often chaotic media environment. Media headlines published within the first six months of his presidency often called his relationship with the press "troubling," "fraught," and "complicated."

American people around a national goal or during a time of crisis. Among the most oft-cited: George Washington's first inaugural address and farewell address, James Monroe's State of the Nation address proclaiming the Monroe Doctrine, Abraham Lincoln's Gettysburg Address, Woodrow Wilson's war message advising Congress to declare war on Germany, Franklin D. Roosevelt's first fireside chat and third inaugural address, John F. Kennedy's inaugural address, Lyndon Johnson's State of the Union address proposing the Great Society program, and Richard Nixon's resignation speech.

Further Reading

BOOKS

GENERAL GOVERNMENT AND POLITICS

Austin, Eric W. *Political Facts of the United States since 1789*. New York: Columbia University Press, 1986.

Carpini Delli, Michael X., and Scott Keeter. *What Americans Know about Politics and Why It Matters*. New Haven, CT: Yale University Press, 1996.

Corwin, Edward S. *The "Higher Law": Background of American Constitutional Law*. Ithaca, NY: Cornell University Press, 1990.

Corwin, Edward, and J. W. Peltason. *Corwin and Peltason's Understanding the Constitution,* 13th edition. Fort Worth, TX: Harcourt Brace, 1994.

Diamond, Larry. *Developing Democracy, Toward Consolidation*. Baltimore, MD: Johns Hopkins Press, 1999.

Eskin, Blake, ed. *The Book of Political Lists*. New York: Villard, 1998.

Fukuyama, Francis. *The Origins of Political Order: From Prehuman Times to the French Revolution*. New York: Farrar, Straus, & Giroux, 2011.

Ganis, Richard. *Politics from A to Z*. Berkeley, CA: Zephytos Press, 2015.

Hamilton, Alexander, James Madison, and John Jay. *The Federalist Papers, 1787–1788*. Reprint, New York: Mentor Books, 1961.

Grisinger, Joanna L. *The Unwieldy American State: Administrative Politics since the New Deal*. New York: Cambridge University Press, 2014.

Huntington, Samuel. *The Third Wave: Democratization in the Late Twentieth Century*. Norman: University of Oklahoma Press, 1991.

Kelly, Alfred, Winfred A. Harbison, and Herman Beltz. *The American Constitution: Its Origins and Development,* 7th edition. New York: W. W. Norton, 1991.

Kenworthy, Lane. *Social Democratic America*. New York: Oxford University Press, 2014.

Mladenka, Kenneth R. *The Unfinished Republic: American Government in the Twenty-first Century*. Upper Saddle River, NJ: Prentice-Hall, 1997.

Page, Benjamin I., and James R. Simmons. *What Government Can Do: Dealing with Poverty and Inequality*. Chicago: The University of Chicago Press, 2000.

Rosenstone, Steven, and John Mark Hansen. *Mobilization, Participation, and Democracy in America*. New York: Macmillan, 1993.

Sandoz, Ellis. A *Government of Laws: Political Theory, Religion, and the American Founding*. Baton Rouge: Louisiana State University Press, 1990.

Skocpol, Theda, and Morris P. Fiorina, eds. *Civic Engagement in American Democracy*. Washington, DC: Brookings Institution Press, 1999.

Sobel, Syl. *How the U.S. Government Works*. New York: Barron's, 2012.

Tocqueville, Alexis de. *Democracy in America*. 1835. Reprint, edited by J. P. Mayer and translated by Phillips Bradley. Garden City, NY: Anchor Books, 1969.

COLONIAL AMERICA AND THE REVOLUTIONARY WAR

Bailyn, Bernard. *The Ideological Origins of the American Revolution*. Cambridge, MA: Harvard University Press, 1967.

Bober, Natalie S. *Countdown to Independence: A Revolution of Ideas in England and Her American Colonies, 1760–1776*. New York: Atheneum Books, 2001.

Boyd, Julian P. *The Declaration of Independence*. Princeton, NJ: Princeton University Press, 1945.

Carman, Harry J., Harold C. Syrett, and Bernard W. Wishy. *A History of the American People: Volume I to 1877*. New York: Alfred A. Knopf, 1960.

Catton, Bruce, and William B. Catton. *The Bold and Magnificent Dream: America's Founding Years, 1492–1815*. Garden City, NY: Doubleday, 1978.

Cogliano, Francis D. *Revolutionary America, 1763–1815: A Political History*. London and New York, Routledge, 2000.

Dinnerstein, Leonard, and Kenneth T. Jackson. *American Vistas*. New York: Oxford University Press, 1991.

Dumbauld, Edward. *The Declaration of Independence and What It Means Today*. Tulsa: University of Oklahoma Press, 1950.

Findling, John E., and Frank W. Thackery, eds. *Events That Changed America in the Eighteenth Century*. Westport, CT: The Greenwood Press, 1998.

Hazelton, John H. *The Declaration of Independence: Its History*. 1906. Reprint, New York: Da Capo Press, 1970.

Hoffer, Peter Charles. *Law and People in Colonial America,* revised edition. Baltimore and London: The Johns Hopkins University Press, 1998.

Kammen, Michael G., ed. *Politics and Society in Colonial America: Democracy or Deference?,* 2nd edition. Huntington, NY: Robert E. Krieger Publishing, 1978.

Lancaster, Bruce. *The American Heritage Book of the Revolution*. New York: American Heritage Publishing Co., 1971.

Maier, Pauline. *From Resistance to Revolution: Colonial Radicals and the Development of American Opposition to Britain, 1765–1776*. New York: Alfred A. Knopf, 1972.

———. *Ratification: The People Debate the Constitution, 1787–1788.* New York: Simon & Schuster, 2011.

McCusker, John J., and Russell Menard. *The Economy of British America, 1607–1789.* Chapel Hill, NC: University of North Carolina Press, 1985.

Middlekauff, Robert. *The Glorious Cause: The American Revolution, 1763–1789.* Vol. 2 of *The Oxford History of the United States.* New York: Oxford University Press, 1982.

Morris, Richard B. *The American Revolution, 1763–1783.* Columbia: The University of South Carolina Press, 1970.

Reich, Jerome R. *Colonial America,* 3rd edition. Englewood Cliffs, NJ: Prentice Hall, 1994.

Rutman, Darrett B. *The Morning of America, 1603–1789.* Boston: Houghton Mifflin, 1971.

Tate, Thad W., and David L Ammerman, eds. *The Chesapeake in the Seventeenth Century: Essays on Anglo-American Society.* Chapel Hill, NC: University of North Carolina Press, 1979.

Taylor, Alan. *Colonial America: A Very Short Introduction.* New York: Oxford University Press, 2012.

Vaughan, Alden T. *America Before the Revolution, 1725–1775.* Englewood Cliffs, NJ: Prentice-Hall, 1967.

Wood, Gordon S. *The Idea of America: Reflections on the Birth of the United States.* New York: Penguin Press, 2011.

FEDERALISM AND STATE AND LOCAL GOVERNMENT

Anton, Thomas. *American Federalism and Public Policy.* Philadelphia, PA: Temple University Press, 1989.

Beer, Samuel H. *To Make a Nation: The Rediscovery of American Federalism.* Cambridge, MA: The Belknap Press of Harvard University Press, 1993.

Burns, Nancy E. *The Formation of American Local Governments: Private Values in Public Institutions.* New York: Oxford University Press, 1994.

Doonan, Michael. *American Federalism in Practice: The Formulation and Implementation of Contemporary Health Policy.* Washington: Brookings Institution Press, 2013.

Dye, Thomas R. *American Federalism: Competition among Governments.* Lexington, MA: Lexington Books, 1990.

Elazar, Daniel. *American Federalism: A View from the States.* New York: Harper & Row, 1984.

Erikson, Robert S., Gerald C. Wright, and John P. McIver. *Statehouse Democracy: Public Opinion and Policy in the American States.* Cambridge, UK: Cambridge University Press, 1993.

Fiorina, Morris. *Divided Government.* New York: Macmillan, 1992.

Peterson, Paul, Barry Rabe, and Kenneth K. Wong. *When Federalism Works.* Washington, DC: Brookings Institute, 1986.

Rivlin, Alice M. "Rethinking Federalism." In Readings in *State and Local Government,* edited by David C. Saffell and Harry Basehart. New York: McGraw-Hill, 1994.

THE LEGISLATIVE BRANCH

Bohn, Michael K. *Presidents in Crisis: Tough Decisions Inside the White House from Truman to Obama.* New York: Arcade Publishing, 2015.

Clinton, Hillary Rodham. *Hard Choices.* New York: Simon & Schuster, 2014.

Congressional Quarterly. *The Presidency A to Z: A Ready Reference Encyclopedia.* 3 vols. Washington, DC: privately printed, 1993.

Crovits, L. Gordon, and Jeremy A. Rabkin, eds. *The Fettered Presidency: Legal Constraints on the Executive Branch*. Foreword by Robert H. Bork. Washington, DC: American Enterprise Institute for Public Policy Research, 1989.

Faber, Charles F., and Richard B. Faber. *The American Presidents Ranked by Performance*. Jefferson, NC: McFarland & Company, 2000.

Goodsell, Charles T. *The New Case for Bureaucracy*. Washington, DC: QC Press, 2014.

Goodwin, Doris Kearns. *The Bully Pulpit: Theodore Roosevelt, William Howard Taft, and the Golden Age of Journalism*. New York: Simon & Schuster, 2014.

Hill, Larry B., ed. *The State of Public Bureaucracy*. Armonk, NY: M. E. Sharpe, 1992.

Kane, Joseph Nathan. *Presidential Fact Book: The Facts on All the Presidents from George Washington to Bill Clinton*. New York: Random House, 1999.

Milkis, Sidney M. *The President and the Parties: The Transformation of the American Party System since the New Deal*. New York: Oxford University Press, 1993.

Nelson, Michael, ed. *The Presidency A to Z,* 2nd edition. Washington, DC: Congressional Quarterly, 1998.

Patella, Lu Ann, and Fred L. *Worth. World Almanac of Presidential Facts*. New York: Pharos Books, 1993.

Pfiffner, James P. *The Modern Presidency*. New York: St. Martin's Press, 1994.

Sisung, Kelle S. *Federal Agency Profiles for Students*. Farmington Hills, MI: Gale Group, 1999.

Sisung, Kelle S., and Gerda-Ann Raffaelle, eds. *Presidential Administration Profiles for Students*. Farmington Hills, MI: Gale Group, 2000.

Spitzer, Robert. *President and Congress: Executive Hegemony at the Crossroads of American Government*. New York: McGraw-Hill, 1993.

Watson, Robert. *The Presidents' Wives: Reassessing the Office of the First Lady*. Boulder, CO: Lynne Rienner Publishers, 2000.

Wilson, James Q. *Bureaucracy: What Government Agencies Do and Why They Do It*. New York: Basic Books, 1989.

Woodward, Bob. *The Agenda: Inside the Clinton White House*. New York: Simon & Schuster, 1994.

THE JUDICIAL BRANCH

Abraham, Henry. *The Judicial Process,* 6th edition. New York: Oxford University Press, 1993.

Ackerman, Bruce. *The Future of Liberal Revolution*. New Haven, CT: Yale University Press, 1992.

Agresto, John. *The Supreme Court and Constitutional Democracy*. Ithaca, NY: Cornell University Press, 1984.

Carp, Robert, and Ronald Stidham. *The Federal Courts*. Washington, DC: Congressional Quarterly Press, 1985.

Congressional Quarterly. *Guide to the U.S. Supreme Court,* 2nd edition. Washington, DC: 1990.

Coyle, Marcia. *The Roberts Court: The Struggle for the Constitution*. New York: Simon & Schuster, 2014.

Goldman, Sheldon, and Thomas P. Jahnige. *The Federal Courts as a Political System*. New York: Harper & Row, 1985.

Hall, Kermitt, L., ed. *The Oxford Companion to the Supreme Court of the United States*. New York: Oxford University Press, 1992.

Healy, Thomas. *The Great Dissent: How Oliver Wendall Holmes Changed His Mind—and Changed the History of Free Speech in America*. New York: Metropolitan Books, 2013.

O'Brien, David M. *Storm Center: The Supreme Court in American Politics,* 5th edition. New York: W. W. Norton, 1999.

Posner, Richard A. *The Federal Courts: Crisis and Reform.* Cambridge, MA: Harvard University Press, 1985.

Rosenberg, Gerald. *The Hollow Hope: Can Courts Bring about Social Change?* Chicago: University of Chicago Press, 1991.

Shapiro, Martin. Courts: *A Comparative Political Analysis.* Chicago: University of Chicago Press, 1981.

Stevens, John Paul. *Six Amendments: How and Why We Should Change the Constitution.* New York: Little Brown and Company, 2014.

Waltman, Jerold L., and Kenneth M. Holland, eds. *The Political Role of Law Courts in Modern Societies.* New York: Macmillan, 1988.

CIVIL LIBERTIES AND CIVIL RIGHTS

Abraham, Henry. *Freedom and the Court: Civil Rights and Liberties in the United States,* 5th edition. New York: Oxford University Press, 1994.

Alderman, Ellen, and Caroline Kennedy. *In Our Defense: The Bill of Rights in Action.* New York: William Morrow, 1991.

———. *The Right to Privacy.* New York: Alfred A. Knopf, 1995.

Alley, Robert S., ed. *The Constitution and Religion: Leading Supreme Court Cases on Church and State.* Amherst, NY: Prometheus Books, 1999.

Brigham, John. *Civil Liberties and American Democracy.* Washington, DC: Congressional Quarterly Press, 1984.

Burns, James MacGregor, and Stewart Burns. *A People's Charter: The Pursuit of Rights in America.* New York: Alfred A. Knopf, 1991.

Constitutional Rights Foundation. "Is a Fair Trial Possible in the Age of Mass Media?" *Bill of Rights in Action 11*, no. 1 (Winter 1994).

Dershowitz, Alan M. *Taking Liberties*. Chicago: Contemporary Books, 1988.

Evans, J. Edward. *Freedom of Religion.* Minneapolis, MN: Lerner, 1990.

Fiss, Owen M. *The Irony of Free Speech*. Cambridge, MA: Harvard University Press, 1996.

Forer, Lois G. *A Chilling Effect: The Mounting Threat of Libel and Invasion of Privacy Actions to the First Amendment.* New York: W. W. Norton, 1987.

Hentoff, Nat. *The First Freedom: The Tumultuous History of Free Speech in America.* New York: Delacorte, 1980.

Mayeri, Serena. *Reasoning from Race: Feminism, Law, and the Civil Rights Revolution.* Cambridge, MA: Harvard University Press, 2014.

Risen, Clay. *The Bill of the Century: The Epic Battle for the Civil Rights Act.* New York: Bloomsbury Press, 2014.

Roleff, Tamara R., ed. *Civil Liberties.* San Diego, CA: Greenhaven Press, 1999.

POITICAL INTEREST GROUPS AND PACS

Cigler, Allan J., and Burdett A. Loomis. *Interest Group Politics,* 3rd edition. Washington, DC: Congressional Quarterly Press, 1991.

Clawson, Dan, Alan Neustadt, and Denise Scott. *Money Talks: Corporate PACs and Political Influence.* New York: Basic Books, 1992.

Day, Christine. *What Older Americans Think: Interest Groups and Aging Policy*. Princeton, NJ: Princeton University Press, 1990.

Holyoake, Thomas T. *Interest Groups and Lobbying: Pursuing Political Interests in America*. Boulder, CO: Westview Press, 2014.

Lewis, Charles, and the Center for Public Integrity. *The Buying of Congress: How Special Interest Groups Have Stolen Your Right to Life, Liberty, and the Pursuit of Happiness*. New York: Avon Books, 1998.

Moe, Terry M. *The Organization of Interests*. Chicago: University of Chicago Press, 1980.

Morris, Dick. *Vote.com: How Big-Money Lobbyists and the Media Are Losing Their Influence, and the Internet Is Giving Power Back to the People*. Los Angeles: Renaissance Books, 1999.

Petracca, Mark, ed. *The Politics of Interests: Interest Groups Transformed*. Boulder, CO: Westview, 1992.

Sabato, Larry. *PAC Power*. New York: W. W. Norton, 1984.

Sisung, Kelle S., ed. *Special Interest Groups for Students*. Farmington Hills, MI: Gale Group, 1999.

Walter, Jack L. Jr. *Mobilizing Interest Groups in America*. Ann Arbor: University of Michigan Press, 1991.

POLITICAL PARTIES

Aldrich, John H. *Why Parties?: The Origin and Transformation of Party Politics in America*. Chicago: University of Chicago Press, 1995.

Coleman, John J. *Party Decline in America: Policy, Politics, and the Fiscal State*. Princeton, NJ: Princeton University Press, 1996.

Gairdener, William D. *The Great Divide: Why Liberals and Conservatives Will Never, Ever Agree*. New York: Encounter Books, 2015.

Geismer, Lily. *Don't Blame Us: Suburban Liberals and the Transformation of the Democratic Party*. Princeton, NJ: Princeton University Press, 2014.

Gould, Lewis L. *The Republicans: A History of the Grand Old Party*. New York: Oxford University Press, 2014.

Kurian, George Thomas, ed. *The Encyclopedia of the Democratic Party*. 2 vols. Armonk, NY: M. E. Sharpe, 1997. See also Kurian's supplement to this work, *Supplement to the Encyclopedia of the Democratic Party*. Armonk, NY: M. E. Sharpe, 2002.

———. *The Encyclopedia to the Republican Party*. 2 vols. Armonk, NY: M. E. Sharpe, 1997. See also Kurian's supplement to this work, *Supplement to the Encyclopedia of the Republican Party*. Armonk, NY: M. E. Sharpe, 2002.

Maisel, L. Sandy, ed. *The Parties Respond: Changes in American Parties and Campaigns*, 3rd edition. Boulder, CO: Westview Press, 1998.

Milkis, Sidney. *The President and the Parties: The Transformation of the American Party System since the New Deal*. New York: Oxford University Press, 1993.

Rockwood, Stephen. *American Third Parties since the Civil War*. New York: Garland Publishing, 1985.

Wattenberg, Martin P. *The Decline of American Political Parties, 1952–1996*. Cambridge, MA: Harvard University Press, 1998.

CAMPAIGNS, ELECTIONS, AND VOTING

Boller, Paul F., Jr. *Presidential Campaigns*. New York: Oxford University Press, 1984.

Congressional Research Service and the Library of Congress. *Presidential Elections in the United States: A Primer.* Washington, DC: Government Printing Office, 2000.

Davis, James W. *U.S. Presidential Primaries and the Caucus-Convention System: A Sourcebook.* Westport, CT: Greenwood Press, 1997.

Flanigan, William H., and Nancy H. Zingale. *Political Behavior of the American Electorate,* 9th edition. Washington, DC: Congressional Quarterly Press, 1998.

Fowler, Linda. *Candidates, Congress, and the American Democracy.* Ann Arbor: University of Michigan Press, 1994.

Ginsberg, Benjamin, and Martin Shefter. *Politics by Other Means: Institutional Conflict and the Declining Significance of Elections in America.* New York: Basic Books, 1990.

Halperin, Mark, and John Heilemann. *Double Down: Game Change 2012.* New York: Penguin Books, 2012.

Lee, Caroline W., Michael McQuarrie, Edward T. Walker, and Craig Calhoun. *Democratizing Inequalities: Dilemmas of the New York Participation.* New York: NYU Press, 2015.

Mattes, Kyle, and David P. Redlawsk. *The Positive Case for Negative Campaigning.* Chicago: University of Chicago Press, 2015.

Morgeson, Forrest. *Citizen Satisfaction: Improving Government Performance Efficiency and Citizen Trust.* New York: Palgrave Macmillan, 2014.

Niemi, Richard, and Herbert Weisberg. *Controversies in American Voting Behavior.* Washington, DC: Congressional Quarterly Press, 1984.

Polsby, Nelson, and Aaron Wildavsky. *Presidential Elections,* 8th edition. New York: Free Press, 1991.

Shields-West, Eileen. *The World Almanac of Presidential Campaigns.* New York: World Almanac, 1992.

Sorauf, Frank. *Inside Campaign Finance: Myths and Realities.* New Haven, CT: Yale University Press, 1992.

Thernstorm, Abigail M. *Whose Votes Count? Affirmative Action and Minority Voting Rights.* Cambridge, MA: Harvard University Press, 1987.

Thomas, Sue, and Clyde Wilcox, eds. *Women and the Elective Office: Past, Present, and Future.* New York: Oxford University Press, 1998.

Wattenberg, Martin P. *The Rise of Candidate-Centered Politics: Presidential Elections of the 1980s.* Cambridge, MA: Harvard University Press, 1991.

PUBLIC OPINION AND THE MEDIA

Brock, George. *Out of Print: Newspapers, Journalism and the Business of News in the Digital Age.* Philadelphia, PA: Kogan Page, 2013.

Burnstein, Paul. *American Public Opinion, Advocacy and Policy in Congress: What the Public Wants and What It Gets.* New York: Cambridge University Press, 2014.

Citrin, Jack, and David O. Sears. *American Identity and the Politics of Multiculturalism.* New York: Cambridge University Pres, 2014.

Erikson, Robert S., Norman Luttbeg, and Kent Tedin. *American Public Opinion: Its Origins, Content, and Impact.* New York: Wiley, 1980.

Fallows, James. *Breaking the News: How the Media Undermine American Democracy.* New York: Pantheon Books, 1996.

Graber, Doris. *Mass Media and American Politics.* Washington, DC: Congressional Quarterly Press, 1989.

McCombs, Maxwell. *Setting the Agenda: Mass Media and Public Opinion.* Malden, MA: Polity, 2014.

Nacos, Brigitte L. *The Press, Presidents, and Crises.* New York: Columbia University Press, 1990.

Owen, Diana. *Media Messages in American Presidential Elections.* Westport, CT: Greenwood, 1991.

Perrin, Andrew J. *American Democracy: from Tocqueville to Town Hall Halls to Twitter.* London: Policy Press, 2014.

Schiffrin, Anya, ed. *Global Muckraking: 100 Years of Investigative Journalism from Around the World.* New York: The New Press, 2014.

Selnow, Gary W. *Electronic Whistle-Stops: The Impact of the Internet on American Politics.* Westport, CT: Praeger Press, 1998.

Spero, Robert. *The Duping of the American Voter: Dishonesty and Deception in Presidential Television Advertising.* New York: Lippincott & Crowell Publishers, 1980.

ONLINE AND PRINT PERIODICALS

The American Spectator (https://spectator.org): Magazine covering what it terms "the New Economy and the New Political Reality."

Brookings Review on JSTOR (jstor.org): Journal containing the scholarly work of the Brookings Institution on public policy.

Congressional Quarterly (cqrollcall.com): Part of a privately owned publishing company called CQ Roll Call that produces a number of publications reporting primarly on the U.S. Congress.

CQ Weekly (https://library.cqpress.com/cqweekly/): Publication providing nonpartisan coverage of Congress.

The Federalist (thefederalist.com/): Email journal providing a survey and analysis of the week's most significant news, policy, and opinion from a conservative perspective.

The Huffington Post (www.huffingtonpost.com/): Online liberal newspaper with extensive political coverage.

Mother Jones (www.motherjones.com/): Magazine committed to social justice through investigative reporting.

The Nation (https://www.thenation.com/): Magazine providing a critical discussion of political and social questions.

National Review (www.nationalreview.com/): Magazine providing coverage and analysis of politics without what it terms a "liberal bias."

The New York Times (www.nytimes.com/): General interest newspaper with extensive political coverage.

Slate Magazine (www.slate.com/): Online magazine providing summaries of top news stories, with particular political coverage.

The Wall Street Journal (wsj.com/): A daily newspaper with a main focus on business news.

The Washington Post (https://www.washingtonpost.com/): General interest newspaper with extensive political coverage.

The Washington Times (www.washingtontimes.com/): General interest newspaper providing coverage of politics and policy.

WEBSITES

About Government (www.aboutgovernment.com/): Provides links to sites covering government, politics, political parties, elections and voting, citizenship, news, icons, landmarks, and traditions.

American Association for Public Opinion Research (https://www.aapor.org/): Provides guides, standards, definitions and recommended and condemned practices for public policy survey data collection.

The American Center for Law and Justice (https://aclj.org/): Engages in litigation, provides legal services, renders advice, counsels clients, and supports attorneys involved in defending Judeo-Christian values.

American Civil Liberties Union (www.aclu.org/): Nonpartisan organization. Works in the courts, legislatures, and communities to defend and preserve individual rights and liberties. Uses staff and volunteer lawyers to handle cases concerning civil rights violations.

American National Election Studies (www.electionstudies.org/): A collaboration of Stanford University and the University of Michigan, producing data on voting, public opinion, and political participation.

Campaigns & Elections (campaignsandelections.com): Focused on the toots, tactics and techniques of the political consulting profession.

Center for American Women and Politics (www.camp.rutgers.edu/): Research, education, and public service center promoting women's participation in politics, government, and public life. From the Eagleton Institute of Politics of Rutgers, the State University of New Jersey.

Center for the Study of the American Electorate (http://csaelectorate.blogspot.com): Nonpartisan research institution focusing on issues surrounding citizen engagement in politics. Issues publications on election night projects, media and politics, campaign finance, voter participation, and other topics.

Center for the Study of the Presidency & Congress (thepresidency.org): Works with leading experts on presidential and congressional history to provide case studies on political leadership, legislative compromise, and national strategy. Publishes the *Presidential Studies Quarterly* (PSQ), an analysis of both the history of the presidency and the current dynamics of the office.

Columbia Journalism Review (www.cjr.org/): Lists major media companies and what they own. Also includes a selected list of articles in CJR about media ownership.

Common Cause (www.commoncause.org/): Nonpartisan citizens' lobbying organization. Promotes open, honest, and accountable government. Publishes investigative studies on the effects of money in politics and reports on issues of ethics and integrity in government.

Congress.gov (https://www.congress.gov/): Provides access to federal legislative information, including bill summary and status, bill text, and public laws by law number; the Congressional Record; roll call votes; and committee information, including House and Senate committee information. Also includes links to other government information and sites.

C-SPAN (www.c-span.org): A public service created by the American cable television industry, providing readers and viewers access to the live gavel-to-gavel proceedings of the U.S. House of Representatives and the U.S. Senate, and to other forums where public policy is discussed, debated and decided—without editing, commentary, or analysis.

Democratic National Committee (https://www.democrats.org/): Provides Democratic Party news and information. Includes voter outreach and registration services, links to other sites, a store, and a job board.

Elections Central (http://www.uspresidentialelectionnews.com): Provides the history of each U.S. presidential election since 1789, including popular and electoral votes, states won, issues, and turnout.

Federal Election Project (www.electproject.org/): Provides timely and accurate election statistics, electoral laws, research reports and other useful information regarding the United States electoral system.

Federal Elections Commission (www.fec.gov): Official federal elections web portal.

FedWorld (www.fedworld.gov/): Gateway to information disseminated by the federal government. Managed by the National Technical Information Service of the U.S. Department of Commerce.

FirstGov (www.firstgov.gov): Official U.S. government web portal. Provides a centralized source for locating information from U.S. local, state, and federal government agency web sites.

Freedom Forum (www.freedomforum.org/): Nonpartisan foundation dedicated to free press, speech, and "spirit for all." Focuses efforts on an interactive museum of news, First Amendment freedoms, and newsroom diversity.

Freedom House (https://www.freedomhouse.org/): Nonpartisan group. Supports democratic values and opposes dictatorships of the far left and far right. Conducts U.S. and overseas research, advocacy, education, and training initiatives that promote human rights, democracy, free-market economies, the rule of law, independent media, and U.S. engagement in international affairs. Original founders include Eleanor Roosevelt and Wendell Willkie.

GPOAccess (https://www.access.gpo.gov/): Provides free electronic access to federal government information, including the Catalog of U.S. Government Publications, the Code of Federal Regulations, the Congressional Record, the federal budget, the Federal Register, public presidential papers, the U.S. code, and the U.S. government online bookstore. A service of the U.S. Government Printing Office.

League of Women Voters (lwv.org): Nonpartisan political organization. Supports the informed and active participation of citizens in government, works to increase understanding of major public policy issues, and influences public policy thorough education and advocacy.

The Libertarian Party (lp.org): Provides Libertarian Party news and information. Includes voter registration services, video clips, and links to other sites.

The Library of Congress (https://www.loc.gov/): Serves as the research arm of the U.S. Congress. Is the largest library in the world, with collections of books, recordings, photographs, maps, and manuscripts. Makes its resources available to Congress and the American people and works to sustain and preserve a universal collection of knowledge and creativity for future generations.

National Archives and Records Administration (https://www.archives.gov/): An independent agency of the U.S. government charged with preserving and documenting government and historical records.

National Center for Policy Analysis (www.ncpa.org/): Nonpartisan public policy research organization. Develops and promotes private alternatives to government regulation and control.

National Center for State Courts (www.ncsc.org/): A nonprofit organization dedicated to improving judicial administration in the United States and around the world.

National Governors Association (https://www.nga.org/): An organization consisting of the governors of the states, territories, and commonwealths of the United States. The NGA's role is to act as a collective voice for governors on matters of national policy, as well as allowing governors to share best practices and coordinate interstate initiatives.

OpenSecrets.org: Tracks money spent in U.S. elections. Website of the Center for Responsive Politics.

Pew Research Center for the People and the Press (www.pewresearch.org/): A nonpartisan American "fact tank" based in Washington, D.C.; provides information on social issues, public opinion, and demographic trends shaping the United States and the world.

Political Advocacy Groups (politicaladvocacy.org/): Provides subject and alphabetical directory listings of lobbyists in the United States.

PollingReport.com (www.pollingreport.com/): Independent, nonpartisan resource on trends in American public opinion. Features highlights from national polls. State-by-state presidential, congressional, and gubernatorial polls, analyses by pollsters, and other data are available to sub-scribers.

Project Vote Smart (votesmart.org/): Offers a library of factual information on 40,000 candidates for public office, including federal, state, and local officials. Covers candidates' backgrounds, issue po-sitions, voting records, campaign finances, and performance evaluations from more than 100 lib-eral and conservative special interest groups.

Reporters Committee for Freedom of the Press (https://www.rcfp.org/): Provides free legal assistance to journalists. Serves as a resource on free speech issues. Issues publications and operates a 24-hour hotline.

Republican National Committee (https://www.gop.com/): Provides Republican Party news and infor-mation. Includes voter registration services, a store, video clips, and links to other sites.

Reuters News (Reuters.com): Reuters is the news and media division of Thomson Reuters, the world's largest international multimedia news agency, providing investing news, world news, business news, technology news, headline news, small business news, news alerts, personal finance, stock market, and mutual funds information available online and on video, mobile, and interactive tele-vision platforms.

Supreme Court of the United States (https://www.supremecourt.gov/): Provides news and information on the Supreme Court. Includes court history, information on current and past justices, case tracking system, oral arguments, bar admissions form and instructions, court rules, case handling guidelines, opinions, orders and journals, public information, details on visiting the court, and links to related sites.

U.S. Electoral College (https://www.archives.gov/federal-register/electoral-college/): Maintains a vari-ety of information and statistics on presidential elections.

U.S. Government Documents Ready Reference Collection (library.columbia.edu/indiv/ usgd.html): Pro-vides a subject arrangement of the most frequently used U.S. government depository document titles at Columbia University Libraries.

U.S. House of Representatives (www.house.gov/): Provides information on House operations, mem-bers, committees, leadership, and other organizations, commissions, and task forces.

U.S. Senate (www.senate.gov/): Provides information on Senate members, leadership, committees, roll call tallies, legislative activities, and nominations.

USCourts.gov: Functions as a clearinghouse for information from and about the judicial branch of the U.S. government, including the Supreme Court, courts of appeals, district courts, and bankruptcy courts.

The White House (https://www.whitehouse.gov/): Official site of the White House. Provides informa-tion on the president, vice president, and their wives; news and policies; speeches; appointments; and history and tours. Also provides general information on the federal government.

The Declaration of Independence

When, in the course of human events, it becomes necessary for one people to dissolve the political bonds which have connected them with another, and to assume among the powers of the earth, the separate and equal station to which the laws of nature and of nature's God entitle them, a decent respect to the opinions of mankind requires that they should declare the causes which impel them to the separation.

We hold these truths to be self-evident, that all men are created equal, that they are endowed by their Creator with certain unalienable rights, that among these are life, liberty and the pursuit of happiness. That to secure these rights, governments are instituted among men, deriving their just powers from the consent of the governed. That whenever any form of government becomes destructive to these ends, it is the right of the people to alter or to abolish it, and to institute new government, laying its foundation on such principles and organizing its powers in such form, as to them shall seem most likely to effect their safety and happiness. Prudence, indeed, will dictate that governments long established should not be changed for light and transient causes; and accordingly all experience hath shown that mankind are more disposed to suffer, while evils are sufferable, than to right themselves by abolishing the forms to which they are accustomed. But when a long train of abuses and usurpations, pursuing invariably the same object evinces a design to reduce them under absolute despotism, it is their right, it is their duty, to throw off such government, and to provide new guards for their future security.

Such has been the patient sufferance of these colonies; and such is now the necessity which constrains them to alter their former systems of government. The history of the present King of Great Britain is a history of repeated injuries and usurpations, all having in direct object the establishment of an absolute tyranny over these states. To prove this, let facts be submitted to a candid world.

He has refused his assent to laws, the most wholesome and necessary for the public good.

He has forbidden his governors to pass laws of immediate and pressing importance, unless suspended in their operation till his assent should be obtained; and when so suspended, he has utterly neglected to attend to them.

He has refused to pass other laws for the accommodation of large districts of people, unless those people would relinquish the right of representation in the legislature, a right inestimable to them and formidable to tyrants only.

He has called together legislative bodies at places unusual, uncomfortable, and distant from the depository of their public records, for the sole purpose of fatiguing them into compliance with his measures.

He has dissolved representative houses repeatedly, for opposing with manly firmness his invasions on the rights of the people.

He has refused for a long time, after such dissolutions, to cause others to be elected; whereby the legislative powers, incapable of annihilation, have returned to the people at large for their exercise; the state remaining in the meantime exposed to all the dangers of invasion from without, and convulsions within.

He has endeavored to prevent the population of these states; for that purpose obstructing the laws for naturalization of foreigners; refusing to pass others to encourage their migration hither, and raising the conditions of new appropriations of lands.

He has obstructed the administration of justice, by refusing his assent to laws for establishing judiciary powers.

He has made judges dependent on his will alone, for the tenure of their offices, and the amount and payment of their salaries.

He has erected a multitude of new offices, and sent hither swarms of officers to harass our people, and eat out their substance.

He has kept among us, in times of peace, standing armies without the consent of our legislature.

He has affected to render the military independent of and superior to civil power.

He has combined with others to subject us to a jurisdiction foreign to our constitution, and unacknowledged by our laws; giving his assent to their acts of pretended legislation:

- For quartering large bodies of armed troops among us:

- For protecting them, by mock trial, from punishment for any murders which they should commit on the inhabitants of these states:

- For cutting off our trade with all parts of the world:

- For imposing taxes on us without our consent:

- For depriving us in many cases, of the benefits of trial by jury:

- For transporting us beyond seas to be tried for pretended offenses:

- For abolishing the free system of English laws in a neighboring province, establishing therein an arbitrary government, and enlarging its boundaries so as to render it at once an example and fit instrument for introducing the same absolute rule in these colonies:

- For taking away our charters, abolishing our most valuable laws, and altering fundamentally the forms of our governments:

- For suspending our own legislatures, and declaring themselves invested with power to legislate for us in all cases whatsoever.

He has abdicated government here, by declaring us out of his protection and waging war against us.

He has plundered our seas, ravaged our coasts, burned our towns, and destroyed the lives of our people.

He is at this time transporting large armies of foreign mercenaries to complete the works of death, desolation and tyranny, already begun with circumstances of cruelty and perfidy scarcely paralleled in the most barbarous ages, and totally unworthy the head of a civilized nation.

He has constrained our fellow citizens taken captive on the high seas to bear arms against their country, to become the executioners of their friends and brethren, or to fall themselves by their hands.

He has excited domestic insurrections amongst us, and has endeavored to bring on the inhabitants of our frontiers, the merciless Indian savages, whose known rule of warfare, is undistinguished destruction of all ages, sexes and conditions.

In every stage of these oppressions we have petitioned for redress in the most humble terms: our repeated petitions have been answered only by repeated injury. A prince, whose character is thus marked by every act which may define a tyrant, is unfit to be the ruler of a free people.

Nor have we been wanting in attention to our British brethren. We have warned them from time to time of attempts by their legislature to extend an unwarrantable jurisdiction over us. We have reminded them of the circumstances of our emigration and settlement here. We have appealed to their native justice and magnanimity, and we have conjured them by the ties of our common kindred to disavow these usurpations, which, would inevitably interrupt our connections and correspondence. We must, therefore, acquiesce in the necessity, which denounces our separation, and hold them, as we hold the rest of mankind, enemies in war, in peace friends.

We, therefore, the representatives of the United States of America, in General Congress, assembled, appealing to the Supreme Judge of the world for the rectitude of our intentions, do, in the name, and by the authority of the good people of these colonies, solemnly publish and declare, that these united colonies are, and of right ought to be free and independent states; that they are absolved from all allegiance to the British

329

Crown, and that all political connection between them and the state of Great Britain, is and ought to be totally dissolved; and that as free and independent states, they have full power to levy war, conclude peace, contract alliances, establish commerce, and to do all other acts and things which independent states may of right do. And for the support of this declaration, with a firm reliance on the protection of Divine Providence, we mutually pledge to each other our lives, our fortunes and our sacred honor.

JOHN HANCOCK, President
Attested, CHARLES THOMSON, Secretary

New Hampshire
JOSIAH BARTLETT
WILLIAM WHIPPLE
MATTHEW THORNTON

Massachusetts Bay
SAMUEL ADAMS
JOHN ADAMS
ROBERT TREAT PAINE
ELBRIDGE GERRY

Rhode Island
STEPHEN HOPKINS
WILLIAM ELLERY

Connecticut
ROGER SHERMAN
SAMUEL HUNTINGTON
WILLIAM WILLIAMS
OLIVER WOLCOTT

Georgia
BUTTON GWINNETT
LYMAN HALL
GEO. WALTON

Maryland
SAMUEL CHASE
WILLIAM PACA
THOMAS STONE
CHARLES CARROLL OF
    CARROLLTON

Virginia
GEORGE WYTHE
RICHARD HENRY LEE
THOMAS JEFFERSON
BENJAMIN HARRISON
THOMAS NELSON, JR.
FRANCIS LIGHTFOOT
    LEE
CARTER BRAXTON.

New York
WILLIAM FLOYD
PHILIP LIVINGSTON
FRANCIS LEWIS
LEWIS MORRIS

Pennsylvania
ROBERT MORRIS
BENJAMIN RUSH
BENJAMIN FRANKLIN
JOHN MORTON
GEORGE CLYMER
JAMES SMITH
GEORGE TAYLOR
JAMES WILSON
GEORGE ROSS

Delaware
CAESAR RODNEY
GEORGE READ
THOMAS M'KEAN

North Carolina
WILLIAM HOOPER
JOSEPH HEWES
JOHN PENN

South Carolina
EDWARD RUTLEDGE
THOMAS HEYWARD, JR.
THOMAS LYNCH, JR.
ARTHUR MIDDLETON

New Jersey
RICHARD STOCKTON
JOHN WITHERSPOON
FRANCIS HOPKINS
JOHN HART
ABRAHAM CLARK

330

Articles

of Confederation

To all to whom these Presents shall come, we, the undersigned Delegates of the States affixed to our Names send greeting. Whereas the Delegates of the United States of America in Congress assembled did on the fifteenth day of November in the year of our Lord One Thousand Seven Hundred and Seventy seven, and in the Second Year of the Independence of America agree to certain articles of Confederation and perpetual Union between the States of New Hampshire, Massachusetts-Bay, Rhode Island and Providence Plantations, Connecticut, New York, New Jersey, Pennsylvania, Delaware, Maryland, Virginia, North Carolina, South Carolina, and Georgia in the Words following, viz.

ARTICLES OF CONFEDERATION AND PERPETUAL UNION, between the States of New Hampshire, Massachusetts-bay, Rhode Island and Providence Plantations, Connecticut, New York, New Jersey, Pennsylvania, Delaware, Maryland, Virginia, North Carolina, South Carolina, and Georgia.

Article I. The Stile of this confederacy shall be, "The United States of America."

Article II. Each State retains its sovereignty, freedom and independence, and every Power, Jurisdiction and right, which is not by this confederation expressly delegated to the United States, in Congress assembled.

Article III. The said States hereby severally enter into a firm league of friendship with each other, for their common defence, the security of their Liberties, and their mutual and general welfare, binding themselves to assist each other, against all force offered to, or attacks made upon them, or any of them, on account of religion, sovereignty, trade, or any other pretence whatever.

Article IV. The better to secure and perpetuate mutual friendship and intercourse among the people of the different States in this Union, the free inhabitants of each of these States, paupers, vagabonds and fugitives from Justice excepted, shall be entitled to all privileges and immunities of free citizens in the several States; and the people of each State shall have free ingress and regress to and from any other State, and shall enjoy therein all the privileges of trade and commerce, subject to the same duties, impositions and restrictions as the inhabitants thereof respectively, provided that such restrictions shall not extend so far as to prevent the removal of property imported into any State, to any other State of which the Owner is an inhabitant; provided also that no imposition, duties or restriction shall be laid by any State, on the property of the United States, or either of them.

If any person guilty of, or charged with, treason, felony, or other high misdemeanor in any State, shall flee from Justice, and be found in any of the United States, he shall upon demand of the Governor or executive power of the State from which he fled, be delivered up, and removed to the State having jurisdiction of his offence.

Full faith and credit shall be given in each of these States to the records, acts and judicial proceedings of the courts and magistrates of every other State.

Article V. For the more convenient management of the general interests of the United States, delegates shall be annually appointed in such manner as the Legislature of each State shall direct, to meet in Congress on the first Monday in November, in every year, with a power reserved to each State to recall its delegates, or any of them, at any time within the year, and to send others in their stead, for the remainder of the Year.

No State shall be represented in Congress by less than two, nor by more than seven Members; and no person shall be capable of being delegate for more than three years, in any term of six years; nor shall any person, being a delegate, be capable of holding any office under the United States, for which he, or another for his benefit receives any salary, fees or emolument of any kind.

Each State shall maintain its own delegates in a meeting of the States, and while they act as members of the committee of the States.

In determining questions in the United States, in Congress assembled, each State shall have one vote.

Freedom of speech and debate in Congress shall not be impeached or questioned in any Court, or place out of Congress, and the members of Congress shall be protected in their persons from arrests and imprisonments, during the time of their going to and from, and attendance on Congress, except for treason, felony, or breach of the peace.

Article VI. No State, without the Consent of the United States, in Congress assembled, shall send any embassy to, or receive any embassy from, or enter into any conference, agreement, alliance, or treaty, with any King prince or State; nor shall any person holding any office of profit or trust under the United States, or any of them, accept of any present, emolument, office, or title of any kind whatever, from any king, prince, or foreign State; nor shall the United States, in Congress assembled, or any of them, grant any title of nobility.

No two or more States shall enter into any treaty, confederation, or alliance whatever between them, without the consent of the United States, in Congress assembled, specifying accurately the purposes for which the same is to be entered into, and how long it shall continue.

No State shall lay any imposts or duties, which may interfere with any stipulations in treaties, entered into by the United States in Congress assembled, with any king, prince, or State, in pursuance of any treaties already proposed by Congress, to the courts of France and Spain.

No vessels of war shall be kept up in time of peace, by any State, except such number only, as shall be deemed necessary by the United States, in Congress assembled, for the defence of such State, or its trade; nor shall any body of forces be kept up, by any State, in time of peace, except such number only as, in the judgment of the United States, in Congress assembled, shall be deemed requisite to garrison the forts necessary for the defence of such State; but every State shall always keep up a well regulated and disciplined militia, sufficiently armed and accounted, and shall provide and constantly have ready for use, in public stores, a due number of field pieces and tents, and a proper quantity of arms, ammunition, and camp equipage.

No State shall engage in any war without the consent of the United States in Congress assembled, unless such State be actually invaded by enemies, or shall have received certain advice of a resolution being formed by some nation of Indians to invade such State, and the danger is so imminent as not to admit of a delay till the United States in Congress assembled, can be consulted: nor shall any State grant commissions to any ships or vessels of war, nor letters of marque or reprisal, except it be after a declaration of war by the United States in Congress assembled, and then only against the kingdom or State, and the subjects thereof, against which war has been so declared, and under such regulations as shall be established by the United States in Congress assembled, unless such State be infested by pirates, in which case vessels of war may be fitted out for that occasion, and kept so long as the danger shall continue, or until the United States in Congress assembled shall determine otherwise.

Article VII. When land forces are raised by any State, for the common defence, all officers of or under the rank of colonel, shall be appointed by the Legislature of each State respectively by whom such forces shall be raised, or in such manner as such State shall direct, and all vacancies shall be filled up by the State which first made appointment.

Article VIII. All charges of war, and all other expenses that shall be incurred for the common defence or general welfare, and allowed by the United States in Congress assembled, shall be defrayed out of a common treasury, which shall be supplied by the several States, in proportion to the value of all land within each State, granted to or surveyed for any person, as such land and the buildings and improvements thereon shall be estimated, according to such mode as the United States, in Congress assembled, shall, from time to time, direct and appoint. The taxes for paying that proportion shall be laid and levied by the authority and direction of the Legislatures of the several States within the time agreed upon by the United States in Congress assembled.

Article IX. The United States, in Congress assembled, shall have the sole and exclusive right and power of determining on peace and war, except in the cases mentioned in the sixth article; of sending and receiving ambassadors; entering into treaties and alliances, provided that no treaty of commerce shall be made, whereby the legislative power of the respective States shall be restrained from imposing such imposts and duties on foreigners, as their own people are subjected to, or from prohibiting the exportation or importation of any species of goods or commodities whatsoever; of establishing rules for deciding, in all cases, what captures on land or water shall be legal, and in what manner prizes taken by land or naval forces in the service of the united Sates, shall be divided or appropriated; of granting letters of marque and reprisal in times of peace; appointing courts for the trial of piracies and felonies committed on the high seas; and establishing courts; for receiving and determining finally appeals in all cases of captures; provided that no member of Congress shall be appointed a judge of any of the said courts.

The United States, in Congress assembled, shall also be the last resort on appeal, in all disputes and differences now subsisting, or that hereafter may arise between two or more States concerning boundary, jurisdiction, or any other cause whatever; which authority shall always be exercised in the manner following. Whenever the legislative or executive authority, or lawful agent of any State in controversy with another, shall present a petition to Congress, stating the matter in question, and praying for a hearing, notice thereof shall be given, by order of Congress, to the legislative or executive authority of the other State in controversy, and a day assigned for the appearance of the parties by their lawful agents, who shall then be directed to appoint, by joint consent, commissioners or judges to constitute a court for hearing and determining the matter in question: but if they cannot agree, Congress shall name three persons out of each of the United States, and from the list of such persons each party shall alternately strike out one, the petitioners beginning, until the number shall be reduced to thirteen; and from that number not less than seven, nor more than nine names, as Congress shall direct, shall, in the presence of Congress, be drawn out by lot, and the persons whose names shall be so drawn, or any five of them, shall be commissioners or judges, to hear and finally determine the controversy, so always as a major part of the judges, who shall hear the cause, shall agree in the determination: and if either party shall neglect to attend at the day appointed, without showing reasons which Congress shall judge sufficient, or being present, shall refuse to strike, the Congress shall proceed to nominate three persons out of each State, and the secretary of Congress shall strike in behalf of such party absent or refusing; and the judgment and sentence of the court, to be appointed in the manner before prescribed, shall be final and conclusive; and if any of the parties shall refuse to submit to the authority of such court, or to appear or defend their claim or cause, the court shall nevertheless proceed to pronounce sentence, or judgment, which shall in like manner be final and decisive; the judgment or sentence and other proceedings being in either case transmitted to Congress, and lodged among the acts of Congress, for the security of the parties concerned: provided that every commissioner, before he sits in judgment, shall take an oath to be administered by one of the judges of the supreme or superior court of the State where the cause shall be tried, "well and truly to hear and determine the matter in question, according to the best of his judgment, without favour, affection, or hope of reward": provided, also, that no State shall be deprived of territory for the benefit of the United States.

All controversies concerning the private right of soil claimed under different grants of two or more States, whose jurisdictions as they may respect such lands, and the States which passed such grants are adjusted, the said grants or either of them being at the same time claimed to have originated antecedent to such settlement of jurisdiction, shall, on the petition of either party to the Congress of the United States, be finally determined, as near as may be, in the same manner as is before prescribed for deciding disputes respecting territorial jurisdiction between different States.

The United States, in Congress assembled, shall also have the sole and exclusive right and power of regulating the alloy and value of coin struck by their own authority, or by that of the respective States; fixing the standard of weights and measures throughout the United States;

regulating the trade and managing all affairs with the Indians, not members of any of the States; provided that the legislative right of any State, within its own limits, be not infringed or violated; establishing and regulating post-offices from one State to another, throughout all the United States, and exacting such postage on the papers passing through the same, as may be requisite to defray the expenses of the said office; appointing all officers of the land forces in the service of the United States, excepting regimental officers; appointing all the officers of the naval forces, and commissioning all officers whatever in the service of the United States; making rules for the government and regulation of the said land and naval forces, and directing their operations.

The United States, in Congress assembled, shall have authority to appoint a committee, to sit in the recess of Congress, to be denominated, "A Committee of the States," and to consist of one delegate from each State; and to appoint such other committees and civil officers as may be necessary for managing the general affairs of the United States under their direction; to appoint one of their number to preside; provided that no person be allowed to serve in the office of President more than one year in any term of three years; to ascertain the necessary sums of money to be raised for the service of the United States, and to appropriate and apply the same for defraying the public expenses; to borrow money or emit bills on the credit of the United States, transmitting every half year to the respective States an account of the sums of money so borrowed or emitted; to build and equip a navy; to agree upon the number of land forces, and to make requisitions from each State for its quota, in proportion to the number of white inhabitants in such State, which requisition shall be binding; and thereupon the Legislature of each State shall appoint the regimental officers, raise the men, and clothe, arm, and equip them, in a soldier-like manner, at the expense of the United States; and the officers and men so clothed, armed, and equipped, shall march to the place appointed, and within the time agreed on by the United States, in Congress assembled; but if the United States, in Congress assembled, shall, on consideration of circumstances, judge proper that any State should not raise men, or should raise a smaller number than its quota, and that any other State should raise a greater number of men than the quota thereof, such extra number shall be raised, officered, clothed, armed, and equipped in the same manner as the quota of such State, unless the Legislature of such State shall judge that such extra number cannot be safely spared out of the same, in which case they shall raise, officer, clothe, arm, and equip, as many of such extra number as they judge can be safely spared. And the officers and men so clothed, armed, and equipped, shall march to the place appointed, and within the time agreed on by the United States in Congress assembled.

The United States, in Congress assembled, shall never engage in a war, nor grant letters of marque and reprisal in time of peace, nor enter into any treaties or alliances, nor coin money, nor regulate the value thereof nor ascertain the sums and expenses necessary for the defence and welfare of the United States, or any of them, nor emit bills, nor borrow money on the credit of the United States, nor appropriate money, nor agree upon the number of vessels of war to be built or purchased, or the number of land or sea forces to be raised, nor appoint a commander in chief of the army or navy, unless nine States assent to the same, nor shall a question on any other point, except for adjourning from day to day, be determined, unless by the votes of a majority of the United States in Congress assembled.

The Congress of the United States shall have power to adjourn to any time within the year, and to any place within the United States, so that no period of adjournment be for a longer duration than the space of six months, and shall publish the journal of their proceedings monthly, except such parts thereof relating to treaties, alliances, or military operations, as in their judgment require secrecy; and the yeas and nays of the delegates of each State, on any question, shall be entered on the journal, when it is desired by any delegate; and the delegates of a State, or any of them, at his or their request, shall be furnished with a transcript of the said journal, except such parts as are above excepted, to lay before the Legislatures of the several States.

Article X. The committee of the States, or any nine of them, shall be authorized to execute, in the recess of Congress, such of the powers of Congress as the United States, in Congress assembled, by the consent of nine States, shall, from time to time, think expedient to vest them with; provided that no power be delegated to the said committee, for the exercise of which, by the articles of confederation, the voice of nine States, in the Congress of the United States assembled, is requisite.

Article XI. Canada acceding to this confederation, and joining in the measures of the United States, shall be admitted into, and entitled to all the advantages of this Union: but no other colony shall be admitted into the same, unless such admission be agreed to by nine States.

Article XII. All bills of credit emitted, monies borrowed, and debts contracted by or under the authority of Congress, before the assembling of the United States, in pursuance of the present confederation, shall be deemed and considered as a charge against the United States, for payment and satisfaction whereof the said United States and the public faith are hereby solemnly pledged.

Article XIII. Every State shall abide by the determinations of the United States, in Congress assembled, on all questions which by this confederation are submitted to them. And the Articles of this confederation shall be inviolably observed by every State, and the Union shall be perpetual; nor shall any alteration at any time hereafter be made in any of them, unless such alteration be agreed to in a Congress of the United States, and be afterwards confirmed by the Legislatures of every State.

And Whereas it hath pleased the Great Governor of the World to incline the hearts of the Legislatures we respectively represent in Congress, to approve of, and to authorize us to ratify the said articles of confederation and perpetual union, Know Ye, that we, the undersigned delegates, by virtue of the power and authority to us given for that purpose, do, by these presents, in the name and in behalf of our respective constituents, fully and entirely ratify and confirm each and every of the said articles of confederation and perpetual union, and all and singular the matters and things therein contained. And we do further solemnly plight and engage the faith of our respective constituents, that they shall abide by the determinations of the United States in Congress assembled, on all questions, which by the said confederation are submitted to them. And that the articles thereof shall be inviolably observed by the States we respectively represent, and that the Union shall be perpetual. In Witness whereof, we have hereunto set our hands, in Congress. Done at Philadelphia, in the State of Pennsylvania, the ninth Day of July, in the Year of our Lord one Thousand seven Hundred and Seventy eight, and in the third year of the Independence of America.

The U.S. Constitution

We the People of the United States, in Order to form a more perfect Union, establish Justice, insure domestic Tranquility, provide for the common defence, promote the general Welfare, and secure the Blessings of Liberty to ourselves and our Posterity, do ordain and establish this Constitution for the United States of America.

ARTICLE I.
Section 1.

All legislative Powers herein granted shall be vested in a Congress of the United States, which shall consist of a Senate and House of Representatives.

Section 2.

The House of Representatives shall be composed of Members chosen every second Year by the People of the several States, and the Electors in each State shall have the Qualifications requisite for Electors of the most numerous Branch of the State Legislature.

No Person shall be a Representative who shall not have attained to the Age of twenty-five years, and been seven Years a Citizen of the United States, and who shall not, when elected, be an Inhabitant of that State in which he shall be chosen.

Representatives and direct taxes shall be apportioned among the several States which may be included within this Union, according to their respective numbers, which shall be determined by adding to the whole number of free Persons, including those bound to service for a term of years, and excluding Indians not taxed, three fifths of all other persons. The actual enumeration shall be made within three years after the first meeting of the Congress of the United States, and within every subsequent term of ten years, in such manner as they shall by law direct. The number of Representatives shall not exceed one for every thirty Thousand, but each State shall have at Least one Representative; and until such enumeration shall be made, the State of New Hampshire shall be entitled to choose three, Massachusetts eight, Rhode Island and Providence Plantations one, Con-

337

necticut five, New York six, New Jersey four, Pennsylvania eight, Delaware one, Maryland six, Virginia ten, North Carolina five, South Carolina five, and Georgia three.

When vacancies happen in the Representation from any State, the Executive authority thereof shall issue writs of election to fill such vacancies.

The House of Representatives shall choose their speaker and other 0fficers; and shall have the sole power of impeachment.

Section 3.

The Senate of the United States shall be composed of two Senators from each State, chosen by the Legislature thereof, for six years; and each Senator shall have one vote.

Immediately after they shall be assembled in consequence of the first election, they shall be divided as equally as may be into three classes. The seats of the Senators of the first class shall be vacated at the expiration of the second year, of the second class at the expiration of the fourth year, and of the third class at the expiration of the sixth year, so that one third may be chosen every second year; and if vacancies happen by resignation, or otherwise, during the recess of the Legislature of any State, the executive thereof may make temporary appointments until the next meeting of the legislature, which shall then fill such vacancies.

No person shall be a Senator who shall not have attained to the age of thirty years, and been nine years a citizen of the United States, and who shall not, when elected, be an inhabitant of that State for which he shall be chosen.

The Vice President of the United States shall be President of the Senate, but shall have no vote, unless they be equally divided.

The Senate shall choose their other officers, and also a president pro tempore, in the absence of the Vice President, or when he shall exercise the office of President of the United States.

The Senate shall have the sole power to try all impeachments. When sitting for that purpose, they shall be on oath or affirmation. When the President of the United States is tried, the Chief Justice shall preside; and no person shall be convicted without the concurrence of two thirds of the members present.

Judgment in cases of impeachment shall not extend further than to removal from office, and disqualification to hold and enjoy any office of honor, trust or profit under the United States; but the party convicted shall nevertheless be liable and subject to indictment, trial, judgment and punishment, according to Law.

Section 4.

The times, places and manner of holding elections for Senators and representatives, shall be prescribed in each State by the Legislature thereof; but the Congress may at any time by law make or alter such regulations, except as to the places of choosing Senators.

The Congress shall assemble at least once in every year, and such meeting shall be on the first Monday in December, unless they shall by law appoint a different day.

Section 5.

Each House shall be the judge of the elections, returns and qualifications of its own members, and a majority of each shall constitute a quorum to do business; but a smaller number may adjourn from day to day, and may be authorized to compel the attendance of absent members, in such manner, and under such penalties as each House may provide.

Each House may determine the rules of its proceedings, punish its members for disorderly behaviour, and, with the concurrence of two thirds, expel a member.

Each House shall keep a journal of its proceedings, and from time to time publish the same, excepting such parts as may in their judgment require secrecy; and the yeas and nays of the members of either House on any question shall, at the desire of one fifth of those present, be entered on the journal.

Neither House, during the session of Congress, shall, without the consent of the other, adjourn for more than three days, nor to any other place than that in which the two Houses shall be sitting.

Section 6.

The Senators and Representatives shall receive a compensation for their services, to be ascertained by law, and paid out of the treasury of the United States. They shall in all cases, except treason, felony and breach of the peace, be privileged from arrest during their attendance at the session of their respective Houses, and in going to and returning from the same; and for any speech or debate in either House, they shall not be questioned in any other place.

No Senator or Representative shall, during the time for which he was elected, be appointed to any civil office under the authority of the United States, which shall have been created, or the emoluments whereof shall have been increased during such time; and no person holding any office under the United States, shall be a member of either House during his continuance in office.

Section 7.

All bills for raising revenue shall originate in the House of Representatives; but the Senate may propose or concur with amendments as on other bills.

Every bill which shall have passed the House of Representatives and the Senate, shall, before it become a law, be presented to the President of the United States; if he approve he shall sign it, but if not he shall return it, with his objections to that House in which it shall have originated, who shall enter the objections at large on their journal, and proceed to reconsider it. If after such reconsideration two thirds of that House shall agree to pass the bill, it shall be sent, together with the objections, to the other House, by which it shall likewise be reconsidered, and if approved by two thirds of that House, it shall become a law. But in all such cases the votes of both Houses shall be determined by yeas and nays, and the names of the persons voting for and against the bill shall be entered on the journal of each House respectively. If any bill shall not be returned by the

339

President within ten days (Sundays excepted) after it shall have been presented to him, the same shall be a law, in like manner as if he had signed it, unless the Congress by their adjournment prevent its return, in which case it shall not be a law.

Every order, resolution, or vote to which the concurrence of the Senate and House of Representatives may be necessary (except on a question of adjournment) shall be presented to the President of the United States; and before the same shall take effect, shall be approved by him, or being disapproved by him, shall be repassed by two thirds of the Senate and House of Representatives, according to the rules and limitations prescribed in the case of a bill.

Section 8.

The Congress shall have power to lay and collect taxes, duties, imposts and excises, to pay the debts and provide for the common defence and general welfare of the United States; but all duties, imposts and excises shall be uniform throughout the United States;

To borrow money on the credit of the United States:

To regulate commerce with foreign nations, and among the several States, and with the Indian tribes;

To establish an uniform rule of naturalization, and uniform laws on the subject of bankruptcies throughout the United States;

To coin money, regulate the value thereof, and of foreign coin, and fix the standard of weights and measures;

To provide for the punishment of counterfeiting the securities and current coin of the United States;

To establish post offices and post roads;

To promote the progress of science and useful arts, by securing for limited times to authors and inventors the exclusive right to their respective writings and discoveries;

To constitute tribunals inferior to the supreme court;

To define and punish piracies and felonies committed on the high seas, and offences against the law of nations;

To declare war, grant letters of marque and reprisal, and make rules concerning captures on land and water;

To raise and support armies, but no appropriation of money to that use shall be for a longer term than two years;

To provide and maintain a navy;

To make rules for the government and regulation of the land and naval forces;

To provide for calling forth the militia to execute the laws of the union, suppress insurrections and repel invasions;

To provide for organizing, arming, and disciplining, the militia, and for governing such part of them as may be employed in the service of the United States, reserving to the States respectively, the appointment of the officers, and the authority of training the militia according to the discipline prescribed by Congress;

To exercise exclusive legislation in all cases whatsoever, over such district (not exceeding ten miles square) as may, by cession of particular States, and the acceptance of congress, become the seat of the government of the United States, and to exercise like authority over all places purchased by the consent of the Legislature of the State in which the same shall be, for the erection of forts, magazines, arsenals, dock-yards, and other needful buildings; And

To make all laws which shall be necessary and proper for carrying into execution the foregoing powers, and all other powers vested by this Constitution in the government of the United States, or in any department or officer thereof.

Section 9.

The migration or importation of such persons as any of the States now existing shall think proper to admit, shall not be prohibited by the Congress prior to the year one thousand eight hundred and eight, but a tax or duty may be imposed on such importation, not exceeding ten dollars for each person.

The privilege of the writ of *habeas corpus* shall not be suspended, unless when in cases of rebellion or invasion the public safety may require it.

No bill of attainder or *ex post facto* law shall be passed.

No capitation, or other direct, tax shall be laid, unless in proportion to the census or enumeration herein before directed to be taken.

No tax or duty shall be laid on articles exported from any State.

No preference shall be given by any regulation of commerce or revenue to the ports of one State over those of another: nor shall vessels bound to, or from, one State, be obliged to enter, clear, or pay duties in another.

No money shall be drawn from the treasury, but in consequence of appropriations made by law; and a regular statement and account of the receipts and expenditures of all public money shall be published from time to time.

No title of nobility shall be granted by the United States: and no person holding any office of profit or trust under them, shall, without the consent of the congress, accept of any present, emolument, office, or title, of any kind whatever, from any king, prince, or foreign state.

Section 10.

No State shall enter into any treaty, alliance, or confederation; grant letters of marque and reprisal; coin money; emit bills of credit; make any thing but gold and silver coin a tender in payment of debts; pass any bill of attainder, *ex post facto* law, or law impairing the obligation of contracts, or grant any title of nobility.

No State shall, without the consent of the Congress, lay any imposts or duties on imports or exports, except what may be absolutely necessary for executing it's inspection laws: and the net produce of all duties and imposts, laid by any State on imports or exports, shall be for the use of the treasury of the United States; and all such laws shall be subject to the revision and control of the Congress.

No State shall, without the consent of Congress, lay any duty of tonnage, keep troops, or ships of war in time of peace, enter into any agreement or compact with another State, or with a foreign power, or engage in war, unless actually invaded, or in such imminent danger as will not admit of delay.

ARTICLE II.
Section 1.

The executive power shall be vested in a president of the United States of America. He shall hold his office during the term of four years, and, together with the Vice President, chosen for the same term, be elected, as follows:

Each State shall appoint, in such manner as the legislature thereof may direct, a number of electors, equal to the whole number of Senators and Representatives to which the State may be entitled in the Congress: but no Senator or Representative, or person holding an office of trust or profit under the United States, shall be appointed an elector.

The electors shall meet in their respective States, and vote by ballot for two persons, of whom one at least shall not be an inhabitant of the same State with themselves. And they shall make a list of all the persons voted for, and of the number of votes for each; which list they shall sign and certify, and transmit sealed to the seat of the government of the United States, directed to the President of the Senate. The President of the Senate shall, in the presence of the Senate and House of Representatives, open all the certificates, and the votes shall then be counted. The person having the greatest number of votes shall be the President, if such number be a majority of the whole number of electors appointed; and if there be more than one who have such majority, and have an equal number of votes, then the House of Representatives shall immediately choose by ballot one of them for President; and if no person have a majority, then from the five highest on the list the said House shall in like manner choose the President. But in choosing the President, the votes shall be taken by States, the representation from each State having one vote; a quorum for this purpose shall consist of a member or members from two thirds of the States, and a majority of all the States shall be necessary to a choice. In every case, after the choice of the President, the person having the greatest number of votes of the electors shall be the Vice President. But if there should remain two or more who have equal votes, the Senate shall choose from them by ballot the Vice President.

The Congress may determine the time of choosing the electors, and the day on which they shall give their votes; which day shall be the same throughout the United States.

No person except a natural born citizen, or a citizen of the United States, at the time of the adoption of this constitution, shall be eligible to the office of President; neither shall any person be eligible to that office who shall not have attained to the age of thirty-five years, and been fourteen years a resident within the United States.

In case of the removal of the President from office, or of his death, resignation, or inability to discharge the powers and duties of the said office, the same shall devolve on the Vice President, and the Congress may by law provide for the case of removal, death, resignation or inability, both of the President and Vice President, declaring what officer shall then act as President, and such officer shall act accordingly, until the disability be removed, or a President shall be elected.

The President shall, at stated times, receive for his services, a compensation, which shall neither be increased nor diminished during the period for which he shall have been elected, and he shall not receive within that period any other emolument from the United States, or any of them.

Before he enter on the execution of his office, he shall take the following oath or affirmation:

"I do solemnly swear (or affirm) that I will faithfully execute the Office of President of the United States, and will to the best of my Ability, preserve, protect and defend the Constitution of the United States."

Section 2.

The President shall be commander-in-chief of the army and navy of the United States, and of the militia of the several States, when called into the actual service of the United States; he may require the opinion, in writing, of the principal officer in each of the executive departments, upon any subject relating to the duties of their respective offices, and he shall have power to grant reprieves and pardons for offences against the United States, except in cases of impeachment.

He shall have power, by and with the advice and consent of the Senate, to make treaties, provided two thirds of the Senators present concur; and he shall nominate, and by and with the advice and consent of the Senate, shall appoint ambassadors, other public ministers and consuls, judges of the supreme court, and all other officers of the United States, whose appointments are not herein otherwise provided for, and which shall be established by law: but the Congress may by law vest the appointment of such inferior officers, as they think proper, in the President alone, in the courts of law, or in the heads of departments.

The President shall have power to fill up all vacancies that may happen during the recess of the Senate, by granting commissions which shall expire at the end of their next session.

Section 3.

He shall from time to time give to the Congress information of the State of the Union, and recommend to their consideration such measures as he shall judge necessary and expedient; he may, on extraordinary occasions, convene both Houses, or either of them, and in case of disagreement between them, with respect to the time of adjournment, he may adjourn them to such time as he shall think proper; he shall receive ambassadors and other public ministers; he shall take care that the laws be faithfully executed, and shall commission all the officers of the United States.

Section 4.

The President, Vice President and all civil Officers of the United States, shall be removed from office on impeachment for, and conviction of, treason, bribery, or other high crimes and misdemeanors.

ARTICLE III.

Section 1.

The judicial power of the United States, shall be vested in one supreme court, and in such inferior courts as the Congress may from time to time ordain and establish. The judges, both of the supreme and inferior courts, shall hold their offices during good behaviour, and shall, at stated times, receive for their services, a compensation, which shall not be diminished during their continuance in office.

Section 2.

The judicial power shall extend to all cases, in law and equity, arising under this Constitution, the laws of the United States, and treaties made, or which shall be made, under their authority; to all cases affecting ambassadors, other public ministers and consuls; to all cases of admiralty and maritime jurisdiction; to controversies to which the United States shall be a party; to controversies between two or more States; between a State and citizens of another State; between citizens of different States; between citizens of the same State claiming lands under grants of different States, and between a State, or the citizens thereof, and foreign States, citizens or subjects.

In all cases affecting ambassadors, other public ministers and consuls, and those in which a State shall be party, the supreme court shall have original jurisdiction. In all the other cases before mentioned, the supreme court shall have appellate jurisdiction, both as to law and fact, with such exceptions, and under such regulations as the Congress shall make.

The trial of all crimes, except in cases of impeachment, shall be by jury; and such trial shall be held in the State where the said crimes shall have been committed; but when not committed within any State, the trial shall be at such place or places as the Congress may by law have directed.

Section 3.

Treason against the United States, shall consist only in levying war against them, or in adhering to their enemies, giving them aid and comfort. No person shall be convicted of treason unless on the testimony of two witnesses to the same overt act, or on confession in open court.

The Congress shall have power to declare the punishment of treason, but no attainder of treason shall work corruption of blood, or forfeiture except during the life of the person attainted.

ARTICLE IV.

Section 1.

Full faith and credit shall be given in each State to the public acts, records, and judicial proceedings of every other State. And the Congress may by general laws prescribe the manner in which such acts, records and proceedings shall be proved, and the effect thereof.

Section 2.

The citizens of each State shall be entitled to all privileges and immunities of citizens in the several States.

A person charged in any State with treason, felony, or other crime, who shall flee from justice, and be found in another State, shall on demand of the executive authority of the State from which he fled, be delivered up, to be removed to the State having jurisdiction of the crime.

No person held to service or labour in one State, under the laws thereof, escaping into another, shall, in consequence of any law or regulation therein, be discharged from such service or labour, but shall be delivered up on claim of the party to whom such service or labour may be due.

Section 3.

New States may be admitted by the Congress into this Union; but no new State shall be formed or erected within the jurisdiction of any other State; nor any State be formed by the junction of two or more States, or parts of States, without the consent of the legislatures of the States concerned as well as of the Congress.

The Congress shall have power to dispose of and make all needful rules and regulations respecting the territory or other property belonging to the United States; and nothing in this Constitution shall be so construed as to prejudice any claims of the United States, or of any particular State.

Section 4.

The United States shall guarantee to every State in this Union a republican form of government, and shall protect each of them against invasion; and on application of the legislature, or of the executive (when the legislature cannot be convened), against domestic violence.

ARTICLE V.

The Congress, whenever two thirds of both Houses shall deem it necessary, shall propose amendments to this constitution, or, on the application of the legislatures of two thirds of the several states, shall call a convention for proposing amendments, which, in either case, shall be valid to all intents and purposes, as part of this Constitution, when ratified by the legislatures of three fourths of the several States, or by conventions in three fourths thereof, as the one or the other mode of ratification may be proposed by the Congress; provided that no amendment which may be made prior to the year one thousand eight hundred and eight shall in any manner affect the first and fourth clauses in the ninth section of the first article; and that no State, without its consent, shall be deprived of its equal suffrage in the Senate.

ARTICLE VI.

All debts contracted and engagements entered into, before the adoption of this Constitution, shall be as valid against the United States under this constitution, as under the confederation.

This constitution, and the laws of the United States which shall be made in pursuance thereof; and all treaties made, or which shall be made, under the authority of the United States, shall be the supreme law of the land; and the judges in every state shall be bound thereby, any thing in the Constitution or laws of any state to the contrary notwithstanding.

The Senators and Representatives before mentioned, and the members of the several State Legislatures, and all executive and judicial officers, both of the United States and of the several States, shall be bound by oath or affirmation, to support this Constitution; but no religious test shall ever be required as a qualification to any office or public trust under the United States.

ARTICLE VII.

The ratification of the conventions of nine States, shall be sufficient for the establishment of this Constitution between the states so ratifying the same.

The word, "the," being interlined between the seventh and eighth lines of the first page, the word "thirty" being partly written on an erazure in the fifteenth line of the first page, the words "is tried" being interlined between the thirty second and thirty third lines of the first page and the Word "the" being interlined between the forty third and forty fourth lines of the second page.

Attest William Jackson Secretary

Done in convention by the unanimous consent of the States present the seventeenth day of September in the year of our Lord one thousand seven hundred and eighty-seven and of the independence of the United States of America the twelfth in witness whereof we have hereunto subscribed our Names,

G°. Washington
Presidt and deputy from Virginia

Delaware
Geo: Read
Gunning Bedford jun
John Dickinson
Richard Bassett
Jaco: Broom

Maryland
James McHenry
Dan of St Thos. Jenifer
Danl. Carroll

Virginia
John Blair
James Madison Jr.

North Carolina
Wm. Blount
Richd. Dobbs Spaight
Hu Williamson

South Carolina
J. Rutledge
Charles Cotesworth Pinckney
Charles Pinckney
Pierce Butler

Georgia
William Few
Abr Baldwin

New Hampshire
John Langdon
Nicholas Gilman

Massachusetts
Nathaniel Gorham
Rufus King

Connecticut
Wm. Saml. Johnson
Roger Sherman

New York
Alexander Hamilton
New Jersey
Wil: Livingston
David Brearley
Wm. Paterson
Jona: Dayton

Pennsylvania
B Franklin
Thomas Mifflin
Robt. Morris
Geo. Clymer
Thos. FitzSimons
Jared Ingersoll
James Wilson
Gouv Morris

The Bill of Rights

CONGRESS OF THE UNITED STATES begun and held at the City of New York, on Wednesday the fourth of March, one thousand seven hundred and eighty-nine.

THE Conventions of a number of the States, having at the time of their adopting the Constitution, expressed a desire, in order to prevent misconstruction or abuse of its powers, that further declaratory and restrictive clauses should be added: And as extending the ground of public confidence in the Government, will best ensure the beneficent ends of its institution.

RESOLVED by the Senate and House of Representatives of the United States of America, in Congress assembled, two thirds of both Houses concurring, that the following Articles be proposed to the Legislatures of the several States, as amendments to the Constitution of the United States, all, or any of which Articles, when ratified by three fourths of the said Legislatures, to be valid to all intents and purposes, as part of the said Constitution; viz.

ARTICLES in addition to, and Amendment of the Constitution of the United States of America, proposed by Congress, and ratified by the Legislatures of the several States, pursuant to the fifth Article of the original Constitution.

Note: The following text is a transcription of the first ten amendments to the Constitution in their original form. These amendments were ratified December 15, 1791, and form what is known as the "Bill of Rights."

AMENDMENT I

Congress shall make no law respecting an establishment of religion, or prohibiting the free exercise thereof; or abridging the freedom of speech, or of the press; or the right of the people peaceably to assemble, and to petition the Government for a redress of grievances.

AMENDMENT II

A well regulated Militia, being necessary to the security of a free State, the right of the people to keep and bear Arms, shall not be infringed.

AMENDMENT III

No Soldier shall, in time of peace be quartered in any house, without the consent of the Owner, nor in time of war, but in a manner to be prescribed by law.

AMENDMENT IV

The right of the people to be secure in their persons, houses, papers, and effects, against unreasonable searches and seizures, shall not be violated, and no Warrants shall issue, but upon probable cause, supported by Oath or affirmation, and particularly describing the place to be searched, and the persons or things to be seized.

AMENDMENT V

No person shall be held to answer for a capital, or otherwise infamous crime, unless on a presentment or indictment of a Grand Jury, except in cases arising in the land or naval forces, or in the Militia, when in actual service in time of War or public danger; nor shall any person be subject for the same offence to be twice put in jeopardy of life or limb; nor shall be compelled in any criminal case to be a witness against himself, nor be deprived of life, liberty, or property, without due process of law; nor shall private property be taken for public use, without just compensation.

AMENDMENT VI

In all criminal prosecutions, the accused shall enjoy the right to a speedy and public trial, by an impartial jury of the State and district wherein the crime shall have been committed, which district shall have been previously ascertained by law, and to be informed of the nature and cause of the accusation; to be confronted with the witnesses against him; to have compulsory process for obtaining witnesses in his favor, and to have the Assistance of Counsel for his defence.

AMENDMENT VII

In Suits at common law, where the value in controversy shall exceed twenty dollars, the right of trial by jury shall be preserved, and no fact tried by a jury, shall be otherwise re-examined in any Court of the United States, than according to the rules of the common law.

AMENDMENT VIII

Excessive bail shall not be required, nor excessive fines imposed, nor cruel and unusual punishments inflicted.

AMENDMENT IX

The enumeration in the Constitution, of certain rights, shall not be construed to deny or disparage others retained by the people.

AMENDMENT X

The powers not delegated to the United States by the Constitution, nor prohibited by it to the States, are reserved to the States respectively, or to the people.

THE 11TH THROUGH 27TH AMENDMENTS TO THE U.S. CONSTITUTION

AMENDMENT XI

Passed by Congress March 4, 1794. Ratified February 7, 1795.

(Note: Article III, section 2, of the Constitution was modified by amendment 11.) The Judicial power of the United States shall not be construed to extend to any suit in law or equity, commenced or prosecuted against one of the United States by Citizens of another State, or by Citizens or Subjects of any Foreign State.

AMENDMENT XII

Passed by Congress December 9, 1803. Ratified June 15, 1804.

(Note: A portion of Article II, section 1 of the Constitution was superseded by the 12th amendment.) The Electors shall meet in their respective states and vote by ballot for President and Vice-President, one of whom, at least, shall not be an inhabitant of the same state with themselves; they shall name in their ballots the person voted for as President, and in distinct ballots the person voted for as Vice-President, and they shall make distinct lists of all persons voted for as President, and of all persons voted for as Vice-President, and of the number of votes for each, which lists they shall sign and certify, and transmit sealed to the seat of the government of the United States, directed to the President of the Senate; the President of the Senate shall, in the presence of the Senate and House of Representatives, open all the certificates and the votes shall then be counted; The person having the greatest number of votes for President, shall be the President, if such number be a majority of the whole number of Electors appointed; and if no person have such majority, then from the persons having the highest numbers not exceeding three on the list of those voted for as President, the House of Representatives shall choose immediately, by ballot, the President. But in choosing the President, the votes shall be taken by states, the representation from each state having one vote; a quorum for this purpose shall consist of a member or members from two-thirds of the states, and a majority of all the states shall be necessary to a choice. And if the House of Representatives shall not choose a President whenever the right of choice shall devolve upon them, before the fourth day of March next following, then the Vice-President shall act as President, as in case of the death or other constitutional disability of the President. *The person having the greatest number of votes as Vice-President, shall be the Vice-President, if such number be a majority of the whole number of Electors appointed, and if no person have a majority, then from the two highest numbers on the list, the Senate shall choose the Vice-President; a quorum for the purpose shall consist of two-thirds of the whole number of Senators, and a majority of the whole number shall be necessary to a choice. But no person constitutionally ineligible to the office of President shall be eligible to that of Vice-President of the United States.

*Superseded by section 3 of the 20th amendment.

AMENDMENT XIII

Passed by Congress January 31, 1865. Ratified December 6, 1865.

(Note: A portion of Article IV, section 2, of the Constitution was superseded by the 13th amendment.)

Section 1.

Neither slavery nor involuntary servitude, except as a punishment for crime whereof the party shall have been duly convicted, shall exist within the United States, or any place subject to their jurisdiction.

Section 2.

Congress shall have power to enforce this article by appropriate legislation.

AMENDMENT XIV

Passed by Congress June 13, 1866. Ratified July 9, 1868.

(Note: Article I, section 2, of the Constitution was modified by section 2 of the 14th amendment.)

Section 1.

All persons born or naturalized in the United States, and subject to the jurisdiction thereof, are citizens of the United States and of the State wherein they reside. No State shall make or enforce any law which shall abridge the privileges or immunities of citizens of the United States; nor shall any State deprive any person of life, liberty, or property, without due process of law; nor deny to any person within its jurisdiction the equal protection of the laws.

Section 2.

Representatives shall be apportioned among the several States according to their respective numbers, counting the whole number of persons in each State, excluding Indians not taxed. But when the right to vote at any election for the choice of electors for President and Vice-President of the United States, Representatives in Congress, the Executive and Judicial officers of a State, or the members of the Legislature thereof, is denied to any of the male inhabitants of such State, being twenty-one years of age,* and citizens of the United States, or in any way abridged, except for participation in rebellion, or other crime, the basis of representation therein shall be reduced in the proportion which the number of such male citizens shall bear to the whole number of male citizens twenty-one years of age in such State.

Section 3.

No person shall be a Senator or Representative in Congress, or elector of President and Vice-President, or hold any office, civil or military, under the United States, or under any State, who, having previously taken an oath, as a member of Congress, or as an officer of the United States, or as a member of any State legislature, or as an executive or judicial officer of any State, to support the Constitution of the United States, shall have engaged in insurrection or rebellion against the same, or given aid or comfort to the enemies thereof. But Congress may by a vote of two-thirds of each House, remove such disability.

Section 4.

The validity of the public debt of the United States, authorized by law, including debts incurred for payment of pensions and bounties for services in suppressing insurrection or rebellion, shall not be questioned. But neither the United States nor any State shall assume or pay any debt or obligation incurred in aid of insurrection or rebellion against the United States, or any claim for the loss or emancipation of any slave; but all such debts, obligations and claims shall be held illegal and void.

Section 5.

The Congress shall have the power to enforce, by appropriate legislation, the provisions of this article.

Changed by section 1 of the 26th amendment.

AMENDMENT XV
Passed by Congress February 26, 1869. Ratified February 3, 1870.

Section 1.

The right of citizens of the United States to vote shall not be denied or abridged by the United States or by any State on account of race, color, or previous condition of servitude.

Section 2.

The Congress shall have the power to enforce this article by appropriate legislation.

AMENDMENT XVI
Passed by Congress July 2, 1909. Ratified February 3, 1913.

(Note: Article I, section 9, of the Constitution was modified by amendment 16.)

The Congress shall have power to lay and collect taxes on incomes, from whatever source derived, without apportionment among the several States, and without regard to any census or enumeration.

AMENDMENT XVII
Passed by Congress May 13, 1912. Ratified April 8, 1913.

(Note: Article I, section 3, of the Constitution was modified by the 17th amendment.)

The Senate of the United States shall be composed of two Senators from each State, elected by the people thereof, for six years; and each Senator shall have one vote. The electors in each State shall have the qualifications requisite for electors of the most numerous branch of the State legislatures.

When vacancies happen in the representation of any State in the Senate, the executive authority of such State shall issue writs of election to fill such vacancies: Provided, That the legislature of any State may empower the executive thereof to make temporary appointments until the people fill the vacancies by election as the legislature may direct.

This amendment shall not be so construed as to affect the election or term of any Senator chosen before it becomes valid as part of the Constitution.

AMENDMENT XVIII
Passed by Congress December 18, 1917. Ratified January 16, 1919. Repealed by amendment 21.

Section 1.

After one year from the ratification of this article the manufacture, sale, or transportation of intoxicating liquors within, the importation thereof into, or the exportation thereof from the United States and all territory subject to the jurisdiction thereof for beverage purposes is hereby prohibited.

Section 2.

The Congress and the several States shall have concurrent power to enforce this article by appropriate legislation.

Section 3.

This article shall be inoperative unless it shall have been ratified as an amendment to the Constitution by the legislatures of the several States, as provided in the Constitution, within seven years from the date of the submission hereof to the States by the Congress.

AMENDMENT XIX
Passed by Congress June 4, 1919. Ratified August 18, 1920.

The right of citizens of the United States to vote shall not be denied or abridged by the United States or by any State on account of sex.

Congress shall have power to enforce this article by appropriate legislation.

AMENDMENT XX
Passed by Congress March 2, 1932. Ratified January 23, 1933.

(Note: Article I, section 4, of the Constitution was modified by section 2 of this amendment. In addition, a portion of the 12th amendment was superseded by section 3.)

Section 1.

The terms of the President and the Vice President shall end at noon on the 20th day of January, and the terms of Senators and Representatives at noon on the 3d day of January, of the years in which such terms would have ended if this article had not been ratified; and the terms of their successors shall then begin.

Section 2.

The Congress shall assemble at least once in every year, and such meeting shall begin at noon on the 3d day of January, unless they shall by law appoint a different day.

Section 3.

If, at the time fixed for the beginning of the term of the President, the President elect shall have died, the Vice President elect shall become President. If a President shall not have been chosen before the time fixed for the beginning of his term, or if the President elect shall have failed to qualify, then the Vice President elect shall act as President until a President shall have qualified; and the Congress may by law provide for the case wherein neither a President elect nor a Vice President elect shall have qualified, declaring who shall then act as President, or the manner in which one who is to act shall be selected, and such person shall act accordingly until a President or Vice President shall have qualified.

Section 4.

The Congress may by law provide for the case of the death of any of the persons from whom the House of Representatives may choose a President whenever the right of choice shall have devolved upon them, and for the case of the death of any of the persons from whom the Senate may choose a Vice President whenever the right of choice shall have devolved upon them.

Section 5.

Sections 1 and 2 shall take effect on the 15th day of October following the ratification of this article.

Section 6.

This article shall be inoperative unless it shall have been ratified as an amendment to the Constitution by the legislatures of three-fourths of the several States within seven years from the date of its submission.

AMENDMENT XXI
Passed by Congress February 20, 1933. Ratified December 5, 1933.

Section 1.

The eighteenth article of amendment to the Constitution of the United States is hereby repealed.

Section 2.

The transportation or importation into any State, Territory, or possession of the United States for delivery or use therein of intoxicating liquors, in violation of the laws thereof, is hereby prohibited.

Section 3.

This article shall be inoperative unless it shall have been ratified as an amendment to the Constitution by conventions in the several States, as provided in the Constitution, within seven years from the date of the submission hereof to the States by the Congress.

AMENDMENT XXII
Passed by Congress March 21, 1947. Ratified February 27, 1951.

Section 1.

No person shall be elected to the office of the President more than twice, and no person who has held the office of President, or acted as President, for more than two years of a term to which some other person was elected President shall be elected to the office of the President more than once. But this Article shall not apply to any person holding the office of President when this Article was proposed by the Congress, and shall not prevent any person who may be holding the office of President, or acting as President, during the term within which this Article becomes operative from holding the office of President or acting as President during the remainder of such term.

Section 2.

This article shall be inoperative unless it shall have been ratified as an amendment to the Constitution by the legislatures of three-fourths of the several States within seven years from the date of its submission to the States by the Congress.

AMENDMENT XXIII
Passed by Congress June 16, 1960. Ratified March 29, 1961.

Section 1.

The District constituting the seat of Government of the United States shall appoint in such manner as the Congress may direct:

A number of electors of President and Vice President equal to the whole number of Senators and Representatives in Congress to which the District would be entitled if it were a State, but in no event more than the least populous State; they shall be in addition to those appointed by the States, but they shall be considered, for the purposes of the election of President and Vice President, to be electors appointed by a State; and they shall meet in the District and perform such duties as provided by the twelfth article of amendment.

Section 2.

The Congress shall have power to enforce this article by appropriate legislation.

AMENDMENT XXIV
Passed by Congress August 27, 1962. Ratified January 23, 1964.

Section 1.

The right of citizens of the United States to vote in any primary or other election for President or Vice President, for electors for President or Vice President, or for Senator or Representative in Congress, shall not be denied or abridged by the United States or any State by reason of failure to pay any poll tax or other tax.

Section 2.

The Congress shall have power to enforce this article by appropriate legislation.

AMENDMENT XXV
Passed by Congress July 6, 1965. Ratified February 10, 1967.

(Note: Article II, section 1, of the Constitution was affected by the 25th amendment.)

Section 1.

In case of the removal of the President from office or of his death or resignation, the Vice President shall become President.

Section 2.

Whenever there is a vacancy in the office of the Vice President, the President shall nominate a Vice President who shall take office upon confirmation by a majority vote of both Houses of Congress.

Section 3.

Whenever the President transmits to the President pro tempore of the Senate and the Speaker of the House of Representatives his written declaration that he is unable to discharge the powers and duties of his office, and until he transmits to them a written declaration to the contrary, such powers and duties shall be discharged by the Vice President as Acting President.

Section 4.

Whenever the Vice President and a majority of either the principal officers of the executive departments or of such other body as Congress may by law provide, transmit to the President pro tempore of the Senate and the Speaker of the House of Representatives their written declaration that the President is unable to discharge the powers and duties of his office, the Vice President shall immediately assume the powers and duties of the office as Acting President.

Thereafter, when the President transmits to the President *pro tempore* of the Senate and the Speaker of the House of Representatives his written declaration that no inability exists, he shall resume the powers and duties of his office unless the Vice President and a majority of either the principal officers of the executive department or of such other body as Congress may by law provide, transmit within four days to the President pro tempore of the Senate and the Speaker of the House of Representatives their written declaration that the President is unable to discharge the powers and duties of his office. Thereupon Congress shall decide the issue, assembling within forty-eight hours for that purpose if not in session. If the Congress, within twenty-one days after receipt of the latter written declaration, or, if Congress is not in session, within twenty-one days after Congress is required to assemble, determines by two-thirds vote of both Houses that the President is unable to discharge the powers and duties of his office, the Vice President shall continue to discharge the same as Acting President; otherwise, the President shall resume the powers and duties of his office.

AMENDMENT XXVI
Passed by Congress March 23, 1971. Ratified July 1, 1971.

(Note: Amendment 14, section 2, of the Constitution was modified by section 1 of the 26th amendment.)

Section 1.

The right of citizens of the United States, who are eighteen years of age or older, to vote shall not be denied or abridged by the United States or by any State on account of age.

Section 2.

The Congress shall have power to enforce this article by appropriate legislation.

AMENDMENT XXVII
Originally proposed Sept. 25, 1789. Ratified May 7, 1992.

No law, varying the compensation for the services of the Senators and Representatives, shall take effect, until an election of Representatives shall have intervened.

Index

Note: (ill.) indicates photos and illustrations.

359

confidentiality, 183
demonstrations on public property, 186–87
Establishment Clause, 178, 179–80
Free Exercise Clause, 178
free press limitations, 184–85
freedom of assembly, 186
freedom of association, 187
freedom of religion, 177–80
freedom of speech, 181–86
freedom of the press, 184–85, 295–96
Internet regulation, 185
Lemon test, 179
lobbyists, 233–34
obscene films, 185
prior restraint, 181–82
public schools and banning of political protests, 187
rap music, 185 (ill.), 185–86
religion and politics, 180
saluting the flag, 183–84, 184 (ill.)
school prayer, 179–80
school vouchers, 180
separation of church and state, 178 (ill.), 178–79
speech codes, 183
"speech plus," 183
strict judicial scrutiny, 182
symbols, 182
"Them's fightin' words," 182–83
time, place, and manner regulations, 186
first lady, 131–32
fiscal federalism, 67
flag, 183–84, 184 (ill.)
Foerstel, Herbert N., 184
Forbes, Steve, 187
Ford, Gerald
  becomes president, 129
  becomes vice president and president after resignations, 145–46
  1976 convention, 266
  1976 debate, 270
  Republican Party, 243
  Rockefeller, Nelson A., 261
  vetoes overridden, 123
  Voice of America, 312
Fourth Amendment, 190, 191–92, 199–200
Franco, Francisco, 5
Frankfurter, Felix, 162
franking privileges, 83
Franklin, Benjamin
  Articles of Confederation, 44
  Constitutional Convention, 48
  as Federalist, 57
  as Patriot, 37

Second Continental Congress, 38
  as signer of Constitution, 49
  Townshend Acts, 29
Franklin, William, 37
Free Exercise Clause, 178
free press limitations, 184–85
Freedom of Access to Clinic Entrances Act (1994), 186–87
freedom of assembly, 186
freedom of association, 187
Freedom of Information Act, 295–96
freedom of religion, 177–80
freedom of the press, 184–85, 295–96
Frémont, John, 242
Friedan, Betty, 210
frontloading, 259
Fuller, Melville W., 159
fundamental values
  American eras, 12–13
  equality, 10–11, 11 (ill.)
  laissez-faire capitalism, 10
  liberty, 10
  political culture, 10
  political equality, 11
Furman v. Georgia (1972), 196

G

Gaddafi, Muammar, 5
Gage, Thomas, 31, 37
Galloway, Joseph, 44, 44 (ill.)
Gallup, George H., 212
Gallup Poll, 212
Garfield, James, 243
Gaspee, 32, 32 (ill.)
Gates, Bill, 287
gay marriage, 200–201, 210
gay men and women in military, 209–10
Geithner, Timothy, 244
General Services Administration, 143, 144
George III, King, 36, 38
Georgia, 25, 25 (ill.), 26
Gerry, Elbridge, 45, 94, 94 (ill.)
Gibbons, Thomas, 63
Gibbons v. Ogden (1824), 63–64
Gideon v. Wainwright (1963), 193
Gingrich, Newt, 311
Ginsburg, Martin, 161
Ginsburg, Ruth Bader, 159 (ill.), 160, 161, 164
Gitlow v. New York (1925), 175–76
Golding, William, 184
Goldman, Ronald, 195
González, Vicente, 85
Gorbachev, Mikhail, 309

Gore, Al, 244 (ill.), 261 (ill.)
  affirmative action, 206
  Gore, Tipper, 186
  ticket balance, 261
  2000 election, 249, 250–51, 279, 281
Gore, Tipper, 186
Gorham, Nathaniel, 49
Gorsuch, Neil, 159 (ill.), 160
government. See also democracy; fundamental values; government, forms of; political ideologies
  Americans' influence on, 18–19, 19 (ill.)
  as bureaucracy, 144
  concepts of, 6–7
  constitutions, 7
  definition, 1
  downsizing, 144
  involvement in daily life, 2, 2 (ill.)
  need for, 3
  politics vs., 1
  public policies, 2–3
  purpose of, 3
government, forms of. See also democracy
  authoritarian government, 5
  authority, 3
  big government, 13
  classification of, 3–4
  constitutional government, 4–5
  definition, 4, 4 (ill.)
  legitimacy, 3
  limited governments, 4–6
government interest groups, 227
governor, 68–70
grand jury, 167, 194
Grand Old Party, 241
Grant, Ulysses S., 242, 243, 301
grassroots lobbying, 229–30
Great Britain, relationship with American colonies, 28–29
Green Party, 249
Greenpeace USA, 226
Griffiths, Martha, 208 (ill.)
Griswold v. Connecticut (1965), 199
Grodzins, Morton, 253

H

Haley, Nikki R., 141
Hall, Gus, 271
Hamilton, Alexander
  Adams, John, criticism of, 299
  economic policy of, 246
  federal courts, 147
  as Federalist, 57
  Federalist Papers, 154
  as signer of Constitution, 49
  Washington, George, speeches of, 303